D0782082

CASS SERIES: STUDIES IN AIR POWER
(Series Editor: Sebastian Cox)

AIR POWER AT THE BATTLEFRONT

CASS SERIES: STUDIES IN AIR POWER
(Series Editor: Sebastian Cox)

AIR POWER
AT THE
BATTLEFRONT

Allied Close Air Support in Europe
1943–45

IAN GOODERSON

FRANK CASS
LONDON • PORTLAND, OR

First Published in 1998 in Great Britain by
FRANK CASS PUBLISHERS
2 Park Square, Milton Park, Abingdon,
Oxon, OX14 4RN

and in the United States of America by
FRANK CASS PUBLISHERS
270 Madison Ave,
New York NY 10016

Transferred to Digital Printing 2005

Website http://www.frankcass.com

© 1998 Ian Gooderson

British Library Cataloguing in Publication Data

Gooderson, Ian
   Air power at the battle front : allied close air support in
Europe, 1943–45. – (Cass series : studies in air power)
   1. World War, 1939–1945 – Aerial operations 2. Close air
support
   I. Title
   940.5'44

ISBN 0-7146-4680-6 (cloth)
ISBN 0-7146-4211-8 (paper)
ISSN 1368–5597

Library of Congress Cataloging-in-Publication Data

Gooderson, Ian.
   Air power at the battlefront : allied close air support in Europe,
1943–45 / Ian Gooderson.
      p. cm. – (Cass series–studies in air power)
   Includes bibliographical references and index.
   ISBN 0-7146-4680-6. – ISBN 0-7146-4211-8 (pbk.)
   1. World War, 1939–1945–Aerial operations. I. Title.
II. Series.
D785.G58 1997
940.54'4–DC21   97-19029
                                                                 CIP

*All rights reserved. No part of this publication may be reproduced in
any form or by any means, electronic, mechanical, photocopying,
recording or otherwise, without the prior permission of Frank Cass and
Company Limited.*

For my mother and father

Contents

Illustrations

(All photographs MOD Crown Copyright. Courtesy of the Air Historical Branch (RAF))

Tables and Diagrams

Editor's Foreword

It is now almost universally accepted that the victories of the Anglo-American armies in western Europe following the Normandy landings were heavily dependent on air power. Images of rocket-firing Hawker Typhoon fighter-bombers and burning German *panzers* are familiar to any student of this campaign. While there have been many histories of the campaign as a whole, and of air power's individual and distinctive part in it, there has previously been little attempt to take the analysis one stage further and investigate in detail the precise effect air power had. By drawing on a wide range of sources, particularly the reports of the Royal Air Force and British Army operational research teams, Dr Gooderson does exactly that and succeeds in bringing some intriguing information to the fore.

In particular, his conclusion that the disruption and demoralisation resulting from air attack was in many ways more important than the physical destruction caused, especially in attacks on armoured units, may be of fundamental importance to our understanding of why and how air power achieves results. Dr Gooderson shows that the psychological impact of air power on both friend and foe was in many instances at least as important as its physical effects. He also offers some valuable conclusions on the most effective types of mission flown by Allied pilots, and the relative efficacy of fighter-bombers and larger bomber aircraft in providing support for the ground forces.

SEBASTIAN COX
September, 1997

Acknowledgements

This study of close air support during the Second World War was made possible by my having been engaged as a researcher on the staff of the Department of War Studies, King's College London, contracted to provide historical data on the effect of air attack on ground forces for the Centre for Defence Analysis (CDA) then at West Byfleet in Surrey. Therefore I should like to express my gratitude to Professor Lawrence Freedman, Head of the Department of War Studies, Professor Brian Bond of the Department, and Mr. David Rowland of CDA for this opportunity. In particular I owe a special thanks to my friend and tutor at King's, Dr. Philip Sabin, for his steadfast support and guidance throughout the years of study.

I am greatly indebted to my Ph.D. examiners, Air Vice-Marshal R.A. Mason and Professor Richard Overy, for their valuable encouragement and advice, and to Mr. Sebastian Cox, the Studies in Air Power series editor and Head of the Air Historical Branch, for his comments and suggestions. I am grateful to Group Captain A.B. Stephens of the Air Historical Branch for reading the manuscript, and to author Jeffery Williams for kindly sparing the time to reply in detail to my letter prompted by his study of Canadian operations in North-West Europe, *The Long Left Flank* (Leo Cooper, 1988).

I also wish to acknowledge the generous and willing assistance rendered to me during my research by the staff of the Public Record Office, Kew, and of the Departments of Documents and Printed Books at the Imperial War Museum. Visits and enquiries made to the Air Historical Branch, the British Library, and the Library of King's College London were also met with great courtesy and a readiness to help in every way.

My grateful thanks go also to publishers Frank Cass & Co., and due appreciation is extended to the *Journal of Strategic Studies* for publishing the material contained in Chapters Five and Six in the June 1991 and September 1992 editions respectively.

Finally, I would like to add that all judgements and opinions concerning the effects and utility of close air support in the period are my own, and should not be construed as reflecting in any way official views held by the Ministry of Defence.

Glossary

AACC Army Air Control Centre (British). Joint RAF/British Army Control Centre for controlling air support.

AEAF Allied Expeditionary Air Force.

AGRA Army Groups Royal Artillery (British). A separate grouping of predominantly medium but also heavy and sometimes field regiments of artillery. Though army troops AGRAs were often under corps control.

ALO Air Liaison Officer (British). Army officer attached to RAF formation or unit for liaison duties.

AOP Air Observation Post (British). These letters are used to designate a light aircraft piloted by an RA officer who controls artillery fire by radio (see FOO and OP below). AOP is also the generic term for the RAF flights and squadrons in which these planes were organized.

ASC Air Support Control. Joint RAF/Army headquarters established at Corps level for evaluating air support requests in the British air-support system developed in North Africa, 1941.

ASPO Air Support Party Officer (USAAF). Pilot attached to US Army Corps, Division, and Armoured Combat Command Headquarters as a liaison officer. (See TALO and TAPO below.)

ASSU Air Support Signals Unit (British). Communications unit attached to Army and RAF formations for relaying air support requests and intelligence. See also TENTACLE.

BAU Bombing Analysis Unit.

CABRANK Method of providing continuous close air support by maintaining standing patrols of fighter-bombers in the battle area ready to be directed against targets by ground control.

CRA Commander, Royal Artillery. Brigadier at Divisional Headquarters advising on use of divisional and any attached artillery.

DAF Desert Air Force (RAF)

FAC Forward Air Controller. RAF or USAAF officer, usually a pilot, attached to ground formations with the role of contacting aircraft and directing airstrikes from the ground.

FASL Forward Air Support Link. RAF team attached to British Army

Brigades and equipped with two-way radio-telephony for relaying air-support requests and for the control of supporting aircraft in the British air-support system developed in North Africa, 1941.

FCP Forward Control Post (British). An air-support control post manned by RAF and Army personnel situated near the battlefront and responsible for controlling air-support in a particular sector.

FOO Forward Observation Officer (British). This is an artillery officer attached to a leading sub-unit of an infantry battalion or armoured regiment with communication links permitting him to call for and direct supporting fire from any number of or even all the artillery units in the sector.

GLO Ground Liaison Officer (US Army). Army officer attached to a USAAF unit as a liaison officer; the equivalent of the British ALO (see above).

HORSEFLY Method of employing airborne Forward Air Controllers in light observation aircraft to direct fighter-bomber strikes. Developed by US forces in Italy and also later employed by US forces in North-West Europe.

IO Intelligence Officer.

LAND MATTRESS Ground-based rocket system for saturation fire, employed by First Canadian Army in North-West Europe.

MATAF Mediterranean Allied Tactical Air Force.

MEW Microwave Early Warning (Radar).

MET (or MT) Mechanised Enemy Transport. Pilots' description of non-armoured enemy vehicles.

MORU
  (i) Military Operational Research Unit (British).
  (ii) Mobile Operations Room Unit (British). An RAF operations centre responsible for co-ordinating the activities of bomber, fighter, and fighter-bomber wings and allocating units for air-support tasks. Employed by the RAF Desert Air Force in Italy, 1944/45.

NCO Non-Commissioned Officer.

OA Operational Analysis (US).

OP Observation Post.

OR Operational Research (British).

ORB Operations Record Book (British). Daily record of operations maintained by RAF Commands, Groups, Wings and Squadrons. Those relating to the Second World War are held at the Public Record Office, Kew.

ORG Operational Research Group (British).

ORS Operational Research Section.

PIG Method of close air support in which fighter-bombers employed strafing attacks only, in circumstances when bombing was inappropriate. Developed by RAF Desert Air Force in Italy.

PRO Public Record Office (Kew).

RA Royal Artillery.

RAF Royal Air Force.

RASL Rear Air Support Link. Two-way radio-telephony communications link in the British air-support system developed in North Africa during 1941 which enabled the ASC to contact RAF airfields.

ROVER Code name for FCPs operating with Allied forces in Italy. Those with British Eighth Army were known as ROVER DAVID and ROVER PADDY, that with the US Fifth Army was known as ROVER JOE. In September 1944 an FCP for directing air attacks upon German artillery positions became operational with Eighth Army and was known as ROVER FRANK.

RP (or R/P) Rocket Projectile (British). Refers to 3 inch rockets carried by Typhoon fighter-bombers.

RSD Radial Standard Deviation. Measure of the scatter of bombs within a bomb pattern.

SA (OR) Scientific Adviser (Operational Research).

SHAEF Supreme Headquarters Allied Expeditionary Force.

SOP Special Observer Party. Operational Research Party set up to investigate the effects of various forms of Allied fire support upon the German coastal defences in Normandy.

TAC Tactical Air Command (US).

TAF Tactical Air Force (British).

TALO or TAPO Tactical Air Liaison Officer or Tactical Air Party Officer (US), same as for ASPO above.

TENTACLE Name given to outstations within the British air-support communications network.

TIMOTHY Method of close air support whereby fighter-bombers attacked targets in relation to a fluid bombline in support of a ground assault. Developed by RAF Desert Air Force in Italy.

VCP Visual Control Post (British). Control posts at the battlefront intended to direct aircraft from a point commanding a view of the battle area. See also FCP.

VHF Very High Frequency.

WINKLE Method of close air support similar to TIMOTHY and employed by RAF fighter-bombers in North-West Europe.

OPERATIONAL CODE NAMES MENTIONED IN TEXT

BLUECOAT British Second Army attack towards Vire, Normandy, 30 July–3 August 1944.

BUCKLAND British Eighth Army attack across the River Senio in Italy, 9 April 1945.

CHARNWOOD British Second Army attack to capture Caen, Normandy, 7–9 July 1944.

CLARION An intensive 24-hour offensive by the Allied air forces against transportation targets in Germany, 22 February 1945.

CLIPPER British XXX Corps attack to secure Geilenkirchen, Germany, 18–19 November 1944.

COBRA US breakout operation, Normandy, 25–29 July 1944.

CRUSADER Unsuccessful British offensive to relieve Tobruk and capture Cyrenaica, November 1941.

CYGNET Operation by British 7th Armoured Brigade to clear a pocket of German resistance along the River Senio near Alfonsine, Italy, 4 January 1945.

DIADEM Allied offensive to liberate Rome during May and June 1944.

GOODWOOD British Second Army attack towards the Bourgébus Ridge, Normandy, 18–21 July 1944.

INFATUATE Operation to capture Walcheren Island, Holland, by First Canadian Army and amphibious forces, 1–8 November 1944.

JUBILEE Raid on Dieppe, 19 August 1942.

MARKET GARDEN Operation by British Second Army and Allied airborne forces to seize bridges at Nijmegen and Arnhem, Holland, 17–26 September 1944. GARDEN was the code name for the Second Army attack, MARKET was the code name for the airborne landings.

OVERLORD Allied liberation of Northern Europe, commencing with Normandy invasion, 6 June 1944.

POINTBLANK Pre-OVERLORD directive for the strategic bombing of Germany, issued June 1943 and designating the German Luftwaffe and its supporting industries as priority targets.

PLUNDER British 21st Army Group crossing of the Rhine, 23–24 March 1945.

QUEEN Offensive by the US First and Ninth Armies towards the River Roer, Germany, November 1944.

STRANGLE Interdiction campaign conducted by the Allied air forces in Italy, March–May 1944.

TORCH Allied landings in French North Africa, November 1942.

TOTALISE First Canadian Army attack towards Falaise, Normandy, 8–11 August 1944.

TRACTABLE First Canadian Army attack towards Falaise, Normandy, 14–16 August 1944.

UNDERGO First Canadian Army operation to capture Calais, 25 September to 1 October 1944.

VARSITY Airborne landings in support of the crossing of the Rhine, March 1945.

VERITABLE First Canadian Army offensive in the Rhineland, 8 February to 10 March 1945.

WELLHIT First Canadian Army operation to capture Boulogne, 17 to 22 September 1944.

WIDGEON Assault on Wesel, Germany, by British 1st Commando Brigade during the crossing of the Rhine, 24 March 1945.

WOWSER Air operations in support of the Allied armies' final offensive in Italy, April 1945.

Introduction

In 1946, shortly after the end of the Second World War, the British Army's Military Operational Research Unit (MORU) initiated a Battle Study to determine the effectiveness of what had been an important feature of operations during that conflict: close air support. Although restricted to the campaign in North-West Europe in 1944–45, the study was intended to be comprehensive, and embraced the roles played by the three general aircraft types that had been employed to support Allied troops; heavy and medium bombers, and fighter-bombers. Whatever their initial hopes regarding the advantages of such a study, the MORU staff evidently found their task both difficult and frustrating, for in the introduction to their eventual report they left the following warning for any future historian of close air support:

> there will be no records of the help it gave to the soldiers, no enemy documents to prove what it cost them in men and equipment, nothing, in fact, to judge the value of it all. He will, of course have glowing testimonies in plenty from Army Commanders, endless mention of the use of air support, and statements of enemy prisoners from Private to Field Marshal indicating how overwhelming and decisive was the air support. But if he is impartial he will remember, too, the tremendous bombings around Caen where it seemed that nothing could survive, and yet where the SS and parachute troops fought on as bitterly as ever. He will remember, too, how the Germans managed to stage an Army Group counter-attack in the Ardennes, almost without air support of their own, and he will remember those Germans, among them Rommel, who claimed that our air superiority was by no means the decisive factor in the North West European Campaign. He will find a surprising lack of concrete factual evidence with which to test the validity of these conflicting statements. He will be able to sum up only by saying, at greater or lesser length, that air support was immensely important,

perhaps vital, but that sometimes it seemed signally to have failed, and that some people held that it was important perhaps, but not particularly so.[1]

Such a statement, from a team of professional military analysts tasked with evaluating the utility and effectiveness of close air support, might suggest that the conclusion to any study of the subject is certain to be equivocal. In the introduction to his recent history of battlefield air attack in the period 1911–45, Richard Hallion echoes somewhat the MORU of 1946 by observing that battlefield air support has been dominated by two opposing but equally fallacious viewpoints – that air support has not been of significance to the land battle and, conversely, that air support has been decisive – whereas the truth is actually to be found in the middle.[2]

As Hallion suggests, close air support has always been, and remains, a contentious subject, and objective conclusions about its advantages and disadvantages are rare. Valuable studies have been produced, including Hallion's work, that written by Peter C. Smith and that edited by Benjamin F. Cooling.[3] The evolution of air-support theory and practice, and developments in aircraft and weapons are well covered in these books, but there has been relatively little attempt to determine precisely the advantages conferred upon troops in combat by the provision of close air support.

By addressing two fundamental questions within the context of the close air support provided for the Allied armies in the campaigns in Italy and North-West Europe in 1943–45 I hope this book will redress the balance. The first question is whether the employment of aircraft in the close-support role provided sufficient military advantage at the battlefront to justify the associated expenditure of effort, and the risk to aircraft and pilots, other than in an emergency. The second is whether air support proved to be of more value when directed against targets beyond the battlefront, such as enemy communications, headquarters, and supplies. As this suggests, the question of close air support is essentially one of cost-effectiveness.

An evaluation of close air support during the Second World War must begin with a definition of the term in the context of its contemporary usage. The term 'Close Air Support' was in use during the war, and in 1944 the Royal Air Force (RAF) defined this type of air support as the immediate availability of aircraft to attack and destroy, in response to army requests, targets engaging or being engaged by the forward British troops, thereby improving the tactical situation of the moment. This was in contrast to 'General Air Support', which was defined as the attacking of targets not in close proximity to friendly troops but immediately behind the battlefront, in order to hamper the fighting capabilities of the enemy's front-line troops. Such attacks included the blocking of road and rail links, the demolition of bridges and tunnels, and the attacking of transport supplying the front line.[4]

A third employment of air power is known as 'Interdiction', a Second World War term remaining in use today, covering air operations intended to isolate the battlefront by destroying, disrupting, and delaying enemy forces, communications and supplies, often in areas far removed from the battle area.[5] The 1944 concept of 'General Air Support' can be seen as interdiction in the tactical area, a mission approximating to, though somewhat wider than, the present concept of 'Battlefield Air Interdiction' (BAI).[6] The subject of this book is close air support, which means the same today as in 1944,[7] though for comparison attention is also given to what was identified in 1944 as 'General Air Support'.

The selection of such a limited time-scale as the campaigns in North-West Europe and Italy in 1943–45 was dictated by the need to be concise. Close air support became an important feature not only of Allied operations in Europe, but also of those in the Middle and Far East and Pacific theatres. The plethora of examples of close air support, the abundance of data regarding the various methods developed for controlling and applying air support, and the aircraft, weapons and tactics employed, meant a line had to be drawn.

Moreover, the campaigns in Italy and North-West Europe offer several advantages to the historian. One is that they saw the culmination of air-support theory and practice in the period, with the British and American forces employing the machinery and methods of air support that had evolved as the direct result of earlier experience and trial and error in previous campaigns. Both campaigns also saw important innovations in the forward control of aircraft and in close air support tactics.

From the analytical point of view, these campaigns are important for two reasons. One is that air superiority enabled the Allies to employ their vast air resources, including heavy bombers of the 'strategic' air forces along with medium bombers and fighter-bombers, to influence the land campaigns without the complication of contending with major German air opposition. The importance of this was later expressed by Air Chief Marshal Sir John Slessor, who

recalled his astonishment when first arriving in the Italian theatre in
early 1944 at the extent to which the Luftwaffe was disregarded,
adding that in North-West Europe the Allied armies were able to
conduct their operations without fear of German air opposition and
consequently with far fewer casualties than would have normally been
expected.[8]

Thus air support can be evaluated within the context of its employment on an unprecedented scale against an army almost totally lacking
in air cover. The same could be said regarding the latter stages of the
Far Eastern and Pacific campaigns after the demise of Japanese air
power over the battlefronts and its concentration, like that of
Germany, to protect the national homeland from strategic air attack.
In these theatres, however, while close air support was extensive, its
effects could be dissipated by terrain and its results are far harder to
evaluate than on European battlefields.

The second reason relates to the availability of data regarding the
effect of air attack. The campaigns in North-West Europe and Italy
offer an advantage lacking in earlier Allied operations and, to a great
extent, those in the Far East – or for that matter Axis close air support
examples. This is that by 1943–45 the scientific discipline of
Operational Research, or Operational Analysis as it was styled by the
Americans, had become an established feature of Allied warfare. The
importance of Operational Research (OR) data to an analysis of close
air support effectiveness cannot be overstated, and the overriding
factor in selecting Italy and North-West Europe for this study was the
extent of OR conducted in these campaigns and its ready availability.

Operational Research Sections (ORS), composed of civilian
scientists in uniform attached to Air Force and Army formations,
investigated some of the most significant air-support operations
(including those in 'close air support', 'general air support' and
'interdiction') shortly after they had occurred. Their battlefield
examinations and subsequent reports, compiled with the intention of
assessing the effectiveness of weapons and tactics, and containing
interviews with Allied troops who had taken part and also their
German prisoners, are especially valuable. They do not provide ready-
made answers to the fundamental questions regarding close air
support that I have outlined. The MORU of 1946, which had access
to this OR data, still found it difficult to arrive at definite conclusions,
as the quotation at the beginning of this chapter reveals. However an
alternative is offered to the glib generalisations regarding air support
which are to be found both in contemporary operational records and
much subsequent post-war historiography.

NOTES

1. Military Operational Research Unit Report No.34 (1946), *The Effects of Close Air Support*, p. 5, PRO WO 291/976.
This report was prepared by Lieutenant-Colonel M.M. Swann, REME, Major C.F. White, RA, and Captain B.G. Fish, RE.
2. Richard P. Hallion, *Strike from the Sky: The History of Battlefield Air Attack 1911–1945* (Shrewsbury: Airlife Publishing, 1989), p. 2.
3. Peter C. Smith, *Close Air Support: An Illustrated History, 1914 to the Present* (New York: Crown Publishers Inc., 1990); Benjamin F. Cooling (Ed.), *Case Studies in the Development of Close Air Support* (Washington, DC: Office of Air Force History, 1990).
4. Royal Air Force (Desert Air Force) paper on air support for ground forces (1944), to be found in *Employment of Fighter-Bombers–Policy*, p. 5, PRO AIR 23/1826.
5. For a useful definition of General Jacob E. Smart, USAF (Rtd), see Richard H. Kohn and Joseph P. Harahan (Eds.), *Air Interdiction in World War II, Korea, and Vietnam*, USAF Project Warrior Study (Washington, DC: Office of Air Force History, 1986), p. 16.
6. See Air Vice-Marshal R.A. Mason, *Air Power: An Overview of Roles* (London: Brassey's Defence Publishers, 1987), p. 66, and AP 3000, *Royal Air Force Air Power Doctrine*, (London: 2nd Edition, 1993), pp. 62–4.
7. Mason, p. 59 and AP 3000, p. 63.
8. Air Chief Marshal Sir John Slessor, *The Past Development of Air Power*, in *The Future of Air Power*, Air Vice Marshal John R. Walker (Ed.), RUSI Military Power Series (Shepperton: Ian Allan, 1986), p. 31.

1

Operational Research

Operational Research is a scientific approach to the problems of determining the likely effects of weapons and tactics and of deciding between varying courses of action. The OR material consulted for this study was compiled by Operational Research Sections serving with British Army and RAF formations in the field, and in order to fully appreciate their work it will be useful to outline briefly their nature, organisation and method. The emphasis has been placed upon No.2 ORS of 21st Army Group and the ORS of RAF 2nd Tactical Air Force in North-West Europe for, as we shall see, these two units were responsible for some of the most important work on air support.

The value of OR had been shown by studies conducted by the Admiralty and Air Department during the First World War, but its potential was more fully realised during the early years of the Second by the extensive work conducted within the RAF to develop Radio Direction Finding (radar) and a fighter interception system for Fighter Command.[1] The need to analyse the effectiveness of the air defence system also led to the beginnings of OR in the Army, and in September 1940 Professor Blackett, Scientific Advisor to the Army's Anti-Aircraft Command, formed a small group of civilian scientists to study the performance of the anti-aircraft defences and to address particularly the problems associated with radar gun-laying.[2]

While the RAF adopted a positive attitude to the utility of OR, with ORS attached to all the operational RAF Commands, the future of Army OR remained for a while questionable after Blackett's departure in March 1941 to RAF Coastal Command. However, after the appointment of a Scientific Advisor to the Army Council in May 1941, this post being taken by the distinguished physicist Sir Charles Darwin, the situation was resolved and by August 1941 an enlarged Army Operational Research Group (AORG) had been created under the command of Lieutenant-Colonel Basil Schonland, the South African physicist. The AORG was intended to serve both the

Ministry of Supply and the War Office, the former with regard to research in the UK, and the latter for research overseas. [3]

On 26 November 1942 the decision was taken to establish ORS for overseas theatres and an establishment for a pool of 36 officers, on the basis of six for each of an estimated six theatres of war, was planned. It is interesting that there was considerable War Office concern at this stage about whether as many as 36 suitably qualified officers could be found, whereas by 1945 a total of no less than 120 officers had served with Army ORS. [4]

The first ORS sent overseas was posted to the Middle East in the summer of 1942 and attached to General Headquarters in Cairo. It encountered the problem that all subsequent ORS had to contend with — the reluctance of operational commands to allow civilian scientists, even in uniform, to conduct work in the battle zone. When it was suggested that the section investigate the effectiveness of anti-tank guns, the response from Eighth Army was that this would necessitate study in the battle area, and that no officer from General Headquarters, with the exception of the Commander-in-Chief, could visit the battle area. [5]

Nevertheless, ORS continued to be prepared for service overseas and on 24 May 1943 No.1 ORS was established and mobilised the following month, eventually to serve in Italy. On 14 August 1943 No.2 ORS was formed, for eventual service with 21st Army Group in North-West Europe. These ORS attached to armies in the field were intended to provide scientific assistance to the Commander in four respects:

a) Advice and assistance in the solving of technical problems arising during operations and advice as to the best use of available equipment.
b) Analysis of the performance of weapons and equipment in battle.
c) Assistance with, and analysis of, trials of British and captured enemy weapons and equipment.
d) Assistance with any problems which might arise requiring a scientific approach to their solution.

The composition of ORS varied according to theatre, but there were important features common to all. One was that the ORS was to be located near to Army headquarters so that it could receive orders directly and that its role might become familiar to the headquarters staff. Each ORS was led by a scientist, normally a Deputy Director of Scientific Research, who was accorded the rank of Colonel in order to have the necessary military status to tender advice to the headquarters staff. An ORS usually contained at least one competent statistician and, when manpower permitted, a number of NCOs (Sergeants) for the task of data collection together with an adequate clerical staff. A basic, far from lavish, scale of transport was also allocated to enable the ORS to operate as a self-contained unit.[6]

While the Army was organising its OR sections for service overseas, so too was the RAF. The ORS attached to RAF 2nd Tactical Air Force in North-West Europe originated in a decision taken in 1942 to create an ORS for Army Co-operation Command, at that time the only RAF formation responsible for practising the weapons and methods of close air support with the Army in the UK. The ORS consisted of two scientific officers and six junior scientific officers, all of whom had been recruited from ORS Fighter Command, with Mr. Graham, another physicist, appointed as officer-in-charge. Close contact with the AORG, particularly with regard to air support problems, was maintained from the outset.[7] In June 1943, Army Co-operation Command was redesignated the Tactical Air Force (TAF), and by the end of the year ORS TAF, as the ORS had become known, was absorbed by the new ORS Allied Expeditionary Air Force (AEAF) created in December under the direction of Mr. Larnder of ORS Fighter Command who was appointed Scientific Adviser (Operational Research) or SA(OR).

The ORS AEAF was a self-contained branch of the Air Staff at Headquarters AEAF and had two main functions:

a) Advise the Air Commander-in-Chief on scientific matters affecting operations,
b) Carry out investigations and analyses for the various Headquarters branches.[8]

Anxious to maintain the identity of an ORS TAF which would be concerned with problems affecting air-to-ground operations, Larnder formed a section which, after the Tactical Air Force had been re-designated the 2nd Tactical Air Force at the end of 1943, became known as ORS 2nd TAF. This was composed of the original ORS TAF members and remained under the control of Graham. Two members of this unit were attached to each of the composite groups within 2nd TAF, while Graham with one assistant was occupied mostly at 2nd TAF's main Headquarters. Scientists attached to ORS AEAF were granted honorary commissions, Larnder being accorded the rank of Group Captain and Graham, commanding ORS 2nd TAF, that of Wing Commander. When serving overseas the ORS personnel wore RAF uniform.[9]

While both the British Army and the RAF had ORS ready to accompany their forces during the liberation of North-West Europe, it would actually be the former's No.2 ORS that carried out the most extensive work on air support. This came about as the result of accident rather than design, and to understand why it is useful to have an idea of how No.2 ORS worked. There are two important factors to consider. First, the size of the Section throughout the campaign was always a factor limiting the amount of work that could be done. Before D-Day it consisted of five officers, three drivers, a clerk, one jeep and two 15 cwt. trucks. When an increase was made, this only amounted to three more officers, an extra jeep, a staff car, and a few more Other Ranks. Second, the work was not carried out by the Section systematically, since it had no clear brief as to what aspects of warfare to investigate. As we shall see, No.2 ORS exercised remarkable initiative regarding the selection of problems to be investigated.

The Section did not go to Normandy as a unit but in instalments. One member, Lieutenant-Colonel Johnson, went to France on D-Day as Radar Adviser to the Anti-Aircraft Brigade, spending the following three weeks evaluating its equipment. Next to reach Normandy was Major Fairlie of the Royal Canadian Artillery who was attached to the Special Observer Party (SOP), a group formed shortly before the landings to study the effects of different forms of attack on the German coastal defences. The SOP spent two weeks working among the beach defences, and one early result of this work was that:

> Whatever induced the Germans to give in, it was not physical destruc-
> tion of their fortifications, for of this there was little or none, despite the
> huge naval and air bombardments.[10]

This indicated that the decisive factor had been the 'morale effect' of bombardment. This was a term used rather loosely in contemporary OR to refer to the prevention of troops under air or artillery bombardment from manning their weapons, and from moving and functioning effectively not only during the bombardment but for varying periods of time afterwards. It was a phenomenon never properly defined, not fully understood, and impossible to quantify. The SOP made no attempt to evaluate it, being concerned only with the physical effects of bombardment, and No.2 ORS did not address the problem until August 1944. The historian of the Section observed:

> To assess the morale effect of a bombardment was...to attempt an utter-
> ly new analysis; though there were many who had suggested doing it,
> there was no one who had ever tried.[11]

No.2 ORS took shape in Normandy towards the end of June when the advance party of two officers (Majors Swann and Sargeaunt), a truck, a jeep, and two drivers landed. This was a week later than intended due to an inauspicious start – the Landing Craft transporting them to France had become separated from its convoy, wandered far off course, and was only saved from entering the Atlantic by observing the course of a German V.1 flying bomb passing overhead. After landing eventually in the American sector, the Section moved to Cruelly, the location of British Second Army Headquarters.

It soon became apparent, however, that the staff of Second Army had little idea of how to employ the ORS, and on its own initiative the Section began to visit the battlefront to assess where it might most usefully contribute. By August the Section had completed surveys into mortar location and the nature of tank casualties, both of which proved valuable in developing appropriate tactics and organisation, in addition to initiating work on such diverse problems as the reliability of the infantry's PIAT (Projector Infantry Anti Tank) anti-tank weapon, which was often fired at German tanks but rarely hit them, and that of the Normandy dust which was rapidly wearing out fighter aircraft engines at the RAF's forward airstrips. The somewhat haphazard nature of OR at this stage is shown by the Section initiating work on these problems without any directives from higher authority, and by the fact that shortly after they had done so the dust problem was taken over, appropriately, by the RAF, and that of the PIAT by the Army's Weapons Technical Staff.[12]

In the meantime, the Section had embarked, equally by chance, upon its extensive work on close air support – initially concentrating on the attacks by heavy bombers. On 7 July 1944, for Operation CHARNWOOD, RAF Bomber Command attacked the northern outskirts of Caen, and nothing shows the spirit of OR and the initiative exercised by the Section better than their own decision to investigate this operation:

> it occurred to us to wonder what this immense effort had...achieved. Conflicting stories abounded, and neither the RAF nor the Army seemed to have any clear idea. Without any directive from above and, with the object more than anything else of satisfying our own curiosity, we set to work to find out what had really happened.[13]

Three members of the Section spent several days amid the ruins of Caen, interviewing troops who had taken part and civilians. Their

Report (No.5) was forwarded to 21st Army Group Headquarters, but the OR team were far from proud of it and only too aware of its limitations. In their view it was merely a study of the physical effects of the bombing, no attempt having been made to study morale effects or conduct prisoner-of-war interrogation or to assess the effect of the bombing on the progress of the British troops, while its conclusions were too indefinite and negative.[14]

Nevertheless, the report was received with interest at 21st Army Group, and particularly by Brigadier Schonland, by then its Scientific Adviser. Some two weeks later, at the start of Operation GOODWOOD, Schonland sent an urgent telegram to No.2 ORS asking them to report on that and all subsequent heavy bombing operations. Report No.6, on GOODWOOD, was equally unsatisfactory in the opinion of the Section. They felt that they had started on the work too late and that the battle had been too large for their small team to cover adequately, while many of the bombed areas remained in German hands.[15]

In the analyses conducted after GOODWOOD, the ORS tried to ensure that work started in good time, that Operation Orders were examined, and that the course of the battle was closely monitored. It was this work on heavy bombing that set the pattern for most of the Section's subsequent work in the campaign:

> our work developed into the search for means to reconstruct and analyse particular battles. Once the missing elements of the battle had been supplied, suggestions for improvement followed; once, for instance, the real value of a particular air attack had been determined, it was not difficult to say whether another type of attack would have been better.[16]

Between 30 July and 20 August 1944 No.2 ORS completed five reports on heavy bombing. The first concerned Operation BLUECOAT, for which the planning and course of the battle were studied in detail, casualties were analysed, and interviews were held with troops who had taken part. In the opinion of the ORS this report (No.7) was the first to indicate clearly the value of the bombing, though it still lacked prisoner interrogation. It was followed by No.8, on TOTALISE, and No.9 on the effects of short-bombing of friendly troops. An idea of the work and method involved in the compiling of these reports, particularly in that the ORS had to commute considerable distances to the front line from where they were based, is given in the Section's history:

Studying these Heavy Bombing attacks was a laborious and depressing
affair, and at the time we prayed that we should never have to do any more
of it. The dust and the appalling quantities of traffic...made travelling to
and fro an exhausting business. Having arrived at the front, we had to
probe about in the desolation of one French village after another, often
uncomfortably close to mortaring, shelling, and the front line, and search
out from their hiding places units which had taken part in the battle.
When we returned there were air photographs to be pored over, and a
thousand and one fragments of information to be assembled.[17]

By this time the Section's work regarding air support had been
extended. Shortly after GOODWOOD, and as a result of an arrange-
ment made by Brigadier Schonland with the Air Branch at
Headquarters 21st Army Group and ORS 2nd TAF, Major Pike, who
had been recalled from No.1 ORS in Italy, arrived from England with
a further jeep and driver. His task was to study the effects of fighter
and fighter-bomber support attacks. As the history of the Section
points out, this work was prompted by lack of knowledge of the effects
of air attack, and such was the extent of this lack of knowledge that it
was subsequently felt that an unduly large proportion of the Section's
time and effort was devoted to the subject.[18]

In fact the question of fighter and fighter-bomber support was
causing considerable rancour between the RAF and Army. Claims
submitted by pilots for the destruction of ground targets were being
regarded with disdain by the Army. Schonland, and particularly
Montgomery's Chief of Staff, De Guingand, needed to know the
truth.[19]

Major Pike's first report (No.3) analysed an attack by RAF
Typhoons on a German column, and was the first case of its kind ever
to be fully examined and documented. His next report (No.4) was far
more extensive and concerned the effect of attacks by RAF rocket-
firing Typhoons against the German armoured counter-attack at
Mortain. Both reports and their conclusions are discussed in Chapter
5 concerning air attack upon armour, but in the context of the work
compiled by No.2 ORS the Mortain report amounted to the first
occasion when attention was drawn to the discrepancy between air
force claims of destruction and the evidence found on the ground.
Consequently the report caused much controversy, and although ORS
2nd TAF also examined the battle area and found the same evidence,
Pike's report was rejected by Headquarters 2nd TAF.

This was only the start of the analyses of fighter-bomber attacks by No.2 ORS. Shortly after the collapse of the Falaise 'Pocket' the Section was directed to the area in order to discover precisely what the Air Forces had achieved during the German retreat. This resulted in the most momentous work of the Section, and it is worth quoting from the Section's history which observes that,

> From the historical point of view, Report 15 *'Enemy Casualties in Vehicles and Equipment during the retreat from Normandy to the Seine'* deserves to be considered as our best work. Into the making of it went the effort of six of us for three weeks, and of one or two for many weeks more. We examined vehicles individually, we counted them in bulk, we interrogated the local French population, we interrogated prisoners of war, we used the reports of air-craft reconnaissance and we examined air photographs. Accepting the limitations of time, there was probably little more we could have done in assessing physical destruction; but we often wished that we had done more on the effect of the Air Forces in causing panic and confusion amongst the enemy.[20]

The result was further controversy with the RAF, as the Section concluded that the Air Forces, despite the destruction that they had inflicted, had failed to achieve effective interdiction and should have been more systematic in their attacks. This is discussed more fully in Chapter 5 below.

In September 1944 the Section had the opportunity to assess the effects of heavy bomber, medium bomber, and fighter-bomber attack all within the context of one operation – the assault on Boulogne. The Section arrived outside Boulogne some days before the assault and so, for the first time, were able to prepare their investigation in detail beforehand using maps and plans. They observed the assault as it progressed, interrogated prisoners as they were brought in and, after the assault, discussed the operation in detail with the Canadian battalions involved. The resulting report (No.16) was the most complete attempt at assessing a battle achieved by the Section during the campaign, though the analysis of the effect of artillery and tanks was acknowledged to be far less detailed than that of air attack due to lack of time. Indeed, the extensive coverage accorded Boulogne prevented the Section from covering – except for a cursory look at the effects of air attack on gun positions – the subsequent assault on Calais.

For much of the autumn and winter of 1944–45 the Section, based in Brussels, was employed in addressing problems related to artillery.

Their most important work in this field, regarding the morale and destructive effect of artillery bombardment, was achieved at this time (see Chapter 7 below). However, in January 1945 the Section was once again called upon to investigate air matters as a result of the German Ardennes offensive. As in Normandy, Allied fighter-bomber pilots were submitting claims for the destruction of German armour which were described by Army Headquarters as 'extraordinary' and, as at that time the US First and Ninth Armies were under the command of 21st Army Group, No.2 ORS was directed to discover what was actually happening as a high priority task.[21] In order to avoid the differences of opinion with the RAF that had occurred in Normandy, the Section was this time directed to work jointly with ORS 2nd TAF. The history of the Section acknowledges that working jointly with the RAF was not an easy process, but that after 'thrashing out reports together' agreement was eventually reached.[22]

Consequently a combined team of eight, including Wing Commander Graham and Squadron Leader Abel of ORS 2nd TAF, was based at Aywaille in the Ardennes salient from where they carried out an extensive ground search for destroyed tanks claimed by the Air Forces. In contrast to their earlier work in Normandy, the ORS were hampered by adverse weather, extreme cold and occasional blizzards, and the fact that much of the ground was covered in snow which prevented tanks from being seen from more than a few yards away. The investigation was therefore slower, and was acknowledged to be less thorough. There was little opportunity to assess RAF attacks as the RAF had not carried out much anti-tank activity, but it soon became clear that, just as with the RAF in Normandy, US fighter-bombers were overclaiming. The ORS reported that,

> For every hundred claims, we could only find one tank indubitably destroyed by air: and, though a few cases turned up where perhaps tanks had been abandoned because of air attack, they were doubtful and went only a very little way to making good the discrepancy.[23]

This investigation resulted in the first Army/RAF ORS joint report, which in turn suggested the need for a fuller study of the role of the Air Forces in defeating the German counter-offensive. A few days after the completion of Joint Report No.1 on aircraft versus tanks, members of both ORSs began to investigate the result of air attacks against the major communications centres in the salient. By ground examination, and extensive interviews with the local Belgian population, a detailed analysis was compiled of the delay and dislocation caused to the Germans by air attack – the result being a comprehensive report by ORS 2nd TAF on the role of the Allied Air Forces in stemming the German thrust. Further joint reports consisted of a valuable assessment of the effectiveness of rocket-firing Typhoons in the close support role, for which many German prisoners were interrogated and extensive interviews conducted with British and Canadian troops, and an analysis of the effectiveness of German flak and Allied counter-flak measures during Operation VARSITY, the airborne assault across the Rhine.

Unlike their Army equivalent, ORS 2nd TAF was never a compact body. Before D-Day the commander of RAF 2nd TAF, Air Marshal Coningham, refused to allow scientists as members of his Headquarters staff and only eventually was he persuaded to allow Wing Commander Graham and his assistant to accompany 2nd TAF's Headquarters to France. Although ORS members arrived at 2nd TAF Headquarters at Le Tronquay on 4 August 1944, it was only after the disbandment of AEAF in October 1944, and the relocation of personnel of ORS AEAF to ORS 2nd TAF that the latter came into its own. On 22 October ORS 2nd TAF, located in Brussels, was reorganised as a team of 15 scientific officers but these were widely distributed throughout 2nd TAF: two were attached to Headquarters, one each to No.2 Group and No.34 Photographic Reconnaissance Wing, two each to No.84 Group and No.6 Film Processing Unit, four to No.85 Group, and one each to Armament Practice Camps. Two further officers were attached to the Bombing Analysis Unit (BAU) recently formed under SHAEF.[24]

Such dispersion made it difficult for ORS 2nd TAF to carry out investigations in the manner of No.2 ORS because they simply could not concentrate officers to deal with a single problem. Had it not been for the centralised organisation of No.2 ORS, the later joint investigations would have been impossible. It was for this reason that the most important work on air support – for example the investigation of the Falaise 'Pocket' – had to be left to the Army. Nevertheless, ORS 2nd TAF managed to conduct some valuable analyses of close support operations, most notably the effect of air attacks on gun positions and strongpoints, and to accumulate much data on fighter-bomber tactics and accuracy.

While the value of wartime ORS material to the historian is unquestionable, it is worthwhile examining the extent to which it was acted upon at the time by those for whom the reports were compiled.

In fact the evidence suggests that the impact of OR at the operational level was slight.

Army and Air Force staffs appear to have held their OR Sections useful for answering questions considered relevant to the sphere of scientific advice. An example of this was the question submitted to No.2 ORS by the staff of 21st Army Group during the planning of Operation VERITABLE enquiring whether the use of aircraft bombs in the battle area would crater the wet ground and render it impassable for tanks. Moreover, as the experience of No.2 ORS shows, they could also be employed to resolve questions such as the accuracy of fighter-bomber pilots' claims of German tank destruction. Such problems were obviously appropriate to the ORS, but their broad analysis of battles also led to conclusions as to the best use of weapons and appropriate tactics. When this type of data, and suggestions, were submitted, they were often either unwelcome, or simply not acted upon.

There were two reasons for this. One was that senior Military and Air Force commanders did not appreciate being told how to conduct their operations – as No.2 ORS discovered. After their extensive field work investigating the heavy bomber operations the Section decided to compile a general report (No.14) on the use of heavy bombers to support the Army which was duly forwarded to 21st Army Group. Their history records that the report had been intended as a simple guide, but was vetoed as being too contentious and outspoken.[25] In fact the 'simple guide' contained some unpalatable conclusions as to the effectiveness of the heavy bombing and, moreover, implicit criticism of the targets selected. The ORS had noted that, despite reports from British troops and prisoners-of-war, the actual amount of damage caused to enemy personnel and equipment by heavy bombing in the four operations reviewed had been small, and that this had been proven by subsequent close ground examination. This was not taken as as an indication of the ineffectiveness of bombs, but due rather to the fact that the Germans practised a very high degree of dispersion and that consequently in several of the areas bombed there had been no Germans at all.[26] This could hardly have been welcomed at 21st Army Group Headquarters, especially in view of the efforts made by the soldiers to secure heavy bomber support, an aspect discussed more fully in Chapter 6 below.

The second reason was that there was simply no mechanism for ensuring that senior commanders, or their subordinates, were made aware of the results of OR studies. Thus the potential usefulness of OR material was often not realised even when it was circulated. The outspoken history of No.2 ORS describes how members of the Section often felt anger and frustration after discovering that their ideas had not been adopted simply because their reports had not been circulated or had not been read, and how this situation arose:

> Much of the trouble lies in the fundamental paradox of the military system: although at the highest formation there is most likely to be the time and temperament to appreciate ORS reports, the opportunity to act on them is in fact least. Although the last say always rests with the top, as regards ways and means of fighting, their influence is remote and their control far less than they may care to admit. The lower formations have the power to act, but less time and less inclination to think, so that ORS reports tend to be regarded as yet more paper from above, and are treated accordingly.[27]

This is no doubt a fair analysis of how the military system functions in war, and an important factor would certainly have been that forces regularly in contact with the enemy proved reluctant to abandon in favour of innovation familiar methods which, whatever their drawbacks, were nevertheless tried and tested in battle. There is, of course, another point which was not made in the history of No.2 ORS, that senior commanders occasionally had good reason to ignore advice from their OR sections even when aware of it. Other evidence and experience sometimes existed to contradict that offered by the ORS who, as will be apparent with regard to their studies of air support, were not always right.

Another contributory factor to the way that OR was received was the extent to which the ORS themselves decided what should be investigated, as they lacked specific instructions as to what was required. To quote once again from the experience of No.2 ORS,

> ...often we were given no directive at all. 'See what you can make of air attack in the Falaise pocket', 'Have a look at the Assault on Boulogne' or 'Follow the armoured drive' were all the direction we ever received for some of the most successful of our reports.[28]

Such a method permitted great freedom of action, and fostered an independence of spirit. This is seen in an example from towards the end of the Normandy campaign, when the Commander of No.2 ORS suggested to the 21st Army Group staff that a member of the Section should accompany the armoured drive through Northern France and Belgium. When asked by the staff what it was proposed that this officer should do, the Commander replied that it would be up to the officer to determine what would be best for him to do when he got there.[29] The detachment was authorised, and in fact some valuable work resulted, but this shows how, in a sense, the ORS were responsible for identifying the need for their own work. It was very easy for such work to be unappreciated by those for whom it was carried out, if the latter did not comprehend the need for it in the first place. The example also shows to what extent initiative and practicality were demanded of the OR worker, and illustrates the point made in the post-war history of OR in the RAF – that while scientific training was necessary (some of the best OR members being engineers or physicists), not all scientists could grasp the principles of operational research.[30]

A related question is the extent to which the conclusions reached by the ORS could be be regarded as reliable, either by military commanders then or by historians now. A salutary warning regarding close air support investigations, based on the experience of ORS 2nd TAF, is given in the post-war history of wartime OR in the RAF. This states that despite the accumulation of a good deal of useful information from prisoner-of-war interrogation, interviews with Army and RAF personnel, the study and analysis of intelligence reports, and ground surveys of battlefields after capture, this data was nevertheless not available in sufficient detail and covered too narrow a range of operations to permit a quantitative study.[31]

Most OR data was certainly based upon particular examples, and this is true of the work of both No.2 ORS and ORS 2nd TAF. Moreover, the few ORS and the small number of scientists in each could not cover a wide range of operations in detail, and, as we have seen, when an attempt was made by No.2 ORS to cover a particular operation in depth some aspect had to be skimmed or neglected altogether due to the volume of work and the pressure of time. Attempts to cover one operation meant that other similar ones could not be studied except in the most cursory sense. Nor, in the experience of No.2 ORS, was OR field work very systematic. As they were attempting much that was unprecedented, there was little direction from higher authority as to what to look at and what to look for; it was a continuous process of discovery determined largely by the initiative of the ORS members themselves. The danger here was that the theoretical aspect of OR work may have been compromised by the ORS itself. Necessarily examining problems at very close range and being unable to cover many such operations in detail, failure to perceive a larger perspective became likely.

Nevertheless, in a practical sense the OR reports hold much that is of value – particularly the ground surveys conducted shortly after operations, during which the ORS examined destroyed and damaged vehicles and equipment, and recorded the number of shell, bomb and rocket craters in the area and their position. In the case of anti-armour operations by Allied fighter-bombers, these provided physical evidence to set against what would otherwise have been misleading claims of destruction. These reports can be considered reliable in the attribution of causes of destruction and damage, for it was not difficult to determine whether tanks and vehicles were destroyed by air or ground weapons, and where there was doubt this was indicated by the ORS. The same is true for the reports examining attacks by fighter-bombers against gun positions and strongpoints, the damage by air weapons being sufficiently obvious to leave little room for doubt.

The investigations of the heavy bomber operations were more complicated. Assessments of the destruction of targets in fixed defence positions, such as gun positions, can be considered accurate – particularly at Boulogne where No.2 ORS, instead of appearing shortly after the operation, were on hand to witness it. It was far harder to evaluate the effect of the bombing in field operations after the ground had been much fought over, and when some of the bombed areas remained in enemy hands. To a greater extent in these operations than in those of fighter-bombers engaging armour the amount of destroyed equipment and the number of enemy casualties found was more likely to reflect precisely that – the amount found rather than that inflicted. In particular the level of casualties caused to German troops as a result of heavy bombing remains, to some extent, questionable.

No.2 ORS found very few German dead after some of the heavy bomber support operations in Normandy, and concluded that such bombing against troops well dug-in did not produce heavy casualties. Taken all round the evidence from such operations supported this view, but the ORS also acknowledged that during one of these investigations a captured German medical officer told them that the Germans always removed their dead before the arrival of Allied troops. They were disinclined to believe him, not only because they thought him an arrogant type whose information was considered unreliable, but also because they felt such a step would normally be impracticable.

Yet in this they were wrong for, when possible, German troops did in fact follow a policy of taking their dead with them when falling back from positions in order to prevent their discovery by the Allies. It seems odd that the ORS were not made aware of this, for the practice should have been known to Military Intelligence as it had been discovered in earlier campaigns. For example, towards the end of the fighting in Tunisia, the British 26th Armoured Brigade captured a number of German troops of the Hermann Goering Division, one of whom remarked to his captors that his unit had received an order to carry back all their dead with them when they withdrew, and that this had had a very bad effect on morale.[32]

Thus there are pitfalls to drawing conclusions from the evidence discovered by the ORS in the battle area, and when using ORS data it must be remembered that the theoretical aspect of their reports, such as the level of casualties inflicted by various methods of attack against different targets and suggestions as to the best method of employing heavy bombers and fighter-bombers in the close support role, were based on deductions made from the evidence available to them. The historian should not regard this evidence as incontrovertible, any more than could the ORS investigator of 1944.

This does not detract from the great value of OR material in that, despite its limitations, an objective attempt was made *at the time* to find out amid the chaos of battle what happened and why. The ORS was on the scene shortly after the conclusion of operations, and sometimes while they were still taking place, and talked to the troops that had taken part while memory and experience remained fresh. Few historians can doubt the worth of having such data as the comments of the British and Canadian infantry officers, given soon after the operation, on why the heavy bombing during CHARNWOOD was of little use to them, the comments of the British tank crews regarding the difficulties of their advance during GOODWOOD; or the descriptions given to an ORS officer by the commanders of American infantry regiments of how fighter-bombers had assisted them at Mortain.

NOTES

1. The role of OR in the RAF is discussed in Air Ministry Publication 3368, *The Origins and Development of Operational Research in the Royal Air Force* (London: HMSO, 1963).
2. British Army Report, *Operational Research in the British Army 1939–1945* (October 1947), p. 1, PRO WO 291/1301.
3. Ibid. See also Terry Copp, *Scientists and the Art of War*, RUSI Journal, Winter 1991, p. 65.
4. *Operational Research in the British Army 1939–1945*, p. 3.
5. Ibid., p. 14.
6. Ibid., pp. 9–10.

7. Air Ministry Publication 3368, *The Origins and Development of Operational Research in the Royal Air Force* (London: HMSO, 1963), p. 128.

8. Ibid., p. 129.

9. Ibid., p. 130.

10. History of the work conducted by No.2 Operational Research Section (British Army) in North-West Europe 1944-45, to be found in *Operational Research in North West Europe*, Introduction, p. i, PRO WO 291/1331.

11. Ibid., p. ii.

12. Ibid., p. iii.

13. Ibid., pp. iii–iv.

14. Ibid., p. iv.

15. Ibid.

16. Ibid.

17. Ibid., p. vii.

18. Ibid., p. v.

19. Copp, *Scientists and the Art of War*, p. 67.

20. *Operational Research in North West Europe*, Introduction, p. ix.

21. Ibid., p. xiii.

22. Ibid.

23. Ibid.

24. Air Ministry Publication 3368, p. 142.

25. *Operational Research in North West Europe*, Introduction, p. vii.

26. No.2 Operational Research Section 21st Army Group, Report No.14, *Heavy Bombing in Support of the Army* (1944), to be found in *Operational Research in North West Europe*, pp. 19–23.

27. *Operational Research in North West Europe*, Introduction, p. xv.

28. Ibid., p. xiii.

29. *Operational Research in the British Army 1939–1945*, p. 16.

30. Air Ministry Publication 3368, p.179.

31. Ibid., p. 160.

32. Prisoner of War Interrogation Report, Tunisia, Appendix B to 26th Armoured Brigade Intelligence Summary No.40, May 1943, PRO WO 175/210.

2

Flawed Instruments:
The Allied Air Support Systems,
1943–45

Close air support required aircraft to become battlefield weapons, but their success in this role depended upon the solution of a considerable command and control problem. There had to be a system enabling troops to request air support, for processing such requests and forwarding them to the air force, for allocating air units in response, and for directing them to the required area of the battlefront. Aerial firepower, when directed at battlefield targets, had to be integrated with the fire and movement of friendly ground forces. Finally, this entire process had to be carried out as quickly as possible if the air support was to be of use to those requesting it. Close air support thus required the creation of an extensive and elaborate joint army/air force machinery for carrying out these various functions, which necessarily employed considerable manpower and equipment resources.

THE BRITISH AIR SUPPORT SYSTEM

Having firmly rejected the concept of close air support during the interwar period, the RAF was inadequately equipped and trained to implement it in 1939. The air support that the RAF was equipped and trained to provide was officially termed 'Army Co-operation' and emphasised reconnaissance. Only one joint RAF/Army School of Army Co-operation existed, at Old Sarum, where under the auspices of No.22 Group junior army officers were trained for liaison duties with the squadrons detailed to support the British Expeditionary Force (BEF) in France by providing tactical reconnaissance (Tac/R), artillery spotting (Arty/R) and photographic reconnaissance (Photo/R).[1]

Fighter cover and bomber support for the BEF were the responsibility of a relatively small number of squadrons despatched to France but remaining under RAF control, these forming an 'Air Component' of fighter and reconnaissance units with the BEF and an independent 'Advanced Air Striking Force' (AASF) of light bomber squadrons. Both were under the aegis of British Air Forces in France Command (BAFF) under Air Marshal Sir Arthur Barratt.[2] During the German invasion of France and the Low Countries which commenced on 10 May 1940 their limited resources were fully stretched, while army requests for their support had to pass through a lengthy and cumbersome chain of command involving assessment at separate army and RAF headquarters.

This system proved hopelessly inadequate for the rapid pace of mobile operations, and effectively broke down after German armoured forces succeeded in breaking through the Allied front and encircling the northern Anglo-French armies. By 21 May most of the 'Air Component' had been withdrawn to operate from bases in southern England, divorced from their RAF headquarters in France, while the AASF withdrew to bases further south which, though beyond German reach, were virtually cut off from communication with the BEF.[3] A chaotic situation prevailed in which army officers in France were telephoning the War Office in London to try to arrange bomber attacks[4], while the RAF units remaining in France found themselves having to escape the German advance by constantly moving, at little notice and with insufficient transport, to ill-prepared and often unsuitable airfields lacking adequate telephone communications.[5]

It was impossible to organise and carry out effective air support under these conditions. There was very little close air support, and such air attacks that could be mounted, which were mainly intended to delay and disrupt the German advance, were usually too late to be of use. For example, on 20 May in response to requests for the bombing of German armoured columns reported approaching the Canal du Nord near Bapaume at 8.30 a.m. the RAF only appeared at 11.30 a.m., by which time the leading German units had already crossed and advanced beyond the canal. Similarly, on the same day, German columns reported approaching Arras at 2 p.m. had advanced considerably by the time the first RAF Blenheim light bombers appeared in the area at 6.30 p.m.[6]

Defeat in 1940 exposed the fundamental weaknesses of the British air-support method; insufficient contact between the army and RAF staffs, a situation exacerbated by their headquarters usually being sited at a considerable distance apart, and the lack of an extensive and reliable communications network. In the summer of 1940, with the UK itself threatened with invasion, the first steps were taken to reorganise the means of providing and co-ordinating air support.

In August 1940 the Air Ministry and War Office sanctioned a number of air-support experiments that were conducted the following month in Northern Ireland under the direction of Group Captain A.H. Wann, who had commanded the AASF light bomber squadrons in France, and Colonel J.D. Woodall, who had been Air Marshal Barratt's Military Staff Officer at Headquarters BAFF. The resulting 'Wann-Woodall Report' had clearly absorbed the lessons of the *Blitzkrieg* by identifying the need for a tactical air force – an RAF formation equipped and trained both to obtain air superiority by offensive air action and to attack battlefield targets in close co-ordination with ground operations.[7] For the latter task the experiments in Ireland saw the birth of the system which, when refined, was that employed by British forces in 1943–45. Essentially, it was an elaborate signals network based upon what Woodall termed 'Tentacles'; light mobile communications links with the forward troops which avoided normal signals channels and which enabled army officers to relay requests for air support direct to a control centre where they could be assessed by a joint Army/RAF staff.[8]

The system was adopted in principle by both the RAF and Army and was set up for further trials under the aegis of the RAF's Army Co-operation Command, which was established in December 1940 under Air Marshal Barratt. The outstanding feature was its extensive communications network, the most vital factor in any air support system, and which even in the experimental stage was found to cut by hours the time hitherto required to arrange air support.[9] The emphasis was placed on joint RAF/Army planning and decision making; Army and RAF Group headquarters were located together and the joint control centre, known as the Army Air Control Centre (AACC) with its own updated battle situation maps and charts of aircraft readiness, was situated as a quadrangle of caravans each connected by telephone. Each headquarters within the Army at Corps, Divisional, and Brigade level had an outstation manned by Royal Corps of Signals operators and an Army Air Liaison Officer (ALO) – this formed a 'tentacle'.

The tentacles were grouped into special units which were at first called 'Close Support Bomber Control' and later 'Army Air Support Control' (AASC). All the tentacles with a division were on the same frequency, and each division also maintained a tentacle at Corps headquarters. Thus all command levels could monitor support requests emanating from the front line, and if necessary cut in and object on the grounds of duplication or danger to friendly troops. This also permitted simultaneous reception of RAF tactical reconnaissance reports, and as adjacent army corps were also 'on net' this data along with the details of the close-support strikes was immediately circulated throughout the Army.

The sanctioning of airstrikes was intended to be the responsibility of the Army Chief of Staff and RAF Senior Air Staff Officer, but practice proved that the control centre itself was capable of handling this responsibility. The procedure was for the joint staff at the control centre to evaluate air-support requests as they came in, checking the proposed targets in relation to the 'bombline' – a line, projected forward of friendly troops and where possible based on physical features easily identifiable from the air, beyond which aircraft were permitted to attack targets. If the target was accepted the squadron designated for the task was then contacted via the direct communications to the airfields, where the ALOs attached to the squadrons were alerted to brief the pilots, who had then to identify their targets by means of photographic maps with grid references.[10]

While this system was being developed in the UK a parallel air-support system was forged in the hard test of battle in North Africa. Mobile warfare in the desert made effective air support particularly difficult. Battles were fought over many miles in a featureless terrain without established front lines, and Army headquarters were often uncertain of the exact positions of their forward troops which rendered bomblines meaningless. Pilots also found the recognition of units from the air problematical, especially as both sides freely employed captured vehicles. These uncertainties inevitably caused delays in the provision of air support, exacerbated by the RAF bomber squadrons usually operating over considerable distances and having to rendezvous with fighter escorts before proceeding to the battle area, where still more time was needed to identify the target. Consequently, the average time between an army request for air support and the bombing of the target could be as much as 2½–3 hours.[11]

The solution to the problem of air support in North Africa came largely through the influence of Air Chief Marshal Sir Arthur Tedder, who became Air Officer Commanding-in-Chief Middle East on 1 June 1941. Tedder reorganised the RAF's No.204 Group in the forward area into a separate 'Air Headquarters, Western Desert' and grouped its fighter, light bomber and reconnaissance squadrons into wings with increased transport for mobility while removing unnecessary equipment and personnel. This streamlining effectively created the RAF's first tactical air force – soon to be known as the Desert Air Force - which in July came under the command of Air Vice-Marshal Arthur Coningham.[12]

Attention was also given to the machinery for requesting, allocating, and providing air support, and in October 1941 a system similar to that being developed in the UK came into operation. A joint RAF/Army staffed Air Support Control (ASC) headquarters was established at each army corps and each armoured division, linked to the forward brigades by a 'tentacle' equipped with two-way wireless telegraphy. An RAF team was also allocated to each brigade, known as a 'Forward Air Support Link' (FASL) and equipped with two-way radio-telephony for the control of supporting aircraft and the reception of reconnaissance broadcasts. Support requests from the brigades were evaluated at the ASC and, if accepted, contact was made with the RAF units at the airfields through a 'Rear Air Support Link' (RASL) (see Appendix).[13]

A fusion of the air-support system developed in the UK with that created in North Africa occurred during 1942, when a UK-trained Tentacle (No.2 AASC) arrived to gain operational experience. No.2 AASC was employed during the Gazala battle, and when called upon proved that the air support response time, from army request to aircraft over target, could be reduced to thirty minutes.[14] Thus, as a result of a combination of theory, experimentation and training in the UK and practical experience in North Africa, a British air support system had been created by the end of 1942, which was to remain essentially the same throughout the war. The principal features of this system and the later refinements in use during 1943–45 are described below.

The vital elements in the communications network linking the Army and RAF were the tentacles. By 1944 they had become the full responsibility of the Royal Corps of Signals and were renamed Air Support Signals Units, or ASSUs. They enabled army formations down to Brigade level to request air support via the combined Army/RAF control centre, and they were standardised to allow their deployment to Corps, Division, or Brigade headquarters. They were also attached to RAF headquarters at Wing and Group Control Centre. Each ASSU tentacle consisted of a vehicle, usually an armoured half-track, a driver/mechanic, and a crew of three operators to man the powerful wireless (WS Cdn.9) working on the tentacle net

DIAGRAM I

SIGNAL DIAGRAM – AIR SUPPORT CONTROL
(BASED ON DIAGRAM IN MIDDLE EAST PAMPHLET No.3A)

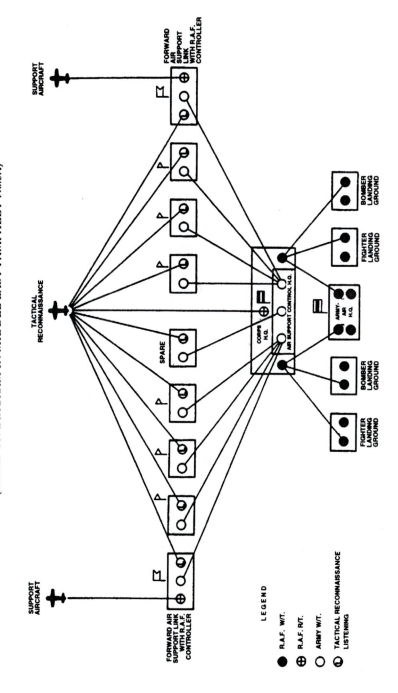

LEGEND

● R.A.F. W/T.

⊕ R.A.F. R/T.

○ ARMY W/T.

◐ TACTICAL RECONNAISSANCE
LISTENING

DIAGRAM II

OPERATIONAL CONTROL FOR A COMPOSITE GROUP – N.W. EUROPE

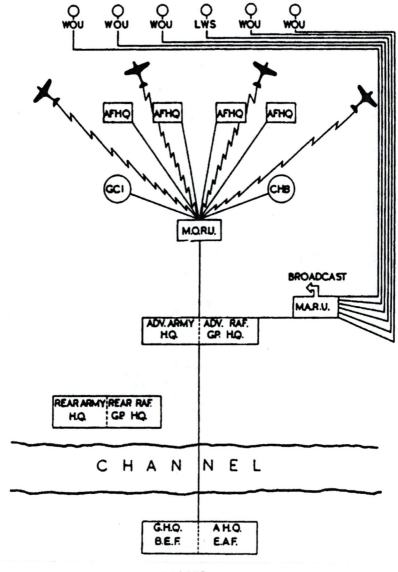

LEGEND

W.O.U. = WIRELESS OBSERVER UNIT
L.W.S. = LIGHT WARNING SET
A.F.H.Q. = AIRFIELD H.Q.
M.O.R.U. = MOBILE OPERATIONS ROOM UNIT
M.A.R.U. = MOBILE AIR REPORTING UNIT

and the remote receiver for reception of RAF tactical reconnaissance broadcasts.[15]

The most important principle regarding the ASSUs was that they should remain rigidly independent of the control of the formations to which they were attached. This prevented wireless sets and their operators being misappropriated by 'on the spot' commanders and diverted from their task of relaying air-support requests and data. Deployed ASSUs came under the command of the formation to which they were attached, but were under the direct control of the 'G' (Operations) staff and never under the jurisdiction of the Signals staff. Tentacle wireless traffic was likewise delivered direct to the 'G' staff, and never passed through ordinary Signals channels where its priority might have been compromised. The formation to which an ASSU tentacle was attached became responsible for its administration, but technical supervision was exercised by mobile servicing detachments sent by a main ASSU headquarters.[16]

The British air support system proved very successful in processing pre-planned air-support strikes, but the more difficult test was how quickly air support could be provided in response to impromptu requests from the forward troops, where speed was vitally important. In this respect, both in Italy and in the early stages of the campaign in North-West Europe, the process was simply not fast enough. A British Army report on air support in late 1944 identified where the problem lay by observing that the failure was not in the communications system itself, but in the number of links in the chain and, particularly, the time spent in discussion between Army and RAF staffs before orders were finally issued.[17]

The solution was to modify the existing machinery and procedure, though ironically this amounted to another link in the air support chain. The original system had envisaged the provision of Visual Control Posts (VCPs) at the battlefront which, as the name implies, were intended for the visual control of aircraft from a position on the ground commanding a view of the battle area. Experience proved that such ground was rarely found, so the VCPs were modified to become small forward air-support controls. They became known as Forward Control Posts (FCPs) and were most significant in the operational development of the ASSUs, as they were intended to decrease the time factor in the provision of immediate close air support.

An FCP was an advanced headquarters, staffed by a senior RAF Controller (often a Wing Commander) and a staff officer from the Army Air Liaison Group, and equipped with ASSU communications enabling them to intercept traffic on the tentacle net and to speak to the tentacles deployed with the forward troops, the RAF/Army Control Centre, and to airborne aircraft by means of VHF. Tentacles with the forward troops could at any time talk direct to the FCP, which could quickly determine the urgency of targets submitted. For a target where speed was not essential the air support system would function in the usual way, with the FCP monitoring but not intervening. However, when it was clear that a target needed to be engaged rapidly the RAF Controller at the FCP could 'step in' and handle the request. In this case the RAF/Army Control Centre was informed by telephone or R/T link that the FCP would deal with that particular target and the requesting army formation contacted by R/T to arrange target details. Strike aircraft, either at airfield readiness or possibly already in or near the battle area were then contacted and briefed in the air. In this way the FCP relieved the main Army/RAF Control Centre of much of the urgent air support workload.[18]

Each FCP was designed to fulfil the requirements of one army corps and was normally sited alongside corps headquarters. When FCPs were required to support more than one corps they were sited to the best wireless advantage at the expense of proximity to any particular headquarters − adequate communications making close physical proximity unnecessary.[19] The FCPs originated with British forces in Italy, where due to their ability to be switched between headquarters without disrupting normal air support communications they were known as ROVER. FCPs operating in support of British Eighth Army were ROVER PADDY and ROVER DAVID. Each FCP required a sizeable commitment of manpower and equipment. In North-West Europe a typical FCP consisted of three 3-ton lorries, an army transmitter vehicle containing the three necessary tentacle sets, an RAF transmitter vehicle and a receiver coach and office.[20] When operating in support of Fifth Army in Italy during late 1944 ROVER PADDY consisted of six officers (two senior Army Air Liaison Officers, two Royal Artillery Liaison Officers, and two RAF Air Controllers) and 34 other ranks. Transport consisted of five jeeps with trailers, two 15-cwt trucks, two armoured cars, and two White scout cars − most fitted with W/T, R/T and VHF communications equipment − in addition to several vehicles equipped with R/T sets specifically for communicating with Air Observation Post (AOP) light aircraft spotting for the artillery.[21]

The FCPs depended upon information sent back from the battle area, but operational experience still exposed the need for a means of controlling aircraft at the battlefront, particularly during mobile operations. The solution was further decentralisation of control – the creation of a modified form of tentacle known as the Contact Car. This consisted either of a White scout car or half-track which, in addition to the normal tentacle wireless (WS Cdn.9), was equipped with two VHF sets (TR.1143) for ground/air communication and another wireless set (WS No.22) for the dual purpose of receiving air-reconnaissance broadcasts and intercepting the air-support control network. Contact Cars were RAF units, and their normal tentacle crew was supplemented by an RAF Wireless Operator/Mechanic whose responsibility was to maintain the VHF equipment. They could function as normal tentacles, but their task was really to enable an RAF Forward Air Controller (FAC) to communicate with aircraft overhead at the battlefront.

Contact Cars were used both to control aircraft obtaining air-reconnaissance data for forward troops and to control strike aircraft. In the case of the former task, an RAF reconnaissance pilot was attached to the Contact Car. A request for a reconnaissance sortie was relayed by the Contact Car to the 'G' staff at Army headquarters responsible for arranging air reconnaissance, who then signalled back to the Contact Car the estimated time of arrival of the aircraft. On arrival over the forward area the pilot was briefed by his fellow pilot attached to the Contact Car, to whom he reported the results of his mission. This was then circulated over the tentacle net to be received simultaneously by all formations listening in. For controlling airstrikes the procedure was slightly different in that the FAC attached to the Contact Car was usually an experienced ground attack pilot, often a Squadron Leader or Flight Lieutenant, able to give the pilots a target briefing and to advise them during the attack using the terms that one pilot would use to another.[22]

During 1944–45 some variations of the Contact Car were developed to meet particular operational requirements. Jeeps equipped with VHF and WS Cdn.9 sets compressed the Contact Car facilities into a small vehicle, and were successfully employed during the crossing of the Rhine in 1945. For the amphibious assault on Walcheren in November 1944 a Weasel amphibian was fitted out as a tentacle and manned by an ASSU crew. However, in contrast to the Americans, the use of contact tanks in offensive operations was never fully developed by British forces. In North-West Europe tanks fitted out as ASSUs were little more than armoured shelters for the controllers to operate their ground/air communications,[23] while in Italy contact tanks as employed by US forces were used for the first time by the British as late as March 1945, when modified Shermans with the North Irish Horse successfully directed airstrikes closely coordinated with the assault on the Comacchio Spit.[24]

The ALOs assigned to RAF units and the joint Army/RAF Control Centre were the chief agents in linking the RAF and Army for close air support operations. This was acknowledged by the RAF, a history of air support in North-West Europe compiled by 2nd TAF observing that the Air Liaison Sections attached to fighter-bomber wings were 'the focal point of the Wing's operations'.[25] Within 2nd TAF in 1944, the air support system as it affected the ALOs with a fighter-bomber Wing functioned as follows:

a) Throughout the day and night Situation Reports ('SitReps') were received from the battle area via ASSU and teleprinter, while any special information was received from the joint RAF/Army Control Centre by telephone. This data flow enabled the ALOs constantly to update their situation and bombline maps. Target details were also received by ASSU or telephone from the Control Centre. When the battlefront was static, an overnight list of likely targets for the following day came through by teleprinter, allowing the ALOs to collect briefing material and thus save some time by anticipation.

b) Executive orders for airstrikes came through RAF channels, and on their receipt the ALOs arranged briefing material (maps and any available photographs) and obtained details as to the estimated time over target from the Wing Commander or flight leader as soon as possible and relayed this immediately to the Control Centre and ASSUs. Pilots were then briefed, it being the ALOs' chief responsibility to ensure that pilots were aware of the position of the bombline and that of friendly troops near the target area.[26] On the return of the pilots the ALOs took part in their debriefing, and a flash report was sent over the ASSU net containing all information of interest to the Army. Details of the mission were also issued in an RAF operations flash signal.[27]

There were weaknesses in this air support system, and consequent inefficiencies that can be seen in several elements of the air-support procedure. One weakness was acknowledged in 2nd TAF's immediate post-war history of air support in North-West Europe. This observed that Contact Cars controlled airstrikes usually as a result of being delegated the task by the FCP controlling that sector, but that the FCP staff did not always choose to delegate despite the obvious advantage of having the airstrike controlled by an observer with the forward troops. This was because it was found that the individual aptitude of Air Liaison Officers and pilots in contact cars varied, and the FCP staffs were often reluctant to authorise local control in cases where the standard of performance was likely to compromise chances of success.[28]

In late 1944 the British Army produced an outspoken report on air support based on the experience gained thus far in North-West Europe.[29] This highlighted another, persistent, problem in the system, that of the correct use of codes and cyphers in air support communications, though it was acknowledged that this was an extremely confusing aspect of the system, and that a balance had to be struck constantly between security and speed and constantly readjusted under changing operational conditions.[30]

During that campaign the Germans had been able to set up a warning system against air attack based on the interception of support requests from British Army units. When this was realised at RAF/Army staff level it created a security scare with, in the opinion of the Army report, 'the result that many unnecessary restrictions were recommended'.[31]

Investigation proved that the Germans had been able to intercept ASSU traffic not as a result of a failure in the system, but because army formations had been misusing it. It was found that some units were using the immediate support request procedure, when messages could be sent in clear, to request air action as much as 24 hours ahead, while all too often units were relaying bombline details which revealed the intentions of the army units in clear rather than in cypher.[32]

Insufficient training, failure properly to understand the procedure, or simply carelessness were all likely to have been contributory factors to this, but another may have been that the ASSUs themselves were being worked to the limit. During both static and mobile operations the volume of signals traffic was immense, yet the number of trained ASSU personnel was limited. In 1944 the Army noted that ASSU tentacle NCOs carried far more responsibility than their ordinary Signals equivalents, that their task was far more demanding, and that a Corporal operator with a British tentacle did essentially the same job as a Canadian Tentacle Officer or a Major with a US Air Support Party.[33]

A characteristic of the British system appears to have been the provision of manpower barely adequate to fulfil assigned tasks, and this was seen in the Army Air Liaison Sections. To carry out the tasks related above, an Air Liaison Section attached to an RAF fighter-bomber wing of several squadrons normally consisted of only four ALOs supported by two clerks, the senior officer being a GSO.2 who also acted as military advisor to the RAF Group Captain commanding the Wing and the Wing Commander (Flying) who planned the Wing's operations. Not surprisingly, the Army firmly resisted RAF attempts to have the task of dealing with cypher traffic at tentacles assigned to the Wing added to the already heavy burden of ALO responsibilities.[34]

More serious failings in the system had been exposed during operations by late 1944, especially with regard to air/ground recognition and bombline discipline, both of which were poor. Correctly identifying friendly troops and vehicles in any terrain from a fighter or fighter-bomber aircraft moving at speed over a battle area obscured by smoke was no easy task, and a great deal of awareness of the problem and the taking of adequate safety measures by both the Army and RAF were required. In both Italy and North-West Europe (but particularly in the latter) this was often lacking. In Normandy the problem was acute, largely because training in air/ground recognition procedure had been severely handicapped before the invasion by delay in the promulgation of agreed methods. The basic principles and recommendations were worked out after extensive trials in Britain some 18 months before D-Day, but final instructions were not issued until shortly before the invasion. As a result, as the Army later acknowledged, no issue of apparatus or painting of vehicle signs had been carried out, and no worthwhile training between the two Services had been possible.[35]

Moreover, there had been a dispute within the Army as to whether identification signs should be painted or carried on vehicles at all – one argument being that if Allied pilots could see them, so could German – and the Armoured Corps at first refused to have any such markings applied. Given that the degree of air superiority attained by the Allied air forces could not be foreseen before D-Day this argument seems reasonable, but it exacerbated an already confused situation.

Poor air/ground recognition procedure inevitably results in aircraft attacking friendly troops and, as events in the Gulf War of 1991 proved only too well, this can have tragic consequences.[36] It is a serious problem which, if not rectified swiftly, can erode confidence and cause bitterness between services and between allies. In 1943–45, and particularly in Normandy, there were frequent occasions when British and Canadian troops were attacked in error by their supporting aircraft during both static and mobile operations. Analysis by the

Army in 1944 found that the number of such incidents peaked during the transition from semi-static to mobile warfare, when Allied forces were advancing and when bomblines became very fluid. For the most part the offending aircraft were flying free-ranging armed-reconnaissance missions as opposed to being detailed for specific close support strikes, and had obviously either failed to identify correctly columns of friendly troops and vehicles or had misjudged the bomb line – though in such operations ground forces often penetrated beyond the bombline.[37]

In Italy and North-West Europe Allied troops were supplied with canisters of yellow smoke with which to identify themselves to friendly aircraft, and it is sobering to read of many instances when air attacks were pressed home against friendly troops carrying out the correct recognition drill by releasing such smoke. On 20 August 1944 in Normandy First Canadian Army produced a report listing 52 separate instances of attacks by fighter bombers – Spitfires, Typhoons, Mustangs, and USAAF Lightnings – against its forward troops that had occurred between 16 and 18 August and which had killed 72 and wounded 191 officers and men and destroyed or damaged 12 vehicles. Some of these attacks had been made despite yellow smoke being released, and in one case despite an Air Observation Post (AOP) artillery spotter plane attempting to ward off the offending Typhoons. Not surprisingly, First Canadian Army called for all possible steps to be taken to reduce such occurrences, warning that otherwise the provision of air support would soon become a deterrent to ground operations rather than the stimulant of which it was potentially capable of being.[38]

This is in fact precisely what happened. The Army report of late 1944 on air support observed that the moral effect of such attacks on friendly troops was great and tended to be out of proportion to the damage and casualties inflicted. Moreover, such attacks left a hangover of some duration in which units became cautious and reluctant to call for air support.[39] Such attacks, though not on such an alarming scale, persisted and the troops developed an acute awareness of the threat. When Beauvais was liberated its French citizens were perplexed to see the passing British Grenadier Guards anxiously glancing skywards, and one of them asked why, when the Allies had air superiority, the British troops should fear air attack. According to the Regimental History the reason was simple – experience had taught the forward troops that during rapid advances friendly aircraft were to be feared more than those of the enemy.[40]

Accurate data regarding the exact location of bomblines was a recurrent problem. Army formations often set bomblines too far ahead of friendly troops. This was erring on the safe side, but had operational disadvantages. One was that many German positions were left within the bombline. Because of an RAF ruling that no target was to be engaged within the bombline unless marked by coloured artillery smoke (a precaution against air attack on friendly troops), these positions could not be attacked by air when smoke was unavailable. Even when smoke was available responsiveness of air support could be reduced, for if a target was to be marked by artillery firing red smoke this alone could sometimes take up to 30 minutes to arrange.[41] Another disadvantage was that, as the Army report of late 1944 admitted, the RAF lost confidence in the bombline as a reliable indication of the position of the forward troops, and were prepared to argue with the Army over the position of the bombline in relation to such troops.[42]

Such disputes threatened to throw the entire air support machinery out of gear by making nonsense of the basic information relayed by the ASSUs and distributed by the ALOs upon which airstrikes were planned. The result was confusion and, in extreme cases, attacks on friendly troops as related above.

That such disputes occurred suggests that the relationship between the RAF and the Army in 1943–45 was an uneasy partnership. From a historical perspective this is surprising, for the RAF had considerable experience of providing air support to the Army during the First World War and in 1917/18 the RFC/RAF had in fact pioneered many of the later techniques of close air support. British aircraft operated with tanks during the Cambrai offensive of 1917, and by 1918, in contrast to 1943–45, air/tank integration for offensive operations was highly developed. Squadrons were attached to the Tank Corps for the specific purpose of dealing with German anti-tank defences, and a system of rotation was introduced whereby Tank Corps officers were assigned to air duty and aircrew to serve in tanks for familiarisation.[43]

Experiments in wireless communication between tanks and aircraft were also conducted, largely by the commander of No.8 Squadron, Trafford Leigh-Mallory – later Air Marshal Sir Trafford Leigh-Mallory and overall commander of the Allied Tactical Air Forces in 1944.[44] The utility of a communications centre linking air and ground units was realised, and in August 1918 the RAF established a wireless information centre near the battlefront which, working from air reconnaissance data and reports from the front line, was able to contact airborne aircraft and direct them to ground targets.[45]

Yet during the Second World War senior airmen were determined
to avoid a commitment to support the Army. This was not only due to
concern that such a commitment would lead to the loss of the RAF's
independent status, but because close support had come to be recognised as a misuse of air power. In May 1941, after experience of the
German use of tactical air power, the War Office demanded that the
RAF be prepared and equipped to provide similar support to the
British Army, particularly against German tanks. This was bitterly
resisted by the Air Ministry, and the Director of Plans, Air Vice-
Marshal Slessor, condemned, with justification, what he saw as the
Army's tendency to ask the RAF to do what it should be doing itself,
adding that it was the job of the Army's anti-tank weapons to destroy
enemy tanks on the battlefield, while the role of the RAF was to prevent enemy forces from functioning due to shortages of fuel, food and
ammunition. In effect Slessor completely rejected close air support
except in the event of an emergency, which in his view should not
occur if the RAF was properly employed from the outset.[46]

Moreover, close air support was considered likely to be very costly.
Group Captain Basil Embry, who had led airstrikes against German
troops in France in 1940, warned the Air Ministry in May 1941 that
the scale and intensity of the German anti-aircraft firepower was such
as to make close support prohibitive, with a potential casualty rate
amongst aircraft out of all proportion to any results achieved.[47]

It is against this background of RAF hostility to the concept of
close support that the British air support system of 1943–45 must be
assessed. The air support machinery was set up and manned by two
independent services, neither of which had had much worthwhile
experience of co-operating closely with the other before 1941–42 as a
result of the dichotomy which occurred after 1918. By 1943–45 Allied
air superiority and the large number of tactical aircraft available made
close support possible and a workable machinery was in place. But it
was manned by an air force whose high command was fundamentally
opposed to the role and an army unused to utilising air support, and
whose General Staff was, for the most part, too unfamiliar with air
power to fully appreciate its potential, and its drawbacks, when
applied to the battlefield. In North-West Europe especially, there was
little RAF/Army commonality at high command level, and a good deal
of bitterness and recrimination.

That this was likely to be a problem in North-West Europe was
foreseen, by none other than Field Marshal Montgomery. In North
Africa Montgomery had been a firm believer in close Army/RAF

relations, and one of his first steps after assuming command of Eighth Army in August 1942 had been to ensure that the Army Headquarters and that of RAF Desert Air Force were located together and that the senior air staff officers shared his mess, a move welcomed by Air Marshal Coningham, commanding Desert Air Force, and Air Marshal Tedder, Air C-in-C Middle East.[48] After his return from Italy in January 1944 Montgomery found a very different situation prevailing in the forces preparing for OVERLORD, and on 4 May he expressed his concern in a letter to the Army Commanders who were to serve under him in Normandy. Observing that there was a 'definite gulf' between the armies and their supporting Air Forces, Montgomery urged that all officers and men be taught to realise that air support was essential for winning the land battle, and that success depended upon each Army and its accompanying Air Force being welded into a single entity.[49]

Yet by this time both Coningham, who was to command RAF 2nd Tactical Air Force in North-West Europe, and Tedder, serving as Deputy to the Allied Supreme Commander, General Eisenhower, were greatly disillusioned with Montgomery. They had resented the prestige and popularity accorded him after Alamein while the air forces had received little recognition; they had also been critical of what they saw as his over-cautious pursuit of Axis forces after Alamein and his failure to take sufficient note in his plans of the need to secure airfields – a criticism that would also be levelled at him in Normandy.

Despite his protestations on the need for close Army/Air Force liaison, Montgomery appears to have done little to remedy the situation in early 1944 when the various Headquarters were situated far apart; 21st Army Group near Portsmouth, the Air C-in-C at Stanmore, and Coningham at Uxbridge. There was also much RAF resentment that, at this period, Montgomery embarked upon a morale-raising tour of camps and factories, leaving his Chief of Staff, De Guingand, to deal with the senior airmen. In short, there was much ill-feeling on the part of senior airmen towards the Army in general and Montgomery in particular, an unpromising atmosphere in which close air/ground integration could hardly flourish and which would worsen during the campaign.[50]

Nevertheless, at the operational level within the air support system where junior officers and men of both services worked together, relations were good, as the Army report of late 1944 admitted:

the difficulties are usually greatest at the higher levels, and decrease at the lower end of the scale. At the first point where practical executive action has to be taken, the difficulties begin to disappear, and from there downwards, in nine cases out of ten, there is no problem.[51]

One example of the tenuous RAF/Army relationship occurred in Normandy, when the Army felt particularly aggrieved by what was seen as a successful attempt by the RAF to deal the authority and influence of the Air Liaison Sections a damaging blow. As a result of an RAF reorganisation of its command structure, the RAF requested that the rank of the senior ALO in an Air Liaison Section be reduced from GSO.2 to GSO.3 in order to be kept in line with the RAF senior Wing Intelligence Officer. This was reluctantly agreed to, but resulted in the senior ALO being equivalent only to a Flight Lieutenant. Not only did this severely reduce prospects of promotion, a move hardly calculated to attract the best talents to the air-support sphere, it was seen by the Army as unjustified. The Army report of late 1944 complained that the post of senior ALO at a wing of five fighter or fighter-bomber squadrons carried considerable responsibility, and justified a second grade appointment.[52]

This was regarded as one manifestation of RAF hostility to Army involvement in air operations. Another Army grievance was the experience of the sections of the 'G' (Operations) staff within British Army formations responsible for coordinating plans for air support. These sections were known as 'G' (Air) and by late 1944 were considered to be functioning effectively, though it was felt that their existence had been resented by the RAF:

> the Air Forces were left with the wrong impression of G (Air) whom they were inclined to regard as pseudo-experts in what they considered purely air matters, and as an unwelcome barrier between themselves and the General Staff. This attitude has subsided during the course of operations, but it did not make the task of G (Air) any easier in the early days.[53]

The Army's principal grievance, however, was that the soldiers had been firmly excluded from any role in decision making as to the weapons and tactics employed in close support. The Army report of 1944 condemned the RAF's apparent disapproval of any attempt on the Army's part to become familiar with the problems of air support, and the prevailing attitude whereby the Army was expected to confine itself to merely stating the problem, while the RAF decided the solution.[54]

Certainly the Army had had no influence in the type of aircraft employed in close support. After the defeats of 1940–41 the Army demanded aircraft capable of providing the same support as enjoyed by German troops, and in particular dive-bombers. This was successfully resisted by the RAF and Air Ministry, senior airmen such as Slessor pointing out that the omnipotence of the German 'Stuka' dive-bomber was illusory and its success due only to German air superiority and the weakness of its opponents' anti-aircraft defences.[55] There is a general consensus among historians that the rejection of dive-bombers was the correct course, but at the time this appeared to the Army to be one of many instances of the RAF being unwilling to provide air support, and fuelled demands for a separate Army air arm.[56]

The result of this decision was that in 1943–45 none of the aircraft providing close support to British troops had been originally developed for the task, being dual-role fighter-bombers as opposed to dedicated ground-attack aircraft, and carrying bombs or rockets in addition to their fixed gun armament. Their effectiveness in this role is discussed in subsequent chapters, but from the Army point of view the fact that they had been designed as interceptor fighters for the defence of Britain meant that they had one major drawback – lack of range. The late 1944 Army report on air support complained, in view of experience in North-West Europe, that the RAF's ability to support the Army during rapid advances had been compromised by the limited range of its fighters and fighter-bombers, particularly during the onset of mobile operations following the breakout from Normandy, and that airfields tended to go out of action just when air support was most needed to assist the momentum of the advance. While longer-range US aircraft had frequently been called upon to cover vital areas and targets on the British front, this in turn had brought problems with recognition, communications and briefing.[57]

The Army also resented a perceived lack of RAF interest in developing and improving the techniques of operating with ground forces. The RAF's knowledge of the Army remained 'depressingly low' with 'little acknowledgement of the fact and no desire to bring about improvement'.

Only one joint school of instruction in air support had been set up and was in the Army's view unsatisfactory, as

> the object of the course has been confined almost entirely to teaching the soldier about the Air Force, a statement which might be qualified by

substituting – to teach the Army what the Air Force thinks the Army ought to know about the Air Force.[58]

This was clearly resentment against what was seen as a patronising RAF attitude towards the Army, but it must also be borne in mind that there was a great lack of comprehension of the entire subject of air support within the Army itself, which can be seen as the result of the Army having little or no experience of utilising it. As the 1944 report admitted, when the G (Air) staffs were created there had been a tendency to treat G (Air) as a new and separate branch of the Staff, and for the General Staff at almost all levels to regard air support as the specialised business of this new branch rather than their own.[59]

Many senior General Staff officers, lacking operational experience of air support, either left all air support problems to their G (Air) sections, thereby giving them little direction as to what was needed, or controlled their activities too rigidly, thereby stultifying what expertise they possessed. The 1944 report identified what was needed to correct this situation, and in doing so highlighted a fundamental weakness in the British Army's conception of air support – that many senior officers shared with many senior airmen the tacit assumption that air support was something other than what they should be concerned with:

> improvement can only come from a recognition of air action as an integral part of Army operations and from experience and study. If this recognition is to take practical form a reorientation of our training will be necessary so that at all stages *and in all staff colleges and schools, supporting air action is taught and studied in the same way and with the same priorities as other operational subjects.*[60]

The British Army of 1943–45 was doctrinally unprepared for such a step, nor would it have been tolerated by the RAF. In 1941 the latter Service had successfully resisted Army attempts to subordinate air operations to those on the ground, and had been vindicated in North Africa. But in 1943–45 the RAF still, as Chester Wilmot observed, laboured under a 'junior service complex', and was constantly eager to assert its equality and independence.[61]

This attitude emanated from the top, and subordinate RAF tactical air commanders who proved willing to co-operate closely with the soldiers in 1943–45, such as Air Vice-Marshal Broadhurst, who had commanded RAF Desert Air Force after Coningham and later 2nd TAF's No.83 Group in North-West Europe, were sometimes censured for this by their seniors.[62] By early 1945 there was also a hardening attitude on the part of the Army. Its report of late 1944 condemned the continuing deference to RAF wishes and, with an eye to the future, advocated a firmer stance:

> in matters of high policy affecting the two Services the Army has deferred to the Air Force in almost every instance... This may have been a question of policy, and was certainly not unconnected with...the advantages conferred on a Service fully engaged operationally at a time when a large proportion of the Army was inactive. The situation has now changed and the Army has come into its own as a war winning factor, but our approach to joint problems does not seem to have been affected, and the policy of appeasement still governs much of our dealings with the Air Force. Whether a policy of appeasement was ever profitable is a matter of opinion... In any case it is difficult to believe in it under the present circumstances where, superficial affability and goodwill on the one hand, and behind the scenes criticisms and backbiting on the other...constitute a poor substitute for genuine co-operation.[63]

THE US AIR SUPPORT SYSTEM

The system of air support employed by the USAAF and Army in North-West Europe and Italy was broadly similar to that of the British. In some respects it was more innovative and flexible, though the same problems that dogged the British system were also evident.

A US Tactical Air Force consisted of several Tactical Air Commands (TACs) composed of fighter, fighter-bomber and reconnaissance squadrons and which approximated to an RAF Group. Thus in early 1945 the Ninth Air Force in North-West Europe comprised the IX, XIX, and XXIX Tactical Air Commands. Each TAC supported a particular Army within the Army Group. As far as possible, Tactical Air Force and Army Group, and TAC and Army, headquarters were located together. When this was not possible, the TACs maintained a small mobile command echelon at the advanced headquarters of the corresponding Army. Air Force headquarters planned the deployment of the TAC's and medium bomber units, controlled the movement of air units, and prepared long range logistical plans. Air Force headquarters also co-ordinated the planning of large scale air operations involving the operations of more than one TAC.

Each TAC planned and coordinated the day to day air support of its corresponding Army. This planning, including the selection of targets and allocation of air effort, was conducted from a 'Combined Operations Center' at TAC/Army headquarters which was manned by joint Air Force and Army staff. Each evening a briefing, known in the Ninth Air Force as the 'Evening Target Conference', was held during which the day's operations and the programme for the following day were outlined. Normal procedure was for the Army G-2 (Intelligence) to summarise ground operations of the day and the Army G-3 (Operations) to describe those planned for the next day and submit a list of request missions. The Air Intelligence Officer (A-2) would then present new items of air intelligence and the A-2 Target Officer outline potential targets for consideration. A weather report would also be given.

After the briefing the Air Combat Operations Officer (A-3) would announce air units available for operations, first deducting units required for special targets ordered by the Tactical Air Force Headquarters and those needed for bomber escort. He would then allocate units for armed reconnaissance missions (see Chapter 8 below) beyond the enemy front line and attacks upon air-designated targets. The balance, less units undergoing maintenance, were allotted to pre-arranged air support missions. This priority accorded to armed reconnaissance was normal during periods when the battlefront was mainly static with few offensive operations by ground forces, a post-war US study observing that air effort was seldom allotted to 'close-in missions' unless the Army was attempting an advance. [64]

Orders were then issued assigning tasks to Groups (the equivalent to RAF Wings), which in turn designated squadrons for particular missions. Plans for major air support operations were drafted at TAC level and submitted to the headquarters of the Tactical Air Force where they were finalised by the joint Army and Air staff. [65]

Air-support requests submitted after 2400 hrs for execution on the same day were evaluated by the Army G-3 according to urgency and the importance of the role of the ground unit making the request in the Army plan. The mission was plotted on a constantly updated situation map and the bomb line checked. This procedure took about 15 minutes, and requests were processed in turn. After checking and approval by the Army G-3, the request was submitted to the Air Combat Operations Officer at an adjacent desk. If it was approved and aircraft were available the A-3 would assign a squadron or group for the task, notifying the group headquarters by telephone or teleprinter. The ground unit making the request was notified of either acceptance or refusal; in the former case the estimated time of arrival of the aircraft was given and in the event of a refusal the reason was stated. Requests for immediate support were also decided upon by the Combat Operations Officer, who could divert aircraft from pre-arranged missions, but mostly such requests, if accepted, were answered by diverting fighter-bombers from armed reconnaissance missions.[66]

Liaison with ground formations was undertaken by Tactical Air Party Officers (TAPOs) – also known as Tactical Air Liaison Officers (TALOs) or Air Support Party Officers (ASPOs) depending upon which TAC they represented. These were pilots whose combat tour had expired and who were attached to the headquarters of Corps, Divisions, and armoured Combat Commands for a period of 90 days in rotation to advise the military commanders on air matters and, in particular, to evaluate the air support targets submitted by the army G-3 (Air) – the staff officer responsible for air support matters. TAPOs were provided with communications personnel and UHF and VHF radio equipment for relaying the air-support requests to the TAC headquarters. The TAPOs also acted as Forward Air Controllers for directing airstrikes, army formations being accorded additional TAPOs for this purpose.[67] In Italy the XII TAC adopted the British ROVER FCP system for controlling airstrikes in support of the Fifth Army, assigning the FCP the codename ROVER JOE.[68]

Army representation with air units was by army staff officers G-3 (Air) and G-2 (Air), the latter responsible for intelligence, being attached to the TAC headquarters. In addition, Ground Liaison Officers (GLOs) were attached to groups and squadrons. Their task was effectively the same as their British ALO counterparts – to keep the air units informed of the situation in the battle area and to maintain the group and squadron battle situation maps. They also played a key role in the pre-mission briefing of aircrew, ensuring that pilots were familiar with the bombline, and also took part in their debriefing.[69]

In some respects the US system of air support reflected a greater spirit of commonality between air and ground forces than was prevalent between the RAF and the British Army, and a consequent mutual willingness to experiment and adopt innovations to improve the system. This is revealed in the relative approaches to the forward control of aircraft. Although this had been pioneered by the British in the Mediterranean, in North-West Europe they were slow to adopt the Visual Control Post method. Before D-Day it had been outlined in an AEAF memorandum that such control of aircraft was most appropriate as part of a prearranged plan, and would only be employed at the discretion of Air Marshal Coningham.[70] As a result, provision of VCPs was scant, amounting to one per Corps, and the British Army report of late 1944 complained that before D-Day the organisation had not included the machinery to control a small reconnaissance/striking force over the advancing columns – a need that consequently had to be met by improvisation.[71] In contrast, each US Air Support Party could function as a forward VCP, and they were allotted on a scale of one per infantry division, and sometimes two or three per armoured division.[72]

Another US innovation, instituted in Italy, was the use of light artillery observation aircraft (Piper L-5 'Grasshoppers') to direct fighter-bombers to close support targets. By June 1944 the XII TAC supporting the US Fifth Army was employing L-5 aircraft equipped with SCR-522 radios and flown by fighter-bomber pilots operating as airborne Forward Air Controllers. This innovation was known as 'Horsefly' and the usual practice was for two L-5s to be assigned to each Corps. They were given distinctive markings for pilots to distinguish them from the L-5s operating as conventional artillery spotters and, in addition to the FAC, carried an infantry observer for the purpose of identifying friendly troops; operating with US armour they carried an observer trained to distinguish US from German tanks. Usually flying at 3,000–4,000 feet, Horseflys used smoke bombs to mark targets and were of particular value when artillery was unavailable for this task. They also provided an easily located orbit point for the fighter-bombers, while the L-5 observer was on hand to rapidly ascertain the results of the airstrike. Horseflys were also successfully employed beyond the battlefront, sometimes roving up to 20 miles behind German lines to direct fighter-bombers against targets of opportunity.[73]

The employment of airborne FACs was not fully adopted by the British despite the necessary machinery being in place – the Air Observation Post (AOP) artillery observation squadrons manned jointly by the RAF and Army and equipped with Auster light observation aircraft (which had been set up despite strong initial RAF/Air Ministry opposition).[74] In Italy during the late autumn of 1944 AOP aircraft were first employed to direct RAF fighter-bombers to close support targets, particularly German tanks. This proved to be successful and the method was much used during the final stages of the campaign.[75] In North-West Europe the AOPs were not officially employed in this way, though the history of the AOP describes how during the crossing of the Rhine a squadron of Typhoons found itself by coincidence to be on the same wireless net as the British artillery below and their attached AOP flight. This enabled some completely unofficial briefings to be given to the Typhoon Flight Leaders, whose pilots were able to destroy a Tiger tank only 300 yards ahead of the British troops after an AOP pilot had pointed it out by radio.[76]

The XII TAC took the Horsefly technique to Western Europe after the invasion of Southern France, and it was subsequently adopted by the US First and Third Armies in that theatre. In fact units of the Third Army later reported that Horsefly had been very successful during the offensive in the Saar and subsequent drive to the Rhine, particularly for indicating targets of opportunity when there had been no time to brief fighter-bomber pilots.[77]

The American air-support system also provided a solution, which originated with XII TAC in Italy, to the problem of German positions being left within the bombline. In Italy the latter was usually fixed between 5 and 10 miles ahead of friendly ground forces, and never closer than a distance estimated as 10 minutes away by infantry advance from the front line. This permitted significant German forces to operate in an area immune from air attack and, in order to prevent this, an additional line known as the 'close co-operation line' was introduced. This was designated immediately in front of friendly troops by the G-3 (Air) at Corps headquarters, who based his positional details on data received from the forward troops. As their positions changed the necessary map references were sent to the senior air controller at Corps whose task was to ensure that airstrikes did not occur within the close co-operation line but remained between the latter and the bombline. This demanded constant updates as to the position of the close co-operation line, which were passed on to the AAF Wings and Groups by the senior air controller at Corps, while the Army G-3 (Air) had the responsibility of informing Army headquarters. Conducting airstrikes close to friendly troops demanded the utmost efficiency in the flow and processing of data from the front line, for it was found that during intensive operations the position of the close co-operation line could change up to ten times in a day. The close co-operation line was also adopted by US forces in North-West Europe.[78]

The US air-support system was also more flexible in the utilization of radar. The British Army report on air support of late 1944 lamented the fact that 2nd TAF had not been able to make use of the SCR-584 precision radar, demonstrated before D-Day, for the navigational guidance of aircraft and for 'blind bombing' in close support, whereas it had been successfully employed by the US Ninth Air Force throughout the campaign.[79] British use of radar was mainly defensive, and it was not employed for 'blind bombing' until 1945. In the US system each TAC had a Tactical Control Center (TCC) sited near the Combined Operations Center. This was a radar control group centred upon a Microwave Early Warning radar (MEW) which was situated 10–30 miles from the battlefront. The MEW was supported by Forward Director Posts (usually three) and three or four SCR-584 Close Control Units. Originally designed for air defence, this network was extensively employed to guide strike aircraft responding to close-support requests to the target area, and sometimes to the target itself, with great precision, and proved of particular value during periods of adverse weather.[80]

The most significant example of the flexibility of the US air support system compared with that of the British was the close integration of air and armour in order to provide continuous air support during mobile operations. This was effected by assigning flights of fighter-bombers to co-operate closely with spearhead armoured units at each stage of an advance, controlled by a FAC riding in a VHF equipped tank. This was known as 'Armored Column Cover' and was introduced by IX TAC (of Ninth Air Force) for the breakout from Normandy. Armored Column Cover is examined in Chapter 4.

For the most part the advantages of the US system were innovations made as a result of operational experience. Yet that same operational experience also revealed serious weaknesses. One was that, as in the British system, insufficient manning levels at times threatened efficiency. In North-West Europe, during September/October 1944, a staff officer (G-3) of US Twelfth Army Group was detailed to conduct an investigation into the efficiency of the air-support system and in that period visited seven corps and thirteen divisions of the US First, Third, and Ninth Armies and their supporting TACs. His investigation revealed considerable variations in available manpower at Army level. The First Army's G-3 Section consisted of four officers, that of the Ninth Army seven, while the Third Army Section had nine. This meant that while the G-3s (Air) of the Third and Ninth Armies were able to spend considerable time at Army headquarters and be involved in the planning of operations, that of the First Army was compelled to be almost constantly at the TAC combined operations room and was consequently less familiar with the overall operational plan. In Ninth Army it was found that a minimum of five

officers was essential to handle the routine functions of a G-3 section
in a 24-hour period, while the four extra officers made possible visits
to GLO sections, consultation with higher and lower echelons, and the
filling of unexpected vacancies in the G-3 or GLO sections.[81]

At corps level manning was adequate, but at divisional level there
were problems. Armoured divisions in the US Army had been recently reorganised, with some still functioning under the old table of
organisation. These had full time G-3 (Air) officers in addition to a
normal G-3 but, surprisingly given the extent to which close air
support was employed, divisions with the new organisation had no
such allotment, the normal G-3 having to act as a G-3 (Air) in addition to his regular duties. A similar situation prevailed in the infantry
divisions, and for the most part the soldiers were of the opinion that
this was detrimental, pointing out that a full time G-3 (Air) had the
opportunity to become thoroughly familiar with air support technique
and procedure as well as relieving an already under-staffed G-3
section of a considerable workload.[82]

Considerable differences in air-support procedure existed among
Army formations, and the relative amount of responsibility assumed
by the G-3 (Air) sections and the Air Support Party Officers (ASPOs)
varied widely. This meant that some G-3 (Air) sections and ASPOs
were very much in touch with the air operations taking place in their
sector of the battlefront, while others could hardly have been less so.
The 1944 investigation described how some corps ASPOs virtually
ran a miniature forward fighter control and supervised the employment of all aircraft operating in the corps area. At the other extreme,
one corps did not employ its VHF radios except during special
operations.[83] To a great extent this came back to the question of manpower, it being found that in most infantry divisions the lack of a full
time G-3 (Air) necessitated the ASPO engaging in staff work to the
detriment of operational duties.[84]

Inadequate staffing and a lack of uniform procedure threatened to
produce inefficiency and poor performance, and there were frequent
examples of this. One was that Army divisions complained that they
were not receiving sufficient notification of the number of aircraft
allotted to them nor of their 'time over target' during pre-planned
close support operations.

This was a serious problem, threatening the fundamental utility of
air support, for without timely notification of these details the army
were not well placed to exploit the air support, and air support if not
exploited on the ground was wasted. This was really due to inefficient

use of the communications network, but the problem reduced army confidence in pre-planned air support. The 1944 investigation observed how difficult it was to integrate air attacks into the following day's operations unless a division was notified prior to midnight what air support it was to receive, and how this was one of the main reasons why ground forces preferred support by armed reconnaissance flights which 'checked in' with the ASPO and which therefore could be employed instantly as the situation demanded.[85] Similarly, Army units complained of an excessive time lapse in notifying them that air support had been denied or cancelled; the elapsed time varied from four to six hours, and in one instance a unit was told that its air support was cancelled nine hours after the original request.[86]

As in British experience, many of the problems in the system were the result of poor performance on the part of individuals. There is evidence to suggest that the US Army was less than satisfied with the efficiency of the GLOs attached to AAF units. In a post-war USAAF study of air-support operations in North-West Europe which invited ground force comments, the VI Corps complained that the GLOs often failed to keep the air units to which they were attached properly informed as to the significance of ground operations and the importance of the air support missions they were assigned. The XII Corps also believed the GLOs to have been too cut off from the battle situation to be of assistance to the fighter-groups, and considered that they had been unable to give them a sufficiently accurate picture of the locations, plans and intentions of the troops they were supporting. The 2nd Armored Division staff suggested that it was the GLOs themselves, rather than the system, which was at fault and observed that too many of them lacked combat experience, and failed to make contact with the combat divisions in order to keep abreast of tactical demands.[87]

In fact such blanket criticism of the GLOs may not have been justified. The 1944 investigation highlighted the problem that the army machinery for disseminating information from the battlefront was itself too slow and did not keep up with the pace of battle, and that the GLO sections did not have the latest information on the ground situation because, despite the efforts of the army G-3 air sections, the situation had often changed by the time the Army had received and disseminated the information. In fact GLO personnel were calling for the G-3s air sections of divisions and corps to send the information direct to them whenever possible.[88]

Yet some individuals lacking aptitude or commitment undoubtedly constituted 'weak links' in the US air support chain. Less than two weeks after D-Day three of the four US Corps Commanders in Normandy had sacked their G-3 (Air), despite there being a shortage of suitably qualified officers to take their place. The best replacements, it was found, proved to be officers drawn from the GLO sections attached to IX TAC airfields.[89]

As with the British system, experience proved that the air-support machinery was often not fast enough to respond adequately to calls for immediate support. In all US divisions the ASPO, whose party was equipped with SCR-522 and SCR-399 VHF radios, submitted air support requests to the G-3 (Air) section at Army headquarters. 'Request missions', those required on the same day but not immediately needed, and 'planned missions', those to be flown on subsequent days, were sent through the G-3 (Air) at Corps to the G-3 (Air) at Army. 'Immediate requests', when air support was required as soon as possible, could be sent direct using the SCR-399. However, as the 1944 investigation discovered, communication by means of the SCR 399 was unsatisfactory when time was a factor due to the slowness of the coding and processing procedures. Even in emergencies, when transmission in clear was authorized, divisions often found it more practicable to call direct to Corps for the air-support request to be forwarded by teletype.[90]

The solution proved to be regular armed-reconnaissance flights, either requested by divisions or allotted without request, 'checking in' with the divisional ASPOs for possible close-support targets before proceeding with their armed-reconnaissance mission beyond the battlefront. That it was necessary to bypass the air-support machinery reveals the inability of the latter to solve the problem of responsiveness, yet the procedure of employing armed-reconnaissance patrols worked. It resulted in a sharp reduction in the number of immediate support requests and was, according to the 1944 investigation, '... the outstanding contribution of the campaign to effective close air support'.[91]

A serious problem, shared with the British, was the propensity of tactical aircraft to attack friendly troops. Air/ground recognition procedure was often poor, and General Bradley describes an incident in Sicily when a flight of A-36 dive bombers persisted in attacking a column of US tanks that were releasing their yellow smoke recognition signal. In self-defence the tanks fired on the aircraft, hitting one and compelling the pilot to bale out. On his landing the soldiers realised that they had been wasting their time releasing the smoke for the pilot had had no idea what it was.[92] On another occasion in Sicily A-36s bombed the headquarters of British XXX Corps, mistaking it for a German strongpoint they were to bomb in close support of US troops attacking near Troina.[93]

Such occurrences persisted both in Italy and North-West Europe. Richard Hallion refers to 'one particularly nasty' incident in Italy when strafing P.40 fighter-bombers inflicted over 100 friendly casualties during the advance on Rome.[94]

The problem was acute during the early stages in Normandy, and between June 8th–17th 1944 aircraft of IX TAC attacked US troops on nine separate occasions.[95] Predictably, ground units became wary of air support and troops soon began to fire at anything in the air. This was bad enough, but the problem worsened when troops, in order to avert friendly attack, displayed their coloured air recognition panels when they were not in front line positions. Pilots may or may not have been given adequate briefing as to where the bombline was, but it was inevitable that in many cases pilots seeing such panels displayed assumed that troops seen ahead of these positions were enemy. One US First Army report noted that a pilot had seen panels all the way back to a corps headquarters.[96]

There was also some concern regarding the execution of close-support strikes. In Italy in October 1944 an outspoken memorandum compiled by XXII TAC revealed several problems in operating the ROVER system, most likely when fighter squadrons unused to close support work were being employed. Flights were often late in engaging their targets and on many occasions flight leaders did not know their assigned mission number and even lacked maps of the target area. Some had not been given alternative targets before take-off and their tactics were inadequate, with bombing runs being too shallow and there being obviously no plan of attack. Radio discipline was also poor, with much unnecessary 'chatter' clogging the ROVER channels.[97]

Many of these problems resulted from inadequate air-support training of both ground and air forces. For example, the US air and ground forces that fought in Normandy had had little opportunity to train together in England before D-Day. The Ninth Air Force was committed to supporting operations of the Eighth (strategic) Air Force until a very late stage and when, in May 1944, it became available for such training it was too late – the ground forces had been sealed into their pre-embarkation marshalling areas and were no longer available for exercises. Few large-scale regimental or divisional exercises involving aircraft had taken place, thus troops were unused to working with aircraft while the fighter-bomber pilots remained unfamiliar with working with troops and were largely untrained in dive-bombing and strafing battlefield targets.[98]

Very little priority and too little thought had been given to close air support, and this was seen not only in the major weaknesses of the system but also in the comparatively minor problems, which could however have far reaching effects. Communications equipment caused problems. The standard VHF radio, the SCR 522, originally developed for aircraft, proved unreliable and unable to stand the rigours of use by ground forces. It was eventually replaced by the sturdier SCR 624, but radios of the period were vulnerable to overheating, dust, and vibration, while spare parts were very difficult to obtain.[99]

A further problem was that confusion resulted in corps and divisions during air support missions due to the channels on ground and aircraft VHF radio sets being lettered differently. Yet another was that both GLOs and ASPOs in 1944 reported difficulty in obtaining adequate equipment from their parent formations to enable them to function properly, in particular tables, maps and acetate. It was also discovered during the 1944 investigation in North-West Europe that the number of VHF radios allotted to divisions varied considerably and affected efficiency. One armoured division had as many as fourteen, enabling it to furnish one to each infantry and armoured battalion, while another had only two, permitting one to each of its two Combat Commands but allowing for no Air Support Party (ASP) at division headquarters.[100]

As with that of the British, the US air support system must be judged in the light of existing Army/Air relations. The USAAF was no more committed to the principle of close air support than the RAF. During the 1930s and throughout the Second World War the AAF leadership pressed for the maximum possible autonomy within the War Department as a step towards eventual independent status for the Air Force.[101] The AAF Tactical School in the pre-war period favoured the strategic bombardment theory, and by 1935 recognised the gaining of air superiority as the single most important aim of air power. Tactical operations were not favoured, though it was acknowledged that after gaining air superiority pursuit (fighter) aircraft might be employed to isolate the ground-battle area by attacking enemy supplies and reinforcements. However, the idea of air units being in any way subordinate to ground forces, or under the control of a ground commander, was firmly resisted. Even the installation of bomb racks on new fighter aircraft was prohibited between 1936 and 1938, and as late as 1941 the Plans Division of the Air Corps remained opposed to any modification of such aircraft for ground-support work.[102]

There were also very few aircraft available specifically for close support. Like their counterparts in the RAF, and for the same reasons, senior airmen rejected US Army calls for the adoption of dive-bombers after the outbreak of war in Europe. This decision was sound, but the fact remains that in 1941 the USAAF possessed no doctrine and no aircraft for co-operation with ground forces.[103] Experience in Morocco and Tunisia following the TORCH invasion in November 1942 led to the introduction of a formal doctrine in May 1943 when the War Department published Field Manual 100-20, *Command and Employment of Air Power.*

Attempts to distribute air assets and subordinate them to ground-force operations had proven unsatisfactory in North Africa, and this gave the AAF the opportunity to declare its independence from such control. FM 100-20 declared air power a co-equal and independent force, the command of which was to be centralised in the hands of a senior air commander responsible only to the overall theatre commander. Mission types were clearly prioritised. First was the need to secure air superiority, while second priority was accorded to attacks on enemy troop concentrations, supplies and communications outside the battle area. Close air support was accorded third priority, but was clearly frowned upon, FM 100-20 warning that such missions would be difficult to control, expensive, and least effective, being only appropriate at critical periods.[104]

Thus the close air support system of 1943–45 was manned by an air force whose senior command felt little commitment to the role. Indeed in 1945 the very term 'support' was declared to be objectionable within Ninth Air Force, and the term 'co-operation' substituted.[105]

This is not to suggest that there were serious problems in the Army/Air relationship at the operational level. In fact there was a greater degree of commonality than in the British system, at least partly due to the fact that the USAAF was part of the Army. One feature of this, seen in both Italy and North-West Europe, was an extensive programme of exchanging air and ground personnel for short periods of time. In the Ninth Air Force alone thousands of air and ground officers, and enlisted men, were attached to parallel ground and air units for familiarisation. The intention was for pilots to see ground combat at first hand and for army personnel to participate in air operations. According to a post-war analysis of the Ninth Air Force this policy brought dividends; air crews developed a keener awareness of air-land warfare and the importance of their role, ground-forces personnel learned at first-hand the extent, power and limitations of air operations, morale in both services improved and goodwill and understanding increased.[106]

In Italy in 1944 the 42nd Bomb Wing, whose medium bombers provided close support during the fighting at Anzio, thereafter instituted an exchange programme and subsequently reported that there was a remarkable difference in the attitude of aircrews when 'close-in' Army targets were to be attacked as oppposed to their normal targets beyond the battlefront. It was observed that crews were prepared to fly through intense flak to attack and destroy a 'close-in' target, whereas the same crews would fly into similarly intense flak to attack a bridge or supply dump but not do such a thorough job.[107]

Such familiarisation was necessary, as much for the soldiers as the airmen. Ground-force commanders often failed to appreciate that air support, to be effective, had to be an integral part of an operation rather than simply appended to it. The 1944 investigation of air support in North-West Europe drew attention to the fact that some air personnel felt that the maximum effectiveness of air support was often not obtained because of the commander's failure to call in G-3 air until after a plan had been already adopted, rather than during the planning stage itself.[108]

Given the opposition of both the RAF and USAAF to the principle of close air-support it is remarkable that the British and US air-support systems were broadly successful in welding together air and ground forces and integrating air and ground operations. This was largely due to a determination to make air support work at the operational level on the part of some of the more junior air commanders, such as Air Vice-Marshal Broadhurst of No.83 Group of 2nd TAF and Major-General Quesada of IX TAC, both of whom were willing to co-operate with the soldiers.

Yet the Allies were also fortunate in 1943–45 in that their air forces had already achieved air superiority over the Luftwaffe, and had an abundance of aircraft available for close support work. Thus the weaknesses in the system could easily be masked by quantitative superiority. The highly critical British Army report of late 1944 on air support observed that it was necessary

... to guard against confusion between quantity and quality and any tendency to allow overwhelming weight to slur over weaknesses in technique and performance which otherwise would be self evident.[109]

This warning is as valid for the historian now as it was for the soldiers and airmen then.

NOTES

1. Charles Carrington, *Soldier at Bomber Command* (London: Leo Cooper, 1987) p. 4.
2. John Terraine, *The Right of the Line* (London: Sceptre: 1988), p. 122.
3. Major L.F. Ellis, *The War in France and Flanders 1939–40* (London: HMSO, 1953), pp. 97–98. See also British Air Ministry, *Air Support, Air Publication 3235 (The Second World War 1939–1945: Royal Air Force)*, pp. 17–18.
4. Carrington, p. 6.
5. Ellis, p. 82. A useful published account of the RAF's role in the Battle of France is also provided by Victor F. Bingham in *Blitzed: The Battle of France May–June 1940* (New Malden: Air Research, 1990).
6. Ellis, pp. 82–3.
7. Shelford Bidwell and Dominick Graham, *Fire-Power: British Army Weapons and Theories of War 1904–45* (London: Allen & Unwin, 1985), p. 264.
   The results of the trials held in Northern Ireland during the autumn of 1940 are detailed in British Air Ministry, *Air Support, Air Publication 3235 (The Second World War 1939–45: Royal Air Force)*, Appendix 1, pp. 189–93.
8. Carrington, p. 10.
9. Ibid., p. 11.
10. Bidwell and Graham, *Fire Power*, p. 265.
11. Terraine, *The Right of the Line*, p. 359.
12. Denis Richards and Hilary St.G. Saunders, *Royal Air Force 1939–45*, Volume II, *The Fight Avails* (London: HMSO, 1954), p. 160.
13. Ibid., p.162; Terraine, p. 346.
14. Bidwell and Graham, pp. 268–9.
15. *The Air Support Signals Unit*, Chapter 4 in *History of Air Support in North West Europe, June 1944 – May 1945* (Unpublished, Chapters 1–8), RAF 2nd TAF 1945, PRO AIR 37/881.
16. Ibid.
17. British Army (1944), *Notes on Air Support, June – Oct. 1944*, p. 5, PRO WO 205/556.
18. HQ British 21st Army Group Report (May 1945), *Air Support for Operations Plunder, Flashpoint, and Varsity*, Part III, *The Forward Control of Aircraft during 'Plunder/Varsity'*, PRO AIR 40/313.
19. *The Air Support Signals Unit*.
20. Ibid.
21. *Memorandum of The Organisation of FACPs Operating with the Eighth Army* (dated 16 January 1945), PRO WO 204/7932.
22. *The Air Support Signals Unit*.
23. Ibid.
24. Air Historical Branch Narrative, *The Italian Campaign 1943–45*, Volume II, *Operations June 1944–May 1945*, p. 253, PRO AIR 41/58.
25. *The Air Liaison Section with a Fighter/Bomber Wing*, in 2nd TAF *History of Air Support*.
26. Ibid.
27. Ibid.
28. British 21st Army Group Report (May 1945), *Air Support for Operations Plunder, Flashpoint, and Varsity*.
29. British Army (1940), *Notes on Air Support, June – Oct. 1944*.
30. Ibid., p. 8.
31. Ibid., p. 9.

32. Ibid.
33. Ibid.
34. Ibid., p. 8. It is also true that at this time the British armed forces, and the Army in particular were labouring under a serious manpower shortage.
35. Ibid., p. 7.
36. On the morning of 24 February 1991 two British Warrior armoured personnel carriers were
hit by Maverick missiles fired by American A-10 Thunderbolt close support aircraft. Nine
soldiers were killed and eleven wounded. John Simpson, *From the House of War* (London:
Arrow, 1991), p. 347.
37. British Army (1944), *Notes on Air Support, June – Oct. 1944*, p. 12.
38. First Canadian Army Report, *Attacks by Allied A/C on Own Tps – 18 and 19 Aug. 1944* (20
August 1944), PRO WO 205/232.
39. British Army (1944), *Notes on Air Support, June – Oct. 1944*, p. 12.
40. Captain N. Nicolson and P. Forbes, *The Grenadier Guards in the War of 1939–45*, Volume
I (Aldershot: Gale & Polden, 1949), p. 104.
41. 2nd TAF *History of Air Support*.
42. British Army (1944), *Notes on Air Support, June – Oct. 1944*, p. 7. In Aug. 1944 Air Marshal
Coningham complained that First Canadian Army had been setting its bombline too far
ahead, thereby depriving his pilots of many profitable targets. Air Marshal Coningham to
Air Vice-Marshal Robb (DCAS Air at SHAEF), 29 August 1944, PRO AIR 37/1132.
43. Brereton Greenhous, *Close Support Aircraft in World War I: The Counter Anti-Tank Role*,
in *Aerospace Historian*, 21, No. 2, Summer 1974, pp. 92–3.
44. Hilary St. George Saunders, *Per Ardua: The Rise of British Air Power 1911–39* (Oxford:
1944), pp. 269, 272–3.
45. Ibid.
46. Air Vice-Marshal J.C. Slessor, *Use of Bombers in Close Support of the Army*, unpublished
memorandum, 6 May 1941, in PRO AIR 20/2970.
47. Group Captain Basil Embry to Air Ministry, 17 May 1941, *Use of Bombers in Close Support
of the Army*, in PRO AIR 20/2970.
48. Nigel Hamilton, *Monty: The Making of a General* (London: Hamish Hamilton, 1981),
p. 638.
49. 21st Army Group/1001/C-in-C, Montgomery to General Dempsey, 4 May 1944, PRO WO
285/2.
50. In Normandy Montgomery refused to deal with Coningham. On tactical matters he preferred to deal direct with Air Vice-Marshal Broadhurst, commanding No. 83 Group and
who was subordinate to Coningham. The hostility of the senior airmen towards
Montgomery is discussed by John Terraine in *The Right of The Line* (London: Sceptre,
1988), pp. 611–19; Chester Wilmot, *The Struggle For Europe* (London: The Reprint Society,
1954), pp. 374–5; Carlo D'Este, *Decision In Normandy* (London: Pan, 1984),
pp. 218–22.
51. British Army (1944), *Notes on Air Support, June – Oct. 1944*, p. 14.
52. Ibid., p. 9.
53. Ibid., p. 10.
54. Ibid., p. 13.
55. Slessor, *Use of Bombers in Close Support of the Army*. An exception to this view regarding
the decision not to adopt dive-bombers would appear to be Peter C. Smith. See his work
Close Air Support: An Illustrated History, 1914 to the Present (New York: Crown Publishers,
1990), p. 64. Other works by this author are listed in the bibliography.
56. See Arthur Bryant, *The Turn of the Tide 1939–43: A Study based on the Diaries and
Autobiographical Notes of Field Marshal the Viscount Alanbrooke* (London: The Reprint
Society, 1958), pp. 194–5, 322.
57. British Army (1944), *Notes on Air Support, June – Oct. 1944*, p.3. The ranges of Allied
fighter-bombers are given in Chapter 3.
58. Ibid., p. 13.
59. Ibid., p. 10.
60. Ibid.
61. Wilmot, *The Struggle for Europe*, p. 374.
62. Air Marshal Broadhurst, then commanding Desert Air Force, was censured by Tedder for
the air support provided for Eighth Army at El Hamma in Tunisia in March 1943 (see

Chapter 7 below). For an example of Tedder chiding him for his willingness to co-operate with Montgomery in North-West Europe see D'Este, *Decision in Normandy*, p. 220. In the summer of 1944 Air Marshal Coningham wanted to sack Air Vice-Marshal L.O. Brown of No.84 Group for what he saw as the latter's 'subservience' to the Army. Air Marshal Coningham to Air Vice-Marshal J. Breen (Air Ministry, 30 August 1944, PRO AIR 37/2.

63. British Army, *Notes on Air Support, June – Oct. 1944*, p. 14.
64. The AAF Evaluation Board in the ETO, *The Effectiveness of Third Phase Tactical Air Operations in the European Theater, 5 May 1944 – 8 May 1945* (USAAF, Feb. 1946), p. 341, PRO AIR 40/1111.
65. Ibid.
66. Ibid.
67. Ibid.
68. US XII TAC Memorandum, *Forward Fighter Bomber Control*, dated 6 May 1944, in *Air Support for Allied Armies in Italy* (1944), PRO AIR 23/1822.
69. The AAF Evaluation Board in the ETO, *The Effectiveness of Third Phase Tactical Air Operations*, pp. 341–3.
70. AEAF/21st Army Group Joint Memorandum, *Direct Air Support*, 23 April 1944, referred to by W.A. Jacobs in *The Battle for France, 1944*, Chapter 6 in Benjamin F. Cooling (Ed.), *Case Studies in the Development of Close Air Support* (Washington, DC: Office of Air Force History, 1990), p.260.
71. British Army, *Notes on Air Support, June – Oct. 1944*, p. 6.
72. W.A. Jacobs, *The Battle for France, 1944*, Chapter 6 in Benjamin F. Cooling (Ed.),*Case Studies in the Development of Close Air Support* (Washington, DC: Office of Air Force History, 1990), p. 260.
73. Richard P. Hallion, *Strike From The Sky: The History of Battlefield Air Attack 1911–45*, (Shrewsbury: Airlife 1989), pp. 181–2; HQ European Theater of Operations US Army Immediate Report No.1 (Combat Observations) (20 Nov. 1944), *Close Air Support Within Twelfth Army Group*, PRO WO 205/556.
74. For details on the development of the British AOP see *Unarmed Into Battle: The Story of the Air Observation Post*, by Major-General H.J. Parham and E.M.G. Belfield, (Chippenham: Picton Publishing, 1986). A useful shorter account is provided by Shelford Bidwell in *Gunners At War: A Tactical Study of the Royal Artillery in the Twentieth Century* (Chapter VIII) (London: Arms & Armour Press, 1970).
75. Parham and Belfield, p. 68.
76. Ibid., p. 96.
77. Kenneth Wakefield, *The Fighting Grasshoppers: US Liaison Aircraft Operations in Europe 1942–45* (Leicester: Midland Counties Publications, 1990), p. 118. It should be noted that Horsefly had its critics, some US officers believing that control of fighter-bombers was better conducted by similar performance aircraft. It was also true that such an employment of slow unarmoured aircraft could only be contemplated in conditions of air superiority.
78. Hallion, *Strike from the Sky*, p.184.
79. British Army (1944), *Notes on Air Support, June – Oct. 1944*, pp. 3–4.
80. The AAF Evaluation Board in the ETO, *The Effectiveness of Third Phase Tactical Air Operations*, pp. 282–93, 370–3.
81. US Army, Immediate Report No.1 (Combat Observations), *Close Air Support Within Twelfth Army Group.*
82. Ibid.
83. Ibid.
84. Ibid.
85. Ibid.
86. W.A. Jacobs, *The Battle for France, 1944*, Chapter 6 in Benjamin F. Cooling (Ed.), *Case Studies in the Development of Close Air Support* (Washington, DC: Office of Air Force History, 1990), p. 261.
87. The AAF Evaluation Board in the ETO, *The Effectiveness of Third Phase Tactical Air Operations in the European Theater*, pp. 341–3.
88. US Army, Immediate Report No.1 (Combat Observations), *Close Air Support Within Twelfth Army Group.*
89. Report by Colonel E.L. Johnson, G-3 (Air) US First Army, 16 July 1944, referred to in W.A. Jacobs, *The Battle for France, 1944*, Chapter 6 in Cooling, *Case Studies in the Development of Close Air Support*, p. 266.

90. US Army, Immediate Report No.1 (Combat Observations), *Close Air Support Within Twelfth Army Group.*
91. Ibid.
92. Omar N. Bradley, *A Soldier's Story* (London: 1952); Albert N. Garland and Howard M. Smyth, *Sicily and The Surrender of Italy*, *U.S. Army In World War II*, Volume II, (Washington, DC: USGPO, 1965), pp. 342, 403.
93. Ibid.
94. Hallion, *Strike from the Sky*, p.184.
95. W.A. Jacobs, *The Battle for France, 1944*, Chapter 6 in Cooling, p. 266.
96. Report by Colonel E.L. Johnson, G-3 (Air) US First Army, 16 July 1944, referred to in ibid., p. 266.
97. HQ, Mediterranean Theater of Operations, Training Memorandum 2, 15 March 1945, *Lessons from The Italian Campaign*; US XXII TAC History, 20 Sept. – 31 Dec. 1944, referred to in Alan F. Wilt, *Allied Cooperation in Sicily and Italy 1943–45*, Chapter 5 in Cooling, pp. 210–11.
98. Wesley F. Craven and James Lea Cate, *The Army Air Forces in World War II*, Volume II, *Europe: Argument to VE Day, January 1944 to May 1945* (Chicago: 1951 and reprinted by the Office of Air Force History, 1984), pp. 135–6.
99. W.A. Jacobs, *The Battle for France, 1944*, Chapter 6 in Cooling, p. 265. The British had similar problems with regard to spare parts for communications equipment. See 2nd TAF, *History of Air Support in North-West Europe.*
100. US Army, Immediate Report No.1 (Combat Observations), *Close Air Support Within Twelfth Army Group.*
101. W.A. Jacobs, *Tactical Air Doctrine and AAF Close Air Support in the European Theater, 1944–45*, in *Aerospace Historian*, 27/1, Spring, March 1980.
102. Ibid.
103. Ibid.
104. US War Department Field Manual FM 100-20, quoted in ibid.
105. Ibid.
106. Headquarters Army Air Forces, Office of the Assistant Chief of the Air Staff-3, Washington, DC, March 1946, *Condensed Analysis of the Ninth Air Force in the European Theater of Operations*, p. 106, PRO AIR 40/1095.
107. USAAF 42nd Bomb Wing (1944), *Air Ground Cooperation*, quoted in Hallion, *Strike from the Sky*, p. 183.
108. US Army, Immediate Report No.1 (Combat Observations), *Close Air Support Within Twelfth Army Group.*
109. British Army, *Notes on Air Support, June – Oct. 1944.*

3

The Fighter-Bomber
Weapon, 1943–45

FIGHTER BOMBING

In Europe in 1943–45 most close air support for Allied troops was provided by fighter-bombers, fighter aircraft which, in addition to their fixed gun armament, were fitted with bombs or rockets for engaging ground targets.

The Germans were the first in the Second World War to employ their fighter aircraft as bombers. In the late summer of 1940, after excessive losses had compelled the withdrawal of medium and dive-bomber units from daylight operations over Britain, Messerschmitt Bf.109E fighters were equipped to carry bombs. By the autumn each fighter group had formed a fighter-bomber squadron (*Jabo Staffel*) equipped with Messerschmitt Bf.109E-4/B aircraft capable of carrying either one 551 lb or four 110 lb bombs.[1] These were employed on 'hit and run' raids across the Channel which caused only limited damage but which were extremely difficult to counter, No.11 Group RAF eventually resorting to the provision of standing patrols to guard against them.[2] While this employment may be seen as 'strategic', the Messerschmitt Bf.109E-4/Bs were later used in the Balkan, Mediterranean, and Russian theatres in the close support role. Tactics were fairly crude, the usual method of attack being a 45° dive with the bomb being aimed by means of the standard Revi reflector gunsight.[3]

After the RAF/Air Ministry rejection of dive-bombers no dedicated ground-attack aircraft were employed operationally by the RAF in Europe or the Middle East and in early 1941 no fighter aircraft were equipped to carry bombs.[4] However, the desirability of providing fighter aircraft with a measure of striking power against ground targets was acknowledged and feasibility tests were conducted with the

Hurricane IIA, later versions of which were equipped with underwing attachments for external fuel tanks which could also house 250 lb general purpose (GP) bombs. Meanwhile in North Africa, during the successful First Libyan Campaign against Italian forces in December 1940 and January 1941, machine-gun ground-strafing attacks had already been carried out, Hurricane pilots being ordered to use their remaining ammunition against any likely ground-target when returning from patrols.[5]

In the UK later in 1941 the Hurricane marks IIA and IIB appeared, the former fitted with twelve .303 inch machine guns and the latter with four 20 mm cannon. These were now designed as bomb carriers with strengthened wing attachments, the IIC being employed by Nos.1 and 3 Squadrons on low-altitude intruder missions ('Rhubarbs') across the Channel. By the autumn two squadrons equipped with the IIB were conducting cross-Channel fighter-bombing raids using tactics developed during the summer by the Air Fighting Development Unit. The RAF's first fighter-bombing attack in Europe was carried out on 30 October 1941 when No.607 Squadron bombed a transformer at Tingry. Other targets included airfields and enemy occupied buildings. These were usually attacked in a low-level approach by pairs of Hurricanes releasing their bombs and pulling up at the last moment, allowing the bombs to continue towards the target. As such attacks increased so did German anti-aircraft (flak) defences, necessitating a change of tactics and a recourse to dive-bombing. Targets were then attacked from slightly different directions at once, in order to split the flak concentrations, in a 65/70° dive with bombs released between 12,000 and 5,000 feet.[6]

By this time thought had also been given to the use of fighter-bombing and strafing attacks in support of troops, with senior Army officers quite enthusiastic. In late 1941 General Sir Alan Brooke, Chief of the Imperial General Staff, was greatly impressed by an RAF demonstration of cannon-equipped fighters attacking lorried infantry and guns, and noted in his diary that such aircraft were clearly destined to play an important ground attack role.[7]

In November 1941 the first RAF fighter-bombers became operational in North Africa, No.80 Squadron with obsolescent Hurricane Is fitted with eight underwing 40 lb fragmentation bombs. They made bombing and strafing attacks upon Axis mechanised transport columns and tank concentrations in support of Operation CRUSADER, with strafing proving more effective, but their losses to flak were prohibitive. On 27 November the squadron ceased strafing attacks, and by mid-January 1942 had reverted to the fighter role on re-equipment with Hurricane IICs.[8]

They were superseded in the fighter-bomber role by a series of US built Curtiss P-40 aircraft, known in the RAF as Kittyhawks, which combined a bombload of up to three 500 lb bombs and the firepower of six .50 inch machine guns. In May 1942 No.112 Squadron became the first of many operational Kittybombers to see service with RAF Desert Air Force in North Africa and later in Sicily and Italy.[9] At this stage fighter-bombers were little employed in close support, and when not attacking lines of communication often reverted to fighter duties. A significant use of fighter-bombers in a close-support role in North Africa occurred on 26 March 1943 in Tunisia, when no less than eighteen Allied squadrons, attacking in waves directly ahead of advancing New Zealand troops, successfully silenced German gun positions in the Tebaga Gap.[10]

There was little opportunity to employ fighter-bombers in close support in Western Europe at this time, but on 19 August 1942, in support of the raid on Dieppe (Operation JUBILEE), Hurricanes of No.174 Squadron carried out fighter-bombing attacks while those of Nos.3 and 43 Squadrons strafed German positions. In the face of effective flak defences the cost was high, No.174 Squadron alone losing five aircraft.[11]

In 1943 the RAF moved to what was to become its close-support workhorse in North-West Europe and its most successful fighter-bomber of the war. Hawker Typhoon fighters, designed as high speed interceptors, became operational in the UK in 1942. Their rate of climb and high-level performance proved disappointing in this role and, initially, a premature operational debut resulted in the aircraft being dogged by an unreliable engine and an alarming tendency for the tail section to fall off in flight.[12] However, the aircraft had a robustness ideal for fighter-bombing and in 1943 was cleared to carry two 500 lb, and later two 1,000 lb, bombs. Many Typhoon squadrons converted to fighter-bombers after the first German V-1 sites were discovered in the Pas de Calais in the Autumn of 1943, and for some months were directed against them. In view of German flak this was quite hazardous, but a 2nd TAF study later observed that it provided excellent training in map reading, pin-pointing small targets, and in the technique of dive-bombing — so that when the time came for tactical operations with the Army the squadrons were already experienced in work of a similar nature.[13] It was also in 1943 that Typhoons were fitted to carry the 3 inch rocket projectile (RP).[14]

The Mediterranean theatre had by then seen the first employment of Spitfire fighter-bombers (in Tunisia). Various marks of Spitfire thereafter served in this role with RAF Desert Air Force until the end of the campaign in Italy, and also in North-West Europe with 2nd TAF.[15]

The USAAF followed the British in rejecting the dive-bomber in March 1943, when a conference held at Wright Field to decide upon fighter-bombers or dive-bombers for air support of ground forces chose the former principally on the grounds that their fighter characteristics enabled them to protect themselves against hostile fighter action.[16] Only one dive-bomber type was employed operationally by the USAAF in Europe, the North American A-36A Invader, with which two USAAF Groups in the Mediterranean theatre were equipped between July 1943 and mid-1944. This aircraft derived from the North American P-51A Mustang fighter and was essentially that aircraft fitted with dive brakes. Most aviation historians agree that these brakes proved unsatisfactory and that they were usually wired shut on operations, the Invaders actually functioning as fighter-bombers.[17] As in the RAF, responsibility for close support and much other ground-attack duty fell primarily upon the fighter types of the USAAF, all of which had fighter-bomber derivatives.

The first operational USAAF fighter-bomber squadrons were those equipped with Curtiss P-40 single-seat, single-engined fighters which arrived in North Africa in late 1942. While as a fighter the P-40 was never an equal match for the German Messerschmitt Bf.109, it had already proven its value as a fighter-bomber in service with the RAF and Commonwealth air forces, as the Kittyhawk. To the USAAF it was the Warhawk, and this aircraft, with the later improved P-40M (Kittyhawk III) and P-40N (Kittyhawk IV) variants, became the principal USAAF fighter-bomber in the Mediterranean theatre until replaced by the P-47 Thunderbolt in 1944. Like their RAF counterparts, the USAAF Warhawks usually carried three 500 lb bombs or occasionally one 1,000 lb bomb in addition to their fixed armament of six 0.50 calibre machine guns.[18] By September 1943 there were no less than thirteen USAAF squadrons equipped with Warhawks serving in the Mediterranean.[19]

The first USAAF Republic P-47 Thunderbolt squadrons arrived in the UK in late 1942, and by the end of 1943 those of the Eighth Air Force returning from bomber-escort missions at low level had begun strafing targets of opportunity with their remaining ammunition. Their success led to the adoption of the P-47 as a fighter-bomber.[20]

The Thunderbolt was the largest and heaviest single-engined single-seat fighter of the Second World War, but it was capable of a maximum speed of 433 mph and, unlike the P-40, proved a highly successful air-combat dogfighter.[21]

Yet, of all the Allied fighter types pressed into service as fighter-bombers, the Thunderbolt was one of the most suited to the role. Its phenomenally rugged construction and air-cooled radial engine enabled it to absorb considerable punishment from ground fire, while it possessed the formidable firepower of eight wing-mounted 0.50 calibre machine guns and the ability to carry up to three 500 lb, or two 1,000 lb bombs, or up to 10 underwing rockets.[22] By June 1944 the Ninth Air Force, preparing to support the US armies during OVERLORD, possessed twelve groups of P-47s, each of three squadrons, in its IX and XIX Tactical Air Commands.[23] In Italy, USAAF fighter-bomber squadrons began to exchange their Warhawks for Thunderbolts in late 1943, there eventually being nine squadrons equipped with Thunderbolts serving in Italy with the Desert Air Force and XXII Tactical Air Command by May 1945.[24]

Another USAAF fighter type that saw service as a fighter-bomber in the Mediterranean and North-West Europe was the Lockheed P-38 Lightning, a single-seat, twin-engined and twin-boomed fighter originally intended as a high-altitude interceptor. The first to see action were P-38Fs which equipped some USAAF squadrons sent to North Africa in November 1942. They took a heavy toll of the German air transports ferrying supplies to Rommel's forces from Italy.[25] An important attribute of the P-38 was its range, and Lightnings were the first USAAF fighters to accompany bombers from UK bases to Berlin.[26] They were effective in the air-combat role, though in German skies they proved to lack the necessary manoeuvrability to tackle on equal terms the German Focke-Wulf 190 fighters and the later types of Me 109 except at the highest altitudes.[27]

Lightnings began fighter-bombing in late 1943, the P-38 variants then operational being able to carry two or more 500 lb, two 1,000 lb or two 1,600 lb bombs or a battery of ten rockets. Their armament of one 20 mm cannon and four 0.50 calibre machine guns concentrated in the nose made them potent ground-strafers, and both in Italy and North-West Europe German troops came to fear *Der Gabelschwanz Teufel* (the fork-tailed Devil), not least because its comparatively low engine noise gave little warning of its approach.[28] In June 1944 the Ninth Air Force possessed nine squadrons of P-38 fighter-bombers (all were in IX TAC), but by early 1945 in both Italy and North-West

Europe the Lightnings had been almost entirely replaced in the ground attack role by single-engined P-47s or P-51s.[29]

The North American P-51 Mustang is widely considered the best US single-seat, single-engined fighter of the Second World War. It possessed the range, with drop tanks, to escort bombers from UK bases all the way to Berlin and the ability to outfight the German Me 109s and Fw 190s.[30] The aircraft was a remarkably successful combination of an American airframe with the British Merlin engine, and the first Merlin-engined P-51B and C Mustangs joined the Eighth Air Force in the UK in December 1943, followed in 1944 by the P-51D with an even more powerful Merlin engine. In early 1944 P-51Bs and Cs entered service with the US Fifteenth (Strategic) Air Force in Italy, and also with the RAF which styled these variants Mustang IIIs. A limited number of P-51Ds were also supplied to the RAF as Mustang IVs. [31]

In March 1944 Mustang IIIs entered service with the RAF Desert Air Force in Italy as fighter-bombers, and by June 1944 there were also two wings (six squadrons) of Mustang IIIs in RAF Second Tactical Air Force, and a similar number in the US Ninth Air Force.[32] As a fighter-bomber the Mustang was able to carry two 500 lb or two 1,000 lb bombs or ten rockets in addition to its six 0.50 calibre machine guns, but it lacked the robustness of the Thunderbolt for ground attack. Hence, the Mustang was regarded as primarily a long-range escort fighter by both the USAAF and RAF. In the USAAF it was the Thunderbolt that became the ground-attack workhorse, while in September 1944 the Mustangs of RAF Second Tactical Air Force were withdrawn from fighter-bombing in order to provide the escorts for Bomber Command's return to a daylight offensive.[33]

FIGHTER-BOMBER CHARACTERISTICS

The fighter-bomber was a versatile weapon, able to accomplish a wide range of tasks. Both in North-West Europe and Italy, in addition to close support, these included short- and long-range fighter sweeps, deep- and shallow-interdiction missions, escort for light/medium bombers, and anti-shipping strikes. In the ground-attack role the fighter-bomber also possessed a tactical versatility denied the dive-bomber, that of being able to deliver bombs and rockets in high-speed low-level passes, which could give a measure of protection from anti-aircraft fire, as well as in steep-dive attacks.

Flexibility was also an important characteristic. Fighter-bomber squadrons were not limited to attack on one particular target, and it was not uncommon for a squadron to carry out, for example, an interdiction mission and follow this with a close air support strike. They could also adapt to last-minute changes of target due to developments in the battle area with a minimum of re-briefing, sometimes by radio while in flight, and they could respond rapidly to target data supplied by tactical reconnaissance (Tac/R) flights. This can be contrasted with light/medium bombers, which were unable to adapt to rapid changes of target due to the length of time needed to re-brief the large number of aircrew and to prepare aircraft and bomb loads.[34]

The critical drawback with fighter-bombers, affecting both versatility and flexibility, was combat radius. Table I shows this for the US fighter types employed in North-West Europe:

TABLE I

COMBAT RADIUS OF US FIGHTERS (NORTH-WEST EUROPE)[35]

TYPE	BOMB LOAD	INTERNAL FUEL CAPACITY (gal.)	EXTERNAL FUEL CAPACITY (gal.)	COMBAT RADIUS (miles) (at 10,000 ft.)
P-38L Lightning	None	410	None	290
	None	410	330 (2 tanks)	600
	2 × 500 lb	410	None	260
	2 × 1000 lb	410	None	250
P-47D Thunderbolt	None	370	None	280
	None	370	188 (1 tank)	400
	2 × 500 lb	370	None	260
	2 × 1000 lb	370	None	230
P-51B/C/D Mustang	None	269	None	350
	None	269	216 (2 tanks)	750
	2 × 500 lb	269	None	325

Table I reveals the difference between the potential long-range fighter and the fighter-bomber, in that carrying bombs and/or rockets considerably reduced combat radius. This table is based on the experience of the US Ninth Air Force in North-West Europe, but Table II is based on an ORS study of Desert Air Force operations in Italy during early 1945 and indicates an even greater limitation. Maximum combat radius with ordnance load is given, taking into account the

need for the aircraft to return to base on internal fuel after an operation and loiter time in the target area:

TABLE II

FIGHTER-BOMBER COMBAT RADIUS, ITALY 1945[36]

TYPE	BOMB LOAD	COMBAT RADIUS (miles)
Spitfire VIII	1 × 500lb (occasionally 2 × 500 lb)	130
Spitfire IX	1 × 500 lb (occasionally 2 x 500 lb)	95
P-51B/C Mustang	2 × 1000 lb 2 × 500 lb	200 250
Kittyhawk IV (US P-40N)	2 × 500lb	140
P-47 Thunderbolt	2 × 500lb plus rockets 2 × 1000lb 2 × 110 gal. Napalm fire bombs	165 165 165

Particularly apparent is the limitation of the British Spitfire compared
with the US fighter types. As shown in Chapter 2, lack of range was a
major British Army criticism of the tactical aircraft with which the
RAF provided air support. The Spitfires of Desert Air Force were
largely restricted to immediate battle area missions as their range
precluded anything else.[37] The Typhoon could do better, with a
maximum range of 510 miles with bombs, but in terms of combat
radius this would have been effectively halved.[38] With regard to close
support, the necessity of airfields not too far removed from the
battlefront is obvious for all the above Allied types.

Also apparent from Table II is the low ordnance load of the
Spitfires, those with Desert Air Force rarely carrying more than one
bomb. By late 1944 those serving with 2nd TAF were carrying a
1,000 lb bomb load (typically one 500 lb centreline and a 250 lb under
each wing) but this was really beyond their capability, it being found
that 60 per cent of all accidents were caused by burst tyres due to the
excessive weight.[39] Here again the Typhoon did better, its sturdier
construction enabling it to carry up to 2,000 lb of bombs or eight
underwing rockets.[40]

As the above tables show, Allied fighter-bombers possessed impressive firepower. In Italy during 1944 the Operations Staff of RAF Desert Air Force outlined the firepower and economy of effort of fighter-bombers in comparison with the other aircraft type employed against ground targets (though, in comparison with fighter-bombers, infrequently in the close-support role), that is to say twin-engined light/medium bombers. This was by reference to the Load/Personnel Factor, whereby the load is expressed as weight of bombs dropped by a Squadron in one day of intensive operations, and the personnel by the number of aircrew and groundcrew required to make this effort possible. The results, shown in Table III, indicate how fighter-bombers compared favourably regarding the number of missions that could be flown, the weight of bombs that could be delivered, and the number of personnel required.

TABLE III

LOAD/PERSONNEL FACTOR

FIGHTER-BOMBERS

Kittyhawk (at 1,500lbs per aircraft) on 3 squadron missions per day = 54,000lbs
Total Personnel required = 243. L/P Factor: 222

Mustang (at 2,000lbs per aircraft) on 3 squadron missions per day = 72,000lbs
Total Personnel required = 243. L/P Factor: 297

LIGHT/MEDIUM BOMBERS

Baltimore (at 1,500lbs per aircraft) on 2 squadron missions per day = 35,000lbs
Total Personnel required = 349. L/P Factor: 104

Marauder (at 4,000lbs per aircraft) on 2 squadron missions per day = 96,000lbs
Total Personnel required = 521. L/P Factor: 184

This question was also investigated by ORS Mediterranean Allied Air Forces, and Table IV shows their breakdown of the manpower-backing required for the aircraft types employed by Desert Air Force which, in addition to fighter-bombers, also included twin-engined Mosquito and Beaufighter strike aircraft, twin-engined Boston and Baltimore light bombers, and heavier twin-engined B-26 Marauder medium bombers.[41]

TABLE IV

MANPOWER PER SQUADRON, DESERT AIR FORCE, NOVEMBER 1944

AIRCRAFT TYPE	AIRCREW (OFFICERS AND NCOs)	GROUND OFFICERS	GROUND PERSONNEL	TOTAL
Kittyhawk Mustang Spitfire }	30	6	208	244
Mosquito Beaufighter }	48	7	334	389
Marauder	156	13	336	505
Baltimore	132	7	249	388
Boston	118	5	256	379

Against most targets, fighter-bombers offered a more profitable return in terms of damage inflicted for effort expended. Although fighter-bombers had their problems with regard to accuracy (see below), they were nevertheless able to tackle most targets with more precision. For example, in the same report Desert Air Force observed that it was extremely difficult for medium-altitude bombers to obtain hits on a bridge due to the narrow target it presented, whereas recent experience had shown that one Squadron of Kittyhawks could succeed where large formations of medium bombers had failed.[42] Moreover, fighter-bombers did not present such good targets to heavy flak batteries as formations of mediums bombing in daylight, the chief threat to fighter-bombers being light automatic flak (see below and Chapter 8). Only targets that required pattern bombing, such as extensive defended positions or gun areas, were more suited to attack by light/medium bombers.

Fighter-bomber squadrons required little more maintenance than those of fighters. A larger armament staff was needed for the fusing and maintenance of bombs, but bomb racks, fusing- and release-mechanisms needed only routine maintenance from squadron armourers. Moreover, fighter-bombers could be armed, fuelled and taxied much easier and faster than light/medium bombers, particularly on rapidly constructed forward airstrips with narrow taxiways and dispersals, while less time was needed for crew briefing. It was mainly this which enabled fighter-bomber squadrons to carry out three, and sometimes more, missions per day as opposed to the usual two of light/medium bomber squadrons.[43]

In 1944 RAF fighter-bomber units were organised into Wings comprising a headquarters and between three and six squadrons. In late 1944 two of the three Typhoon wings serving in No.84 Group of RAF 2nd TAF each had four squadrons while the third comprised three. The same situation prevailed in No.83 Group.[44] In Italy at this time, No.239 (Fighter-Bomber) Wing consisted of six squadrons. According to Desert Air Force this enabled the wing to maintain intensive operations as a whole, or if split into two groups for any reason. However, maintaining such a large strike force under the administrative and operational control of a single headquarters brought problems, the DAF study observing that the chief disadvantage was accommodation both for aircraft and personnel – a considerable amount of ground being required for some 96 aircraft and 1,600 personnel.[45]

In fact there was a serious problem of airfield congestion in Italy in the winter of 1944–45 which adversely affected fighter-bomber operations, particularly at Fano, where six British and three US squadrons were based, and Forli from where six British squadrons operated. The usual airfield procedure was for aircraft to take off and land in either direction, in order to bring aircraft as close to their dispersals as possible and minimise the distance over which they had to taxi.

Usually a single taxi strip would be used for two squadrons, over which there was an alternating flow of aircraft to and from the main runway. It normally took some six minutes for each flight to leave dispersal, taxi to the runway, and take off. The problem in 1944–45 was that the taxi strips were too narrow, and in winter (and spring) aircraft were confined to them due to mud. The taxi strips were thus packed, delaying take-off times, while squadrons returning from operations often had to orbit for up to 40 minutes before they could land, pilots having to allow for this eventuality by reducing time in the battle area. This obviously affected air-support timings, as aircraft could not take off on schedule nor arrive in the battle area when expected, and it was estimated that pre-arranged support missions were delayed by at least one hour. Moreover, as an airfield was expected to handle between 200–220 sorties in a ten-hour day, it was estimated that this congestion reduced the number of missions flown by 20 per cent.[46]

Command of a fighter-bomber wing was exercised by a wing commander (usually holding the RAF rank of Group Captain) who was responsible for the wing's administrative and operational efficiency. The running of the Wing Operations Room and flying operations were the responsibility of his second-in-command, the Wing

Commander (Flying). There was also a Squadron Leader attached to assist in administration duties and an Intelligence Officer, usually a Flight Lieutenant, responsible for obtaining and disseminating all information regarding enemy movements, positions, tactics, and the location of flak positions in the battle area and for maintaining a stock of maps. Operations Officers, usually three with the rank of Flight Lieutenant or Flying Officer, manned the Wing Operations Room on a 24 hour basis. Their task was to maintain details of squadron states (serviceability of aircraft and states of readiness) and to take details of impending operations and to warn the squadrons concerned. They also briefed pilots and, in wings of which the squadrons were frequently employed in close support, worked closely with the attached Army Air Liaison Officers. The total personnel strength of a wing headquarters was about 140, organised as in Diagram I.[47]

DIAGRAM I

RAF FIGHTER-BOMBER WING HEADQUARTERS

Commanding Officer

(Administrative side)　　　　　　　(Operational side)

Squadron Leader (Administrative)　　Wing Commander (Flying)

Wing Headquarters　　　　　　　　Wing Operations Room

Signals, Medical, Store, Cyphers & Motor Transport Sections

3 Operations Officers (1 Flying Control)
Intelligence Officer & Clerk
3 Army Air Liaison Officers & Clerk

Squadron Headquarters　　　　　　Squadrons

A fighter-bomber squadron consisted of a headquarters and two flights of aircraft with approximately 12 pilots to each flight. A squadron could be expected to keep 12 aircraft available for operations with 4 more as an immediate reserve, though during operations the number of aircraft and pilots available varied considerably from day to day. Operations of squadron strength were usually carried out by a maximum of 12 aircraft, experience having shown that this was an efficient and manoeuvreable formation whereas anything larger was unwieldy.[48]

Apart from the pilots, most of the other squadron personnel were responsible for servicing aircraft and loading weapons and ammunition, total personnel amounting to approximately 240. The

DIAGRAM II

RAF FIGHTER-BOMBER SQUADRON HEADQUARTERS

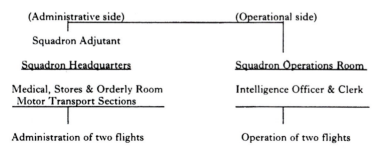

Squadron Commander

(Administrative side)   (Operational side)

Squadron Adjutant

Squadron Headquarters   Squadron Operations Room

Medical, Stores & Orderly Room   Intelligence Officer & Clerk
Motor Transport Sections

Administration of two flights   Operation of two flights

organisation of a typical squadron headquarters is shown in Diagram
II.

Command was exercised by a Squadron Leader responsible for both
the administrative and operational running of his squadron, though
his duties were primarily leading his pilots and keeping them up to the
mark in tactics and operational efficiency. He would have had a senior
Flight Commander as second-in-command, usually a Flight
Lieutenant, whose duties were predominantly flying, the burden of
administrative work falling upon the Squadron Adjutant who was
generally also a Flight Lieutenant. Each squadron also had an
Intelligence Officer, usually with the rank of Flying Officer, responsible for running the squadron's own operations room and for taking
details of operations from Wing and briefing pilots. His primary duty
was the debriefing of pilots on their return from operations and the
compiling of operations reports to be forwarded to the Wing
Intelligence Officer. In squadrons engaged in close support he worked
closely with the attached Army ALOs in maintaining maps of the
battle area and updating bombline data.[49]

As in the RAF, the basic operational unit of the USAAF was the
squadron. However, US fighter-bomber squadrons had an authorised
establishment of 25 aircraft plus five in reserve, and a personnel
establishment of some 57 officers and 245 men; both varied considerably during operations. Squadrons were organised into Groups (the
equivalent of RAF Wings) of, usually, three squadrons. The number
of personnel in a Group was some 200 officers and 800 enlisted men.[50]

FIGHTER-BOMBER TACTICS

Close-support missions were usually carried out by the RAF with flights of between six and eight aircraft, whereas the USAAF favoured the four-plane flight as the basic fighter-bomber unit.[51] Larger formations of Wing (RAF) and Group (USAAF) strength, involving a number of squadrons, were employed to attack particularly formidable or important targets, especially in support of major ground operations. Infantry and gun positions, strongpoints, tanks, and defended buildings were engaged in either dive or low-level attacks depending upon weather and visibility conditions, and the amount of flak in the target area. For attacks to be effective, visibility had to be at least 2,000 yards and the cloud base no lower than 5,000 feet for bombing or 3,000 feet for strafing. During bombing or rocket-firing a strong wind would dictate the direction of approach, often preventing pilots from taking advantage of such factors as the position of the sun and of friendly troops. It would also adversely affect accuracy.[52]

The chief danger confronting fighter-bomber pilots in 1943–45 was not the Luftwaffe, which was rarely seen over the battlefront in daylight, but German anti-aircraft firepower – flak – the presence and variations of which determined tactics both during the flight to the target and the attack. Ground-attack pilots often had to contend with formidable concentrations of small calibre flak that was very effective up to 3,000 feet and the fire of which was not visible to them; therefore they were briefed to come below 3,000 feet only when carrying out their attacks. Heavy calibre automatic flak (20 mm–40 mm) was effective up to 6,000 feet and its explosions were easily seen by pilots; fighter-bomber formations usually flew at 7,500–8,000 feet which was just out of range of this, yet where the heavier non-automatic flak (such as 88 mm) tended to be inaccurate.[53] The effective range of German guns, and particularly that of automatic flak, was often the subject of controversy between pilots and their Intelligence Officers. Bill Colgan, who served as a fighter-bomber pilot with the US 79th Group in Italy, remembers that pilots were often disdainful when told of the effective range of German guns, especially after seeing rounds from such guns exploding at higher altitudes.[54]

As fighter-bomber pilots were primarily trained as day-fighter pilots, they flew fighter formations. RAF formations flew in sections of four aircraft flying nearly line abreast, with 50–75 yards between aircraft, and with each section of four stepped up or down 500–1,000 feet depending on the position of the sun.[55] In a 16-plane USAAF squadron the four flights flew in two sections, one flying 300 yards behind the other and from 500 to 1,000 feet higher. In a 12-plane USAAF squadron the flights usually flew in a loose, shallow V, with 200–300 yards between them.[56]

Dive bombing attacks were made by both British and US fighter-bombers at steep angles, usually between 45° and 60°, with the pilots following their leader into the attack and releasing their bombs at 2–3,000 feet. With single-engined aircraft, as the RAF discovered particularly with the Typhoon, it was very difficult for the pilot to see straight down to the ground without tipping up the wing. In Typhoon squadrons the usual procedure was for the pilot flying as the leader's No.2 to be briefed to fly a little further away in order to enable the leader to tip his wing when over the target so that he could judge the exact moment at which to roll over for the dive. Correctly identifying targets was crucial but rarely easy, and it was common for the leader to give a quick final briefing to his pilots by R/T, such as,

> The target is the white building with the red roof just North of the river bank.

Sometimes extraordinary measures were taken by troops to indicate targets for their supporting aircraft – in Italy in April 1945 No.87 (Spitfire) Squadron reported a dive-bombing attack on seven German tanks laagered near Felice which was indicated by someone wearing a white shirt standing 200 paces to the east of their position.[57]

When satisfied that the target was correctly identified, the leader would warn his pilots when he was about to dive by announcing 'Bomb switches on' followed by 'Going down in 10 seconds' and 'Going down now'. A 2nd TAF report on tactics stated that a steep dive was essential for accuracy, and that it was best not to roll over into the dive too fast, but to run up to the target in a gentle dive and then gradually pull up, thereby losing speed before finally rolling over; if this was not done then too much speed was gained early on in the dive and insufficient time given to line up the aircraft and reduce 'skid'.[58]

Diagram III (see Appendix) shows an example of a dive bombing attack as carried out by bomb carrying Typhoons or Spitfires against a lightly defended target from 12,000–7,000 feet or below. In such an attack, when in the target area, the fighter-bombers would have changed from their approach formation into echelon starboard. When over the target, the leader would have allowed it to pass under the leading edge of his port wing as shown in Phase 2 of the diagram. As the target reappeared at the trailing edge, the leader would have executed a semi-stalled turn to port, followed by the others of the section. This allowed for a line-astern attack at a steep angle on the reciprocal of the original course, as shown in Phase 3. After releasing bombs, all aircraft would have made a violent evasive turn in a pre-arranged direction before reforming in line abreast. Diagram IV (see Appendix) shows a heavier scale of attack from 12,000–7,000 feet by two sections against a heavily defended target. In this case an attempt would have been made to reduce flak effectiveness by attacking from out of the sun and from two directions in order to split concentrations of flak fire.[59]

Low-level attacks were usually carried out in a dive at about 30° with the bombs released at about 800 feet and the aircraft flying at high speed in order to escape small calibre and light flak and the burst and debris from their own bombs. Typhoons usually attacked in pairs, using bombs fitted with short-delay fuses so that each pair attacked just after the previous pair's bombs had exploded. However, such tactics could be hazardous against targets heavily defended by flak, and an RAF report warned that in such circumstances four aircraft going down in two pairs was all that could reasonably expect get away with this type of attack.[60]

Against targets such as strongpoints in buildings or headquarters, mixed tactics of low-level and dive-bombing attacks were employed. The usual procedure was to commence with low-level bombing against the most prominent buildings, followed by dive bombing immediately the low-level aircraft were clear. The RAF found that rocket-firing aircraft, which could also attack either in steep dives or at low level, were particularly successful when employed in such mixed attacks due to the incendiary effect of their rockets.[61]

Fitting Typhoons with underwing rails, enabling each aircraft to carry eight 3 inch rockets, each with a 60 lb high-explosive warhead, gave them tremendous firepower. The rockets also had several advantages; being self-propelled they had a much greater impact velocity, while the rocket motor created no recoil on leaving its carrier, enabling the warhead to be considerably heavier and of greater calibre than an orthodox airborne cannon shell.[62]

The rocket was crude in its simplicity, consisting of a cast-iron pipe with a 3 inch diameter motor and with the 60 lb warhead screwed on the front. Four cruciform stabilising fins were attached to the rear and the rocket was connected by lugs to the Typhoon's launching rails. On firing the rocket left the aircraft with a velocity of about 150 feet per second, its cordite propellant burning for 1½ seconds during which time the rocket could accelerate to over 1,000 feet per second over a distance of 500 yards, thereafter gradually slowing over the next 500 yards as it approached its target.[63]

As with bombing, rocket-firing tactics were determined by weather and by the amount of flak. Against heavily defended targets pilots were usually instructed to make a steep 60° dive at 7–8,000 feet and fire all eight rockets in a salvo at about 4,000 feet at a range of some 1,700 yards. If the target was lightly defended, pilots were encouraged to make a shallow dive of 20° or 30° at 3–4,000 feet and to fire their rockets by 'rippling' them in pairs from 1,500 feet at a range of about 1,000 yards.[64] However, such procedures were often disregarded on operations and squadrons soon evolved their own tactics. A former Typhoon pilot recalls that the common practice was to fly down to low level in a shallow dive, aim at 600 or 700 yards, then fire cannon and rockets together at close range which was sometimes 250 yards.[65]

If a target was heavily protected by flak, only one attack could be attempted and pilots were briefed never to attack such targets twice. If a repeat attack was essential, then pilots were briefed to attack again from a different direction to minimise the risk of the previously-alerted flak gunners waiting to pick off the returning aircraft.[66]

US fighter-bombers were also equipped with air-to-ground rockets both in Italy and in North-West Europe. In the latter theatre the first P-47 Thunderbolts equipped with rockets became operational in July 1944. They lacked the firepower of the Typhoons, each aircraft carrying only four 5 inch HVAR (High-Velocity Aircraft Rocket) projectiles.[67] This was later increased, P-47s being fitted with rails for up to ten rockets, but in fact US fighter-bombers in Europe never employed rockets on a large scale. Those of Ninth Air Force fired only 13,959 during the war as opposed to the 222,515 fired by fighter-bombers of RAF 2nd TAF.[68] In Italy during late 1944 some P-47s were fitted with underwing infantry-type bazooka tubes to house 4.5 inch rockets (a cluster of three under each wing). These missiles, equivalent to a 105 mm howitzer shell, proved extremely effective in attacks on buildings, but the rocket was not a popular fighter-bomber weapon in this theatre even with the RAF. The only RAF fighter-bombers of Desert Air Force equipped with rockets in 1945 were the Mustangs of No.260 Squadron, but each aircraft carried only four 3 inch rockets, two under each wing on special rails enabling one rocket to be housed underneath the other.[69]

Napalm fire-bombs, often auxiliary fuel tanks filled with petroleum jelly and fitted with a fused igniter, were extensively used by US fighter-bombers in both campaigns. Their delivery demanded special tactics, the object being to tumble the napalm tanks on to the target. In hilly terrain the tanks were usually delivered in shallow dives, while against targets on fairly flat terrain they were dropped in level flight from minimum altitude – creating long swathes of fire that edged towards and engulfed the target area.[70]

While fighter-bomber pilots frequently fired their machine-gun and/or cannon armament during bombing or rocket-firing, they were also called upon to carry out specific 'strafing' attacks. These too demanded appropriate tactics, and speed and co-ordination were essential as the aircraft were coming down to low level where they were perilously vulnerable to flak. RAF fighter-bombers usually approached their target from a wide turn and with a loss of height that ensured they were at average speed and not higher than 1,500 feet when levelling out for the attack. After steadying their aircraft and getting the target in the sights, pilots would open fire at a height of 700 feet at a range of about 500 yards and at an angle of 25° to 30°.[71]

The guns of fighter aircraft were harmonized for the rounds to converge at a point ahead of the aircraft. This was an air-to-air combat consideration and in 1943–45, for both the RAF and USAAF, the distance was some 250 yards. At this range the rounds fired would impact the target together, and when pilots were strafing individual targets, such as tanks or vehicles along a road, this was desirable. Low-level strafing of such targets, however, could be perilous for fighter-bomber pilots. Apart from the risk of flak, a slight misjudgement or target-fixation on the part of the pilot could send the fighter-bomber hurtling into the target or into nearby trees and obstructions. Should the pilot have selected as his target a lorry or railway waggon which proved to be carrying ammunition or explosives, this could literally blow up in the pilot's face, hurling debris such as slabs of roadway, lorry or waggon parts, or unexploded ammunition, into the path of his aircraft. Strafing area targets was less hazardous, for then close-in firing was a disadvantage and pilots opened fire at wider ranges in order to cover the target area.[72]

FIGHTER-BOMBER ACCURACY

The free-fall bombs and air-to-ground rockets of 1943–45 were highly inaccurate and barely adequate for use against precision targets. This was suspected at the time, and eventually proven in a series of Army and RAF ORS investigations.

The British 3 inch rocket was very difficult to place accurately, and delivering it with a fair chance of hitting its target demanded considerable skill. Due to their weight, and how it was distributed, the rockets had a curved trajectory which meant that they needed to be fired within a range of 1,000 to 2,000 yards. Beyond that range the trajectory curve was so severe as to make accurate firing almost impossible. The relatively low launching-speed also meant that, if the aircraft skidded slightly or turned at the moment of release, a considerable error could result.

Typhoon pilots of 2nd TAF were given initially a three-week course in rocket-firing, followed by regular refresher periods at Armament Practice camps in the UK. During attendance at the latter it was found that pilots consistently tended to undershoot the target either as a result of releasing the rockets at too long a range or through flying too slowly at the lower dive-angles. In particular pilots had to learn to calculate accurately the effect of wind before firing, it being discovered that, for example, a 10 mph wind could result in a 5 yard shift in line and a 3 yard shift in range at the Mean Point of Impact (MPI). This could easily mean the difference between a hit and a near-miss if the target was relatively small, such as a tank or single gun position.[73]

TABLE V

TYPHOON SCALE OF EFFORT NECESSARY
AGAINST TYPICAL TARGETS[74]

TARGET	SIZE	HORIZONTAL PROJECTED AREA (45° DIVE)	% SHOTS HITTING TARGET	FOR 50% CHANCE OF HIT	
				ROCKETS NEEDED	SORTIES
Small gun position	5 yards diameter	19 square yards	0.2	350	44
Panther tank	22' 6" × 10' 9" × 9' 10"	50 square yards	0.5	140	18
Large gun position	10 yards diameter	80 square yards	0.8	88	11
Army hut	60' × 30' × 20'	270 square yards	2.8	24	3
Large building	120' × 54' × 50'	1,000 square yards	10.0	7	1

Pilot accuracy showed significant improvement after a session at Armament Camp, but could never compensate adequately for the weapon's inherent inaccuracy or the lack of an effective sight through which to aim the rockets. The modified Mk.IID gyroscopic sight, which allowed for the initial gravity drop of the rockets as well as for the effect of wind and movement of the target, was not available until late 1944.[75] Average Typhoon pilots in trials, firing all eight rockets in a salvo, had roughly a four per-cent chance of hitting a target the size of a German tank.[76] On operations, with targets camouflaged and difficult to identify, and with pilots under anti-aircraft fire, accuracy could be even further reduced.

In 1945 a joint British Army/RAF ORS study of the effectiveness of rocket-firing Typhoons in the close air support role, outlined the scale of Typhoon attack necessary to obtain hits on typical targets. This was based on operational data and is shown in Table V.

Very apparent is the high number of sorties and rockets considered necessary to secure a reasonable chance of hitting such relatively small targets as tanks and gun positions. Yet these were, as the report indicated, characteristic of many close support targets.

The advent of the improved sight made some difference, and after comparing the accuracy of rocket-Typhoon attacks against German-occupied buildings in Holland in 1944 with attacks upon similar targets in Germany in 1945 ORS 2nd TAF discovered that the distance of the mean point of impact of the rockets from the aiming point had decreased from 62.5 yards to 43 yards.[77]

Despite their inaccuracy, rockets could be placed with more precision than free-fall bombs. Table VI shows the number of instances during attacks by Spitfires and Typhoons upon gun positions and strongpoints in 1945 where rockets and bombs actually landed within 150 yards of their target. The targets were all field positions and were attacked at the request of British troops during mobile operations in Germany. The results reflect the difficulty of landing a bomb on or near a pinpoint target.[78]

TABLE VI

BOMBING AND ROCKET ACCURACY

	ROCKETS	BOMBS
NUMBER OF ATTACKS	37	11
NUMBER WITHIN 150 YARDS	33 (89%)	5 (45%)

Also in 1945 ORS 2nd TAF examined the accuracy of Typhoon bombers in operations between October 1944 and April 1945, nine pin-point bombing targets were analysed by plotting bomb distributions from air reconnaissance photographs and by ground examination. The average radial error for these attacks was 158 yards, with only 50 per cent of the bombs falling within 130 yards of the target. For the same investigation seventeen railway line targets were examined, for which a total of 320 bombs dropped by Typhoons and Spitfires were plotted. It was found that the average line error was 69 yards, with only 50 per cent of the bombs falling within fifty yards either side of the target.[79] At least targets such as bridges and road/rail crossings could be seen by pilots, whereas many of the close-support targets, being small and camouflaged, could not – the pilots being able to aim only at the coloured smoke fired by friendly artillery to indicate the target.

The most accurate weapons possessed by fighter-bombers were their cannon and machine gun armament. This was illustrated by the British Army's Operational Research Group in 1945, when they compared 20 mm aircraft cannon with the 3 inch rocket and outlined the number of rounds that could be fired per attack per aircraft against ground targets and the probable number of hits secured:

TABLE VII

STRAFING ACCURACY

WEAPON	ROUNDS PER ATTACK PER AIRCRAFT	HITS ON 10 FEET SQUARE NORMAL TO LINE OF FLIGHT PER ATTACK PER AIRCRAFT
20 mm Cannon	120	32
3 inch Rocket	8	0.045

This suggests that the greater number of rounds fired by machine-guns and/or cannon ensured that some were likely to strike the target.[80] However, the question remained whether such rounds were powerful enough to inflict serious damage or destruction, and this problem is discussed in the following chapters.

THE FIGHTER-BOMBER COMPONENT

By 1944–45 fighter-bombers were, for the most part, the largest component of the Allied Tactical Air Forces operational in Italy and North-West Europe. This is shown in Table VIII. Squadrons designated as day-fighter have been bracketed with those designated fighter-bomber because operational roles were not always clearly defined but depended upon circumstances.[81] Day fighters frequently flew armed-reconnaissance missions and carried out ground-strafing

TABLE VIII

FIGHTER AND FIGHTER-BOMBER COMPONENT
OF THE ALLIED TACTICAL AIR FORCES

ITALY

RAF DESERT AIR FORCE (1945)   NUMBER OF SQUADRONS

          Fighter/Fighter-Bombers: 22 (52.6%)   including 3 US P-47
                                                    Squadrons attached
          Light/Medium Bombers: 7 (16.6%)
    Night-Bombers & Night-Fighters: 6 (14.2%)
          Air Observation Post: 5 (11.9%)
              Reconnaissance: 2 (4.7%)

US XII AIR SUPPORT COMMAND (JANUARY 1944)
          Fighter/Fighter-Bombers: 23 (57.5%)
    Fighter/Dive-Bombers (A36A):   6 (15.0%)
          Light/Medium Bombers: 4 (10.0%)
              Night-Fighters: 3 (7.5%)
              Reconnaissance: 3 (7.5%)
          Radio Counter-Measures: 1 (2.5%)

NORTH-WEST EUROPE

RAF 2nd TACTICAL AIR FORCE (1945)
          Fighter/Fighter-Bombers: 49 (61.2%)
          Light/Medium Bombers: 13 (16.2%)
              Reconnaissance: 9 (11.2%)
          Air Observation Post: 9 (11.2%)

US 9th AIR FORCE (1945)
          Fighter/Fighter-Bombers: 45 (42.8%)
          Light/Medium Bombers: 45 (42.8%)
              Night Fighters: 2 (1.9%)
              Reconnaissance: 13 (12.3%)

US 1st TACTICAL AIR FORCE (1945)
          Fighter/Fighter-Bombers: 24 (50.0%)
          Light/Medium Bombers: 14 (29.1%)
              Reconnaissance: 8 (16.6%)
              Night Fighters: 2 (4.1%)

attacks in the battle area, particularly during German withdrawals, such as at Falaise, and large scale interdiction operations such as STRANGLE (May 1944) in Italy and CLARION (February 1945) in North-West Europe. Moreover, as the campaigns progressed and the likelihood of encountering the Luftwaffe decreased, many fighter squadrons were converted to fighter-bombers. Specific fighter-bomber squadrons were similarly often required to fly fighter missions, by acting as escort for medium bombers or by providing fighter patrols. To sum up, by 1944 the fighter aircraft fitted with bombs or rockets constituted the principal tactical air weapon. Its effectiveness in the close support role is examined in the following chapters.

NOTES

1. Christopher Shores, *Ground Attack Aircraft of World War II* (London: Macdonald & Jane's, 1977), pp. 46–7.
2. Donald L. Caldwell, *JG26: Top Guns of The Luftwaffe* (New York: Orion Books, 1991), pp. 64–5.
3. Shores, p. 50.
4. The only dive bombers employed operationally by the RAF during the Second World War were US-built single-engined, two-seater, Vultee Vengeance aircraft which equipped four RAF squadrons (Nos. 45, 82, 84, and 110) and two RIAF squadrons in the Far East, being first employed in Arakan in late 1942. They carried a 1,000 lb bomb load (two 500 lb or four 250 lb bombs), and usually attacked targets in a steep dive. Missions were usually flown by formations of six or twelve aircraft, and very often fighter escorts were provided. Vengeances proved successful in the close-support role, though a report comparing dive bombers and fighter-bombers in close support compiled by RAF 3rd Tactical Air Force (of Air Command South-East Asia) in Sept. 1944 noted that 4th Corps considered Hurricane fighter-bombers more accurate. (PRO AIR 23/2514). Detailed analyses of Vengeance operations are Air Headquarters India Tactical Memorandum No.35, *Vengeance Operations In Arakan* (May 1943) and South-East Asia Command Tactical Memorandum No.1 *Employment of Vengeance Aircraft* (compiled by No.168 Wing RAF in Dec. 1943), both in Air Command South-East Asia reports on dive bombing, PRO AIR 23/2514. Air Command South-East Asia Tactical Memorandum No.5, *Dive Bombing* (Feb. 1944), compares operational experience of Vengeance aircraft in Australasia with that of Dauntless dive bombers in the Solomons, in *Dive Bombing: Combined Operational Data 1944*, PRO AIR 23/2830. Vengeance operations are described in two works by Peter C. Smith, *Jungle Dive Bombers At War* (London: John Murray Ltd., 1987), and *Vengeance – The Vultee Vengeance Dive-Bomber* (Shrewsbury: Airlife Publishing, 1986). See also *Deadly Diving Accuracy*, his interview with Arthur Murland Gill (Officer Commanding No.84 Squadron RAF 1942–44) in *Military History*, Vol. 4, No. 6, June 1988, pp. 18–24.
5. Shores, p. 52. In Dec. 1940/Jan. 1941 No.274 (Hurricane) Squadron flew some eighty operations of which ten (12%) were specific strafing attacks against Italian troop convoys and airfields. No.274 Squadron Operations Record Book, Dec. 1940/Jan. 1941, PRO AIR 27/1588.
6. No. 607 Squadron Operations Record Book, Oct. 1941, PRO AIR 27/2093; Shores, p. 103.

7. Arthur Bryant, *The Turn Of The Tide 1939–43: A Study Based on the Diaries and Autobiographical Notes of Field Marshal The Viscount Alanbrooke, K.G., O.M.* (London: The Reprint Society, 1958), p. 194.
8. No. 80 Squadron RAF, Operations Record Book, Nov. 1941–Jan. 1942, PRO AIR 27/669.
9. Bill Gunston, *The Illustrated Encyclopedia of Combat Aircraft of World War II* (London: Tiger Books, 1990), pp.210–13; Operations Record Book of No.112 Squadron RAF, May 1942, PRO AIR 27/873.
10. Air Historical Branch Narrative, *The North African Campaign, November 1942*–May 1943, pp. 175–9, PRO AIR 41/33.
11. No.174 Squadron RAF Operations Record Book, Aug. 1942, PRO AIR 27/1108.
12. Between July and Sept. 1942 it was estimated that at least one Typhoon failed to return from each mission due to one or the other of these defects. See William Green, *Famous Fighters of the Second World War* (London: Macdonald, 1960), p. 103. Details of the problems experienced when first converting the Typhoon to a bomber are in an RAF Report of 1944 entitled *Typhoon Bomber*, PRO AIR 37/798.
13. RAF 2nd TAF Report, *Tactics used by Typhoon Day Fighter/Bomber Squadrons of 2nd TAF* (1945), in PRO AIR 37/871.
14. Shores, *Ground Attack Aircraft of World War II*, p. 111.
15. Ibid., p. 66 and p. 152.
16. Peter C. Smith, *Close Air Support: An Illustrated History, 1914 to the Present* (New York: Crown Publishers, 1990), p. 82.
17. Ray Wagner (Ed.), *American Combat Planes* (New York: Doubleday, 1968), pp. 84–5; Richard P. Hallion, *Strike From The Sky: The History of Battlefield Air Attack 1911–45* (Shrewsbury: Airlife Publishing, 1989), p. 177. Peter C. Smith refutes the view that dive brakes on the A-36A were usually wired shut. He quotes a former A-36A pilot who served with the US 525th Fighter Bomber Squadron, John B. Watson, who told him that he could not recall participating in any mission when the brakes were not used on bomb runs between 8,000 and 12,000 feet when the dive was vertical. See *Close Air Support*, p. 96.
18. Enzo Angelucci with Peter Bowers, *The American Fighter: The Definitive Guide to American Fighter Aircraft from 1917 to the Present* (Yeovil: Haynes Publishing, 1987), pp. 163–4 and pp. 166–7; Green, *Famous Fighters of the Second World War*, pp. 46–9; Gunston, *The Illustrated Encyclopedia of Combat Aircraft*, pp. 210–13.
19. Order of Battle, Royal Air Force and United States Army Air Forces, Appendix 4(a) to C.J.C. Molony, *The Mediterranean and Middle East*, Vol. V (London: HMSO, 1973), pp. 874–5. Neither the RAF nor the USAAF employed the P-40 operationally in North-West Europe. In Italy in 1945 some RAF and Commonwealth squadrons were still equipped with the later Kittyhawk variants, but by this time USAAF squadrons in Italy had converted to the P-47 Thunderbolt.
20. Green, *Famous Fighters of the Second World War*, p. 88.
21. Ibid., p. 84 and p. 88.
22. Ibid., p. 88; Gunston, *The Illustrated Encyclopedia of Combat aircraft*, pp. 249–50; Angelucci and Bowers, *The American Fighter*, pp. 390–1 and pp. 394–6.
23. Shores, *Ground Attack Aircraft of World War II*, p. 140.
24. Ibid., pp. 134–5. Some RAF squadrons were equipped with the Thunderbolt, but not in Europe. In Sept. 1944 P-47s became operational with No.261 Squadron in Burma, and by the end of the year seven RAF squadrons in Burma had similarly converted from Hurricanes. These squadrons were extensively employed in close support, and a study of their ORBs provides a good insight to the nature of close air support in that theatre, not least because their ORBs tended to be written-up in more detail than those of RAF squadrons serving in Europe. See for example the ORBs of Nos. 5, 79, 134, 123, 258, and 146 Squadrons for April 1945 detailing VCP-controlled airstrikes in close support of British and Indian troops clearing the Japanese-held villages of Kandaung, Thabyebin, Sadaung, Kalaywa, Thazi, Yamethin, Hletaikon, Kokkogaing, Pyinbongyi, Thamin, and Ingon (PRO AIR 27/66, AIR 27/666, AIR 27/947, AIR 27/917, AIR 27/1531, and AIR 27/989 respectively). These provide detailed target descriptions, map references, the height at which bombing and strafing was carried out, the locations where individual bombs fell and an assessment of results, and the number of rounds fired in strafing the target.
25. Green, *Famous Fighters of the Second World War*, p. 75.

26. Ibid., p. 77.
27. Ibid.
28. Ibid. In 1944 an Allied Prisoner of War report observed that the Lightning was more feared than the Thunderbolt. This was because the Thunderbolt had a loud engine which could be heard from sufficient distance to give some warning of attack, whereas the Lightning approached with little noise, even at low level, and was often able to surprise men and vehicles in the open. Prisoner of War Interrogation Report A.D.I. (K), No. 382/1944 (Normandy, 24 July 1944), in PRO AIR 37/760
29. Shores, *Ground Attack Aircraft of World War II*, p. 152.
30. Green, *Famous Fighters of the Second World War*, p. 91 and p. 96.
31. Ibid., pp. 96–7.
32. Shores, pp. 139–40.
33. Ibid., p. 146.
34. RAF Desert Air Force Study (1944), *Fighter-Bombers* in *Employment of Fighter-Bombers (Policy)*, PRO AIR 23/1826.
35. Table based on The USAAF Evaluation Board in the European Theater of Operations, Report 33, *Tactics and Techniques of the Tactical Air Commands in the ETO* (1946), reproduced in William A. Jacobs, *Tactical Air Doctrine and AAF Close Air Support in the European Theater, 1944–45*, Aerospace Historian, 27/1, Spring, March 1980, p. 47.
36. Headquarters Mediterranean Allied Air Forces ORS Report No.32 (1945), *Observations on the Strength and Balance of Desert Air Force*, PRO AIR 23/7513.
37. Ibid.
38. Gunston, *The Illustrated Encyclopedia of Combat Aircraft*, p. 109.
39. Shores, *Ground Attack Aircraft of World War II*, p. 152.
40. Gunston, p. 109.
41. RAF Desert Air Force Study (1944), *Fighter Bombers*; ORS MAAF Report No.32 (1945) *Observations on the Strength and Balance of Desert Air Force*.
42. RAF Desert Air Force Study (1944), *Fighter-Bombers*.
43. Ibid.
44. Orders of Battle for RAF 2nd TAF, Aug.-Dec. 1944, PRO AIR 16/964 & PRO AIR 16/965.
45. RAF Desert Air Force Study (1944), *Fighter-Bombers*, in *Employment of Fighter-Bombers (Policy)*, PRO AIR 23/1826.
46. ORS MAAF Preliminary Report (Jan. 1945), *Effect of Airfield Congestion on Operations of DAF Fighter and Fighter-Bomber Squadrons*, in PRO AIR 23/7513. Airfield congestion also meant that accidents, if they occurred, were likely to destroy or damage more aircraft. At Fano, four instances of an aircraft swinging on take-off had resulted in the destruction of ten aircraft and several damaged.
47. RAF Desert Air Force Study (1944), *Fighter-Bombers*.
48. Ibid.
49. Ibid.
50. Bill Colgan, *World War II Fighter Bomber Pilot* (Blue Ridge Summit, PA.: Tab Books, 1985), p. 36; Alan F. Wilt, *Allied Cooperation in Sicily and Italy*, Ch. 5 in Benjamin F. Cooling (Ed.), *Case Studies in the Development of Close Air Support* (Washington, DC: Office of Air Force History, 1990), p. 198.
51. The AAF Evaluation Board in the ETO, *The Effectiveness of Third Phase Tactical Air Operations in the European Theater, 5 May 1944–8 May 1945* (Feb. 1946), p. 378, PRO AIR 40/1111.
52. RAF 2nd TAF 1945, *Tactics used by the Squadrons of the 2nd Tactical Air Force*, p. 5., PRO AIR 37/871.
53. Ibid., p 4.
54. Colgan, pp.103–4.
55. RAF 2nd TAF 1945, *Tactics used by the Squadrons of the 2nd Tactical Air Force*, p. 3, PRO AIR 37/871.
56. The AAF Evaluation Board in the ETO, *The Effectiveness of Third Phase Tactical Air Operations*, p. 378.
57. No.87 Squadron RAF, Operations Record Book, April 1945, PRO AIR 27/713.
58. RAF 2nd TAF 1945, *Tactics used by the Squadrons of the 2nd Tactical Air Force*.

59. Diagrams III and IV are based on those contained in Appendices to RAF Air Fighting Development Unit Report on fighter-bombing (1944), *Fighter-Bomber Tactics*, in PRO AIR 23/7479.
60. RAF 2nd TAF 1945, *Tactics used by the Squadrons of the 2nd Tactical Air Force*, p. 4., PRO AIR 37/871.
61. Ibid.
62. Desmond Scott, *Typhoon Pilot* (London: Arrow, 1988), p. 94.
63. Alfred Price, *The 3 inch Rocket: How Effective was it against the German Tanks in Normandy?*, Royal Air Force Quarterly, Summer 1975, p. 129.
64. RAF Tactical Bulletin No.45, *Tactical Employment of R P Aircraft*, Headquarters No.38 Group RAF, Oct. 1944, PRO AIR 37/415.
65. Charles Demoulin, *Firebirds: Flying The Typhoon in Action* (Shrewsbury: Airlife, 1986–87), p. 70.
66. H.G. Pattison (former Flying Officer, No.182 Sqn RAF) quoted in Norman Franks, *Typhoon Attack* (London: William Kimber, 1984) p. 150.
67. Brereton Greenhous, *Aircraft versus Armor: Cambrai to Yom Kippur*, in Tim Travers and Christan Archer (Eds.), *Men at War* (Chicago: Precedent, 1982), pp. 105–6.
68. Shores, *Ground Attack Aircraft in World War II*, p. 155. Rocket use by US fighter-bombers was more extensive in the Pacific and Far East, especially after the more efficient zero-length underwing rocket rails became available in greater quantity during early 1945. See ibid, pp. 179–80.
69. Ibid., p. 124 and p. 133. Rocket-equipped Hurricane IVs of No.6 Squadron arrived in Italy in March 1944, but operated mainly over the Adriatic and Yugoslavian coast against shipping. They carried an asymmetric load; a 45 gallon auxiliary fuel tank under one wing and four rockets under the other. Hurricane IVs also equipped No.20 Squadron in Burma in 1944–45, serving as rocketeers providing close support for British troops, but by European war standards the aircraft were then obsolete.
70. Colgan, *World War II Fighter-Bomber Pilot*, pp. 130–1.
71. RAF 2nd TAF 1945, *Tactics used by Spitfire Day Fighter/Bomber Squadrons of 2nd TAF*, pp. 9–10, in PRO AIR 37/871.
72. Colgan, op.cit., p.44.
73. ORS 2nd TAF Report No.20 (1945), *The Accuracy of Rocket Firing at Armament Practice Camps*, PRO WO 291/1349.
74. ORS 2nd TAF/No.2 ORS 21st Army Group Joint Report No.3 (1945), *Rocket Typhoons in Close Support of Military Operations*, in *Operational Research in North-West Europe*, PRO WO 291/1331.
75. M.M. Postan, D. Hay, and J.D. Scott, *Design and Development of Weapons* (London: HMSO, 1964), p. 119.
76. Price, *The 3 inch Rocket*, p. 129.
77. ORS 2nd TAF Report No.36 (July 1946), *The Operational Accuracy of 2nd TAF Fighter-Bomber and R P Aircraft, Oct. 1944–April 1945*, PRO AIR 37/61.
78. ORS 2nd TAF Report No.32 (Dec. 1945), *Fighter-Bomber Attacks on Guns and Strong Points in the Closing Phase*, PRO AIR 37/61.
79. ORS 2nd TAF Report No.36, *The Operational Accuracy of 2nd TAF Fight Bomber and R/P Aircraft*. These figures give a different impression from the observation made by RAF Desert Air Force referenced at note 42 above. Some squadrons became adept at bombing after pilots had gained experience, though targets such as bridges were in fact very difficult to destroy. Group Captain D.E. Gillam, who commanded No.146 (Typhoon) Wing in North-West Europe recalled that bridges were very difficult to damage or destroy even with 1,000 lb bombs, and that pilots were very lucky to obtain a hit as the bombs usually glanced off and fell into the river. Quoted in Franks, *Typhoon Attack*, p. 215. Sometimes squadrons were lucky. Typhoons of No.198 Squadron, each with two 1,000lb bombs, destroyed the bridge at Vianen near Utrecht on 5 Jan. 1945 after attempts by several squadrons had previously failed. In May 1944, twelve P-47s of the US 365th Fighter Group bombed the railway bridge at Vernon, France, with such success that details were circulated throughout the Allied tactical air forces. See Headquarters 365th Fighter Group Report (14 May 1944), *Report on Low-Level Attack on Railway Bridge at Vernon, France*, PRO AIR 37/805.

80. British Army Operational Research Group Memorandum No.495 (1945), *Attack on Army Targets by Fighter Aircraft*, PRO WO 291/811.
81. ORS MAAF Report No.32 (1945), *Observations on the Strength and Balance of Desert Air Force*; L.F. Ellis, *Victory In The West*, Vol. II, *The Defeat of Germany*, Appendix V, *The Allied Air Forces* (London: HMSO, 1968), pp. 389–96; Hilary St. G. Saunders, *Royal Air Force 1939–45*, Vol. III, *The Fight is Won*, Appendix XI (London: HMSO, 1954), pp. 412–17.

4

The Flying Spearhead:
Close Support for Allied Mobile
and Airborne Operations

Close air support by fighter-bombers was of vital importance during operations when Allied troops possessed limited firepower; namely armoured thrusts and airborne operations. Such operations saw artillery relegated to a secondary role in favour of air power. In the case of armoured thrusts this was because the tanks, if they succeeded in breaking through German defensive positions, would penetrate beyond the range of their supporting artillery, the bulk of which would also be outpaced by the advance.

The solution to this problem was the provision of continuous close air support for armoured spearheads during daylight. Particularly by the Americans in North-West Europe, the fighter-bomber and the tank were welded into an effective offensive combination that exceeded even the German developments in air/tank integration during 1940–42.

Regarding airborne operations conducted beyond the range of positioned friendly artillery, artillery support was limited to those pieces which could be transported to the dropping zone; in 1944 these were few and of relatively light calibre.[1] This was in line with the nature of airborne operations, which were essentially *coup de main* tasks demanding the rapid seizure of limited but important objectives and their retention until early relief. Once landed, however, lightly equipped airborne units were extremely vulnerable to counterattack by conventional troops supported by comparatively heavy weapons. Close air support was then the only means of delivering essential fire support for these forces.

THE FIGHTER-BOMBER/TANK COMBINATION

Successful deep penetration by armour depended upon maintaining the momentum of the attack after the initial breakthrough. Beyond the range of friendly artillery, armoured units depended upon speed and their intrinsic firepower to bypass (preferably) or, if necessary, overcome resistance. During 1940–42 the Germans demonstrated that this firepower could be successfully augmented by close air support, aircraft acting as 'flying artillery' to strike at targets in the path of the advance. Luftwaffe liaison officers in radio-equipped armoured cars accompanied the panzer columns, and were able to call upon Ju.87 'Stuka' dive-bombers that were already over the battle area or waiting at readiness on the airstrips hastily occupied in the wake of the advance.[2] The invasion of Russia in June 1941 saw the panzer units accompanied by Luftwaffe tank liaison officers, riding in their own radio-equipped tanks and in contact with air units.[3] This enabled targets to be bombed shortly after being encountered, and in 1942 RAF Intelligence estimated that Stuka attacks could be carried out within 15/20 minutes of the original support request, though this was considered 'exceptional'.[4]

The campaigns in Italy and North-West Europe in 1943–45 were characterised by the need to break a stubborn German defence through a lengthy and costly process of attrition.[5] However, there were occasions when, after German defence zones had been broken, mobile operations were possible. The problem then was how to sustain an advance before German forces could form a new defensive line. During the breakout from Normandy in July/August 1944, Operation COBRA, when US armour had to penetrate through and beyond the hedgerow-lined roads of the *bocage*, which were ideally suited to defence, success was largely due to an innovation in air support carried out by the US Ninth Air Force and which became known as 'Armored Column Cover'.

Introduced on the initiative of Major-General Quesada of IX TAC, Armored Column Cover was the provision of continuous air support for the US armour. Flights of four P-47 Thunderbolts, relieved by another flight approximately every 30 minutes, were maintained over the armoured spearheads during daylight. Controllers in the leading tanks communicated with the flight leaders by VHF radio and could thus call down strikes when required or request searches of the roads ahead of the column. The usual procedure was for the arriving fighter-bomber flight to check in by radio with the ground controller and, when relieving another flight, with the leader of the flight already present. This allowed any targets encountered to be attacked at once, and enabled the incoming pilots to be warned of likely areas of German resistance. During periods of rapid advance and little German ground opposition, the flight leaders often patrolled ahead of the column, sometimes at a distance of up to 30 miles along the axis of advance, searching for any German troops, tanks or gun positions.[6]

Armored Column Cover was put into effect on 26 July 1944, the second day of COBRA, and immediately proved effective in overcoming the *ad hoc* German defensive positions and strongpoints hastily thrown together to halt the US advance. The fighter-bombers cleared the roads ahead of the US tanks, a typical example being the air support provided for Combat Command A of the US 3rd Armored Division on 31 July. A task force commanded by Colonel Doan had succeeded in cutting the Villedieu–Granville road late in the afternoon when a message was received from VII Corps ordering Doan to proceed a further 12 miles to the final objective, hill 242 near Brécy. When his force approached a defended railway embankment Doan requested his column-cover P-47's to strafe the tracks, their last mission for the day as light was fading. As the US tanks crossed the embankment unopposed their crews saw several unmanned German anti-tank guns. The morale effect of air attack coupled with the shock of an immediate armoured follow-up had induced their crews to remain under cover, though they subsequently returned to man their guns against the following US infantry.[7]

The main problem with Armored Column Cover was that implementing it required the commitment of considerable air effort. On 28 July 1944, the third day of its employment, column cover absorbed 22 per cent of the IX TAC's total available air resources, which in turn amounted to 61 per cent of the total of those resources allocated to close air support.[8] Further use of column cover on occasions in North-West Europe saw these totals increase. A post-war USAAF study noted that the air effort that a TAC could make available for column cover rarely exceeded the requirements of three armoured columns, and that this commitment absorbed between 30 per cent and 60 per cent of the available air strength of a TAC, or approximately the equivalent of one fighter group per armoured division.[9] Nevertheless, in Army opinion this air effort was both necessary and worthwhile. A post-war report compiled by the Twelfth Army Group observed that the decision by the Ninth Air Force to give high priority to armoured column cover during mobile operations in North-West Europe was a major factor in enabling the US armour to break through German defences and also gave the armour far more flexibility than would otherwise have been possible.[10]

British armoured forces received similar, if not quite so closely integrated, close air support by fighter-bombers on CABRANK. This was a method of providing continuous close air support during intensive, mostly large-scale, operations and was first employed in Italy during the assault to clear the line of the River Sangro in November 1943. It was devised by the (then) commander of the Desert Air Force, Air Vice-Marshal Broadhurst. Flights of fighter-bombers were detailed to proceed to an area of the battlefront likely to require air support. This area was called the CABRANK and on arrival the aircraft reported to the ROVER controlling that sector. They then patrolled the area awaiting a call from the ROVER giving them a target. When this occurred, the pilots were able to attack after a short target-briefing had been given by the ROVER, and often after the target had been indicated by coloured smoke rounds. It was usually possible for targets to be attacked within 10 minutes of the original request and for repeat-attacks, if required, to be made within 30 minutes by subsequent flights arriving in the battle area. In the event of the ROVER not assigning a target, the fighter-bomber pilots attacked a target for which they had been pre-briefed. [11]

That British armour was capable of successfully exploiting fighter-bomber support when provided on CABRANK can be seen in two operations, Operation GARDEN in North-West Europe and Operation CYGNET in Italy. Operation GARDEN was the offensive launched by British Second Army as part of MARKET GARDEN in Holland on the afternoon of 17 September 1944. For this operation the Guards Armoured Division was to spearhead the XXX Corps advance intended to relieve successively the three Allied airborne divisions that had been landed to seize a series of river crossings leading to the Rhine at Arnhem. This, the objective of 1st British Airborne Division, was some 60 miles from the Allied front lines.

In order to facilitate an armoured breakout along a single axis of advance, lined on each side by streams and marshy ground preventing the deployment of armour and by woods concealing German anti-tank guns and infantry, the Corps commander, General Horrocks, decided to employ an extensive artillery programme supplemented by close air support by rocket-firing Typhoons.[12] One Typhoon squadron was to attack along the road immediately after the barrage ended, while a further ten squadrons were thereafter to maintain CABRANK for the armour. The 2nd Irish Guards (tanks) were to spearhead the attack along the road, while the flanks were to be cleared by infantry of the 2nd Devons.[13]

At 2.15 p.m. the artillery barrage began, a belt of fire one mile wide and five miles deep timed to work its way across the German positions ahead of the Guards' tanks and their supporting infantry. Fire was provided by ten field regiments, three medium regiments, one heavy battery of 8 inch guns and a regiment of heavy anti-aircraft guns employed in the ground role.[14] This fire was impressive, and the troops waiting to advance could see the shells exploding among the German positions along the road ahead.[15]

Then followed the arrival of the Typhoons, flights arriving approximately every five minutes to rocket and strafe each side of the road. At 2.35 p.m. the Irish Guards began the advance, their lead tanks following the barrage closely. For the first ten minutes the advance went smoothly, the tanks gaining over 1,000 yards and the German defences apparently subdued by the combined weight of artillery and airborne firepower.[16] However, shortly afterwards the crews of the leading tanks heard the thump and clanging of anti-tank action behind them.

The Germans had concentrated a battle group under the command of Oberst (Colonel) Walther to block the approaches to Eindhoven. *Kampfgruppe Walther* consisted of some ten weak infantry battalions, supported by self-propelled guns and 88 mm anti-tank guns, but the defence of the road leading to Valkenswaard along which the British tanks were advancing had been entrusted to Major Kerrutt. Kerrutt had immediately to hand a battalion of infantry supported by a battery of howitzers. On 13 September he had been reinforced by a troop of 88 mm guns, and also some triple-barrelled 20 mm anti-aircraft guns. Kerrutt's troops were well dug-in and camouflaged in trenches cut into the verges on both sides of the road and along the fringes of the woods, with their fields of fire crossing in enfilade.[17]

On the afternoon of 17 September they had held their fire until the barrage and the leading British tanks had passed them, and had then proceeded to knock out nine of the following tanks within two minutes. The situation for the Irish Guards was at once radically transformed. A half-mile gap littered with burning tanks lay between the leading tanks and the following squadrons, the latter being unable to deploy off the road due to the marshy ground and dense woodland and unable to advance due to the wrecks blocking the road and the waiting German guns. The armoured thrust had been stopped cold, and artillery fire could not be brought down on the German positions due to the proximity of the British tanks.[18]

This was precisely the situation in which prompt close air support could make the difference between success and failure. The RAF controller in the contact car with the Irish Guards immediately called down the Typhoons waiting above on CABRANK. Within a few minutes, as the Guards' tanks began firing red smoke rounds to indicate the German positions, the Typhoons started to dive. The Irish Guards' War Diary describes how throughout the next hour the Typhoons made very low and accurate attacks, in some cases their rockets striking within 100 yards of the Guards' tanks which were burning their yellow recognition smoke.[19]

The Typhoon attacks quickly and utterly demoralised the German troops. The Irish Guards War Diary recorded that the effect of the rockets was almost instantaneous, and that German troops came running out of their trenches 'trembling with fright' in order to surrender.[20] The 2nd Devons started to comb the woods and verges in the wake of the Typhoon attacks, and found many dazed and frightened German troops still crouching at the bottom of their slit trenches. They also found a self-propelled gun abandoned in such haste that its engine had been left running.[21] The Typhoons were clearly more effective than supporting artillery fire could have been under the circumstances, and their morale effect more marked. By 3.30 p.m., within an hour of the start of the advance, the Irish Guards and 2nd Devons had taken 250 prisoners. This was a remarkable turn of fortune in what had been a very doubtful situation.

However, the advance was not immediately resumed due to the Guards requesting a further medium artillery barrage and, as they were within 200 yards of its intended start line, they pulled back 500 yards. This barrage, of 20 minutes duration, was not put down until 5.39 p.m., the tanks resuming the advance only at about 6 p.m.[22] Typhoons remained in support, but were now streaking above the road well ahead of the Guards engaging any targets they could see, clearing the route ahead in the same manner as with US Armored Column Cover. As they advanced the Irish Guards witnessed the effect of the Typhoon attacks on the morale of the German troops as the prisoners began to come in. One of them, an officer from an anti-tank unit, told his captors that he had commanded ten 7.62 mm Russian guns before the battle and that all had been knocked out with very few of his crews left alive. He was unable to say which had been worse, the rocket fire or the strafing, and was sent back along the road weeping.[23] Four German 88 mm guns of the 602nd Heavy Anti-Aircraft Battalion with their towing vehicles were also captured intact, and the Guards reported that their surviving crews were found in a great state of fear.[24]

This demoralisation was achieved, in some cases, without rockets or cannon being fired, as the Typhoons stayed with the Guards even though they had expended their rockets and cannon ammunition, making dummy attacks on the German positions that proved equally effective in subduing them. This was greatly appreciated by the Guards, who subsequently signalled their gratitude to the squadrons involved.[25]

The German force defending the road to Valkenswaard had been overwhelmed by the combined air and ground assault. In the early afternoon the headquarters of *Kampfgruppe Walther* reported unusually heavy Allied fighter-bomber activity in Major Kerrutt's sector. All vehicle movement as far as Eindhoven came to a halt as a result of their presence, and Oberst Walther's own combat headquarters near Valkenswaard was attacked several times from the air. Further reports came of a very heavy British artillery barrage falling on the defence positions along the road, and soon afterwards telephone communication with Kerrutt was lost. At 2.30 p.m. a staff officer sent forward from Walther's headquarters reported that British tanks had broken through on both sides of the road and had overrun one of Kerrutt's infantry companies. They were being engaged by Kerrutt's supporting anti-tank guns, with the German guns coming under heavy fire.

By 5 p.m. it was known at Walther's headquarters that a further company of Kerrutt's infantry had been overrun and that his 88 mm guns, lacking the mobility to change positions under fire, had been lost and their commanders killed. British artillery fire was now falling close to Valkanswaard and Major Kerrutt, with the remains of two infantry companies and a few of his howitzers and 20 mm guns that had been extricated, was attempting to organise new positions. At about 7 p.m. Walther's headquarters reported to their parent formation, First Parachute Army, that the remaining forces near Valkenswaard were too weak to sustain any defence.[26]

By 7.30 p.m. the Irish Guards reached Valkenswaard, where they were to halt for the night, although Eindhoven had been the day's intended objective. They had lost nine tanks destroyed at the outset of the attack, with eight men killed and several wounded. The 2nd Devons had lost twelve men killed and twenty-two wounded.[27]

Typhoons had ceased to operate on the XXX Corps front at 7.26 p.m., as dusk was falling; No.83 Group had flown 233 close-support sorties.[28]

On 17 September the air-tank combination showed what it could achieve, and can be contrasted with subsequent days when air support was unavailable. On 21 September at 11 a.m. the Irish Guards were ordered to advance north along the main road from Nijmegen to Arnhem. Once again they were confronted by a road defended by German infantry dug-in with anti-tank guns. According to the subsequent British narrative, the advance started at 1.30 p.m. and ended at 1.50 p.m., when the three leading tanks were knocked out as they came into view of German positions.[29] Only one regiment of field guns was available to support this attack, and its fire was ineffective. Inexplicably, no artillery FOO able to direct fire appears to have been with the Irish Guards.[30] Moreover, while Typhoons were above on CABRANK, they could not be called down because at first the VCP control-set broke down, and then later in the afternoon the fly-in of Polish airborne reinforcements to the Arnhem area automatically banned the use of close-support aircraft.[31] Infantry of 3rd Irish Guards, who had been riding on the tanks, tried to advance but were repulsed, as was an attempted right-flanking movement. Finally, at 6.30 p.m. the Irish Guards drew back 1,000 yards to harbour for the night.[32]

GARDEN was an operation largely compromised by the fact that XXX Corps had to advance for a considerable distance (some 46 miles) along a single axis. When air support was not available due to the complication of airborne drops, poor weather, or simply bad luck as on 21 September, then little, if any, progress was made.[33]

An operation in Italy in early 1945 was more successful due to its limited objective. By early January 1945 the British V Corps of Eighth Army had closed up to the line of the River Senio except where a pocket of German resistance remained around Alfonsine, 10 miles NW of Ravenna. This pocket, roughly box-shaped with sides about 4,000 yards long, was held by some four battalions of infantry of the German 278th Infantry Division supported by about six tanks and self-propelled guns. From north to south, the pocket was contained by the 1st Canadian, 56th British, and 2nd New Zealand Divisions.[34]

Despite the importance of eliminating the pocket, V Corps could not mount an assault due to a severe shortage of artillery ammunition in Eighth Army. For this reason a planned full-scale attack involving the Canadians and New Zealanders had been cancelled. Moreover, due to a shortage of replacements, V Corps ordered that 56th Division, which consisted of only two infantry brigades, should not itself attempt a major effort. After 56th Division had mounted a series of 'nibbling' attacks, which the Germans stubbornly and successfully resisted, its commander, Major-General Whitfield, was directed to prepare a plan for eliminating the pocket using the only reinforcements that could be spared. This was an armoured brigade and, for their first employment in Italy, sufficient kangaroos (armoured personnel carriers) to carry a battalion of infantry.[35]

The result was Operation CYGNET, an armoured sweep through the pocket by 7th Armoured Brigade with two armoured regiments, 10th Royal Hussars on the right and 2nd Royal Tank Regiment on the left, with a battalion of infantry, 2/6th Queens Royal Regiment, following the tanks in kangaroos and prepared to debus rapidly to mop up points of resistance. Success depended upon two factors. The first was surprise. A series of heavy frosts permitted the cross-country employment of tanks, but the Germans, who had mined the main routes, did not expect such a weight of armour to be deployed against them and remained unaware of 7th Armoured Brigade's concentration. The second factor was a heavy scale of close air support. To compensate for the lack of artillery the Desert Air Force provided extensive fighter-bomber cover, commencing with a heavy strike on the German positions at the outset of the armoured advance and following this with CABRANKS of Spitfires continuously on call, through the ROVER tentacle at 7th Armoured Brigade Headquarters, to bomb and strafe just ahead of the leading tanks.[36]

CYGNET started at first light on 4 January and proved highly successful, a subsequent Royal Armoured Corps study noting that the German defenders were paralysed by surprise as the armoured force swept through them from an unexpected direction.[37] The German defence was certainly thrown off balance by the combined air and armoured assault, and those German troops who attempted resistance were soon overcome either by the tanks or the waiting fighter-bombers. The extent to which the air support was relied upon during the attack, and how close to the British armour the fighter-bombers engaged targets, is indicated by the *History of the 2nd Royal Tank Regiment*, which recorded that air support was called down upon almost every house as it was reached, with the fighter-bombers attacking between 100 and 200 yards ahead of the leading tanks.[38]

In an operation lasting some 10 hours the Desert Air Force had flown 116 fighter-bomber sorties in support of the British armour, which had secured 12,000 square yards of territory and taken over 300 prisoners. Casualties to the attackers were extremely light; 3 tanks bogged down and 6 men slightly wounded in 10th Hussars, 5 tanks (3 later recovered) and 10 men wounded (one of whom later died) in 2nd RTR, and 7 infantrymen of 2/6th Queens wounded.[39] The most important factor in preventing any organised German resistance, and thereby maintaining the momentum of the advance, had undoubtedly been the airstrikes made in immediate response on potential or actual opposition. The subsequent Royal Armoured Corps study of CYGNET observed that whenever air support had been provided, it had caused a temporary disorganisation of the German troops occupying the houses, and therefore had enabled the British tanks to close in without casualties.[40]

Armored Column Cover and both GARDEN and CYGNET indicate that in mobile operations close air support was more appropriate and effective than artillery, because fighter-bombers were able to deliver fire support with greater accuracy in close proximity to friendly troops under fluid battle conditions. They could also keep pace with a rapid advance whereas artillery often could not, not least because of transport and maintenance difficulties. In North-West Europe, during the pursuit after the crossing of the River Seine, British Second Army covered 250 miles in six days but to make sufficient transport available an entire Corps (the VIII) and most of the army artillery had to be left behind around the Seine for some weeks.[41]

An obvious question is whether self-propelled (SP) artillery offered an alternative solution to the problem of fire support for mobile operations. US armoured divisions were equipped with three battalions of SP guns, each with eighteen M.7 105 mm howitzers on Sherman chassis. Their British counterparts had only one regiment of twenty-four Sextons, self-propelled 25-pounders on the chassis of the Canadian Ram tank, the other regiment being of conventional towed guns.[42]

SP guns offered important advantages over towed pieces. One was that they combined mobility and firepower with protection for the gunners, enabling the guns to provide close-in support from hull-down positions without the delay caused by unlimbering and digging gunpits. They could deploy quickly, and change position rapidly in action if necessary, while on the move they took up less road space. However, on occasions when speed was essential they still took time to deploy and register targets, and there was always the factor of the limited supply of ammunition carried on board and the frequent need to replenish. In North-West Europe, as the numbers of available US tanks increased, US armoured divisions relied increasingly on the armament of their tanks, with artillery required only in set piece operations. Hence their reliance on Armored Column Cover when tanks could not generate sufficient firepower.[43]

In British experience, the principal drawback with SP guns was the level of maintenance required to keep them roadworthy. Tracked vehicles were susceptible to mechanical breakdown, and the guns were usually either in action or on the move a high proportion of the time. Moreover, breakdown meant shortage of a gun, whereas with towed pieces another tractor was simply hooked on to the gun. Another problem was that SP guns had a high profile and were difficult to conceal.[44]

To sum up, SP artillery did not obviate the need for close air support during mobile operations. Had SP 25-pounders been present with the forward tanks of Guards Armoured on 17 September they would not have been able to extricate them as had the Typhoons, not least because of the limited traverse of their guns, and, like the tanks, they would have been unable to deploy off the road. They would also have been as vulnerable, indeed more so, to the German anti-tank fire. During CYGNET they might have provided close-in support for the tanks as strongpoints were encountered, but in fact they would still have been subject to the severe shortage of 25-pounder ammunition that had dictated the nature of the operation. There were also different morale and proximity characteristics between artillery and close air support, and these are considered in Chapter VII below.

AIRBORNE OPERATIONS

The defining characteristic of airborne operations was that their execution was dependent upon air capabilities; delivery to the drop/landing zone, sustaining of the landed airborne forces with supplies and reinforcements, and the augmenting of firepower by air support all depended upon the air forces. Experience in North-West Europe indicated that with regard to the latter task Allied airborne forces were poorly served. However, this must be qualified by some general observations with regard to airborne operations.

First, it was impossible to provide close air support for airborne troops when they most needed it – when they were at their most vulnerable while dropping out of the sky. Air attacks upon enemy defensive positions could immediately precede a drop, but the risk to the airborne troops was too great to permit airstrikes either during the drop or immediately afterwards, when the scattered airborne troops were organising. Thus if the defending troops had been unaffected by the preliminary air bombardment, or had recovered from its effects, those paratroops unfortunate enough to land among them stood little chance of survival. This was a lesson learnt by all combatants who employed airborne forces.[45]

Second, even after paratroops and/or glider-borne troops had landed, had organised as far as possible, and were attempting to take their assigned objective, it was still by no means straightforward to provide close air support. This was because pilots could not be expected easily to distinguish friend from foe on the ground in a battle taking place beyond the established front lines, and were thus reliant upon the airborne troops indicating their own and the enemy's positions by pre-arranged signals or radio communication. However, this was a process fraught with danger. During the German airborne invasion of Crete in May 1941 British and Commonwealth troops soon learnt that engaging the German paratroops closely meant that German aircraft, ever overhead in daylight, could not intervene in the fighting for fear of hitting their own men. It was even sometimes possible to imitate the paratroops' Very light signals to their supporting aircraft, and on at least one occasion in Crete the Luftwaffe was induced to attack German troops.[46]

Third, whereas the German airborne troops had relied on a series of light signals for contacting aircraft, Allied airborne forces by 1944–45 relied on radio equipment manned by air-contact teams landed with the airborne troops. Here too was a risk, for airborne forces had to anticipate casualties as a result of jumping accidents or glider mishaps before coming into contact with the enemy, while losses to strength due to scattered drops – often miles away from the intended landing zone as had occurred in Sicily – were another hazard. A misplaced air-contact team, or radio equipment lost or damaged in the drop, could mean no communication with aircraft and no air support.

The first major Allied use of airborne forces in North West Europe during the Normandy campaign indicated that little consideration had been given to the provision of close air support. A frank post-war US study observed of the airborne landings in Normandy that it had been fortunate that the airborne troops had been able to link-up with the beachhead forces on 8 June, since both fighter-bomber support and aerial reconnaissance had been insufficient to assist the lightly-armed and isolated airborne units.[47]

Most missions flown in support of the airborne forces were in the nature of pre-planned strikes against bridges and lines of communication leading to the airborne landing areas, in effect battlefield air interdiction. This no doubt reduced the potential number of German troops and their supporting armour to be confronted, but had small effect upon those German forces already in position in the landing area. There was little close support, not because the aircraft were lacking, but because the command and control machinery was not in place. As the same US study pointed out, there had been very few request missions on critical close-support targets and those that were carried out had been 'stolen' from other tasks by circumventing the unwieldly procedure and channel set up, and by 'talking the pilot' into the target. An important factor had been casualties to TALOs and equipment during the airborne drop, which reduced ability to call for and control air support, but the study nevertheless considered that losses to the airborne units through lack of close air support were out of proportion considering the number of fighter-bombers over the invasion area.[48]

That little had been done to solve the problem of command and control of close air support for airborne forces became apparent during Operation MARKET in September 1944. It seems remarkable that the airborne forces remained unfamiliar with the air-support system by then in regular use by Allied troops on the Continent. The most likely explanation for this is, as Shelford Bidwell and Dominick Graham suggest, that the airborne divisions remained isolated from the mainstream of military experience.[49] In any event, as late as September 1944 First Allied Airborne Army had no Air Support Signals Unit (ASSU) or training in air/ground cooperation, and although a staff officer from 1st British Airborne Division had been sent to Normandy to learn at first hand how air support was arranged, nothing had resulted.[50]

At the outset of the operation, each airborne division was allocated two US air-support parties, while one was allocated to First Airborne Corps Headquarters. This was much in the nature of an afterthought. These parties had no experience of working with the troops they were to accompany, and the operators were even unfamiliar with their radio sets. Those that accompanied 1st Airborne Division to Arnhem proved a failure; neither ever succeeded in contacting aircraft by radio and both were put out of action by German mortar fire.[51] This alone would have been enough to rule out effective close support for, as a US study later observed, without the ability to control aircraft from the ground and direct them to targets, the bomb line became a restriction denying the close support which the airborne units needed.[52]

Apart from the inability of the airborne troops to communicate with aircraft, there was another major factor in the lack of close air support. This was the fact that the experienced Allied tactical air forces already established on the Continent, in particular No.83 Group of RAF 2nd TAF and the IX TAC of US Ninth Air Force, were prevented from intervening at crucial periods during the operation not only by the weather but because of a ruling that prohibited them from operating in the battle area when troops or supplies were being landed or dropped, the aim being to prevent close-support aircraft of the tactical air forces becoming mixed up with the fighter escort from England with unfortunate result.[53]

Responsibility for the preliminary bombardment of German flak batteries en route to and in the landing areas, and for the escort of the transport and supply aircraft, was assigned to the US Eighth (Strategic) Air Force, whose UK-based fighter groups had no experience of ground-support operations. In effect, tactical air force operations were controlled from England, and when adverse weather prevented the take-off of transports there, or during the frequent changes in planned programmes for airdrops and landings, the close-support aircraft remained grounded too. The result was that close air support for the Airborne Corps during the operation from 17 to 25 September was scant and irregular, being provided on only five days. On the 18 September, close-support sorties flown for the US 82nd Airborne Division around Nijmegen totalled 97, while on 22 September some 119 sorties were flown in close support of the US 101st Airborne Division fighting near Eindhoven. British airborne troops at Arnhem saw supporting Typhoons for the first time on 23 September, when a few sorties were provided by No.83 Group, but they received their first significant close support only on the following day, a week after the start of the operation, when 22 sorties were provided. A further 81 Typhoon sorties were provided on 25 September.[54]

No.83 Group was well aware of the plight of 1st Airborne at Arnhem, fighting for its life against the troops and tanks of 9th and 10th SS Panzer Divisions, through the 'Y' army radio-intercept service, but its repeated pleas to be able to release the Typhoons standing armed and ready on its forward airfields were disregarded.[55] However, given that the German infantry and their supporting tanks were closely engaging the British airborne troops in the town, it is unlikely that the Typhoons could have identified their targets adequately enough for them to intervene directly in the fighting – particularly in view of the lamentable state of 1st Airborne's communications.[56] Nevertheless, they could initially have assisted the paratroops to seize their objectives, and afterwards struck at the German tank and troop concentrations in and around the town, harassing movement. This had been expected by the commander of 1st Airborne Division, Major-General Urquhart, who later wrote that he had been surprised by the lack of close support and that fighter-bomber attacks upon German armour would have greatly assisted his men.[57]

As it was, the Germans destroyed 1st Airborne Division largely unmolested from the air. Appearing over Arnhem in any strength only on 24 September, the Typhoons were too late to affect the ultimate outcome of the battle. Moreover, in the absence of direct ground-air communications, support requests had to be channelled from First Airborne Division through 64th Medium Regiment Royal Artillery (attached to XXX Corps), whose guns were then in range), to Airborne Corps, thence to Second Army, then to Headquarters 2nd TAF and finally to No.83 Group. Even under these circumstances their morale effect was remarkable. A witness later recalled that when they were overhead German mortarmen and gunners were reluctant to man their weapons, and that their presence greatly boosted the morale of the airborne troops.[58]

On 24 March 1945 the Allied assault across the River Rhine was spearheaded by the landing of the British 6th and US 17th Airborne Divisions. On this occasion, the last large-scale use of airborne forces in North-West Europe, the lessons of previous operations appear to have been learned.

Control of air support was easier than during MARKET due to the fact that the airborne landing zones occupied a narrow belt on the far bank of the Rhine. Three Forward VCPs were landed by glider with 6th Airborne Division, one being in operation directing air support from 2nd TAF within two hours of landing.[59] Although this was a vast improvement on Arnhem, communications still left something to be desired and air support did not function without some difficulty, as seen in an example from 25 March. The 6th Airborne Division tentacle requested aircraft on CABRANK to attack some German tanks positioned in an orchard. Two air attacks were unsuccessful because the ground controller was unable to describe exactly the position of the target. As the German tanks were only 250 yards from its positions, the FCP staff eventually decided to deal with 6th Air Landing Brigade direct, but the latter had no ground to air communications. In the event the FCP Controller used a reconnaissance photograph of the area as a guide to his briefing of the aircraft, and he was kept informed of the result of the attacks by means of a running commentary from the forward tentacle. After seven attacks directed in this cumbrous manner the German tanks eventually dispersed.[60]

The US airborne units had also been better equipped with ground-air communications for the Rhine operation, an air-support party with 17th Airborne Division being operational on the afternoon of 24 March, while on the next day several close-support strikes were directed, one within 10 minutes of the original request.[61]

Experience in 1944–45 suggested that close air support was a prerequisite for successful armoured thrusts, particularly when the axis of advance was narrow and when any significant opposition was likely. The main value of fighter-bomber attack appears to have been in its morale effect, the neutralization of German defences, albeit temporary, rather than actual destruction or casualties caused. By being able to engage targets closely, sometimes to within 100 yards of friendly tanks, fighter-bombers could offer greater opportunity to exploit this neutralization than was permitted by artillery fire. Moreover, they offered the only means of providing continuous support throughout an advance.

Similarly, close air support offered the only means of augmenting the firepower of airborne troops operating beyond the range of friendly artillery. Yet the importance of air support for such troops does not seem to have been sufficiently realised by Allied air and ground commanders in 1943–45. While there were command and control problems with providing close air support for troops operating far beyond the battlefront, these could be solved, mainly by the provision of adequate ground-air communications, as the Rhine crossing proved. Without such support, or a very rapid link-up with friendly ground formations, airborne troops were likely to be destroyed – perhaps the most obvious lesson from the Arnhem debacle.

NOTES

1. At Arnhem British 1st Airborne Division had only its Light Regiment of air-portable 75 mm howitzers, firing a comparatively light shell. Major-General R.E. Urquhart, *Arnhem* (London: Pan, 1960), p. 21.

   Ammunition supply for airborne artillery was also a problem. In Normandy, supplies for British 6th Airborne Division were outstripped by expenditure; the US 82nd and 101st Airborne Divisions found the same, necessitating a reliance on fire support from non-airborne formations whose guns were in range and long range naval gunfire. J.B.A. Bailey, *Field Artillery and Firepower* (Oxford: The Military Press, 1989), p. 78n.

Recoilless artillery, allowing for a very light gun carriage, offered a solution to the problem of fire support for airborne forces, but such weapons were not developed in quantity by any of the belligerents in the Second World War. In Crete in May 1941 German paratroops were supported by several experimental 7.5 cm recoilless guns, which were never introduced in numbers despite their usefulness. The only use of such weapons by Allied airborne troops in Europe occurred during the last days of the war when several M.20 75 mm recoilless rifles were employed by the US 17th Airborne Division near Essen. Ian V. Hogg, *British and American Artillery of World War 2* (London: Arms & Armour, 1978), pp. 242–3.

2. RAF Intelligence Report, *Co-operation Between the German Air Force and the Army* (March 1942), PRO AIR 40/2054.
3. Karl Hecks, *Bombing 1939–45* (London: Robert Hale, 1990), p. 114.
4. RAF Intelligence Report, *Co-operation Between the German Air Force and the Army*.
5. The nature of the campaigns in Italy and North West Europe is discussed by John Ellis in *Brute Force: Allied Strategy and Tactics in the Second World War* (London: André Deutsch, 1990), Ch. 6, 7 and 8.
6. General Omar N. Bradley and the US 12th Army Group Air Effects Committee, *Effect of Air Power on Military Operations, Western Europe*, Wiesbaden, Germany: US 12th Army Group Air Branches of G-3 and G-2, 15 July 1945, pp. 41–2, PRO AIR 40/1131.
7. US 3rd Armored Division Combat Command A, After Action Report, July 1944, quoted in Martin Blumenson, *Breakout and Pursuit* (Washington, DC: Department of the Army, 1961), p. 309.
8. First United States Army and IX Tactical Air Command Operations Summary, 28 July 1944, quoted in ibid, p. 333.
9. The USAAF Evaluation Board in the ETO, *The Effectiveness of Third Phase Tactical Air Operations in the European Theater, 5 May 1944–8 May 1945* (1946), p. 343, PRO AIR 40/1111.
10. Bradley and the US 12th Army Group Air Effects Committee, p. 42.
11. RAF Desert Air Force Report (1944), *Fighter Bombing*, in *Employment of Fighter-Bombers – Policy*, PRO AIR 23/1826; Section IX, *The Rover Tentacle*, in RAF Intelligence Report (1944), *Italy – Fighter and Bomber Tactics, Sept. 1943 – Feb. 1944*, PRO AIR 40/304; *Memorandum on the Organisation of FACPs Operating with the Eighth Army* (16 Jan. 1945), in PRO WO 204/7932. See also Air Historical Branch Air Publication 3235, *Air Support*, Air Ministry 1955, pp. 115–16.
12. War Office Narrative, *Liberation Campaign North-West Europe*, Book III, Chapter V, *Phase 5 The Advance from the Seine to the Siegfried Line and the Battle for Arnhem 29 Aug.–30 Sept. 1944*, p. 27, PRO CAB 44/254; Guards Armoured Division War Diary, Appendix C, Notes on road from Dutch frontier to Arnhem, Sept. 1944, PRO WO 171/376.
13. War Office Narrative, *Liberation Campaign NW Europe*, p. 43.
14. Ibid., p. 40.
15. Captain The Earl of Rosse, MBE, and Colonel E.R. Hill, *The Story of the Guards Armoured Division* (London: 1956), p. 127.
16. War Diary, 2nd (Armoured) Irish Guards, 17 Sept. 1944, PRO WO 171/1256.
17. *Battle Group Walther*, German account of the defence of the Valkenswaard area, compiled post-war, copy held at the Imperial War Museum, London; Anthony Farrar-Hockley, *Airborne Carpet* (London: Macdonald, 1970), p. 104; Robert J. Kershaw, *It never snows in September* (Marlborough: Crowood Press, 1990), pp. 45–6.
18. Rosse and Hill, p. 128.
19. War Diary, 2nd (Armoured) Irish Guards.
20. Ibid.
21. War Diary, 2nd Battalion the Devonshire Regiment, 17 Sept. 1944, PRO WO/171/1278.
22. War Office Narrative, *Liberation Campaign NW Europe*.
23. War Diary, 2nd (Armoured) Irish Guards.
24. Ibid.
25. H. Ambrose (Former Flight Lieutenant, No.175 Squadron RAF), quoted in Norman Franks, *Typhoon Attack* (London: William Kimber: 1984), p. 156.
26. German account, *Battle Group Walther*.
27. War Diary, 2nd (Armoured) Irish Guards; War Diary, 2nd Devons.
28. No.83 Group Daily Intelligence Summary, 17 Sept. 1944, PRO AIR 25/705.
29. War Office Narrative.

30. Ibid.
31. Ibid.
32. Ibid.
33. The question of whether the British armour displayed a lack of necessary drive and deter-mination to reach Arnhem is discussed by Geoffrey Powell in *The Devil's Birthday: The Bridges to Arnhem 1944* (London: Papermac, 1985), pp. 162–3 and pp. 239–40.
    The armour was clearly unwilling to advance without assured artillery and/or air support and it was accepted doctrine in British and Commonwealth armies by 1944 that such support was essential for an armoured advance. Commanders willing to risk advancing with-out it were censured. During a tactical exercise in Italy run by the 5th Canadian Armoured Division, which postulated that its 5th Brigade had seized an objective and was contemplat-ing further advance in the face of a disorganized enemy, the Brigade Commander (Brigadier Bradbrook) queried the need to wait for supporting artillery to move up when he already had over 150 guns – on his tanks. He was subsequently fired by his divisional Commander, Lieutenant-General G.G. Simonds, who was to command 2nd Canadian Corps in North-West Europe. See John A. English, *The Canadian Army and the Normandy Campaign: A Study of Failure in High Command* (New York: Praeger, 1991), pp. 271–2.
34. Royal Armoured Corps Pamphlet: *Armoured Operations in Italy, May 1944 – January 1945*, p. 77.
35. Ibid.
36. Ibid.; Air Historical Branch Narrative, *The Italian Campaign 1943–45*, Volume II, *Operations June 1944–May 1945*, PRO AIR 41/58.
37. Royal Armoured Corps Pamphlet, p. 78.
38. *Seconds Out, A History of The 2nd Royal Tank Regiment*, by Sergeant Chadwick (undated), Volume II, p. 283.
39. *The 10th Royal Hussars in the Second World War 1939–45*, the Regimental Committee (Aldershot: Gale & Polden, 1948), p. 158; Major R.C.G. Foster, *History of the Queen's Royal Regiment*, Volume VIII, 1924–48 (Aldershot: Gale & Polden, 1953), p. 456; 2nd Royal Tank Regiment Report (1945), *Account of Operation 'CYGNET'*, PRO WO 204/7989.
40. Royal Armoured Corps Pamphlet, p. 81.
41. A.L. Pemberton, *The Development of Artillery Tactics and Equipment* (London: The War Office, 1951), p. 234.
42. B.T. White, *Tanks and other Armoured Fighting Vehicles 1942–45* (Poole: The Blandford Press, 1975), pp. 104 and 119.
43. Bailey, *Field Artillery and Firepower*, pp. 195, 206.
44. British 21st Army Group Report (undated, but likely 1945), *Self-Propelled Artillery in 21st Army Group: Analysis of Opinions and Criticisms*, PRO WO 291/1336.
45. One example is the virtual destruction of the German III Parachute Battalion which landed on and near the positions of the 23rd New Zealand Infantry Battalion near Maleme during the invasion of Crete on 20 May 1941. Some 400 of this force of 600 paratroops are thought to have been killed either while descending or immediately on landing. Another example is the heavy casualties suffered by the US 3rd/505th Parachute Infantry landing in the face of an alerted German defence at Ste. Mère Église in Normandy early on 6 June 1944. I. McD. G. Stewart, *The Struggle For Crete* (Oxford: 1966), pp. 164–5, and John Keegan, *Six Armies In Normandy* (London: 1982), pp. 93–4.
46. Commonwealth troops also captured and used German ground indicator panels during the fighting in Crete.
    A first-hand account of a spirited, aggressive and highly successful defence against paratroop attack by the Australian officer who directed it is *Report by Lt.-Col. I.R. Campbell, DSO, AIF on the Defence of Retimo Aerodrome, Crete, 20–30 May 1941* (1945), PRO CAB 106/382. This was written by Lt.-Col. Campbell on his release from German captivity in 1945. His account provides an example illustrating the difficulty faced by ground-attack pilots in identifying battlefield targets. During the fighting in Greece and Crete German pilots identified British troops by their dish-shaped steel helmets. In Crete, a party of British troops were taken prisoner at Canea, and immediately their German paratroop captors made them throw away their helmets into a nearby wadi. According to Campbell, 'from then on this collection of helmets received a great number of bombs and machine gun bullets from German airmen'.
47. General Bradley and the US 12th Army Group Air Effects Committee, pp.143–4.
48. Ibid., p. 144.

49. Shelford Bidwell and Dominick Graham, *Fire-Power: British Army Weapons and Theories of War 1904–45* (London: Allen & Unwin, 1985), p. 273.

50. Ibid.

51. Powell, *The Devil's Birthday: The Bridges to Arnhem, 1944*, pp. 171–2.

52. General Bradley and the US 12th Army Group Air Effects Committee, p. 144.

53. Allied tactical aircraft were frequently attacked in error by friendly aircraft, US and British pilots often failing to recognise each other's aircraft types. In his study of the Normandy campaign Max Hastings observes that British pilots were nervous of their American counterparts, who tended to attack any aircraft in the sky that they could not at once identify, and that RAF Typhoons were quite regularly attacked by US Mustangs and Thunderbolts. See *Overlord* (London: Michael Joseph, 1984), p. 274. In fact it was all too easy for such incidents to occur; in an interview conducted by the USAF for Project Warrior, General John W. Vogt, Jr., who commanded a squadron of Eighth Air Force P-47 Thunderbolts in 1944, recalled an occasion when his squadron very nearly engaged British Tempest II aircraft near Paris, believing them at first to be German Bf.109 fighters. The US pilots had not been briefed about the existence of the Tempest II and had not expected to encounter British aircraft in the area. See Richard H. Kohn and Joseph P. Harahan (Eds), *Air Interdiction in World War II, Korea and Vietnam*, USAF Warrior Studies (Washington, DC: Office of Air Force History, 1986), pp. 29–30.

	Awareness of this problem no doubt influenced the planning for MARKET-GARDEN. That pilots of the Allied tactical air forces, which often co-operated, frequently made such errors suggests the havoc likely to have ensued if UK-based fighter squadrons, tasked with the protection of the airborne forces from German fighters, but unfamiliar with operating in the tactical area, had encountered unfamiliar continental-based tactical air force squadrons.

54. Powell, *The Devil's Birthday: The Bridges to Arnhem, 1944*, p. 209.

55. Bidwell and Graham, *Fire-Power: British Army Weapons and Theories of War 1904–45*, pp. 274–5; RAF 2nd TAF Operations File and Reports, PRO AIR 37/615.

56. One of the first German units to confront the British airborne troops after they had landed near Arnhem was 16th SS Panzer Grenadier Depot and Reserve Battalion, commanded by *Sturmbannführer* (Major) Sepp Krafft. In his subsequent report, Krafft stated: 'We knew from experience, that the only way to draw the teeth of an airborne landing with an inferior force, is to drive right into it.' Krafft's account shows that at no time was the deployment and movement of his troops influenced by any threat of air attack. War Diary, SS Panzer Grenadier Depot and Reserve Battalion 16, *The Battle at Arnhem 17 Sep 44 – 7 Oct 44* (Sturbannführer Sepp Krafft), translated copy, PRO AIR 20/2333.

57. Urquhart, *Arnhem*, pp. 205–6.

58. Powell, p. 209.

59. Headquarters British 21st Army Group Report (May 1945), *Air Support for Operations Plunder, Flashpoint, and Varsity*, Part III, *The Forward Control of Aircraft During PLUNDER/VARSITY*, PRO AIR 40/313.

60. Ibid.

61. Ibid.

5

Allied Fighter-Bombers Versus German Armoured Forces: Myths and Realities

MYTHS AND REALITIES

A widely accepted historical view of the campaign in North-West Europe in 1944–45 is that Allied fighter-bombers inflicted heavy losses upon German armour. A former RAF Typhoon pilot has recorded that by August 1944 his squadron alone was credited with the destruction of 112 tanks and the damaging of a further 215; not surprisingly he suggests that the Typhoon was 'decisive in beating the panzers'.[1]

Yet an unquestioning acceptance of such levels of destruction by historians can distort perceptions of the effectiveness of fighter-bomber attack upon armour. This is because, in terms of numbers of tanks actually destroyed, the Allied fighter-bombers were far from being effective tank-killers. The most significant, large-scale, anti-armour operations conducted during the campaign by the Allied tactical air forces were each the subject of investigations carried out shortly afterwards by Allied Operational Research Sections. Their battlefield examinations suggest that, while great destruction was inflicted upon German 'soft-skin' motor transport (MT) by air attack, the traditional image of fighter-bombers inflicting heavy losses upon German armoured columns, even under ideal attack conditions when the columns were caught vulnerable to air attack along the roads and unable to deploy, is open to question.

There was a wide discrepancy between the level of destruction of armour claimed by fighter-bomber pilots and the level of destruction that could be attributed to air action discovered on the ground. Often, high claims of tank 'kills' were made which could not be upheld, and the evidence suggests that even a heavy scale of fighter-bomber attack upon armour in the period 1944–45 was likely to result in only a low level of destruction.

This is not to suggest that such attacks were ineffective, but that their effectiveness should not be measured in terms of the amount of destruction alone. The contemporary operational research suggests it was not necessary for the fighter-bombers to achieve a large number of tank 'kills', but the level of firepower that they were able to concentrate upon their targets and the consequent disruption and demoralization their particular form of attack could cause were often sufficient to obtain decisive results.

The Allied fighter-bombers of 1944–45 were not equipped with specially designed anti-armour munitions. However, possession of the 3 inch rocket ensured that the Typhoons of 2nd TAF gained the reputation of being the principal Allied 'tank-buster'. A major draw-back with the rocket was its inaccuracy (see Chapter 3), but it did not lack hitting power. Its ability to destroy or seriously damage even the heavier type of German tank was proven in a trial conducted by the RAF in 1944.

A Panther tank, captured intact in Normandy, was set up as a stationary target for two separate attacks each by four rocket-firing Typhoons. A total of 64 rockets were fired, the aircraft making steep dive attacks and releasing their rockets between 3,000 and 2,500 feet. On the first shoot of 32 rockets only one hit was obtained but this pen-etrated the tank's engine cover and exploded inside, igniting the remains of oil and petrol. On the second shoot two hits were obtained, one rocket stricking the side of the turret and exploding, while the other struck the tank's gun barrel. These hits showed that the rocket could penetrate all but the frontal armour of the Panther hull or turret, the thickness of which was 80–100 mm, but it was thought a hit on either of these points would render the tank inoperative by causing casualties to the crew, while a hit on the tracks would immobilise the tank. The rocket had no near-miss value, with blast and splinters of nearby ground strikes causing no damage.[2]

The trial, with only three hits scored on a stationary and easily identifiable target, emphasised how difficult it must have been for Typhoon pilots to hit individual tanks on the battlefield which were camouflaged, often protected by flak, and whose crews would have been seeking to get their tank under cover as soon as the aircraft appeared. Concentrations of tanks offered better targets, and against these the Typhoon pilots usually made vertical dives, releasing their rockets in salvo to saturate the area; their 20 mm cannon ammunition was generally reserved for MT targets. When armoured columns were caught moving along a road, attempts were made to block the road and seal off any escape route by attacking the front and rear of the column, thereby trapping those vehicles in between.[3]

Given its inaccuracy, the 3 inch rocket appears to have been a totally inadequate weapon for engaging tanks. Admittedly this was not the rocket's only or even primary role, but that it was the best the RAF had for the job in 1944–45 is nevertheless surprising, for despite its doctrinal opposition to aircraft intervening on the battlefield the RAF had earlier in the war acknowledged the need for air action against German armour and had employed a much more potent specific anti-tank weapons system.

In June 1942 Hurricane IID aircraft arrived in North Africa, nine of them becoming operational with No.6 Squadron. These Hurricanes were each fitted with two 40 mm Vickers 'S' cannon guns in underwing fairings. That they were very effective against German armour was confirmed by German tank crewmen taken prisoner during the Gazala battles later in 1942. One told his British captors that the tank-busters 'caused panic whenever they appeared', while another told of an occasion when twelve tanks had been attacked by them and six knocked out by cannon hits on their engines, ammunition stowage areas, or fuel tanks.[4] Field Marshal Rommel certainly took them seriously. When illness compelled his return to Germany after the battle of Alam Halfa in September 1942 he took with him a sample of the armour-piercing shells that the Hurricane IID's had been firing at his tanks, though his concern was ignored by the German High Command, including Reichsmarshall Goering.[5]

Despite their undoubted effectiveness, due largely to the accuracy of the cannon and the penetration capability of the 40 mm rounds, the Hurricane IID's found little favour with the RAF. Only two units, No.6 and No.7 (South African Air Force) Squadrons were equipped with them but operations proved prohibitively expensive. The Hurricanes had to attack at low level, yet the weight of the cannon packs reduced speed and armour plate was sacrificed to compensate for this. The result was an aircraft perilously vulnerable to groundfire, and losses were high. After the second battle of Alamein in October 1942 losses were such that both squadrons were withdrawn but No.6 Squadron, with the remaining aircraft, reappeared in Tunisia in early 1943. Yet between 21 and 25 March 1943 the squadron lost 16 aircraft to groundfire, six of them on one mission on 25 March. Fortunately, due to the less hazardous nature of a forced landing in desert conditions, pilot losses were not high, but in April the Squadron was withdrawn. It was the end of the Hurricane IID's operational service against German tanks.[6]

Thereafter British attention turned to the development of rockets, and no further tactical aircraft with a heavy cannon armament suitable for the anti-tank role appeared in the RAF. This was a cause of some regret in Army circles, but there could have been no question of employing such a vulnerable aircraft as the IID or any similar type in the flak-intensive environment expected, and encountered, in North-West Europe.

While the 3 inch rocket gave the RAF something specific to use against enemy tanks, in 1944/45 the Americans had to rely mainly upon the general purpose high explosive bombs and heavy machine guns of their fighter-bombers for attacking armour. Thunderbolt pilots generally employed a 45° attacking dive against such targets, but dive-bombing or low-level bombing of individual tanks or even groups of armoured vehicles demanded a higher level of accuracy than could normally be expected with free-fall bombs. Strafing armoured vehicles with his six wing-mounted .50 inch calibre machine guns offered the Thunderbolt pilot a greater chance of scoring hits. Yet, while this firepower could prove devastating to soft-skin or lightly armoured vehicles, especially when incendiary ammunition was used, its effect upon tanks was less certain. A former US fighter-bomber pilot observed that merely spraying German medium tanks (such as PzKw IVs) and heavy tanks (such as Panthers and Tigers) with .50 calibre bullets was useless, and described how pilots strafing tanks needed to hit them with the simultaneous fire of all their guns, aiming for vulnerable points such as engine louvres and air vents. When tanks were caught on a hard road surface, attempts were made to ricochet rounds up into the tanks' more lightly armoured bellies.[7]

In July 1944 the first US P-47 squadron equipped with air-to-ground rockets became operational in Ninth Air Force, each P-47 carrying four 5 inch High Velocity Aircraft Rockets (HVAR) of a type originally developed by the California Institute of Technology for air-to-air combat. These were usually delivered in either low-level attacks, releasing the rockets at a range of 600–1,000 yards, or in a 30° dive in which the rockets were released at a range of 1,000 yards or over. By September this unit had flown 323 sorties and fired 1,117 rockets at ground targets, many of which had been German tanks for the squadron's claims included:

TABLE I

P-47 SQUADRON CLAIMS

	DESTROYED	DAMAGED	TOTALS
Tanks	85	29	114
Armoured Cars	15	1	16
Motor Vehicles	164	23	187

Although these P-47's carried only half the number of rockets carried by a Typhoon, and their pilots lacked the same degree of rocket training as their RAF counterparts, the unit was regarded as successful. A Ninth Air Force study reported that the rockets could be fired from longer range than the .50 calibre guns which reduced the danger from flak. They also had more penetration capability than bullets or the general purpose bombs that tended to break up on contact with targets, and they proved more accurate than dive-bombing.[8] Despite this study, advocating further rocket use, the Ninth Air Force never employed rockets on a large scale.[9]

Later in the campaign, Ninth Air Force made increasing use of napalm fire bombs. Napalm could be effective against even heavy tanks, burning them out by very near misses as well as by direct hits, but its use against targets close to friendly troops involved considerable risk. Certainly in Normandy, it would appear Ninth Air Force felt the lack of an airborne anti-armour weapon of more precision that could be employed against German tanks in close proximity to friendly troops. On occasions when heavy concentrations of German armour were encountered by American forces, recourse was had to the RAF for rocket-Typhoons to operate in the American sector and engage them.

CASE STUDIES

In the wake of the Allied breakout from Normandy, Operation COBRA which began on 25 July 1944, large German forces in the Cotentin peninsula were forced to risk air attack by moving in daylight to avoid being encircled by the American armour. Just south of Coutances, near Roncey, some six German divisions were cut off in what became known as the Roncey 'Pocket'. Choking the roads, the German columns became ideal targets for attacks by Allied fighter-bombers whose attacks succeeded in preventing any organised break-out. On the afternoon of 29 July P-47's of the American 405th Fighter Group observed this dense mass of German transport, including tanks, on the roads near Coutances and on the road between St. Denis-le-Vêtu and Roncey they saw a column extending for over three miles blocked by American armour to the east and west. Between 3.10 and 9.40 p.m. the P-47s of the 405th Group systematically bombed and strafed this column, returning to their base to rearm and refuel before returning to the attack. Two days later American ground forces found the road impassable, and discovered 66 German tanks, 204 vehicles, and 11 guns destroyed, and 56 tanks and 55 vehicles damaged. This destruction, though, was the result of the combined firepower of P-47s and the artillery and tanks of nearby American ground units.[10]

Some indication of the destruction caused specifically by air weapons is provided by an RAF anti-armour operation on the same day. Rocket Typhoons of 2nd TAF were requested by US forces to attack a concentration of some 50 German tanks observed in the Roncey area, near Gavray. Consequently Typhoons of No.121 Wing of No.83 Group flew 99 sorties in the area between late afternoon and dusk, and claimed the destruction of 17 tanks with a further 27 damaged. The pilots reported that there was little sign of life or movement during their attacks and the area was littered with damaged and burning tanks, making target selection difficult. There was no flak, and pilots were able to attack at very low level. Only one Typhoon was lost, hit by flying debris and forced to crash-land.[11]

The Typhoon effort had been concentrated mainly against a German column near the village of la Baleine, and shortly after the air attacks this area was investigated by the British Army's No.2 ORS. The column had been a formidable mix of armour and transport, including Panther tanks, and after examining the tanks and vehicles the ORS outlined the causes of destruction. This is shown in Table II.

The surrounding terrain was heavily wooded and dissected by deep, narrow, valleys and the column had used a side road which descended to la Baleine where a bridge crossed the river Sienne. On one side of this road was a steep, wooded cliff and on the other a sheer drop to the river; caught by fighter-bombers at this point the vehicles had been unable to pull off the road. P-47's had attacked the area with 500 lb bombs before Typhoons had been called for, and the bridge over the river had been sufficiently damaged by their bombs to prevent heavy vehicles from crossing.

Squadron Leader R.A. Sutherland, DFC, and Major Colin Gray at their Visual Control Post in Normandy.

The following four photographs were taken in Normandy during a demonstration of rocket-firing Typhoons attacking a captured German tank.

The target was a Panzer Mk. V which had been drained of all ammunition, petrol and oil.

Rockets exploding on the target.

Air Vice-Marshal H. Broadhurst filming the burning tank.

Air Marshal Sir Arthur Coningham (nearest camera) and Air Vice-Marshal Broadhurst view the results.

RAF ground crews of No.247 Squadron loading a Typhoon with rocket projectiles at B6, Coulombs.

Armourer fitting an electrical rocket-firing plug.

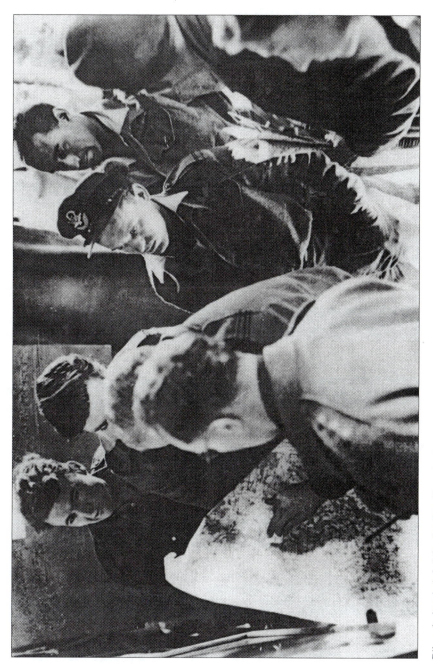

Pilots being briefed in the Intelligence tent.

Normandy: RAF Typhoons attack enemy armour in woods north of Rocquancourt.

Typhoons of the No.175 Squadron at B5, Le Fresne Camilly.

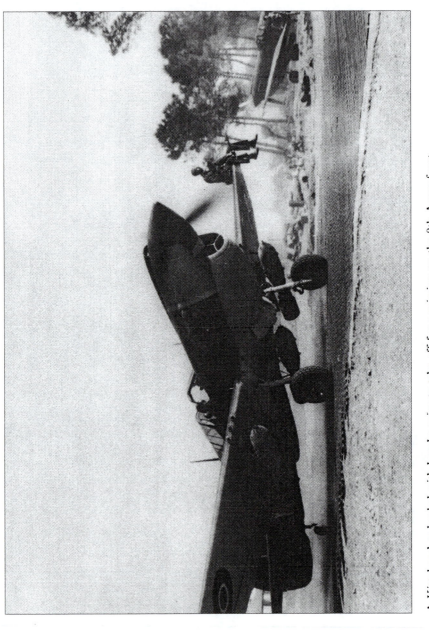

A Kittybomber loaded with bombs prior to take off for a mission on the 8th Army front.

TABLE II

LA BALEINE – LOSSES AND CAUSES[12]

Destroyed by	Rockets	Possibly Rockets	Unknown Shells	Unknown Causes	Crew	Abandoned	Totals
Panthers	1	–	1	–	3	3	8
PZ Mk IV Special	1	–	–	–	–	–	1
Armoured Cars	–	1	–	–	–	–	1
Armd. troop carriers	5	–	–	–	–	–	5
75 mm SP guns	–	–	–	1	–	1	2
50 mm Anti-Tank Guns	–	–	–	–	1	1	2
Howitzers	–	1	–	–	–	1	2
Rocket launchers	–	–	–	–	–	1	1
Lorries	–	–	–	8	–	–	8
Cars	–	–	–	10	–	–	10
Totals:	7	2	1	19	4	7	40

The motor transport was so mangled that identification of the cause of destruction was impossible and the ORS acknowledged their 'unknown causes' table to be unduly loaded. They suggested that a more accurate picture would be provided by the motor transport being spread over the table in the same proportion as the other losses. Although rockets appear as the biggest single known cause of destruction, the amount attributed to them is small compared to the relatively high number of Panthers destroyed by their crews or abandoned intact. How they had been left suggested abandonment in haste, almost certainly as a result of air attack or the threat of such attack, and possibly even before the arrival of the Typhoons. Craters of 500 lb bombs were found in an orchard within 50 yards of two Panthers; neither tank had been hit but the crews obviously baled out and later set fire to the tanks, one of the guns being destroyed by a high-explosive round left in the chamber.

Although lack of fuel in a retreat could be expected to result in the abandonment or destruction of tanks by their crews, this was not the case at la Baleine; near similar bomb craters two Panthers were found completely undamaged, their fighting ability unimpaired with full complements of petrol and ammunition. One of the 75 mm self-propelled guns, its armour reinforced with concrete, was found abandoned undamaged 35 yards from a bomb crater. As it had not been set on fire by its crew it was considered more likely to have been abandoned in haste rather than left as a deliberate roadblock.

Possibly the tanks had been abandoned or destroyed by their crews because they could not negotiate the damaged bridge. The ORS noted that the German crews could have forded the river further down-stream, as American Sherman tanks later succeeded in doing, but this ignores the fact that in their hurry to escape encirclement the Germans probably had little time to reconnoitre the area. That all the troop carriers discovered had been destroyed by rockets suggests the possibility that other similar types may have escaped over the bridge, not needing to be abandoned like the heavier tanks. At la Baleine the most significant evidence of demoralisation was that there were no German graves. Only one German corpse was found and local civilians, many of whom were interviewed, confirmed that it was of a sniper killed after the air attacks, while no evidence could be found that American forces had removed bodies for burial. This suggests that the German troops may have dispersed from the column when it became obvious air attack was imminent, which squares with the Typhoon pilots observing little German activity during their attacks.

La Baleine was the first ORS investigation of its type, and certainly reflects the shortcomings of air-to-ground weapons against tanks. Despite the craters none of the tanks or self-propelled guns had been knocked out by bombs, and the number destroyed by rockets is unimpressive. Nevertheless, there was a good deal of evidence discovered by the ORS at la Baleine to suggest that air attack was responsible, even if indirectly, for the disruption and abandonment of the column, and that the German crews preferred to abandon or destroy their armour rather than invite further air attack by attempting to salvage combat-worthy tanks.[13]

Similar evidence of German tanks being abandoned under air attack is seen in the example of the only large-scale German armoured offensive mounted in Normandy. Early on the morning of 7 August 1944, the strike force of XLVII Panzer Corps, the 1st SS, 2nd SS, and 2nd Panzer divisions, attacked positions held by the US 30th and 9th Infantry divisions near Mortain with the ultimate objective of reaching the Cotentin coast at Avranches and cutting off American armoured spearheads from their supplies. Although tank strength was depleted after weeks of heavy fighting the Germans mustered 70 Panthers, 75 Mk IVs, and 32 self-propelled guns for the attack.[14] By noon on 7 August they were within nine miles of Avranches after penetrating the front of 30th Division to a depth of about three miles. Having arrived in Mortain only the day before, 30th Division had nothing but its 57 mm towed anti-tank guns and 3 inch gun tank-destroyers with which to engage the German tanks at close range. Despite its determined defence, the credit for bringing the German attack to a decisive halt on the afternoon of 7 August is generally regarded as belonging to Allied fighter-bombers, particularly the RAF Typhoons, which were called to intervene.

The response of the Allied tactical air forces to the German attack was swift. The Typhoons of No.83 Group RAF were made available, and plans co-ordinated directly between the headquarters of No.83 Group and IX Tactical Air Command. Rocket Typhoons were to engage the German tanks, while American fighter-bombers were to attack transport moving to and from the battle area. The Ninth Air Force was also to provide a fighter screen to intercept German aircraft, a vital task as the *Luftwaffe* had planned to make an all-out effort to support the attack with some 300 planes.[15] The German command had relied upon fog, prevalent on previous days and which had been fore-cast for 7 August, to protect their armoured spearheads from air observation and attack, but at about 11 am that day the fog over the battle area began to clear.

At about midday the first Typhoons took off for the American sector from their advanced landing grounds, and went into action just before 1 p.m. against a concentration of some 60 tanks and 200 vehicles observed along a hedge-lined road near Mortain. The tanks, some heavily camouflaged, were grouped closely together as if unpre-pared for the rapid lifting of the fog.[16] After overflying at low level to confirm them as German, the Typhoons commenced dive attacks upon the front and rear of the column, which was immediately brought to a halt. The pilots observed that their attacks caused great confusion, and saw German tank crews baling out and running for cover regardless of whether or not their tanks were left blocking the road.[17] Also at this time the first American fighter-bombers arrived in the area, with P-47s, including the squadron equipped with rockets, attacking German transport.[18]

The weather remained clear and between 2 p.m. and 8 p.m. flights of five or six Typhoons were taking off roughly every 20 minutes to

attack, returning to refuel and rearm before setting off again for
Mortain. As the afternoon wore on the pilots found the task of locat-
ing the German tanks increasingly difficult due to their dispersion and
to clouds of dust and smoke in the battle area, but the forward movement of the German attack had been halted. By the end of the day
No.83 Group had flown 294 sorties and IX Tactical Air Command
200 sorties in the Mortain area. Three Typhoons and pilots had been
lost. Though the level of flak had initially been light, it had increased
during the day with box-like patterns being put up over the tanks, and
many of the Typhoons were found to have suffered damage from this
and small-arms fire.[19]

German accounts clearly attribute the failure of their attack on 7
August to the fighter-bombers. The commander of 2nd Panzer
Division, von Luttwitz, later recalled that his tanks had made a swift
advance of about ten miles when suddenly the fighter-bombers
appeared,

> They came in hundreds, firing their rockets at the concentrated tanks
> and vehicles. We could do nothing against them and we could make no
> further progress.[20]

Hans Speidel, then the Chief of Staff of the German Army Group B,
later wrote of Mortain that

> it was possible for the Allied air forces alone to wreck this Panzer oper-
> ation with the help of a well co-ordinated ground-to-air communica-
> tions system.[21]

The German troops received no air support on 7 August. Their
aircraft attempting to reach the battle area were intercepted by strong
American fighter patrols and none reached within 40 miles of
Mortain.[22] Although fighting continued in the area for several days,
with Mortain being recaptured by American forces on 12 August, the
Germans made no further attempt to reach Avranches after 7 August.
Typhoons took no part in the battle after that date, with responsibil-
ity for air support reverting to the IX Tactical Air Command. The
claims made by the Allied fighter-bomber pilots for the period 7–10
August are impressive, and are shown in Table III below.

Yet these claims are misleading and cannot be substantiated.
During 12–20 August the Mortain battle area was examined by two
separate British ORS teams; No. 2 ORS and ORS 2nd TAF. No
German vehicles were missed by the investigation as the areas was not
extensive; moreover the area was examined from an observation

TABLE III

ALLIED FIGHTER-BOMBER CLAIMS, 7–10 AUGUST 1944

	Destroyed	Probably Destroyed	Damaged	Total
ARMOUR				
2nd TAF	8	35	21	140
9th AF	69	8	35	112
MOTOR TRANSPORT				
2nd TAF	54	19	39	112
9th AF	94	1	21	116

aircraft at low level with no further vehicles discovered. The destruction attributed to various weapons can be tabulated as shown in Table IV, which is a compilation of both the RAF and Army reports. This shows that a total of only 46 German tanks and self-propelled guns were actually found in the battle area, and of these only nine were considered to have been destroyed by air weapons.

It was not possible to discriminate between victims of British and American aircraft as the latter had also fired some 600 rockets. Many of the 'unknown causes' were found some distance from any sign of air attack – such as cannon and machine gun strikes on the ground and rocket or bomb craters – and could not be considered as possible air victims. An obvious question is whether the Germans had been able to recover any of their tanks. The presence of a German tank recovery vehicle would seem to confirm they had but, while it is likely that some tanks were recovered, this can hardly be an adequate explanation for the discrepancy between air claims and the destruction found. Armoured and motor vehicles destroyed by air weapons were invariably burnt out, and for recovery purposes damaged and abandoned vehicles had priority over such. German prisoners, many of whom were questioned on this subject, consistently stated that burnt out tanks were never salvaged.[23] In effect, a tank hit by a rocket or bomb was not worth recovering and the ORS should have found what was left of it.

Another question is whether German accounts of the fighting can shed more light on the number of tanks and vehicles destroyed by air attack. The histories of the German divisions that fought at Mortain, compiled post-war, stress how decisive the intervention of the fighter-bombers had been, but are ambiguous with regard to the question of

TABLE IV

DESTRUCTION ATTRIBUTED TO VARIOUS WEAPONS,
MORTAIN AREA, AUGUST 1944

TYPE   FORM OF DESTRUCTION OR NEUTRALISATION

	Rockets	Cannon/ MG	Bomb	Abandoned intact	Crew	US Army	Unknown	Total
Panther	5	–	1	6	4	14	3	33
Mk IV	2	–	1	1	–	5	1	10
SP Guns	–	–	–	–	–	1	2	3
Armd Troop Carriers	7	4	–	1	–	3	8	23
Armd Cars	1	–	–	1	–	5	1	8
Armd recov. veh.	–	–	–	–	–	1	–	1
88 mm Guns	–	–	–	–	–	1	1	2
75 mm Guns	–	–	–	–	–	1	–	1
50 mm Guns	–	–	–	1	–	–	–	1
Cars	2	2	–	–	–	4	3	11
Lorries	–	6	–	1	1	2	20	30
Ambulances	–	2	–	2	–	–	1	5
Motor Cycles	–	–	–	1	–	1	2	4
Totals	17	14	2	14	5	38	42	132

losses. That of the 2nd Panzer Division states of the Typhoons that they attacked with great accuracy and succeeded in knocking out even the heaviest tanks, but the number of tanks actually lost in this way is not given.[24] The history of the 1st SS Panzer Division (*Leibstandarte Adolf Hitler*) is similarly unclear as to the the actual number of tanks knocked out from the air, though it implies that the number was considerable and quotes an account of the air attacks by a panzer grenadier who recalled seeing many black oil clouds indicating the positions of destroyed tanks.[25] Also quoted is a panzer grenadier officer who, after describing how a fighter-bomber shot down by flak crashed onto a tank and put it out of action, adds that most of the other tanks and armoured personnel carriers also fell victim to the intense, hour-long, low-level attacks.[26]

Yet such German accounts attributing heavy tank and vehicle losses to air attack are misleading. They take little cognizance of the losses inflicted by US ground forces which, though almost certainly overestimated at the time in the confusion of battle, were none the less considerable. American accounts of the fighting indicate that, on 7 August, the forward troops of the US 30th and 9th Divisions claimed the destruction of at least eighteen German tanks, fourteen of them by the 30th Division's attached 823rd Tank Destroyer Battalion alone.[27] Moreover, the ORS confirmed that US troops accounted for more heavy German armour than the fighter-bombers, the destruction of twenty of the total of forty-six tanks and SP guns found being attributed to US ground weapons.

The principal reason why such German accounts should be regarded with caution, however, is that they provide no explanation as to what had become of the tanks and vehicles destroyed by the fighter-bombers by the time the ORS examined the battle area. Nor do they explain the not inconsiderable number of tanks found abandoned or destroyed by their own crews. To some extent, German attribution of tank losses to air attack may stem from the confusion of battle, but it may also suggest both a reluctance to acknowledge the morale effect of such attack, and a desire to ascribe the halting of the armoured thrust, which was much in the nature of a forlorn hope, to Allied air power rather than to defeat at the hands of US ground forces.[28]

Despite the toll taken of the German armour by US ground weapons, the commanders of the US units engaged on 7 August later confirmed that it was the fighter-bombers that brought the German thrust to a halt. At the time of the ground survey, a member of ORS 2nd TAF visited the headquarters of the US 9th Division's 39th Infantry Regiment. He was told by the Commander how the German attack had cut off part of his regiment from its headquarters and how his anti-tank guns had been insufficient to halt such a large number of tanks. He also told how he had remained 'vulnerable and anxious' until Typhoons arrived to attack the German spearhead. A visit was also made to the the Commander of the 30th Division's 117th Infantry Regiment, which had been in the path of the 2nd Panzer and 1st SS Panzer Divisions on 7 August. He recalled that when the mist lifted at about 12.30,

> Thunderbolt and Typhoon aircraft came in immediately and attacked, Typhoons attacking for what seemed to him to be about two hours. This, added to the resistance of the ground forces, stopped the thrust.[29]

Such appreciation of the close air support on 7 August is significant in view of the tendency of Allied aircraft to attack friendly positions inadvertently in what was a very fluid ground battle. The US 30th Division recorded that the Typhoons and P-47s often attacked its positions, the 120th Regiment alone receiving ten such attacks during the day.[30]

Given the lack of tank destruction by air weapons, the undoubted effectiveness of the sustained fighter-bomber assault on 7 August must have been largely the result of completely disrupting the German attack by compelling tanks to seek cover or their crews to abandon them. The level of destruction attributed to air weapons by the ORS is too insignificant to have been decisive, and even if the unknown causes for destruction of both armour and motor transport were added to the air attack totals the number would only be a quarter of those claimed. Yet no fewer than ten of the 33 Panthers found, or 30 per cent, had been abandoned or destroyed by their own crews. This was an important discovery at the time, and a contemporary RAF tactical study stressing the demoralising effect of the 3 inch rocket projectile – or RP as it was generally called – offered this explanation for the German abandonment of tanks and vehicles at Mortain:

> Interrogation of prisoners has shown without question that German tank crews are extremely frightened of attacks by RP...Crews are very aware that if an RP does hit a tank, their chance of survival is small. It is admitted that the chances of a direct hit are slight; nevertheless, this would hardly be appreciated by a crew whose first thought would be of the disastrous results if a hit was obtained.[31]

Prisoner of war data further confirmed the demoralising effect of air attack upon tank crews. German tank crewmen questioned for the later joint RAF/British Army study of Typhoon effectiveness indicated an irrational compulsion among inexperienced men to leave the relative safety of their tank and seek alternative cover during air attack:

> The experienced crews stated that when attacked from the air they remained in their tanks which had no more than superficial damage (cannon strikes or near misses from bombs). They had great difficulty in preventing the inexperienced men from baling out when our aircraft attacked.[32]

It is certainly plausible that tank crews under a heavy scale of air attack would be induced to bale out, despite the interior of the tank being possibly the safest place to be, and in this way the bombs and rockets did not need to strike the tanks to be effective. When asked for an opinion by the ORS on the number of abandoned tanks in the Mortain battle area, an experienced NCO of a US anti-tank unit replied,

> There is nothing but air attack that would make a crack Panzer crew do that.[33]

The retreat of the German army towards the River Seine in order to escape encirclement in the Falaise 'Pocket' in August 1944 also provided the Allied tactical air forces with an abundance of targets, and great claims of destruction were made. On 18 August RAF 2nd TAF alone claimed 1,159 vehicles destroyed and 1,700 damaged together with 124 tanks destroyed and 100 damaged. On the same day the Ninth Air Force claimed 400 vehicles destroyed.[34]

During the period of this retreat nearly 9,900 sorties were flown by the RAF. Destruction was claimed of 3,340 soft and 257 armoured vehicles or some 36 targets destroyed for every hundred sorties.[35] The USAAF claimed 2,520 soft and 134 armoured vehicles destroyed during nearly 2,900 sorties, or some 91 successes per hundred. Overall claims therefore amount to a successful strike approximately every second sortie.[36] (See Appendix.)

Shortly after the 'Pocket' had been closed No.2 ORS conducted an extensive investigation in the area to determine the German losses caused by air attack and the effectiveness of air-to-ground weapons.[37] The principal roads taken by the Germans were patrolled in three areas; the 'Pocket' itself around Falaise, the area at the mouth of the pocket near Chambois and referred to as the 'Shambles', and the area known as the 'Chase' which led to the Seine crossings.

Of the 133 armoured vehicles of all types located by the ORS in the 'Pocket', only 33 had been the victim of any form of air attack. The remaining 100 had been destroyed by their crews or simply abandoned. Air attacks were far more effective against soft-skinned vehicles. Of 701 cars, trucks and motor cycles found in the 'Pocket' 325 had been the victim of attack from the air, and of these 85 per cent were hit by cannon or machine-gun fire – a testament to the effectiveness of this form of attack. The fact however remains that of a total of 885 vehicles of all types lost by the Germans in the Falaise pocket nearly 60 per cent were destroyed or abandoned by their crews rather than as the direct result of attack from the air. (See Appendix.)

The large number of armoured and motor vehicles abandoned or destroyed by their crews is hardly surprising in such a retreat, and it was thought many of those destroyed by air weapons had already been abandoned. Air attack, though, was considered responsible for much of the abandonment as a result of causing disorganisation; moreover, destroyed vehicles had completely blocked roads. Cannon and machine gun attacks had proved to be extremely effective against the densely-packed motor transport. Such vehicles hit by cannon or machine gun rounds were invariably burnt out, and the report noted that where pock marks of strikes appeared in the roads a burnt vehicle was usually to be found.[38]

In the 'Shambles' so many German vehicles were found that it was impossible to examine each in detail; they were classed either as burnt or unburnt as an indication of whether they had been hit by air weapons or abandoned. A total of 1,411 tanks and vehicles were classed as burnt, and 1,380 as unburnt. Of the 187 tanks and SP guns found in this area, 82 were examined in detail, of these only two were destroyed by attack from the air and eight by ground fire, while all but one of the remainder were either burnt by their crews or merely abandoned. There was no evidence – such as rocket craters – to suggest that any appreciable number of those burnt tanks and SP guns not examined had been destroyed by air weapons. (See Appendix.)

A sample of 330 of the softskin vehicles, and 31 of the lightly armoured vehicles, found in the 'Shambles' were also examined in detail. Of the softskin vehicles, 110 were found to have been destroyed by air weapons and 135 abandoned intact, while of the lightly armoured vehicles 6 were credited to air weapons and 13 were found abandoned intact. The effectiveness of strafing against soft-skin and light armoured vehicles was again confirmed, this being the greatest known cause of destruction.

The 'Chase' area yielded a count of 3,648 vehicles and guns, and of 3,332 light armoured and soft-skin vehicles, 2,390 were classed as burnt and 942 unburnt. The ORS were unable to cover every road in such an extensive area, so the absolute number of vehicles and guns was unknown but thought to be less than twice that recorded. Of the 150 tanks and self-propelled guns 98 were examined. None were found to have been destroyed by rockets, nor were there any craters to suggest rocket attacks had been made in the area. Most, amounting to some 81 per cent, had been destroyed by their crews or abandoned. (See Appendix.)

To allow for the possibility of German vehicles and guns being missed in wooded terrain or along unchecked roads, No.2 ORS estimated that the Germans had lost some 10,000 vehicles and guns during the retreat, a figure not thought to be in error by more than 2,000 either way. This was broken down as 1,500 in the 'Pocket' area,

3,500 in the 'Shambles', and 5,000 in the 'Chase'. As it was estimated that the Germans must have had a total of some 30,000 vehicles it was considered that two-thirds, including about 250 tanks and SP guns, had escaped across the Seine.[39] This was regarded as the result of the air forces attempting general destruction rather than trying to achieve interdiction by attacking key 'choke' points, a charge strongly refuted by 2nd TAF as taking no account of weather, flak levels, or bomblines set by friendly ground forces.[40] In fact No.2 ORS overestimated the number of German tanks that had escaped, as on 22–23 August the German Army Group B, reporting on the state of its eight surviving Panzer divisions, listed only some 72 tanks.[41]

The retreat to the Seine clearly reveals the limitations of Allied air-to-ground weapons against tanks, particularly the 3 inch rocket. Only ten out of 301 tanks and SP guns examined, and three out of 87 armoured troop carriers examined, were found to have been destroyed by this weapon – these figures must be compared with the 222 claims of armour destruction made by Typhoon pilots alone. In contrast is the marked effectiveness of cannon and machine guns, and to a lesser extent bombs, against soft-skin transport vehicles. By destroying large numbers of these, thus blocking roads and increasing congestion, the fighter-bombers indirectly caused the abandonment of many tanks.

Moreover, many of the tanks and SP guns were found abandoned without petrol, not least because trucks carrying their fuel had been shot up from the air. German prisoners described how the threat of air attack restricted movement to the hours of darkness until congestion and haste compelled movement by day. They also told how whenever aircraft appeared crews stopped to take cover and vehicles were driven off the main roads into side roads which in turn became blocked.[42] In effect, the almost continuous fighter-bomber attacks in daylight, within a restricted area upon retreating troops, caused a great deal of demoralisation and delay which prevented many tanks and vehicles escaping.

IDENTIFICATION OF KILLS

The influence of Allied tactical air power upon German ability to carry out large-scale armoured operations was so great by the end of 1944 that the timing of the German Ardennes offensive was dictated by the occurrence of bad weather. In the early stages of the offensive, which began on 16 December 1944, fog and low cloud protected the tank spearheads from aerial observation and attack. Then the weather cleared and Allied fighter-bomber pilots were presented with targets such as they had not seen since Normandy and, as in Normandy, they made large claims for the destruction of armour. Between 17 December 1944 and 16 January 1945 the IX and XIX Tactical Air Commands of Ninth Air Force and RAF 2nd TAF claimed a total of 413 German armoured vehicles destroyed in the Ardennes salient, 324 of which were claimed as tanks. In early January No.2 ORS began an investigation of these claims, in the middle of the month they were joined by ORS 2nd TAF and a joint report was produced.[43]

Although hampered by thick snow which prevented the discovery of rocket craters and burnt patches caused by napalm bombs, the ORS were able to examine 101 armoured vehicles – the practice being to search an area within 2–3 kilometres of each claim. The claims for destruction within the salient are shown in Table V:

TABLE V

ALLIED AIR CLAIMS FOR GERMAN ARMOUR DESTROYED
IN THE ARDENNES SALIENT

	IN AREA EXAMINED BY ORS			IN WHOLE SALIENT		
	Tanks	Armd. Vehicles	Total	Tanks	Armd. Vehicles	Total
IX TAC	62	23	85	140	69	209
XIX TAC	2	0	2	176	19	195
2nd TAF	2	1	3	8	1	9
Totals	66	24	90	324	89	413

The air weapons used were general purpose high-explosive bombs, fragmentation bombs, napalm fire bombs, and rockets. Many of the tanks claimed by Ninth Air Force had also been engaged by machine guns, some only by this means.

For the 101 tanks and armoured vehicles examined, damage was attributed as in Table VI. Considering that this represents the investigation of claims for the destruction of 66 tanks and 24 armoured vehicles the effect of air attack seems unimpressive; a maximum of seven out of 101 vehicles examined, some six per cent. It was found that fighter-bomber attack had also involved some wastage, with bombs dropped among tanks already knocked out by American troops, and it is revealing that even when these bombs landed within 15 yards of the tanks no additional damage was done.[44] Not surprisingly, the report concluded that, while the contribution of the air forces to

TABLE VI

ATTRIBUTABLE DAMAGE TO SAMPLE OF 101 TANKS
AND ARMOURED VEHICLES, ARDENNES SALIENT

	Tiger II	Panther	Mk IV	SPGun	Light Armour	Total
AIR:						
Bomb	1	–	–	–	–	1
Possibly air attack	–	3	–	2*	1	6*
GROUND:						
Armour-Piercing Shot	1	16	1	9*	8	36*
High-Explosive Shell	–	3	–	1	4	8
Demolition	2	10	1	–	4	17
Abandoned	1	10	–	4	7	22
Other Cause	–	–	1	1	–	2
Unknown Cause	–	5	2	1	2	10
TOTAL:	5	47	5	18	26	101

* One other SP Gun also had armour-piercing penetrations but has been attributed to a rocket strike.

stemming the German offensive had been considerable, this

> was not by the direct destruction of armour, which appears to have been
> insignificant; but rather by the strafing and bombing of supply routes,
> which prevented essential supplies from reaching the front.[45]

While the lack of destruction of armour in these examples from
Normandy and the Ardennes may be explained by the shortcomings
of the air-to-ground weapons employed, something must also be said
about the high number of claims made by the air forces. This was
almost certainly the result of the difficulties experienced by pilots
engaged in the ground-attack role. One reason is that pilots were very
likely to misinterpret the results of their attacks. Flashes from exploding cannon shells, ricochet sparks, and smoke emitted from the
exhausts of revving tanks could all be mistaken for evidence of tank
kills.[46] A former Typhoon pilot, describing an attack on a German
column in the Falaise 'Pocket', describes how within a few seconds a
stretch of road could be left blazing under rocket and cannon fire.[47]
Such conditions could not have made accurate damage assessment
very easy, and pilots regularly reported their claims as 'smokers' or
'flamers'. It seems fair to assume that much of the smoke and flame
was not actually the result of tanks being hit. There was also the

problem of accurate target identification by pilots hurtling at low level over a mass of vehicles obscured by smoke and flames. Under such conditions all types of armoured vehicles, and perhaps even some soft-skin vehicles, could be mistaken for tanks. In the snows of the Ardennes it was found that even small buildings such as huts which stood out against the white background could be mistaken by pilots for tanks and vehicles.[48] Moreover, what constituted a tank was often loosely defined by pilots, a former American fighter-bomber pilot admitting that assault guns, armoured artillery, and tank destroyers were all identified as by pilots as 'tanks'.[49]

Another most important reason for the number of claims was duplication. Unless a tank or armoured vehicle was burning, smoking, or an obvious wreck, pilots had no way of knowing whether it had been the target of a previous attack. When conducting its ground survey of the Falaise area, No.2 ORS discovered an armoured troop carrier abandoned in a particularly prominent position and were told by local civilians it had been the target of twelve separate strafing attacks; it very likely figured in twelve separate claims.

As regards the reliability of the ORS ground surveys, one may wonder if tanks attributed to destruction by ground weapons had in fact been knocked out by aircraft and subsequently used as target practice by Allied troops. However, such mistakes were very unlikely. Bombs and rockets were hardly ever, if at all, used singly, and near vehicles destroyed by such weapons were always found the craters of near misses. Moreover, rocket craters were distinctive, oval in shape and usually with part of the rocket tube or fins in or near them. Parts of the rocket were also often found in tanks or vehicles destroyed by the weapon. In or near tanks and vehicles destroyed by their crews were often found the metal cases that had contained German demolition charges, these being placed in a specific part of the tank, such as under engine hatches. Pock marks on roads or holes roughly six inches in diameter in the ground indicated machine gun or cannon attacks, and tanks and vehicles that had been strafed bore holes or dents on upper surfaces. It is possible that tanks abandoned intact were subsequently used for target practice, and attributed to a particular ground weapon, but this has little relevance to the effectiveness of air weapons.[50]

The ORS investigations help to set the achievements of the Allied fighter-bombers into perspective. By attacking soft-skin supply vehicles they were able to choke the arteries feeding fuel and ammunition to the Panzer divisions and, although their weapons were inadequate for engaging tanks directly, their rockets and bombs could strike at a more vulnerable part of a tank than its armour plate – the morale and will to fight of its crew. At Falaise the fighter-bombers proved a tank is so much scrap without fuel or ammunition, or if abandoned along a hopelessly blocked road. At Mortain, in an example of rapidly concentrated aerial firepower, the fighter-bombers proved a tank to be equally useless in battle even if fully armed and fuelled if its crew were sheltering in a ditch, or desperately trying to get the tank into cover, as a result of air attack.

NOTES

1. Charles Demoulin, *Firebirds: Flying The Typhoon in Action* (Shrewsbury: Airlife, 1986/87), p. 138.
2. No.83 Group Operations Record Book, Appendices July–August 1944, Appendix F, *Trial to Determine the Effect of an RP fitted with a 60 lb HE Shell on a German Panther Tank*, PRO AIR 25/704. Panther armour details from Eric Lefèvre, *Panzers in Normandy Then and Now* (London: After The Battle, 1983), p. 27.
3. Synopsis of Typhoon tactics by Lt. Col. R.A. Lallement in Christopher Shores, *Ground Attack Aircraft of World War II* (London: Macdonald & Jane's, 1977), pp. 157–9.
4. British Army Prisoner of War Interrogation Reports, Serials 1332 and 1339 (Nov. 1942), copies in No.6 Squadron RAF, Operations Record Book, Jan. 1943, PRO AIR 27/76.
5. B.H. Liddell Hart (Ed.), *The Rommel Papers* (London: Collins, 1953), p. 295.
6. No.6 Squadron RAF, Operations Record Book, PRO AIR 27/76. In Dec. 1943 Hurricane IID's began ground attack operations in the Far East with No.20 Squadron. They were successful in this less hazardous environment, though few Japanese tanks were encountered. However, during the siege of Imphal in June 1944 a detachment of the Squadron engaged twelve Japanese tanks and destroyed them all, losing one aircraft. On 19 February 1945 thirteen Japanese heavy, medium and light tanks were caught and destroyed by the Squadron in the village of Paunggadaw – as British troops later confirmed. The effectiveness of the Hurricane IID against Japanese armour is outlined in RAF ORS (Air Command South-East Asia) Report, *Air Firing Trials Against Captured Japanese Tanks at Thinunggei* (August 1944), PRO AIR 37/1236.
7. Bill Colgan, *World War II Fighter Bomber Pilot* (Blue Ridge Summit, PA: Tab Books, 1985), pp. 181–2.
8. ORS Ninth Air Force Report No.59 (19th Sept. 1944), *Rocket Status in 9th Air Force*, PRO AIR 37/956; see also Brereton Greenhous, *Aircraft versus Armor: Cambrai to Yom Kippur*, in *Men at War*, Tim Travers and Christan Archer (Eds.) (Chicago: Precedent, 1982), pp. 105–6.
9. See Chapter 3 above.
10. Wesley F. Craven and James L. Cate (Eds.), *The Army Air Forces in World War II*, Vol. III, *Argument to VE Day* (Chicago: 1951), p. 242.
11. No.83 Group RAF Operations Record Book (ORB), 29th July 1944, PRO AIR 25/698; ORBs of Nos. 175, 245, and 174, Squadrons, 29 July 1944, PRO AIR 27/1111, AIR 27/1482, and AIR 27/1109 respectively.
12. No.2 ORS Report No.3, *Investigation of an Attack on a German Column near La Baleine*, in *Operational Research in North West Europe*, PRO WO 291/1331.
13. Ibid.
14. Max Hastings, *Overlord: D-Day and The Battle for Normandy 1944* (London: Michael Joseph, 1984), p. 285.
15. Air Historical Branch Narrative, *The Liberation of North West Europe*, Vol. III, *The Landings in Normandy*, pp. 85–6, PRO AIR 41/24.
16. Appendix C to No.83 Group RAF ORB, *Report on Attacks by R/P Typhoons of 83 Group in Avranches Area – 7 Aug. 1944*, PRO AIR 25/704.
17. Ibid.

18. Air Historical Branch Narrative, p. 86, PRO AIR 41/24.
19. Appendix C to No.83 Group RAF ORB; Craven and Cate, *The Army Air Forces in World War II*, p. 249; John Golley, *The Day of the Typhoon* (Patrick Stephens Ltd., 1986), p. 128.
20. Quoted in Milton Schulman, *Defeat in the West* (London: 1948), p. 148.
21. Hans Speidel, *Invasion 1944: Rommel and the Normandy Campaign* (Chicago: 1950), p. 131.
22. Air Historical Branch Narrative, p. 87, PRO AIR 41/24.
23. No.2 ORS Report No.4, *Air Attacks on Enemy Tanks and Motor Transport in the Mortain Area, Aug. 1944*, in *Operational Research in North-West Europe*.
24. Franz Joseph Strauss, *Geschichte der 2 (Weiner) Panzer Division* (Neckargmünd: Kurt Vowinckel Verlag, 1977), p. 171 (CDA translation).
25. Rudolf Lehmann and Ralf Tiemann, *Die Leibstandarte*, Band IV/1 (Osnabrück: Munin Verlag, 1986), pp. 207–8 (CDA translation).
26. Ibid., p. 209.
27. US Army 823rd Tank Destroyer Battalion Unit Report, 7 Aug. 1944, quoted in Martin Blumenson, *Breakout And Pursuit* (Washington, DC: Department of the Army, 1961), p. 474.
28. German commanders were pessimistic regarding the outcome of the Mortain operation. Graf von Schwerin, commanding the 116th Panzer Division, refused to commit his division to the attack. He was later replaced for his insubordination. See James Lucas and James Barker, *The Killing Ground: The Battle of the Falaise Gap August 1944* (London: Batsford, 1978), pp. 17–18.
29. ORS 2nd TAF Report No.1, *Investigation of TAF Aircraft in the Mortain Area – 7 Aug. 1944*, PRO AIR 37/61.
30. Robert L. Hewitt, *Workhorse of the Western Front: The Story of the 30th Infantry Division* (Washington, DC: Infantry Journal Press, 1946), p. 59.
31. Headquarters RAF No.38 Group, Tactical Bulletin No.45, Oct. 1944, *Tactical Employment of R.P. Aircraft*, PRO AIR 37/415.
32. ORS 2nd TAF/No.2 ORS Joint Report No.3, *Rocket Typhoons in Close Support of Military Operations*, in *Operational Research in North-West Europe*.
33. ORS 2nd TAF Report No.1, *Investigation of TAF Aircraft in the Mountain Area*.
34. Dispatch by Air Chief Marshal Leigh-Mallory, Air Operations 15 Nov. 1943 to 30 Sept 1944, PRO CAB 106/980.
35. No.2 ORS Report No.15, *Enemy Casualties in Vehicles and Equipment during the Retreat from Normandy to the Seine*, in *Operational Research in North-West Europe*.
36. Ibid.
37. Ibid.
38. Ibid.
39. Ibid.
40. Comments from RAF 2nd TAF, Addenda to Ibid.
41. Hastings, *Overlord: D-Day and the Battle for Normandy, 1944*, p. 313.
42. No. 2 ORS Report No.15.
43. No.2 ORS/ORS 2nd TAF Joint Report No.1, *Air Attack on Enemy Armour in the Ardennes Salient*, in *Operational Research in North-West Europe*.
44. Ibid.
45. Ibid.
46. Richard P. Hallion, *Strike from the Sky: The History of Battlefield Air Attack 1911–45* (Shrewsbury: Airlife Publishing, 1989), p. 226.
47 Desmond Scott, *Typhoon Pilot* (London: Arrow, 1988), p. 122.
48. No.2 ORS/ORS 2nd TAF Joint Report No.1, *Air Attack on Enemy Armour in the Ardennes Salient*.
49. Colgan, *World War II Fighter Bomber Pilot*, pp. 181–2.
50. Air Ministry Air Publication 3368, *The Origins and Development of Operational Research in the Royal Air Force*, Appendix 4, *The Examination of A Battlefield* (London: HMSO, 1963) pp. 203–8.

6

Heavy and Medium Bombers in the Close Support Role

A MATTER OF PRIORITY

In March 1944 General Eisenhower, as Supreme Allied Commander, obtained direction of the Allied heavy bomber forces, RAF Bomber Command and the US Eighth Air Force, for Operation OVERLORD. He later recalled that

> We had no intention of using the Strategic Air Forces as a mere adjunct to the Tactical Air Command.

But he also recalled that, by the time of the breakout by the Allied armies from the Normandy beachhead in late July 1944,

> the emergency intervention of the entire bomber force in the land battle had come to be accepted almost as a matter of course.[1]

In fact the diversion of the Allied heavy bomber forces from the strategic air campaign against Germany and their employment against battlefield targets in close proximity to friendly ground forces was the most audacious form of air support provided for Allied troops in the Mediterranean and in North-West Europe. It was also the most controversial. Equipped and trained for the bombing of large area targets by night or, in the USAAF case, for the mass bombing of strategic targets in daylight, the heavy bombers had become committed to providing tactical close air support, the antithesis of their intended role. In Normandy they supported no less than six major attacks by Allied troops, and later supported operations to clear the Channel Ports, to clear the Scheldt Estuary, to cross the Rhine, and to breach the Siegfried Line.

This was not without determined opposition from most senior airmen and, before examining the effectiveness of close support bombing, a brief examination of the strategic commitments of the heavy bomber forces and the command set-up whereby they could be called upon to operate in the tactical role may be helpful.

The Combined Chiefs of Staff directive of March 1944 gave Eisenhower 'strategic direction' of the heavy bomber forces, not outright command. These forces included RAF Bomber Command, commanded by Air Chief Marshal Sir Arthur Harris, and the United States Strategic Air Forces in Europe (USSTAF), including the Eighth Air Force in the UK and the Fifteenth Air Force in Italy, commanded by Lieutenant-General Carl Spaatz. Eisenhower's principal link with these Headquarters was his deputy, Air Chief Marshal Sir Arthur Tedder. While Tedder could represent Eisenhower's wishes with respect to the employment of the strategic forces, he was not an overall air commander and firmly rejected the notion that he was an 'Air Commander-in-Chief'.[2]

In fact there was no such post, nor was there an overall air headquarters to control and co-ordinate the tactical and strategic air forces. The two Allied tactical air forces supporting OVERLORD, the US Ninth commanded by Major-General Lewis Brereton and Air Marshal Sir Arthur Coningham's 2nd TAF, were under the direction of Air Chief Marshal Sir Trafford Leigh-Mallory's Allied Expeditionary Air Force (AEAF) Headquarters. Demands for air support could be met from their resources, but Leigh-Mallory had no authority over the strategic air forces and his requests for their support had in practice to be endorsed by Tedder.[3]

Thus no effective command machinery existed for employing the strategic forces in tactical operations and, while both Harris and Spaatz were obliged to support OVERLORD, neither wished to see their forces diverted from what they saw as their decisive bombing offensives against Germany. An earlier Combined Chiefs of Staff directive, POINTBLANK, issued in June 1943, had given them the priority task of attacking the Luftwaffe and those industries supporting it.[4] Both Harris and Spaatz believed that bombing by itself could defeat Germany, and that the landing of Allied armies on the Continent was unnecessary. Both had unsuccessfully resisted any subordination of their forces to Eisenhower for operations in support of OVERLORD.[5]

In April and May 1944 RAF Bomber Command was increasingly committed to attacking communications targets in France and the

Low Countries as part of the 'Transport Plan' to sever communications to the projected OVERLORD battle area. The US Eighth Air Force was involved on a lesser scale as its daylight offensive against the Luftwaffe was maintained. Moreover, by this time the Americans believed that they had found the critical target upon which to concentrate the bomber offensive – Germany's synthetic oil plants. Spaatz's staff had prepared plans for their systematic destruction, and in April Eisenhower sanctioned experimental attacks. With the Allied armies established in France the attacks on oil refineries gathered pace, and as early as 8 June Spaatz informed the Eighth and Fifteenth Air Forces that their primary strategic aim was the denial of Germany's oil supplies. Bomber Command too was committed to this task, with the ten synthetic oil plants in the Ruhr being given as targets.[6]

While the airmen prepared to resume their strategic offensives after the OVERLORD aberration, the soldiers had been thinking on very different lines. Montgomery's Chief of Staff, Major-General Sir Francis De Guingand, later recalled that in early 1944 the Army in England preparing for OVERLORD was giving much thought to the subject of how the heavy bombers could be used in close support, and that while the soldiers appreciated the primary strategic role of the bomber forces they were nevertheless planning to employ them in close support on occasions.[7]

A study was made of the problems involved, and two senior soldiers at the War Office, General Rowell, the Director of Tactical Investigation, and General Crawford, Director of Air, were involved in discussions with the Air Ministry. They met with little enthusiasm, but it is interesting that well before D-Day the Army was considering such questions as accuracy, levels of destruction, appropriate bomb fuses, safety precautions, and the risks of craters causing obstruction to friendly troops.[8]

In Italy, heavy bombers had already appeared over the battlefield in direct support of Allied troops. On 15 February, in support of an attack by 4th Indian Division, they had reduced the monastery at Monte Cassino. Their assistance had been requested again and on 15 March, in close support of New Zealand troops, they had returned to bomb Cassino town (see below). Events in Italy indicated that when confronted with stubborn and formidable German defences Allied soldiers would request heavy bomber support in order to overcome them. This is what occurred in North-West Europe, where such support was not provided without bitter recriminations being made by senior airmen against the Army and its willingness to fight and,

particularly in Normandy, against Montgomery's competence. This
theme underlies the following analysis of how effective heavy bombing was in close support of troops.

The principal tactical advantage derived from employing heavy
bombers against targets within the range of friendly artillery, or beyond
it, was the tremendous weight of high explosive they could deliver in a
comparatively short period of time. The Avro Lancaster, by 1944 the
principal RAF four-engined heavy bomber, and its US counterpart the
B-17 Flying Fortress, had normal individual bomb loads of 14,000 lb
and 6,000 lb respectively.[9] As No.2 ORS observed in 1944, a heavy
bomber formation had an immediate barrage capacity

> out of all comparison with that attainable by any artillery concentration
> that can at present be contemplated.[10]

Twin-engined medium bombers provided a similar advantage, but
lacked the capacity of the heavy bombers. The B-26 Marauder and
B-25 Mitchell, two medium types extensively used by both the
USAAF and RAF, each had individual bomb loads of 4,000 lb.[11]
Unlike heavy bombing, medium bombing was a form of air support
used from early in the war and large numbers of mediums were
included in the Allied tactical air forces. Their principal role was to
bring under attack targets beyond fighter-bomber range, such as headquarters and supply and ammunition dumps, and targets in the battle
area which required pattern bombing, such as gun areas and troop
concentrations.[12]

Mediums bombed in small formations, usually of six aircraft,
releasing their bombs simultaneously with the formation leader. They
flew tighter formations than heavy bombers and usually bombed from
a lower altitude, though in the presence of flak this was rarely lower
than 10,000 feet. Heavy bombers usually bombed in greater numbers
and in looser formation, creating larger bomb patterns. They often
flew at an altitude of 20–25,000 feet but for some close support
missions bombed from 12,000 feet or lower. On such missions RAF
'heavies' carried 500 lb and 1,000 lb bombs. Each bomber had a
carrying capacity of 5½ tons and had 14 bomb hooks, a typical load
being ten 1,000 lb and four 500 lb bombs. Each of the USAAF heavy
bombers had a bomb load of some 2 tons but they had 40 bomb hooks,
and in addition to 500 lb and 1,000 lb bombs could carry 250 lb, 260
lb, and 100 lb bombs as well as 90 lb or clusters of 20 lb fragmentation bombs. A B-17 could thus deliver over two hundred 20 lb
fragmentation bombs as an alternative load.[13]

For close support both heavy and medium bombers were employed tactically either to bomb German 'Fortress' positions with the aim of destroying fixed defences and gun batteries in preparation for Allied assaults, or to support breakthrough operations in the field. The latter took the form of saturation or 'carpet' bombing on the frontage of Allied attacks with the aim of destroying or paralysing the German forward defences to a depth of some 2,000 yards, or of bombing specific areas behind the forward German line in order to neutralise gun areas, sever communications, and isolate the forward German troops from their headquarters and rear echelons. German defence localities on the flanks of a proposed Allied advance were also bombed with the aim of isolating the German troops on the attack frontage and preventing their reinforcement and supply.[14]

There was a significant difference between Allied heavy bombing techniques. The RAF bombed in succession with each bomber aiming individually, usually at a Target Indicator previously laid by a specialist 'Pathfinder' aircraft, and with an airborne 'Master Bomber' directing the crews by radio-telephone. The USAAF bombed in fixed formations, or boxes, of varying size, with only the formation leader aiming his bombs while the rest of the box released at the same time as the leader. The RAF method was slightly more accurate. Operational research proved that an RAF attack resulted in a pattern of bomb strikes much more dense at the centre of an objective than at the periphery, while a US bomber box achieved a fairly even density of strikes – to achieve the cumulative ground pattern of an RAF attack several boxes of US bombers had to have the same aiming point.[15]

Against pinpoint military targets, such as gun positions, heavy bombing proved too inaccurate to be relied upon to achieve destruction. Assessments of bombing accuracy against such targets were made by estimating the displacement in yards of the mean point of impact of the bombs from the aiming point, and the radial standard deviation – a measure of the scatter of bombs within a bomb pattern. The smaller the radial standard deviation, the more concentrated were the bombs around the mean point of impact. Table I shows the accuracy achieved by RAF heavy bombers on ten targets in three close-support operations in Normandy. For these attacks the average radial standard deviation of the bomb pattern was 620 yards, and was found to be of a similar order for USAAF attacks. With this order of accuracy, bomb density at the assigned aiming point and over the whole bomb pattern simply depended upon the number and calibre of the bombs employed.[16]

TABLE I

BOMBING ACCURACY IN NORMANDY

TARGET AREA	CODE	DISPLACEMENT OF MEAN POINT OF IMPACT IN YARDS	RADIAL STANDARD DEVIATION OF BOMB PATTERN IN YARDS
CAUMONT	B	730	750
	E	340	550
	F	360	450
CAEN AREA	1	290	370
	2	390	590
OP. 'GOODWOOD'	A1	100	810
	A2	200	910
	H1	670	560
	H2	610	560
	M	390	680

Operational research found that 100 RAF heavy bombers achieved a density of some 10 bombs per acre at the centre of their bomb pattern but that only 30 per cent of the ground at the centre of the pattern was cratered. In view of the fact that the destructive effect of a high-explosive bomb extended little beyond the crater this seems unimpressive. Despite their greater number of bombs US bombers achieved even less.[17]

The accuracy of medium bombing depended upon the aim of the formation leader and the tightness of the formation's bomb pattern. This varied considerably. Between June and August 1943 mediums of RAF Desert Air Force were bombing point targets with an overall probable radial error of 330 yards, whereas in June 1944 the mediums of the Mediterranean Allied Tactical Air Force (MATAF) were found to be bombing point targets with an overall probable radial error of 170 yards.[18] In fact the radial error of medium bombing was roughly two-thirds that of heavy bombers and, for a given number of bombs, the bomb density on point targets achieved by mediums was generally 2½ times greater than that of heavy bombers. But bomb density in the target area did not necessarily mean the target was likely to be hit. From operational data compiled in the Mediterranean theatre it was calculated that to ensure a 95 per cent chance of a hit on a bridge target occupying 6,000 square feet the mediums of MATAF needed to drop 600 bombs; those of the RAF Desert Air Force were required to drop 2,400 bombs.[19]

It was evidently difficult for mediums to hit such targets as small gun positions, occupying an area of little over 1,000 square feet, and attempts to bomb such targets were wasteful. In North-West Europe the US 9th Bombardment Division reported that medium bombardment was inappropriate for small targets because,

> to guarantee a reasonable probability of destruction, eighteen aircraft will normally have to be assigned, resulting at best in wasting the major part of the bomb load.[20]

That mediums were considered 2½ times more effective than heavy bombers against such targets indicates that neither form of bombing could have been relied upon to destroy them.

DESTRUCTION AND OBSTRUCTION

The use of bombers as a form of siege artillery against troops dug-in in urban areas represented another form of air support. The Cassino bombings, particularly that of the town, offered valuable lessons for those contemplating such employment of heavy bombers further. Between 8.30 a.m. and noon on 15 March 1944 278 heavies and 177 mediums of the Allied Mediterranean strategic and tactical air forces delivered 992 tons of high explosive bombs on the town, where the Allied advance was being held up by stubborn German resistance. This was followed by an eight hour artillery programme for which 890 guns of all calibres fired 195,969 rounds at pre-selected targets.[21] The heaviest concentration of air power and artillery yet seen in Italy, it was in close support of General Freyberg's New Zealand Corps, who were to attack the town immediately after the bombing. A subsequent bomb plot found that 47 per cent of the bombs fell within a mile of the town centre and 53 per cent in the general town area, but despite the weight of air and artillery firepower the attack failed, for two reasons.

The first was the resilience of the German garrison. Some 950 paratroops of First Parachute Division held Cassino on 15 March, supported by a battery of five assault guns. The 2nd Battalion, in the northern part of the town, caught the full weight of the unexpected bombing, and of some 300 men, at least 160 were killed and four assault guns buried under rubble. Some companies were reduced to only a few men and many small parties of troops were isolated by debris and signal communications were cut.[22] Yet, as a result of sheltering in a large cave during a pause between bomber waves, most of the reserve company survived, while others took shelter in deep cellars and the bell-shaped pillboxes that had been sunk at various points in the town. These were of steel, several inches thick, and were intended to accommodate two men. As many as six crowded into them during the bombing and they seem to have offered adequate protection. A subsequent Allied Air Force appreciation reported that

> Bombs falling three to four yards from a pill-box lifted it out of its position without seriously harming the men inside.[23]

Those German troops that survived the bombing were undoubtedly shaken, but such was the quality of the paratroops that they soon recovered and emerged from cover to engage the New Zealanders. More importantly, many of them had ample time to recover – and to dig themselves out from under the debris thrown down upon their shelters – before they were threatened by the New Zealanders' approach.

This leads to the second, and most important, reason for the failure of the attack – that the Army had insisted upon an urban area being bombed. General Ira C. Eaker, Commander of the Allied air forces in the Mediterranean, had sanctioned the bombing reluctantly and doubted its usefulness in such terrain. He warned Freyberg that the resulting debris would obstruct his tanks but was assured that this was acceptable as German armour would also be obstructed and that bulldozers would be used to clear routes,[24] an indication that the soldiers had little conception of the scale of obstruction such bombing would cause.

Instead of the planned advance rate of 100 yards in 10 minutes, the attack of the 25th New Zealand Battalion barely managed 100 yards in an hour as the assault troops tried to advance over or around bomb craters and masses of debris. Their supporting tanks of 19th Armoured Regiment fared even worse. As Eaker predicted, they could not negotiate the huge piles of rubble, and attempts by their crews to use pick and shovel or to use tanks to ram the obstacles availed little. By evening the attack was far behind schedule. The infantry had broken into the town but, while two troops of tanks were caught up amid the ruins, the rest of the armour was jammed along the only two roads leading into the town from the north. This congestion prevented engineers getting forward to clear rubble, and the single company that did reach the town could not use their unarmoured bulldozers because of close range German fire. The extent of the rubble was such that one Brigadier subsequently estimated that even without German resistance it would have taken 48 hours for bulldozers to clear a single route through the town.[25] Attempts by two further infantry battalions to overcome German resistance failed.[26]

Bombing Cassino had been counter-productive. The assault troops were impeded, their supporting armour prevented from deploying, and the surviving German troops provided with a series of new, well-concealed positions. The bombing may have enabled the New Zealanders to break into Cassino with fewer casualties than otherwise – the 41 sustained by the 25th Battalion were not excessive for such an attack. The obstruction it had caused, however, prevented them from exploiting the single most important advantage that bombing could bring to the attack – the initial disruption of the German defence. Eaker's doubts had been vindicated, and he afterwards asserted that heavy bombers should never be employed in close support when an adequate tactical air force was available.[27]

Cassino proved that bombing was effective in causing obstruction and the scale of bombardment necessary to achieve a complete blockage of a 100 yard circle in various forms of terrain, particularly in built-up areas, was not prohibitive. Five bombs per acre, the product of fifty British bombers, would suffice in heavily built-up areas, whereas twice this might be needed to cause obstruction in close country with villages and woods. In open country areas and outlying suburbs no less than forty bombs per acre and 400 aircraft would be required.[28] (See Appendix.) However, the resultant obstruction threatened to be more disadvantageous to an attacker needing to make rapid progress than to the defender. Cassino inevitably became the byword of those senior airmen opposed to meeting Army demands for heavy bomber support,[29] but it is remarkable that after Cassino the soldiers still requested heavy bombing of urban areas in the path of their attacks. When such bombing was carried out it proved of little advantage.

Operation CHARNWOOD, an attack by the 3rd British, 59th British, and 3rd Canadian Divisions supported by two armoured brigades, was intended to clear the city of Caen as far as the west bank of the river Orne and to seize the crossings. The first use of heavy bombers to support an offensive in Normandy, it exceeded the errors of Cassino.

By mid-June 1944 there was much air force criticism of Montgomery and his failure to secure Caen and the Caen–Falaise airfield sites which the airmen had considered vital. Concern was voiced by both Coningham and Tedder at the Allied Air

Commanders' Conference at Stanmore during 14–16 June, and the former demanded that the Army press on with more urgency.[30] Leigh-Mallory had already rejected Montgomery's proposal to drop the 1st Airborne Division near Caen to loosen German resistance but, anxious to assist the Army, he flew to Montgomery's headquarters on 14 June and suggested instead a bombardment of the German positions by heavy and medium bombers on a front of 5,000 yards behind which the Army could advance. This proposal was accepted with enthusiasm, but a conference at General Dempsey's Second Army Headquarters at Bayeux to discuss the plan on the following day was broken up by the arrival of Tedder and Coningham, the latter furious that he had not been consulted. Moreover, neither strategic air force, whose representatives were present, favoured the operation. The task was considered the responsibility of the tactical air forces, and Leigh-Mallory was only just dissuaded by his staff from resigning immediately in protest.[31] While acknowledging that the Army had not prepared its case well, De Guingand later admitted his disappointment, as the soldiers had been 'most anxious to try out the machinery'.[32]

Three weeks later, with Second Army still held before Caen, Montgomery requested heavy bombing of the city's Northern approaches and its suburbs in support of CHARNWOOD. Eisenhower was present at the Air Commanders' Conference on 7 July which agreed to the bombers being employed that evening. Tedder had objected, and the AEAF historical record noted his view that the heavy bombers should not be employed in the ground battle except in exceptional circumstances to prevent a crisis. Tedder's fear was that agreeing to the Army's request would encourage the soldiers to make further demands for heavy bomber support, with the result that the strategic forces would be unduly diverted from their proper tasks.[33]

It has been suggested that the decision to employ the bombers was born of the need finally to secure Caen, which had actually been a British objective for D-Day.[34] Substance is given to this view by the fact that the bombing targets were the same as those proposed earlier but rejected by Coningham and Tedder not only on principle but because it was felt that there was little in the proposed bombing zone for them to hit.[35]

The German defence was centred on a belt of mutually supporting positions in several villages in an arc three miles north and north-west of Caen, held mostly by the extremely tough 12th SS Panzer Division. When, on the evening of 7 July, 467 aircraft of Bomber Command delivered 2,276 tons of bombs these strongpoints were not targeted. Instead a rectangular bombing zone 4,000 yards wide and 1,500 yards deep, including the northern part of the city and an open area to the north-west, was hit. This was to minimise the risk of bombs falling on friendly troops, as none were to fall within 6,000 yards of the forward British positions, but meant that those strongpoints immediately in the path of the attack were not touched and had to be neutralised by artillery. Moreover, a forecast of adverse weather at the time of the attack, 4.20 a.m. on 8 July, meant that the bombing occurred between 9.50 and 10.30 p.m. on the previous evening thus giving the German troops six hours in which to recover from the worst effects of demoralisation and disruption.[36]

Poor targeting and timing ensured that the bombing did little to assist the pace of the attack or reduce casualties, some British battalions losing 25 per cent of their strength in the two days of fighting needed to break through the defended villages to the outskirts of Caen. On 9 July troops of 3rd British and 3rd Canadian Divisions met in the city, but armoured units attempting to rush the bridges were impeded by the huge masses of masonry thrown down by the bombs and against which even bulldozing proved ineffective. During a subsequent investigation, conducted by Professor Zuckerman and Air Commodore Kingston-McCloughry, the staff of 3rd British Division stressed that bomb craters and rubble had blocked the direct route into Caen and had impeded their advance. They questioned the decision to bomb the city and did not believe that the bombing had destroyed any German positions, as their troops had found no German dead or destroyed equipment.[37] Canadian and British infantry officers told No.2 ORS that the bombing had made Caen harder to take by denying access to armour while giving cover for German snipers and restricting the number of entrances that the Germans had to defend.[38]

It is not clear how many German troops in the city were killed by bombing. One prisoner stated that a headquarters had been destroyed, and others were found still stunned by vibratory shock two days later; but the ORS investigation suggested that German casualties had been relatively light. The urban area, occupied by the 31st Luftwaffe Field Regiment, had been struck by some 300 aircraft whose bombs fell at a density of 10 to 15 per acre in the suburbs and 5 per acre in the town. Here the ORS found the bodies of only three German troops, although more were thought to be buried under rubble, but no destroyed vehicles or equipment. The open area, struck by about 160 aircraft whose bombs fell at a density of 10 per acre, had been held by part of the 26th SS Panzer Grenadier Regiment supported by 15 assault guns of 21st Panzer with about 40 vehicles and some flak guns. Here were found the bodies of two German troops, one wrecked 88mm gun, and ten destroyed or damaged vehicles.[39]

The bombing certainly prevented those German troops in the urban area being supplied and reinforced, yet they resisted for longer than those units holding the approaches to Caen, mainly because the resulting obstruction denied them a route of withdrawal – here too the bombing may have been counterproductive. This obstruction also prevented a rapid seizure of the Orne bridges (all of which were found to have been blown) and further advance into the city's Eastern suburbs. Uncoordinated with the ground assault, the CHARNWOOD bombing was futile and, as many French civilians were killed, tragic. It is best summed up by the Zuckerman–McCloughry report which warned that it was

> idle to expect the best the air can provide by calling in heavy bombers as a frill to a ground plan already made.[40]

Closer air-ground co-ordination was seen when Bomber Command made its last raid of the war in close support of British troops. As in CHARNWOOD, the target was urban, and obstruction caused similar problems for the assault troops. The bombing in support of Operation WIDGEON, the assault on the town of Wesel by 1st Commando Brigade during the crossing of the Rhine on 24 March 1945, saw perhaps the finest precision bombing carried out in close support by Bomber Command. Two raids were made on Wesel on 23 March. In the first, between 5.31 and 5.41 p.m., 77 Lancasters dropped 435 tons of bombs. In the second, closely co-ordinated with the Commando assault, 184 bombers dropped nearly 1,000 tons between 10.35 and 10.43 p.m. This latter raid was intended to blast a way into the northern part of the town for the Commandos, who were waiting only 2,000 yards from the bombers' aiming point.[41]

Due to the proximity of the Commandos, meticulous precautions were applied by the bombers. No bombs were to fall after 10.45 p.m. and the Master Bomber was to permit bombing by reference to the marker previously laid by Pathfinders only when completely satisfied. No crews were to bomb unless they had positively identified the Target Indicators. Consequently the raid was very accurate, with no instance of short bombing. Soon afterwards the Commandos attacked. By 3 a.m. on 24 March they had penetrated into the town and by daylight the entire Brigade was established in Wesel. There was only one instance of determined resistance, when the German garrison commander and his staff, who had sheltered in cellars during the bombing, defended their headquarters. In this action the German commander was killed. In all, 330 German troops surrendered in Wesel, which was secured with only 44 Commando casualties.[42]

Yet it was not the bombing that had prevented a costly urban battle. Of the 3,000 German troops defending the Wesel area only 350 were in the town itself, mostly low-grade *Volksturm* of poor morale, and the number of prisoners suggests that few had been killed by the bombing. Few showed signs of bomb-shock, such as inability to coordinate limbs or uncontrolled shaking, and many had sheltered in cellars. The majority of German troops in the area, for the most part better quality, was deployed outside the town, untouched by the bombing. Consequently, a British Army study later admitted that bombing '...was not essential to the success of the operation'.[43] Moreover, the obstruction made movement for the Commandos difficult and very slow, particularly at night. Officers reported that they lost their bearings as landmarks that they had been trained to recognise on maps and models no longer existed, and movement within the town had to be by compass.[44] It was the poor quality of the garrison that enabled the town to be taken quickly. Against determined troops bombing Wesel could have produced another Cassino.

Despite their limited effectiveness against pinpoint targets, heavy and medium bombers were consistently directed upon them when attacking German defence systems or 'Fortress' positions, such as the Channel ports. Targets were mostly gun or battery positions, but success was negligible.

On the Mediterranean island of Pantelleria in June 1943 6,400 tons of bombs were dropped upon a target area occupying only eight square miles in 5,218 heavy, medium and fighter-bomber sorties, but of some 130 guns in the defences only 16 were subsequently found to have been destroyed or damaged. The German coastal batteries in the British assault area in Normandy were each targeted by 100 heavy bombers and at least 5,000 tons of bombs were dropped on 5 and 6 June 1944, but of 116 guns on seven beach sectors only three were later found to have been destroyed or damaged by bombs. At Le Havre much of the 9,631 tons dropped by Bomber Command in 1,846 sorties during September 1944 was directed at reported German battery positions, but subsequent investigation showed that of 76 German guns bombs had accounted for only eight. In the same month at Boulogne 710 tons were aimed at batteries, but bombs destroyed or damaged only six guns out of a total of 110. At Walcheren the German gun positions in the area assaulted by British Commandos were the target of some 5,500 bombs during October 1944, but of the 26 guns only two were hit.[45]

To bomb such targets with any hope of achieving destruction was prohibitively expensive in terms of sorties and bomb tonnage. Pantelleria proved that attacks equivalent to 70–100 heavy bombers per battery could achieve a maximum reduction in firepower of only 10–15 per cent of guns in concrete casemates. Against guns in the open, the same scale of attack could only put 25 per cent of the guns out of action, some permanently and some for periods of up to six hours.[46] At Boulogne, for 840 bombs dropped by mediums, only one gun had been destroyed and two slightly damaged. Yet No.2 ORS subsequently admitted that the RAF had bombed

> as accurately and effectively as they could be expected to ... and produced as much material damage as might be expected.

No battery had been put out of action at Boulogne by bombing, and it was calculated that to put half the guns in an open battery, regardless of size, out of action, 180 heavy bombers or, since they were more accurate, 150 mediums were needed. To ensure destruction of all the guns, three or four times these numbers of aircraft would have been required.[47] After the assault on Walcheren, it was calculated that 720 heavy bombers delivering some 9,360 bombs would have been required to secure a 50 per cent chance of destroying a casemated battery of 6 guns.[48]

This was due not only to inaccuracy, but also to the invulnerability of gun positions protected by concrete and steel to the bombs available in 1943–45. At Le Havre the weight of air attack had been equivalent to 20–40 heavy bombers unloading 100–200 tons on each of 12 batteries. But even direct hits had only slightly damaged the protection, up to 3 feet of reinforced concrete, of covered gun positions, and a British Bombing Analysis Unit later reported that nowhere had bombing hindered the normal working of the fortress.[49] On 25 August 1944 Bomber Command sent 316 aircraft to bomb eight German coastal batteries in support of the US VIII Corps assault on the defended port of Brest, but it was later found that damage had been slight, with even the heaviest calibre bombs having little effect. The US Official History states that the Brest defences were not vulnerable to air attack, that no concrete emplacements had been so destroyed, and it describes how a 12,000 lb RAF 'Tallboy' bomb had made a huge crater 200 yards from a German gun emplacement yet had failed to damage it.[50]

A British Army ORS study of close support bombing noted in 1945 of the Walcheren operation that the bombing of the German batteries was expected to destroy many of the guns, and somewhat bitterly observed that the lessons of earlier operations had been ignored, despite the results of previous experience being available to those responsible for planning the operation.[51]

The limitations of bombing when directed against widely spaced or well-protected military targets was apparently never appreciated by the planners of such operations. By the time of Walcheren control of the strategic air forces had reverted to the Allied Chiefs of Staff, allowing the airmen to reassert their strategic targeting priorities, and there has been much Army bitterness that consequently the Walcheren batteries did not receive a sufficient weight of bombs. Major-General Essame observes that in October 1944 Bomber Command directed 21,930 sorties and some 56,612 tons of bombs against strategic targets, whereas only 1,616 sorties and 9,728 tons were provided in Army support. Citing the effectiveness of the Bomber Command attacks on the Normandy defences on D-Day, he suggests that the strategic bombing of Germany could have been suspended for a few days in order to enable the Walcheren forts to be dealt with adequately.[52]

Yet the bombing of the Normandy defences had been effective not because of the damage inflicted or the number of guns destroyed, but because the bombing had occurred shortly before the Allied assault. The German batteries had not been destroyed, but they had been prevented from firing at their full effectiveness; if bombs did not destroy guns they at least kept the German gunners in their shelters, severed communications, and disrupted fire-control apparatus at this crucial time. In 1945 the British Joint Technical Warfare Committee reported of the fire support for the Normandy landings that

> bombing had reduced the potential rate of fire of the coastal batteries ... while naval gunfire was the only means available for producing a further appreciable but temporary reduction in enemy fire.[53]

But this was quite pointless unless immediately exploited by Allied ground action. In their investigation of the air support at Boulogne No.2 ORS concluded that the only worthwhile object of bombing in periods before an assault was launched was the attempted destruction of German guns, as any damage to fortifications could be repaired before the assault while any short-lived morale effect upon the German garrison could not be exploited.[54] Given the inability of the air forces to destroy guns, well known to the ORS, this amounted to saying that bombing was only cost-effective when closely followed by ground action, and that bombs dropped in raids uncoordinated with such action were wasted.

The operational evidence regarding destruction does indeed suggest that the only advantage bombing could have brought in support of operations against fixed defences was that of causing temporary disruption by drenching the target with bombs. The tragedy of Walcheren was not that the RAF failed to bomb the batteries sufficiently in the days before the assault, but that the one crucial raid, when they were to be bombed shortly before the British Commando assault on 1 November 1944, was prevented by adverse weather. In the event the German batteries, with communications damaged in earlier raids repaired, came into action and sank or badly damaged 19 of the 27 naval craft supporting the landing and inflicted 458 casualties.[55]

By contrast, Operation WELLHIT, the assault on Boulogne by 3rd Canadian Infantry Division between 17 and 22 September 1944, indicated that heavy bombing could be effective against German defence works when closely co-ordinated with a ground assault. The bombing was an integral part of the assault plan which intended to exploit fully its morale and disruptive effect. Brigadier Rockingham, commanding 9th Canadian Infantry Brigade and tasked with the capture of the heavily defended Mont Lambert feature, was initially reluctant to have heavy bomber support. Concerned with the risk of 'short bombing', and that the Germans would have time to recover and man their weapons before his men had reached the objective, he suggested to General Simonds, commanding Canadian II Corps, that the approach could be made closer with just artillery support. Simonds responded by assigning to 9th Brigade an RAF Group Captain, who would be in contact with the bombers during the attack. It was also arranged for the bombers, having dropped their loads, to fly over the German positions once again with their bomb doors open to ensure that the German troops remained in cover. Rockingham later admitted of the attack by 692 heavy bombers which preceded the assault by his battalions that the control system and the 'dummy run' certainly worked; the German troops remained in their shelters, enabling the Canadian battalions to approach with fewer casualties.[56]

The time taken by the Canadian battalions to clear their objectives depended upon such factors as defence strength and the extent of minefields and other obstacles, while some of the casualties sustained by the attackers were caused by fire from areas adjacent to the objective. Nevertheless a quantitative indication of how the bombing contributed to the success of the assault is given by the experience of the attacking battalions. The St. Martin area was bombed and the Stormont, Dundas and Glengarry Highlanders secured its southern part in less than half a day with about four casualties, while the Queen's Own Rifles secured the northern part in a day without sustaining any. By contrast, the Régiment de la Chaudière took five days and 58 casualties to secure Bon Secours and the North Shore Regiment three days and 54 casualties to secure La Tresorerie; neither target had been bombed.[57]

The effectiveness of the air support at Boulogne was investigated by No.2 ORS shortly after the assault. Those battalions that had received heavy bomber support were enthusiastic, particularly the Stormont, Dundas, and Glengarry Highlanders who had been able to take their first objectives within an hour of the bombing. The bombing had caused few German casualties, but it had kept the defenders in their shelters at the critical time. Some 9,500 German troops surrendered, and all those subsequently questioned by the ORS stated that they had sheltered from the bombs and had made no attempt to man their weapons until the aircraft had departed. Officer prisoners described how bombing had made control and cohesion very difficult, with telephone lines cut and communication dependent upon wireless, while others told how bomb craters had enabled the Canadian troops to approach their positions unseen. Whereas some prisoners stated that the Canadian artillery had prevented them from recovering from the effects of the bombing, the ORS emphasised that the disruptive and morale effect of bombing was only temporary, and had to be followed-up rapidly by the assault troops. They confirmed of the defenders that 'Everybody in the bombed areas was severely shaken and those of poor morale became worse', but also warned that 'Those of better morale all said that the effect was only temporary and that they regained heart'.[58]

BOMBING IN SUPPORT OF BREAKTHROUGH OPERATIONS

One limiting factor to the effectiveness of heavy and medium bombing of German defence localities in close support of attacks in open terrain was the paucity of targets offered by troops usually well dispersed. This meant that the number of German casualties and amount of equipment destroyed or damaged was unlikely to be decisive, and that sufficient troops and equipment were likely to survive to offer effective resistance.

Heavy and medium bombers were first employed against such field positions in Italy in a defensive rather than offensive context. In February 1944 heavy, medium and fighter-bombers were committed to support Allied troops defending the Anzio beachhead against determined German counterattacks. On 17 February they flew 724 daylight sorties, delivering 833 tons of bombs upon German positions and troop concentrations in the Anzio–Nettuno battle area.[59] This effort, supplementing artillery and naval gunfire, was considered by the Allies to have been very effective, and the US Fifth Army later reported that the bombing kept the German troops pinned to the ground, retarded their movement and prevented the full power of their attack from developing. Moreover, the German artillery fire had ceased as the gunners went into and stayed in their dugouts.[60]

The bombing obviously had an impressive morale effect but, in fighting a defensive battle, Allied troops had little opportunity to learn to what extent bombing had inflicted casualties and damage. In fact neither had been as great as observers believed. General Erich Ritter von Pohl, commanding all German anti-aircraft artillery in Southern Italy, witnessed the bombing of the German positions around Nettuno and later recalled that the density of the bombing led observers to expect the complete annihilation of the units under attack, but on entering the position shortly afterwards it was found that most of the artillery pieces, machine guns, and observation instruments were intact, and that even the effect on morale wore off after the initial experience.[61]

By August 1944 the Allies had sufficient experience to be aware of this phenomenon. This is shown in an assessment by No.2 ORS of one of the Normandy operations – TOTALISE. Launched on the night of 7/8 August 1944, TOTALISE was an attempt by II Canadian Corps to reach Falaise and was supported by 642 RAF heavy bombers dropping 3,460 tons of bombs on to five German defence localities flanking the attack. Afterwards, using as examples the known German defence strength in two villages in the battle, No.2 ORS outlined the level of casualties and destruction likely to be caused by bombing. La Hogue was held by 250 troops supported by seven guns deployed at a density of some 125 troops and three guns per 1,000 square yards. The ORS calculated that, targeted in two raids each of 100 heavy bombers, bombing would have caused about 30 German casualties and destroyed one gun. Rocquancourt was defended by some 700 troops supported by 26 guns deployed at a density of 175 troops and seven guns per 1,000 square yards. If targeted in four raids each by 50 heavy bombers, the ORS calculated the bombs would have caused 45 casualties and destroyed at most two guns.[62]

Another limiting factor was that bombing could only assist the initial break-in phase of an attack. German troops beyond the bombing zone remained unaffected and success depended upon how rapidly resistance in the bombing zone could be overcome before the arrival of German reserves to seal the break-in. Much depended upon maintaining the momentum of the attack, but experience proved that this could be eroded by the survival in the bombed area relatively few troops, able to offer resistance. Appropriate bomb types were another problem. Crater bombing could impede German movement but also jeopardise the advance of Allied troops, while fragmentation bombing risked the German reserves being insufficiently obstructed.

That heavy bombing could be negated by defence in depth was seen in Operation GOODWOOD, an attempted breakout from the Orne bridgehead in Normandy by three British armoured divisions along a 'tank-run' blasted through German defences by saturation bombing. GOODWOOD was supported by the heaviest air strike yet provided in close support: 1,512 heavy bombers and 343 mediums,[63] delivering a total of 6,000 one thousand pound and 9,600 five hundred pound bombs.[64] Montgomery's request for maximum air support was supported by Eisenhower, and granted by the senior airmen, including Tedder and Coningham, on the assumption that this was to be the breakout from Normandy. That this did not occur caused much recrimination against Montgomery, and left not only the senior airmen but also Eisenhower feeling that they had been duped.[65]

Bomber Command had 942 aircraft deliver 5,000 tons of crater bombs on villages flanking the tank run, which were cleared by infantry, while 650 tons of instantaneous-fused bombs, to avoid cratering, were released on Cagny, the most strongly held village in the tank-run. The latter, some 1,500 yards wide and stretching for 4 miles south of the bridgehead beyond the Caen–Vimont railway to the Bourgébus ridge, was the target of fragmentation bombing by mediums of the US 9th Bomber Command. These were to neutralise the German anti-tank guns, as the British tanks were not supported by infantry and, towards the end of its length, the tank-run lacked suitable terrain for fire-and-movement tactics. By this method advancing tanks were covered by others, usually hull-down behind a crest, providing fire support, but the last 4,000 yards of the tank-run lacked crest cover. South of the tank-run 570 B-24 Liberator heavy bombers of the Eighth Air Force targeted the main German gun area with 1,429 tons of fragmentation bombs, while beyond the heavy and medium bombing zones RAF fighter-bombers attacked German reserves and artillery.[66]

The bombing occurred in three waves between 5.30 and 8.30 a.m. on 18 July 1944. Unexpected by the Germans, it inflicted considerable destruction. In the Colombelles suburb of Caen, flanking the tank-run, Bomber Command's 1,000 lb bombs struck German infantry and anti-tank gun positions, and large numbers of damaged 75 mm guns and German dead were later found.[67] Here a regiment of the 16th Luftwaffe Division was overrun without serious resistance, with many of the prisoners taken suffering from bomb shock. When being escorted to POW cages many had to stop and sit by the road to recover before they could walk in a straight line, and 70 per cent of them remained stone deaf for 24 hours.[68] Similarly dazed German troops were found by the infantry clearing the villages flanking the tank run.

At Cuverville the Mk.IV tank battalion of 21st Panzer Division and Tiger tanks of the 503rd Heavy Tank Battalion were caught undispersed by the carpet of 500 lb and 1,000 lb bombs. They were part of a battle group commanded by Colonel von Luck, who later recalled that even some of the 56 ton Tigers were overturned by blast and that craters 30 feet wide made the area impassable.[69] Later examination by an RAF Bombing Analysis Unit found 15 tanks, armoured cars, and many transport vehicles in various states of destruction, some half-buried in bomb craters. The 11 acre orchard had received 145 bombs, about 13 per acre, which had caused multiple ground shocks, blast waves, and the movement of debris of the order of 40,000 tons.[70]

British tank crews, who advanced at 7.45 a.m., later told No.2 ORS that the bombing in the first part of the tank-run had been effective and that they had not been delayed by craters. They were unanimous that the bombing had been of particular assistance in frightening and dazing the German anti-tank gun crews.[71] In fact German gunners were found still sheltering in slit trenches and were killed by grenades, this was later confirmed by the following British infantry who discovered the bodies. This emphasis on the morale effect of the air attack is important, as no evidence was found that German anti-tank guns had been destroyed by bombs. Only three guns were found in the area, and all had been destroyed by tank shells.[72]

Yet the German defence was not sufficiently neutralised to allow a rapid advance. In Cagny, five 88 mm guns and several tanks survived to knock out 16 British tanks and a regiment had to be left to screen them; further south the British armour also came under fire from anti-tank guns positioned in the villages targeted by mediums. Only one of these had totally escaped the bombing, but in each case destruction had been partial only and sufficient guns survived to hold the British armour. German fire also came from nearby woods, and it was later calculated that the bombing, concentrated upon the villages, had insufficiently covered these strongpoints.[73]

It was 11 a.m. before the first three miles of the tank-run had been cleared, and its final stretch, where most of the British tank casualties occurred, was not reached until ten hours after the bombing. By then the British armour was being held by anti-tank guns on the Bourgébus ridge and by German tanks which had moved up from beyond the bombing zone firing from hull-down positions on the crest and able to block every offensive move with their superior range. British tank crews told the ORS that the last stretch of the tank-run should not have been bombed until they were ready to attack it, and advocated that bombing should take place in a series of waves preceding an advance. In fact the tactical air forces had offered to return in the afternoon to bomb the Bourgébus ridge, which at the extreme range of British artillery was an obvious air target, but the Staff of British Second Army refused on the grounds that by then their tanks should have reached it.[74]

This highlights the dilemma facing the planners of such operations. Staggered bombing might have been of more assistance to the attackers, but increased the risk of them penetrating into areas prior to a bomber strike and incurring casualties through short-bombing, while to halt a successful advance in order to await a prearranged air strike risked the loss of valuable momentum. The solution was the provision of tactical air support by fighter-bombers able to respond immediately to requests for support as the battle progressed. In GOODWOOD the British tank crews were denied this. They could not call down the RAF's rocket-firing Typhoons which were overhead because their only contact car had been knocked out and the RAF controller wounded. It is a reflection on the low priority accorded to this form of immediate support, while the provision of only one communications link reveals how little consideration had been given to a possible need for such support after the bombing.[75]

When GOODWOOD ended two days later only seven miles had been gained, while British casualties totalled 4,011. Tank losses amounted to 493 or 36 per cent of the total of 1,369 available.[76] Harris observed that he had dropped a thousand tons of bombs to advance the Army one mile, and that at that rate it would take him 600,000 tons to get them to Berlin.[77] Eisenhower was also heard to remark that the Allies could hardly expect to advance through France expending a thousand tons of bombs per mile.[78] Such remarks took little account of the depth of the German defence confronting GOODWOOD. This had been seriously underestimated by the Second Army staff, who believed that the depth of the German defence extended for only four miles, and consisted of the 16th Luftwaffe Division and some 1,000 troops and 50 tanks of 21st Panzer, with the depleted 12th SS Panzer as the only reserve.

Instead there were five belts of defences with a depth of ten miles including villages strongly held by companies of infantry supported by anti-tank guns and tanks and a main gun line of 90 dual-purpose heavy anti-aircraft/anti-tank guns. Further fire support was provided by 194 field guns and 272 six-barrelled mortars, while in reserve were 45 Panther tanks of 1st SS Panzer Division and two battle groups of 12th SS Panzer Division each with 40 tanks.[79] Without the bombing GOODWOOD could hardly have penetrated as far as it did. Against a defence of such depth however even the heaviest bombing could not be decisive, and GOODWOOD failed because it could be contained even after the initial break-in.

In contrast, Operation COBRA succeeded in breaking out from the Normandy beachhead because of the lack of depth of the German defences opposite US forces in the St.Lô sector. COBRA was intended to breach the German defence line five miles west of St.Lô in an attack by three infantry divisions of the US VII Corps on a front of 6,000 yards preceded by saturation bombing of an area measuring 3,000 by 7,000 yards south of the Périer–St.Lô road. This air effort was to consist of 1,500 US heavy bombers delivering high-explosive and fragmentation bombs in three waves each over a 15 minute period, followed by a 30 minute attack by 396 mediums delivering 500 lb general purpose and 260 lb fragmentation bombs. In addition over 700 fighter-bombers in two waves, each wave attacking for about 20 minutes, were to attack with high-explosive, fragmentation, napalm and white phosphorus bombs.[80]

Of the 30,000 Germans in the attack sector only 5,000 were combat troops and positioned near the front. Some 3,200 were of General

Bayerlein's Panzer Lehr Division and attached parachute regiment, holding a front of about three miles in a series of tank/infantry/anti-tank gun strongpoints. Panzer Lehr, depleted by previous fighting, had only some 40 combat-ready tanks, and the depth of the defence did not exceed 4 miles. In reserve there were only several infantry companies and a few tanks.[81]

Despite poor air-ground co-ordination causing heavy casualties to US troops through short-bombing, the air strike proved effective, particularly in the destruction wreaked upon German troops. This was because Panzer Lehr was caught unusually concentrated in the bombing zone. COBRA was set for 1 p.m. on 24 July 1944 and an unexpected postponement came too late to prevent over 300 heavy bombers and three fighter-bomber groups dropping 685 tons of bombs. Only 15 per cent of the bombs were on target, and some fell short causing casualties to US troops, but Panzer Lehr suffered 350 casualties and lost ten armoured vehicles in the bombing and subsequent fighting. Bayerlein, convinced that a major US attack had been repulsed, moved more troops and tanks into the forward area in anticipation of a renewed US offensive. Their positions almost exactly corresponded to the bombing zone when COBRA was renewed the following day.[82]

On 25 July 1,490 B-17s and B-24s delivered over 3,370 tons of bombs, with over 50 per cent falling on target, while 380 mediums and over 550 fighter-bombers also attacked. Some three per cent of the bombs delivered by heavy bombers and some medium loads fell short, causing disproportionately high losses among the concentrated US troops, but, according to Bayerlein, Panzer Lehr was decimated. He subsequently described how the bomb carpets unrolled in great rectangles, and with direct hits knocked out half his flak guns while silencing the rest. After an hour his communications, including radio, were cut, and he estimated that some 70 per cent of his troops were out of action – dead, wounded, crazed or numbed. All his forward tanks were knocked out, and the roads were rendered impassable.[83] Panzer Lehr had some 1,000 casualties on 25 July, Bayerlein later asserting that 50 per cent of them were caused by bombing and 30 per cent by the integrated US artillery fire. He also noted the effect of the bombing on the morale of his men, saying that many survivors soon surrendered to the US troops or abandoned their positions for the rear. Command and control broke down and communications became dependent upon motorcycle messengers whose journeys were disrupted by craters and roving fighter-bombers.[84]

Craters also slowed the progress of the US troops, but so did stubborn pockets of German resistance. Bayerlein may have exaggerated the effects of the bombing, for his account apparently does less than justice to his men. The history of the US 30th Infantry Division, one of those spearheading the VII Corps attack, is even somewhat dismissive of what the bombing had achieved. It acknowledges that some German troops were shaken and some damage inflicted, but most had adequate shelters and emerged to engage the advancing US troops with the usual combination of dug-in tanks and infantry.[85] That the short-bombings may have soured the appreciation of the US troops for the heavy bomber support is understandable. Moreover, many had expected the weight of air attack to eliminate all resistance, which was unrealistic.[86] Nevertheless, American accounts do confirm that 25 July was a day of hard fighting, by the end of which VII Corps had advanced less than two miles.[87]

Yet the back of the German defence was broken, and the limited progress of VII Corps could be exploited because beyond the Périers–St.Lô road there was no organised German defence zone, only a vacuum. With the US armour committed to the attack on 26 July, preceded by further medium bomber strikes and supported by fighter-bombers patrolling the main roads, an advance developed which within three days threatened to turn the left flank of the German forces in Normandy.[88]

Five days after COBRA Operation BLUECOAT, a thrust by British Second Army with the object of securing Vire and the 1,100 foot Mont Pinçon, indicated that bombing, quickly exploited, was of tactical value in assisting troops to secure limited objectives in open terrain. Opposing Second Army were three German infantry divisions, unsupported by tanks but well dug-in on the slopes and ridges of a terrain favouring defence. Bomber Command sent 692 aircraft to support the attack, launched on 30 July 1944, but cloud over the target permitted only 377 aircraft to bomb and only two of the six assigned target areas were covered.[89] The German positions facing the 43rd and 50th British Infantry Divisions were not bombed and neither progressed much beyond their start lines.

The 15th Infantry Division attacked at 7 a.m., before the bombing, when two battalions without timed artillery support but accompanied by tanks secured the first objectives of Sept Vents and Lutain Wood within two hours. Each battalion had about 80 casualties. The bombing occurred between 9 and 10 a.m. and was followed by an attack on the high ground at Les Loges by 2nd Argyll & Sutherland

Highlanders and tanks of 3rd Scots Guards, and on Hervieux village by 10th Highland Light Infantry and tanks of 4th Grenadier Guards. Each assault was preceded by a timed artillery programme and by midday both objectives were taken. But this time the casualties were at least 43 per cent less. One of the objectives was not directly bombed but the casualties to the assault troops were only 35; the other battalion whose objective had been directly bombed had only 20 casualties.[90]

In the afternoon the final objective, Point 309, was attacked. The inflexibility of prearranged bomber support caused the assault troops to wait some hours for an airstrike timed for between 4 and 5 p.m. While waiting, 3rd Scots Guards lost 12 tanks to German self-propelled guns. Tank crews later interviewed by No.2 ORS were critical of this imposed delay, but the bombing appears to have brought dividends. When the tanks of the Coldstream Guards and infantry of 2nd Glasgow Highlanders attacked they made such progress that the timed artillery support was cancelled as unnecessary. By 6 p.m. the tanks were on the objective, followed an hour later by the infantry, who had only 35 casualties. British tank losses in support of 15th Division totalled 50, including 12 lost to mines and the 12 lost by 3rd Scots Guards while waiting for the bombers. Of the remaining 26 tank losses most were caused by German anti-tank guns firing from beyond the bombing zone for, as in GOODWOOD, tank crews found German anti-tank gunners still sheltering in their trenches after the bombing. A subsequent British Army study of the 15th Division's attack acknowledged that the casualties were low compared with similar attacks in Normandy.[91]

SHORT BOMBINGS

Many heavy bomber support operations were marred by aircraft inadvertently releasing bombs over friendly troops. Such short bombings invariably caused heavy casualties as, unlike their enemy, dug-in and dispersed for defence, Allied troops were concentrated and often in the open waiting to attack. They were subjected to short-bombing on five occasions, the resulting casualties being some 339 men killed and 1,245 wounded (see Appendix).[92]

Apart from killed and wounded, many troops suffered concussion and shock. During COBRA General Hobbs' US 30th Infantry Division, which suffered short-bombings on both 24 and 25 July, reported 164 cases of such 'combat exhaustion.' Morale could be severely affected and confidence in the air forces eroded. When the 30th Division was held by a German strongpoint on 25 July, General Collins, commanding VII Corps, suggested a further medium bomber strike. Hobbs, unwilling to risk more short-bombing, refused and warned Collins that any further such incidents and the troops would be finished.[93] For the rest of the war Hobbs was opposed to his Division receiving heavy bomber support.[94] During TOTALISE some Allied guns actually fired on the errant bombers, and troops were heard to cheer as hits were scored.[95]

Short-bombings were the consequence of insufficient integration and co-ordination of air and ground planning. That there was a lack of adequate liaison, mutual understanding, or even sympathy, between air and ground staffs was seen during the planning for COBRA, when such a fundamental question as the bombers' approach to the target was subject to misunderstanding. At a conference to discuss the air support held on 19 July General Bradley, commanding US First Army, advocated a parallel approach and that his troops be withdrawn 800 yards. The airmen wanted a perpendicular approach because a lateral bombing run would lead the bombers over German flak. They also wanted the troops withdrawn 3,000 yards. Soldiers were understandably reluctant to relinquish hard-won ground, and a compromise was reached whereby the troops would withdraw 1,200 yards while the heavy bombers and mediums were to bomb no closer to them than 1,450 yards. But no assurances were given as to the bombers' direction of approach. In fact the bombers made perpendicular approaches on both 24 and 25 July, leading Bradley to accuse the air command of a serious breach of good faith. [96]

Similar lack of commonality existed between the British Army and RAF Bomber Command. Charles Carrington, the Army's Liaison Officer at Bomber Command, refers to the RAF's insistence that the Army accept cratering on some operations as insolence, because of the implication that, if the heavy bombers were to be diverted from a strategic operation to assist the Army, at least they would not also have to study the problem and reload with an appropriate type of bomb, but could use their normal bombload, which usually consisted of 1000 lb bombs with delayed-action fuses designed to destroy the foundations of solid masonry.[97]

Poor air-ground liaison also affected such fundamentals as the provision of adequate methods of air-ground identification and communication. Those employed for COBRA were based on experience with fighter-bombers or small numbers of mediums and consisted in the marking of the US front line with fluorescent panels, the indicating of German positions by artillery firing red smoke shells, and the marking of US tanks and vehicles with cerise panels and repainting of their white star markings; all were totally inappropriate for high altitude heavy bombers. After the first bombings on 25 July the resulting dust and smoke obscured the aircrews' view of the battle area, even of the prominent Périers–St.Lô road, while a five knot wind misplaced the red smoke rising from the targets. The most serious omission was that the US troops had no means of contacting the heavy bombers. Some tanks and vehicles had radios for contacting fighter-bombers, but no such VHF link with the heavy bombers was provided.[98] Unlike with artillery, the US troops had no means of correcting aim and when the leaders of three bomber formations began to bomb short, inducing following aircraft to do likewise, they were helpless to avert disaster.

Canadian and Polish troops were similarly helpless when, during the second phase of TOTALISE, two formations of B-17s mistook their positions for the target and straddled them with nearly 1,000 90 lb fragmentation bombs – with devastating effect against troops caught in the open.[99] The only occasion when RAF Bomber Command caused heavy casualties by short-bombing occurred during Operation TRACTABLE when, on 14 August 1944, 805 bombers were sent to support a further attack towards Falaise by Canadian II Corps. Pathfinders in the second wave failed to check their timed run from the French coast accurately and mistook a wood four miles, or one minute's flying time nearer the coast, for the German strongpoint of Quesnay Wood. Some seven per cent of the bombs fell on Canadian and Polish troops, who also had no means of contacting the bombers. The error was compounded by a particularly unfortunate occurrence. In desperation the troops fired yellow smoke, the standard method of indicating their positions to friendly tactical aircraft but the bomber crews, not of the tactical air forces, assumed the smoke to be the yellow target indicators generally employed by Bomber Command.[100] After TRACTABLE no special technique for close support bombing was developed by Bomber Command, but the provision of an air-to-ground communications link during WELLHIT and the standard of bombing during WIDGEON showed that the lesson had been learned.

After COBRA, the Eighth Air Force developed an elaborate ground-to-air marker and communications system enabling heavy bombers to identify aiming points and the location of friendly troops with minimal risk of short-bombing. This was successfully employed during Operation QUEEN, an offensive by the US First and Ninth Armies towards the Roer river on 16 November 1944. For QUEEN 1,204 heavy bombers dropped 4,120 tons of fragmentation bombs on the fortified towns of Eschweiler and Langerwehe in the path of the US troops. Most of the bombers were equipped to receive signals from a vertical SCS-51 localiser transmitter beacon placed a short distance behind the US front line, and from two marker beacons. The SCS-51 indicated to the bomber crews their exact position in relation to the front line and the bomb release point, while the marker beacons kept the bombers on course. A ground control station was set up in radio contact with the bomber stream, and the aircrews had been given detailed briefings.

Extensive measures on the ground included a series of large panel markers indicating the approach to the front line and a line of low altitude captive balloons, flown at 2,000 feet at 300 yard intervals, placed 4,000 yards behind the front line perpendicular to the bombers' approach. Four batteries of 90 mm anti-aircraft guns placed 8,000 yards behind the front line fired a line of red smoke shells on the same line as and above the balloons, These were timed to give eight simultaneous bursts every 15 seconds at a height 2,000 feet below the altitude of the bombers, the timings co-ordinated by direct telephone and radio link between an air controller and the batteries.[101]

Consequently no bombs fell on US troops during the approach to the target, and although the bombing was from 18,600–24,000 feet due to cloud over the target and flak, all targets received a high proportion of hits. The unexpected bombing caused heavy casualties among some German units caught in the open as they were being relieved (the 1st Company of the 981st Infantry Regiment had 30 per cent losses) and the US troops initially encountered only weak resistance. But by late afternoon the Germans had begun to recover and resistance stiffened. QUEEN failed to become a breakthrough, for three reasons.

First was the depth of the German defence system; it took 3 days for the US troops to break through the outer defences and by then the effect of the initial air bombardment had been lost. Second, November gave limited hours of daylight for fighter-bombers to prolong the effect of air attack. Whereas COBRA on 25 July had 16¼ hours of daylight, QUEEN had only seven hours, and much of this was disrupted by poor weather with the result that only 349 sorties were flown. But the third and most important reason was that, although the Americans had done much to solve the problem of short bombing, the memory of COBRA prevented complete confidence among the air and ground staffs in deciding how far the heavy bomber targets should be from the US troops. Their caution ensured that the US troops were unable to exploit fully the most important effect of the bombing. As a subsequent US study of QUEEN acknowledged, in view of the safety and accuracy aids employed, the bombing could have been placed much closer to the front line to enable the the US infantry to take full advantage of the shock effect.[102]

However, that the most elaborate precautions could minimise, but not eliminate, the risk of short bombing was shown during the opening phase of Operation BUCKLAND, the attack across the River Senio by the V British and II Polish Corps in April 1945, which was the Eighth Army's role in the final Allied ground offensive in Italy. Heavy bomber support was provided by the Fifteenth Air Force, whose aircraft were also to support US troops as part of a general air operation code-named WOWSER.

The safety precautions for WOWSER/BUCKLAND surpassed those for QUEEN. In addition to a series of large white ground markers placed along the bombers' route to the target area and indication lines of anti-aircraft shell bursts at pre-arranged heights, arrangements were made for a possible last-minute cancellation of the bombing. In the American sector this took the form of a VHF forward radio control established at the headquarters of the Army's supporting Tactical Air Force (XXII TAC), while in the British sector a series of flak bursts forming the letter 'X' was to indicate that the heavy bombing had been cancelled. Moreover, a familiarisation programme was conducted in the days before the offensive whereby the bombardiers and navigators of the leading planes of the heavy bomber groups were flown over the Allied troop positions and the route to the target area in reconnaissance aircraft, the experienced pilots of which pointed out the front line and target markers. Some 175 such flights, each of over one hour's duration, were flown.[103]

BUCKLAND commenced on the afternoon of 9 April, some 825 B-17's and B-24's carpeting German positions along the Senio with 1,692 tons of (mostly) fragmentation bombs. This was followed by fighter-bomber attacks on specific gun positions and command posts. The bombing was well concentrated and was, for the most part, followed up quickly on the ground, a subsequent report noting that many Germans in the attack zones were so confused and demoralised by the bombing that they offered no resistance to advancing Allied troops and surrendered without a struggle.[104]

However, not all the bombs landed among German positions. Through aircrew error one formation of 18 heavy bombers unloaded over the concentration area of a Polish battalion, causing heavy casualties. Eighth Army later admitted that casualties would have been fewer if more attention had been paid to ensuring that troops took cover during the heavy bomber attacks, but rightly added that this did not excuse the complete error in bombing made by the aircraft concerned.[105]

OPPORTUNITY COSTS

Close air support accounted for only a small fraction of the Allied heavy bomber effort. From D-Day to the end of the war in Europe RAF Bomber Command flew 182,549 operational sorties, of which less than 10,000 sorties were provided in close support. Even if sorties directed against targets other than in close support but which were related to the ground battle, such as attacks on communications, are included in the total of sorties, this still represents less than 24,000 altogether.[106] During the same period the Eighth Air Force flew over 227,000 operational sorties of which less than 10,000 were in close support.[107]

Moreover, heavy bomber losses in close support operations were far from prohibitive. They encountered little or no air opposition, while the flak encountered was either effectively smothered by the bomb carpet or silenced by friendly artillery. For a total of some 14,826 sorties losses amounted to only 53 aircraft, or 0.35 per cent.[108] This can be contrasted with the losses sustained on other types of mission. Bomber Command losses in raids upon communications (mostly railway) targets in France and synthetic oil plants in Germany during June 1944 alone, amounted to 210 aircraft in 3,840 sorties, or 5.4 per cent. Eighth Air Force losses in raids against strategic targets in Germany during June and July 1944, including returned aircraft written-off through damage, were 276 aircraft in 12,664 sorties, or 2.1 per cent.[109]

Yet the important questions are to what extent the diversion of effort to close support hindered persistence with the strategic campaign, and whether this could be justified.

Unlike, for example, the bombing of communications targets in France during the spring of 1944 as a prelude to OVERLORD, the relatively small heavy bomber effort accorded to close support in 1944-45 did not result in a significant reduction in the level of attack upon strategic targets. Nevertheless, further escalation of close support missions, the trend toward which was seen in Normandy before the breakout, did pose a potentially serious threat to the effectiveness of the strategic offensive. This would have been hard to justify because, although hampered by disputes over targeting priorities, the bomber offensive ultimately proved to have decisive results.

One result was that the bombing of oil targets, with particular emphasis upon those plants producing aviation fuel, brought the Luftwaffe to the point of collapse. In April 1944 German production of aviation fuel stood at 175,000 tons, by June it was reduced to 55,000 tons, in July it was 35,000 tons, falling to 16,000 tons in August and only 7,000 tons in September. The resulting fuel famine compelled the Luftwaffe to cease initial flying training, and nearly all medium and heavy bomber units were disbanded, while aerial reconnaissance and army support were severely curtailed. This, along with the need to concentrate air resources on defence of the Reich, meant that the Luftwaffe virtually disappeared from the battlefronts.[110] The strategic offensive was thus a major contributary factor to the air superiority enjoyed by the Allied tactical air forces.

Moreover, the Luftwaffe's fighter force, almost totally committed to defence against the daylight bombing of Germany, was relentlessly destroyed through air-combat attrition. A post-war RAF analysis of fighter losses in defensive operations examined the Luftwaffe's battle against the USAAF daylight offensive over Germany between November 1943, when long-range US fighters began to accompany the bombers deep into Germany, and August 1944. It observed that

> The GAF [German Air Force], at the beginning of the period, was numerically inferior to the attack and this inferiority increased steadily throughout the period. The average exchange rate between defence and attack was about ten German fighters to eight USAF aircraft, and this in the circumstances, worked very much to the detriment of the defence. The GAF attempted to respond to the increased frequency of attack but only by decreasing the average size of the fighter force deployed for any given raid. In other words the defence was wasting away, and was probably a beaten force even before petrol shortage became an important factor.[111]

Over a thousand German fighter pilots were lost between January and April 1944 alone, among them many irreplaceable experienced operational commanders.[112] Such losses inevitably brought a decline in quality and fighting efficiency as inadequately trained pilots were committed to battle, which in turn invited heavy casualties.[113]

The effect of bombing upon the German economy and its capacity to wage war was difficult for Allied strategists to determine accurately at the time, but subsequent research has confirmed that it was great. With regard to industrial output Richard Overy has pointed out that the bombing imposed a ceiling on German war production which was considerably less than what Germany, with skilful and urgent management of its resources, was capable of producing after 1943.[114]

In late 1944 there began an increased emphasis upon the bombing of transportation targets within Germany. In October Tedder had argued that the primary Allied air objective should be German communications, this being the one common factor in the entire German war effort at all levels.[115] Tedder's plan was adopted by SHAEF and ratified by the Combined Chiefs of Staff on 1 November, the result being that communications targets were accorded second priority after oil. The effectiveness of the subsequent offensive upon German communications, particularly the German railway system, has been analysed by Alfred C. Mierzejewski, who observes that the repeated bombing of marshalling yards, canals, and viaducts succeeded in denying resources both to German industry and to the armed forces, besides preventing the distribution of coal, disorganising the exchange of components, and compelling German industry to consume its reserves.[116]

The attrition of the Luftwaffe, the destruction of German oil producing capacity, and the disruption of German industry and communications could only be achieved and maintained by a continuous bombing offensive. It was not enough to bomb such targets as factories, oil refineries and marshalling yards once; if they were to remain inoperative repeat attacks were necessary at intervals when the weather allowed. Thus the strategic air forces might be faced with a choice between assisting the armies or putting an oil refinery out of action for several weeks. In view of this, Army demands for heavy bomber support, and the level of such support that was provided, appears of far greater consequence than the number of sorties might suggest. While there was some scope for a limited diversion of heavy bomber effort to assist the armies without seriously compromising the bomber offensive, further escalation could only have been at the expense of achieving strategic goals.

Hence the bitter recriminations of the airmen when, in their opinion, the Army wasted or misused bomber support, and their concern at increasing Army demands for such support. In October 1944 the British Chief of the Air Staff, Air Chief Marshal Portal, wrote to Tedder that the frequent intervention of the heavy bombers in the land battle was not essential and was only intended to save casualties, a process that would lead to the demoralisation of the Army. Tedder agreed, and observed that the Army had indeed been 'drugged with bombs'.[117]

The airmen were acutely aware of the need to maintain the pressure upon Germany, but the soldiers were primarily concerned with their need to overcome German defences at less cost, for which they were willing to risk the drawbacks of employing the heavy bombers and even short-bombing. The result was a bitter divergence of views, exacerbated by unfortunate timing. In 1944–45 Army demands for bomber support occurred at the time when the strategic air offensive was at last starting to show positive results. Yet the soldiers were aware that, in both Italy and North-West Europe, but particularly the latter, infantry casualties were proving far heavier than had been anticipated, and for the British and Canadians reached crisis proportions due to the lack of replacements.[118]

The operational results of employing the strategic air weapon in a tactical role were mixed. No close-support operation by heavy bombers was ever completely successful, being marred by short bombing, by the infliction upon the Germans of insufficient casualties and damage to be decisive, or by the consequent obstruction hindering the Allied troops. The reason was that, as the senior airmen knew, heavy bombers were poor battlefield attack aircraft. They lacked flexibility to respond to the changing patterns of the land battle. Unlike the tactical air forces, trained to work in close liaison with ground forces, heavy bombers could not be called up at short notice by the forward troops to assist the progressive stages of an advance; Lancasters and B-17s could not fly cab-rank.

Heavy bomber strikes from bases distant from the battlefront required detailed planning and staff work, the briefing of crews and aircraft preparation, and various different headquarters, geographically separated, had to be involved. The intervention of the heavy bombers brought a rigidity to the battle area, with troops having to relinquish often hard-fought ground in order to accommodate bomblines much more restrictive than those imposed by tactical aircraft. As a consequence the heavy bomber contribution to offensive operations could only be made in the initial stage of a set-piece attack.

The object of bombing was then to render German forces vulnerable to attack and incapable of resisting effectively by causing the maximum possible destruction, obstruction, and demoralisation. Bombing undoubtedly had the potential to inflict heavy casualties upon German troops and to destroy much of their equipment, but only when they were concentrated in the bombing zone. Such occurrences were rare. In open areas German forces were too well dispersed to offer profitable targets. The bomb pattern achieved in an attack by RAF heavy bombers on any one target, regardless of the weight of attack, remained fairly constant, with nine-tenths or more of the bombs falling within a 1,000 yard radius. Against widely dispersed targets this was uneconomic. Some positions were overhit while others remained untouched, and many bombs fell where there were no German positions at all.[119]

For the same reason pinpoint targets were very difficult to destroy by bombing and required a prohibitively high investment of sorties and bomb tonnage to offer a reasonable chance of destruction. This explains the small amount of equipment found destroyed and the relatively few German dead subsequently found by ORS investigations, though with regard to the latter there is reason to believe that the Germans removed their dead before the arrival of Allied troops whenever opportunity allowed.

With the possible exception of Panzer Lehr during COBRA, the level of casualties and destruction caused by bombing was never enough to be in itself decisive. However with regard to COBRA the critical factor in the success of the operation was the lack of depth of the German defence. Bombing was more successful in causing obstruction. On 30 June 1944, for example, 266 aircraft of Bomber Command delivered 1,100 tons of bombs on a road junction at Villers-Bocage in Normandy through which tanks of the German 2nd and 9th Panzer Divisions would have to pass in order to counter-attack the Allied beachhead. The resulting obstruction ensured that no such attack took place.[120] This was an example of what heavy bombing alone could achieve, but in close support the causing of such obstruction also hindered the progress of Allied troops. Yet when, as in the GOODWOOD tank-run, fragmentation bombs were employed in order to avoid this, the amount of destruction inflicted upon the well dug-in German troops was less than could have been achieved with high-explosive crater bombs. This dilemma could never be satisfactorily solved, and the only workable method evolved was to use fragmentation bombs in the path of an attack while crater bombing was employed on German rear areas and on the flanks to obstruct German counter-attacks.

The principal advantage of heavy and medium bombing in close support was that of rendering German troops and equipment temporarily incapable of functioning as a result of vibratory shock and also, temporarily, reducing the morale and will to fight of troops subjected to intense and prolonged bombardment. As Charles Carrington observed, German troops were dazed and deafened rather than killed.[121] Bombing came with little warning, and to the effect of surprise was added the shock caused by the tremendous concentration of firepower that the bombers could deliver in a short time. Even if few troops were killed or wounded, many were left reeling from the effects of such bombardment, communications with headquarters were often cut and, though few guns and tanks were actually destroyed, many were unmanned and buried under debris. In the period immediately after sustained heavy bombing the whole machinery of defence was disrupted and left vulnerable to attack.

One example of the weight of high explosive that the bombers could deliver is seen by comparing the bomb tonnage and weight of artillery employed at the start of WELLHIT. In an initial fireplan lasting 85 minutes 328 guns fired 19,324 shells, or 524 tons, whereas 690 heavy bombers dropped 3,356 tons, the weight of shells being less than 20 per cent of that of the high explosive delivered by the bombers.[122] This was vital to the success of the operation, as the supporting artillery was insufficient to silence the German batteries which caused most of the 634 casualties sustained by 3rd Canadian Division during the assault.[123] Without the bombing the Canadian artillery would have been overcommitted, unable both to neutralise the German defences at the outset of the attack and engage in counter-battery fire, causing Canadian casualties to be consequently heavier or the operation postponed.

When its disruptive and morale effects could be rapidly exploited by the assault troops, as at Boulogne and during BLUECOAT, heavy bombing could save both time and casualties. The available artillery alone could not have smothered the German forward defences to the extent necessary for operations on the scale of GOODWOOD or COBRA to be mounted, and tactical aircraft, while more appropriate than heavy bombers for rapid-response and progressive close air support, lacked sufficient bomb carrying and delivery capability. The value of fighter-bombers, and even mediums, lay in extending and prolonging the effects of bombardment initiated by the heavy bomber

strike. Both GOODWOOD and QUEEN would have progressed
further had tactical aircraft been able to intervene more effectively,
while during COBRA the provision of continuous fighter-bomber
cover for the US armour was a decisive factor in the subsequent success of the breakout.

However a further commitment to close air support by the heavy
bombers, beyond supporting the armies at the outset of a limited
number of major operations, could not have been justified. It would
have meant a reduction in the strategic offensive for which they had
been developed and trained, and the wasting of a major asset, in that
a strategic weapon would have been, as the airmen feared, frittered
away in a tactical role when there already existed large tactical air
forces. Results on the battlefield would not have justified such a step,
while to abate the strategic offensive would have almost certainly permitted Germany to continue the war beyond May 1945. A greater
commitment to close support would have been equally inappropriate
for medium bombers, for they enabled the tactical air forces to strike
at targets beyond fighter-bomber range, and at battle area targets
requiring a greater weight of attack.

On occasion, heavy and medium bombers could and did provide an
important increment to the firepower available to Allied troops. The
problem in 1944–45 was that on such occasions their value was compromised by poor air-ground liaison. The drawbacks with such
support were not inevitable. Operations BLUECOAT, WELLHIT,
COBRA, and even GOODWOOD – though it ultimately failed –
proved that German defence effectiveness could be significantly, if
temporarily, reduced, while both WELLHIT and QUEEN proved
that the risk of short bombing could be minimised. Though it would
have been unsound to devote valuable time and effort to train the
heavy bomber forces for close support, a greater degree of liaison during the planning and execution of operations would have ensured both
that the bombing was better exploited and that fewer Allied troops
were killed by Allied bombs. That this did not occur until a late stage
was the responsibility of both the senior airmen and the senior
soldiers, the former because the bomber support was only grudgingly
provided, and the latter because they failed to comprehend and adjust
to its inherent characteristics.

NOTES

1. Eisenhower, *Crusade In Europe* (London: William Heinemann, 1948), pp. 245, 297.

2. Vice Chief of the Air Staff to Chief of the Air Staff, 24 Aug. 1944, PRO AIR 20/5308; SHAEF (Air) Historical Record, PRO AIR 37/1436.
3. Solly Zuckerman, *From Apes to Warlords* (London: Collins, 1988), p. 347.
4. Max Hastings, *Bomber Command* (London: Pan, 1981), pp. 221–2.
5. Ibid., pp. 327–8. There was also a prestige factor as far as the USAAF was concerned. As Spaatz explained to Professor Zuckerman, subordination of the strategic air forces to AEAF control and therefore to Army operations would compromise the fight for an independent air force. Journal of Professor Solly Zuckerman, 9 July 1944, quoted in Carlo D'Este, *Decision in Normandy* (London: Pan, 1984), p. 215.
6. Alfred Price, *Battle Over the Reich* (London: Ian Allan, 1973), p. 138.
7. Major-General Sir Francis De Guingand, *Operation Victory* (London: Hodder and Stoughton, 1947), p. 400.
8. Ibid., pp. 400–1.
9. Bill Gunston, *The Illustrated Encyclopedia of Combat Aircraft of World War II* (London: Tiger Books, 1990), pp. 79, 200.
10. No.2 ORS Report No. 14, *Heavy Bombing In Support of the Army*, in *Operational Research in North West Europe*, PRO WO 291/1331.
11. Gunston, pp. 229, 247.
12. ORS MAAF Report No.32 (1945), *Observations on the Strength and Balance of Desert Air Force*, lists aircraft types and roles, PRO AIR 23/7513.
13. MORU Report No.34 (1946), *The Effects of Close Air Support Part I, Medium and Heavy Bombers*, PRO WO 291/976; The USAAF Evaluation Board in the ETO, *The Effectiveness of Third Phase Tactical Air Operations in the European Theater, 5 May 1944 – 8 May 1945*, (1946), pp. 385–6, PRO AIR 40/1111.
14. British 21st Army Group Draft Report, 14 Aug. 1944, *Use of Heavy Bombers in a Tactical Role*, PRO WO 232/51.
15. MORU Report No.34 (1946).
16. Ibid.
17. Ibid.
18. Ibid.
19. Ibid.
20. Quoted in the USAAF Evaluation Board in the ETO, *Effectiveness of Third Phase Tactical Air Operations*, p. 385.
21. Brigadier C.J.C. Molony, *The Mediterranean and Middle East*, Volume V (London: HMSO, 1973), pp. 785–6.
22. Mediterranean Allied Air Forces (MAAF) Report (1944), *The Bombardment of Cassino 15 March 1944*, PRO AIR 8/1358; Rudolf Böhmler, *Monte Cassino* (London: Cassell, 1964), p. 214.
23. MAAF Report, *The Bombardment of Cassino*.
24. Molony, *The Mediterranean and Middle East*, pp. 777–9.
25. MAAF Report, *The Bombardment of Cassino*.
26. Molony, pp. 786–7.
27. Quoted in Molony, p. 853
28. No.2 ORS Report No. 14, *Heavy Bombing in Support of the Army*.
29. When Zuckerman presented him with a paper proposing the use of strategic bombers in direct support of the Army, Tedder replied that he was not interested as he was not concerned with 'Cassinos' or with agriculture. Zuckerman Journal, 9 July 1944, quoted in D'Este, *Decision in Normandy*, p. 310n.
30. Minutes of the Allied Air Commanders' Conference, 14 to 16 June 1944, AEAF Historical Record, PRO AIR 37/1057.
31. This incident is fully described in D'Este, *Decision in Normandy*, pp. 226–8.
32. De Guingand, *Operation Victory*, p. 401.
33. AEAF Historical Record, July 1944.
34. Air Commodore Kingston-McLoughry's suggestion that the decision to bomb Caen was political is discussed in D'Este, *Decision in Normandy*, pp. 310–13.
35. Zuckerman Journal, 9 July 1944, quoted in D'Este, p. 316.
36. Chester Wilmot, *The Struggle For Europe* (London: The Reprint Society, 1954), p. 387; Montgomery of Alamein, *Normandy to the Baltic* (London: Hutchinson, 1958), pp. 72–3.
37. Air Commodore E.J. Kingston-McCloughry and Professor S. Zuckerman, *Observations on RAF Bomber Command's Attack on Caen July 7th 1944* (Report on visit to Caen, 12 July

1944), PRO AIR 37/1255; S. Zuckerman, *From Apes to Warlords* (London: Collins, 1988), pp. 275–6.

38. No.2 ORS Report No.5, *Heavy Bombing in Operation Charnwood*, in *Operational Research in North-West Europe*.
39. Ibid.
40. Kingston-McCloughry and Zuckerman Report, July 1944.
41. MORU Report No.12 (1945), *The Assault on Wesel*, PRO WO 291/955
42. Ibid.
43. Ibid.
44. Ibid.
45. Data from: Allied Force Headquarters, 12 July 1943, *Lessons from Operations against Pantelleria*, PRO WO 232/54; Molony, *The Mediterranean and Middle East*, p. 49; MORU Report No.34 (1946); No. 2 ORS Report No.16, *Air and Ground Support in the Assault on Boulogne*, in *Operational Research in North-West Europe; Report on the Bombing of Le Havre By Bomber Command* (Sept. 1944), Summary, Map, and Photographic Interpretation Reports, PRO WO 233/29; British Army Operational Research Group Report No. 299, *Walcheren 1 to 8 Nov. 1944*, PRO CAB 106/1090.
46. *Lessons From Operations Against Pantelleria*.
47. No.2 ORS Report No.16.
48. Army Operational Research Group Report No. 299, *Walcheren*.
49. MORU Report No.34 (1946).
50. Craven and Cate (Eds.), *The U.S. Army Air Forces in World War II*, Volume III, *Argument to V-E Day* (Chicago: 1951), pp. 263–4.
51. MORU Report No.34 (1946).
52. H. Essame, *The Battle for Germany* (London: Batsford, 1970), pp. 48–9.
53. Quoted in S. Roskill, *The War at Sea 1939-45*, Vol.III, Part II (London: HMSO, 1961), p. 53n.
54. No. 2 ORS Report No.16.
55. Army Operational Research Group Report No. 299, *Walcheren;* L.F. Ellis, *Victory in the West*, Vol.II (London: HMSO, 1968), p. 122; B. Fergusson, *The Watery Maze* (London: Collins, 1961) p. 359. Casualty figures from Gerald Rawling, *Cinderella Operation: The Battle for Walcheren 1944* (London: Cassell, 1980), p. 122 This seems to supersede earlier conflicting sources. Rawling served in the Naval Support Squadron, and apparently includes all wounded rather than just severe cases (p.126).
56. Quoted in Jeffery Williams, *The Long Left Flank* (London: Leo Cooper, 1988), p. 64.
57. No.2 ORS Report No.16, *Air and Ground Support in the Assault on Boulogne*.
58. Ibid.
59. Molony, *The Mediterranean and Middle East*, p. 746.
60. US Fifth Army G-2 Evaluation of the bombing in support of the Anzio beachhead, quoted in Headquarters 12th USAAF Report (15 April 1945), *Medium Bomber Operations*, detailing operations of the USAAF 42nd and 57th Bomb Wings, Jan. to Aug. 1944, PRO AIR 23/7603.
61. Quoted in Wynford Vaughan-Thomas, *Anzio* (London: Pan Edition, 1963), p. 181.
62. No.2 ORS Report No. 14, *Heavy Bombing in support of the Army*.
63. Richard P. Hallion, *Strike From The Sky: The History of Battlefield Air Attack 1911–45* (Shrewsbury: Airlife, 1989), p. 207
64. AEAF Preliminary Report (July 1944), *Preliminary Analysis of Air Operations – 'GOOD-WOOD', July 1944*, PRO AIR 37/762.
65. The recriminations over GOODWOOD are discussed in D'Este, *Decision in Normany*, pp. 391–9.
66. Wilmot, *The Struggle for Europe*, pp. 394–5; John Keegan, *Six Armies in Normandy* (London: 1982), pp. 192–3; Max Hastings, *Overlord* (London: Michael Joseph, 1984), pp. 230–3; Montgomery, *Normandy to the Baltic*, p. 81; No.2 ORS Report No.6, *Bombing in Operation Goodwood*, in *Operational Research in North West Europe*.
67. *Operation Goodwood – 18 July 1944*, Appendix G in *Report on Tactical Bombing* (based on reports by the Scientific Adviser, 21st Army Group), PRO WO 205/232.
68. Report on Heavy Bombing in support of the Army by Lieutenant-Colonel Carrington, Liaison Officer at RAF Bomber Command, in PRO WO 233/60; *Report On Tactical Bombing*; Keegan, *Six Armies in Normandy*, p. 202.

69. Hans von Luck, *Panzer Commander: The Memoirs of Colonel Hans von Luck* (New York: Praeger, 1989), p. 154.

70. RAF Bombing Analysis Unit (BAU) Report No.22 (11 Jan. 1945) quoted in Army Operational Research Group Report No.282 (July 1945), *A Study of Casualties and Damage to Personnel and Equipment Caused by some Air and Artillery Bombardments in European Operations*, PRO WO 291/262.

71. No.2 ORS Report No.6, *Bombing in Operation Goodwood*.

72. Ibid.

73. *Report On Tactical Bombing*.

74. Wilmot, *The Struggle for Europe*, p. 395.

75. Ibid., p. 399.

76. MORU Report No.23 (Oct. 1946), *Operation Goodwood*, PRO CAB 106/1024

77. Quoted in Charles Carrington, *Soldier at Bomber Command* (London: Leo Cooper, 1987), p. 163.

78. Stephen E. Ambrose, *The Supreme Commander* (London: Cassell, 1970), p. 439.

79. Wilmot, pp. 395–6.

80. The USAAF Evaluation Board in the ETO, *The Effectiveness of Third Phase Tactical Air Operations*, pp. 85–9.

81. Martin Blumenson, *Breakout And Pursuit* (Washington, DC: Department of The Army, 1961), pp. 227–8.

82. Ibid., p. 238.

83. US Army Interrogation quoted in Wilmot, p. 434.

84. Hallion, *Strike from the Sky*, p. 213. This work also contains interesting quotes from Bayerlein's Interrogation. See also The USAAF Evaluation Board in the ETO, *The Effectiveness of Third Phase Tactical Air Operations*, p. 259.

85. Robert L. Hewitt, *Workhorse Of The Western Front, The Story of The 30th Infantry Division* (Washington, DC: Infantry Journal Press, 1946), p. 37.

86. Blumenson, *Breakout and Pursuit*, pp. 244–5.

87. Wilmot, *The Struggle for Europe*, p. 434.

88. Ibid., pp. 435–6.

89. No.2 ORS Report No.7, *Bombing In Operation Bluecoat*, in *Operational Research In North West Europe*; MORU Report No.34, *The Effects of Close Air Support*.

90. No.2 ORS Report No.7.

91. Ibid.

92. Data from: Molony, *The Mediterranean and the Middle East*, p. 785; Böhmler, *Monte Cassino*, p. 212; The AAF in the ETO, *Effectiveness of Third Phase Tactical Air Operations*, p. 91, PRO AIR 40/1111; No.2 ORS Report No.9, *The Effect of 90 lb Fragmentation Bombs*, in *Operational Research In North West Europe*; British 21st Army Group Report to Air Commodore E.J. Kingston-McCloughry giving revised figures for casualties inflicted on Allied troops during TRACTABLE (20 Aug. 1944), PRO WO 205/232; Air Narrative to Eighth Army History, April 1944 – May 1945 (1945), PRO WO 204/8120. (See Appendix.)

93. Hewitt, *Workforce of the Western Front*, p. 40.

94. *First United States Army Report of Operations 20 Oct. 1943–1 Aug. 1944*, Book I, p. 99; Eisenhower, *Crusade in Europe*, p. 297.

95. Hastings, *Overlord*, p. 298.

96. Blumenson, *Breakout and Pursuit*, p. 231.

97. Carrington, *Soldiers at Bomber Command*, p. 159.

98. General Omar N. Bradley, Military Advisor USSBS and Air Effects Committee, *Effect of Air Power on Military Operations, Western Europe*, US 12th Army Group, July 1945, pp. 104–5, PRO AIR 40/1131.

99. No.2 ORS Report No.9, *The Effect of 90 lb Fragmentation Bombs*.

100. Sir Brian Horrocks with Everley Belfield and H. Essame, *Corps Commander* (London: 1977), p. 44; Carrington, *Soldier at Bomber Command*, p. 166.

101. Bradley, *Effect of Air Power on Military Operations*, pp. 106–7.

102. Ibid., p. 108.

103. Headquarters 15th USAAF, Report (31 May 1945), *'Operation Wowser': The Participation of Heavy Bombers in the Final Victory in Italy*, PRO AIR 23/7605.

104. Ibid.

105. Air Narrative to Eighth Army History (1945).

106. Martin Middlebrook and Chris Everitt (Eds.), *The Bomber Command War Diaries* (London: Penguin, 1990).
107. Roger Freeman with Alan Crouchman and Vic Maslen (Eds.), *The Mighty Eighth War Diary* (London: Arms And Armour Press, 1990).
108. Middlebrook and Everitt; Freeman, Crouchman and Maslen.
109. Ibid.
110. Price, pp. 138 and 144.
111. Research Branch, Fighter Command, Report No. 710 (May 1952), *The Trend of Defensive Day Fighter Losses in Intensive Air Operations in World War 2*, PRO AIR 16/1218.
112. Price, p. 131.
113. The attrition of the Luftwaffe in 1945 is detailed in Werner Gerbig, *Six Months To Oblivion* (London: Ian Allan, 1975).
114. R.J. Overy, *The Air War 1939–45* (London: PaperMac, 1987), p. 123.
115. Tedder, *Notes on Air Policy* (Oct. 1944), PRO AIR 37/1013.
116. Alfred C. Mierzejewski, *The Collapse of the German War Economy* (University of North Carolina Press, 1988), p. 120.
117. Quoted in C. Webster and N. Frankland, *The Strategic Air Offensive Against Germany*, Vol.III (London: HMSO, 1961), pp. 68–9.
118. The manpower question in Normandy is discussed in D'Este, *Decision in Normandy*, pp. 252–70.
119. No.2 ORS Report No. 14, *Heavy Bombing in Support of the Army*.
120. Middlebrook and Everitt, *The Bomber Command War Diaries*, p. 536.
121. Observations on heavy bomber support for the Army, 27 July 1944, PRO 205/232.
122. British 21st Army Group Report, *Spectacular Examples of Massed Artillery and Air Bombardment* (March 1945), PRO AIR 37/644.
123. Second Canadian Corps Counter-Battery Intelligence Summary No.6 (Boulogne), Sept. 1944, quoted in C.P. Stacey, *The Victory Campaign* (Ottawa: 1960), p. 344.

7

Fighter-Bombers and Artillery:
A Comparison of Effectiveness

The campaigns in Italy and North-West Europe in 1943–45 saw developments in air/ground communications and control, which resulted in an improved level of responsiveness and air/ground integration between the Allied armies and their supporting tactical air forces. Both campaigns also saw the results of similar, and parallel, improvements in communication and responsiveness within the ground forces' intrinsic close-support arm – the artillery. A comparison should enable us to determine the relative merits of artillery and tactical aircraft in the close-support role, and to address the question of why, when both the British and US artilleries had become proficient at rapidly concentrating firepower in the immediate support of infantry and armour, close air support was considered necessary.

CHARACTERISTICS

The most important advantage of artillery was that it could provide fire support in all weathers, day or night. In contrast, the fighter-bombers of 1944/45 were unable to operate effectively at night, while their employment in daylight could be prevented or considerably reduced by adverse weather, even in summer. Normandy in June and July 1944 saw more cloud, wind and rain than at any time recorded since 1900 and on many days air missions could not be flown. For example, between 26 June and 24 July the US IX TAC was able to fly only 900 sorties in support of US First Army, it being calculated later that the weather had cancelled as much as 50 per cent of the potential air support.[1]

In winter, with fewer daylight hours and the increased likelihood of poor flying weather, a reduction in available air support was inevitable. The experience of RAF Desert Air Force in Italy may be taken as typical. In November 1944 there were nine days during which the weather permitted only 180 sorties to be flown; in December there were at least 10 days when operations were completely suspended or confined to weather reconnaissance sorties and a further eleven days when operations were restricted. In January 1945 there were seven days when flying was impossible, while a further three days were confined to weather reconnaissance sorties.[2]

Artillery, moreover, could command a considerable area – including the zone within 7,000/8,000 yards of the line of contact where close air support was likely to be required. Shelford Bidwell has observed that the 25-pounder gun/howitzer, the principal British and Commonwealth field gun of World War II with a fighting range of 11,000 yards and an arc of 90°, when positioned 3,000 yards behind the front line, could dominate 30 square miles of enemy territory.[3] The principal British and US artillery equipments of 1943–45 are shown in Table I.[4]

TABLE I

PRINCIPAL BRITISH AND US ARTILLERY EQUIPMENTS

	TYPE	RANGE IN YARDS/MILES		RATE OF FIRE
British	25-pounder gun/howitzer	13,500	(7.6 miles)	4 rounds per minute
	5.5 inch gun/howitzer	16,200	(9.2 miles)	1 round per minute
	7.2 inch howitzer	16,900	(9.6 miles)	1 round per minute
US	105 mm howitzer	12,500	(7.1 miles)	4 rounds per minute
	155 mm gun	25,715	(14.6 miles)	1 round per minute
	155 mm howitzer	16,000	(9.0 miles)	2 rounds per minute

The ranges of these guns show to what extent artillery could dominate the battle area, and in the early stages of both campaigns it was an avowed principle of the Allied Tactical Air Forces not to engage targets within artillery range. In 1944 the RAF Desert Air Force in Italy reported that

> When it is possible to put smoke on to a target by shell fire, it will usually be found that [the] request for air support against that particular target will be refused, the reason being that it will be considered to be an artillery target.[5]

This was also the view of the USAAF. A former US fighter-bomber pilot recalls of a spell of duty as a forward air controller in Italy that a basic ground-rule was that air strikes were not to replace artillery, and that attempts had to have been made to engage targets by artillery, or reasons given why this was not possible, before air strikes were sanctioned.[6]

Yet, for the air forces to refuse all targets within artillery range would have ruled out close air support. That this did not happen was initially the result of necessity. A US study of air support compiled by the Twelfth Army Group in 1945 admitted that

> the previous air force conception that fighter-bomber aircraft should not be used on targets within the range of ground artillery should not be an inflexible rule. Early in...Normandy it became apparent to staff officers in the combined air-ground operations centers that various factors affected this preconceived tenet, and that each request should be considered from all angles.[7]

One of these factors was whether enough guns were available to engage a target successfully. In 1944 RAF Desert Air Force acknowledged that, even if a target could be indicated by artillery, it would be attacked by fighter-bombers if insufficient guns could be brought to bear.[8] Linked to this was the question of whether the terrain in the battle area allowed for suitable artillery deployment, an acute problem in the mountainous areas of Italy.

There were occasions when it was imperative for fighter-bombers to act as a substitute for artillery. One such occurred in late June 1944, after storms swept the OMAHA and UTAH landing beaches in Normandy and disrupted the scheduled arrival of artillery units and ammunition. Fighter-bombers of the US Ninth Air Force had to be employed in close support against what normally would have been regarded as artillery targets. This proved successful, the Twelfth Army Group study pointing out that a refusal of requests from corps and divisions for close air support against targets within artillery range at this time would have seriously compromised the Army's ability to consolidate the beachhead and capture the port of Cherbourg.[9] Another reason why close support from fighter-bombers was sometimes essential was shortage of artillery ammunition. For example, the participation of the Desert Air Force fighter-bombers in Operation CYGNET in Italy in January 1945 (see above, Chapter 4) had been requested primarily because of the severe shortage of artillery ammunition in Eighth Army at that time which saw the 25-pounders restricted to only 10 rounds per gun per day.[10]

Close support, either by fighter-bombers or artillery, consisted of prearranged airstrikes or artillery bombardments laid on either as preparation for a planned attack or as impromptu support provided in response to developments at the battlefront. The latter, to be of use to those requesting it, had to be provided quickly. Fighter-bombers, flying from landing-grounds often considerable distances from the target area, could not normally provide such support as rapidly as artillery positioned at or near the battlefront. Such support was the primary task of artillery, and both British and US divisions possessed considerable organic artillery firepower.

Each US infantry division had three battalions of field artillery, each with twelve 105 mm howitzers, and one battalion of twelve 155 mm medium howitzers. Its British counterpart had three regiments of field artillery, each of twenty-four 25-pounders subdivided into three batteries of eight guns, which in turn were subdivided into troops of four guns. British and US armoured divisions were equipped with self-propelled artillery (see Chapter 4 above).[11]

By 1944 Allied gunners were able to concentrate the fire of these guns in response to support requests with remarkable speed. In the British and Commonwealth forces this was due to the adoption of a fire control system which enabled support requests to be rapidly answered by the fire of massed guns, the principal factor being an efficient network of radio communication. Each troop and battery commander of a British artillery regiment was equipped to form an obervation post (OP) and, while remaining independent, batteries became affiliated to support particular battalions. This inculcated the battery commander and his OP officers with a strong commitment to support 'their' battalion, and they usually became regarded as as much a part of the battalion as its company commanders.[12]

By radio the Forward Observation Officers (FOOs) attached to the forward troops, those with armoured regiments riding in their own tanks, could call direct for fire support from, if required, every gun within range, since troops, batteries and regiments all operated on the same radio network, or 'net'. It was equally possible for listening headquarters to intervene and order other units to join in the engagement of a target – functioning in much the same way as the RAF's Forward Control Post in the broadly similar Air Support Signals Unit system.

This method was pioneered by Major-General H.J. Parham when serving as Commander Royal Artillery (CRA) of the 38th Division in England in 1941. By dispensing with the hitherto 'hierarchical' chain of command in dealing with support requests (that is, from troop to battery to regiment to headquarters for approval and back) much time was saved. Moreover, Parham dispensed with the lengthy pursuit of extreme accuracy in artillery fire when dealing with such requests, realising that speed was of more importance. In a conventional fire control system the fire of a battery could be corrected quite rapidly by adjusting to left or right or longer or shorter by the battery's own sights, but in other batteries engaging the same target compensating corrections had to be calculated. In Parham's system this was obviated, a new type of fire order being introduced using compass points. Shelford Bidwell describes how guns could be instructed to shift their fire, say, to a point 400 yards north-east of where it was falling, by the simple order 'Go N.E. 400', an order immediately applicable to every battery regardless of their position or that of the OP. The resulting spread of shot when engaging a target simultaneously with three or four regiments compensated for initial inaccuracy in spotting the target.[13]

The system became known by the letters of the phonetic alphabet employed; 'UNCLE' for 'U' was a call for support from the entire divisional artillery, and 'MIKE' for 'M' called for the fire of a regiment. It was not intended to replace more traditional methods, such as the accurate survey which was vital in the preparation of fireplans for predicted fire, but it did provide a means of handling massed artillery as a single fire unit, able to switch fire rapidly from point to point by radio control in response to any emergency. Its simplicity enabled infantry and tank officers to understand and use it if their accompanying FOO became a casualty, and it could be extended to call on the guns of not just one division but also those of other divisions, and of the separate groupings of field, medium and heavy artillery of the Army Groups Royal Artillery (AGRAs) that were usually attached to Corps. Furthermore it was fast: divisional concentrations could usually be put down within five minutes of the radio alert of 'Uncle Target'.[14] Even when further extended the system remained swift. The attack on the HITLER LINE in Italy by I Canadian Corps on 23 May 1944 saw the first employment of the WILLIAM TARGET, calling on the guns of an entire army corps, and on one occasion a call for support was answered by 19 field, nine medium, and two heavy regiments engaging the target simultaneously with 668 guns – 3,509 rounds, or 92 tons of high explosive, being delivered within 33 minutes of the original request.[15]

The system employed by the US artillery differed in that forward observation officers were precisely that; they observed, reported, but could not order fire. Decisions as to whether a target was to be engaged, the number of guns and scale of fire to be employed were taken by more senior officers at a fire direction centre behind the battlefront. This meant that decisions were based on much wider intelligence than was available to a single British FOO in the front line caught up in his own particular battle, but the response time could be slower than in the British system.[16] However, against targets that had been previously registered the US artillery could respond very quickly, concentrating fire in a few minutes upon the receipt of the appropriate code word.[17]

By 1943 the effectiveness of both the British and US artilleries had been further increased by the provision of specially trained observers flying over the battlefront in light observation aircraft and in direct communication with the guns. Targets that would not have been observed from the ground could be rapidly engaged once spotted from the air. This is seen in an example from the fighting for the Anzio beachhead in Italy in February 1944. During a German counterattack on 18 February Captain William H. McKay, a US artillery observer flying over the battle area in an L-4 Cub observation aircraft, spotted over 2,000 German troops supported by tanks moving to exploit a breach made in the Allied line. He radioed this information to the artillery of the US 45th Division, and within 12 minutes the VI Corps Fire Control Centre had concentrated the fire of over 200 guns – including some British – on the target, which shattered the German force; within the next 50 minutes McKay caused four further German attempts to be similarly broken up.[18] Such was the success of air- observed fire that by this time many missions were directed in this way, for example the US 1st Armored Division's Air OPs were directing more than 50 per cent of all observed missions.[19]

In general, fighter-bombers having to fly to the battle area could not equal artillery response times, though it is true that the distance from fighter-bomber airfields to the battlefront varied considerably as the campaigns progressed. In the early stages of the Normandy campaign, due to the shallowness of the beachhead, Allied fighter-bombers occupied hastily constructed airfields very close to the front line; Desmond Scott recalls that when his Typhoon wing (No.123) moved to Normandy in mid-June 1944 their airfield, near Caen, was only four miles from German positions and often under shellfire.[20] In such circumstances fighter-bombers were able to take off, attack their targets, and return in a matter of minutes, and sometimes airfield personnel were able to watch the aircraft attacking the targets that were so close.[21] Frequently, however, fighter-bombers had to attack targets many miles from their airfields. In France during August and September 1944 the US Third Army was advancing eastward from Normandy and also reducing German garrisons in Brittany. This required units of the supporting US XIX TAC to be widely deployed in order to be able to attack targets that were sometimes 500 miles apart.[22]

In Italy and North-West Europe in 1943–45 it was found that a request for air support from the forward troops took an average of about 75 minutes to fulfil. This could be more or less, depending upon such variables as distance from the forward airfields to the battle area, and the availability of aircraft and their state of readiness.[23] Typically it might take nine minutes for the request to reach Army/Air joint HQ, a further 12 minutes for a decision on an estimated time on target, and half an hour or so on matter such as pilot briefing. A flying time to target of about 20 minutes would then account for the 75 minute average speed of response quoted above.

Much depended upon how quickly a fighter-bomber squadron could become airborne after having been detailed to attack a target. In 1944 RAF Desert Air Force outlined the time breakdown for a squadron at 45 minutes readiness, meaning that all aircraft could become airborne 45 minutes after receipt of the target by the Wing Operations Room, as follows:

1) Target is received at Wing Operations Room from the Air Support Control and MORU.
2) Wing Operations Room alerts the Squadron Operations Room for briefing; while they are en route the Wing Commander, ALO's, and Intelligence Officer gather the necessary information for the briefing.
3) Pilots are briefed, requiring at least 15 minutes providing no further information is required from Air Support Control.
4) Pilots proceed to dispersal and board their aircraft, arrange maps and flying gear, start up and move up to the assembly point on the runway, all this taking at least 10 minutes.
5) The squadron takes off, forms up, and sets course for the target. As only one aircraft could usually take off at a time at least 12 minutes elapsed before course was set for the target. The squadron then had to reach the target, which could take anything up to an hour depending on the distance from the airfield to the battlefront.[24]

Moreover, after returning from a sortie a considerable time elapsed before a squadron of fighter-bombers could become airborne again in response to a further request. This was due to the time needed for refuelling aircraft and rearming them with ammunition and bombs, or 'turning around' a squadron as it was called. In 1944 the Desert Air

Force found that it took one hour to 'turn around' a squadron of
Kittyhawk IV's, the time divided as follows:

> Total time for refuelling squadron (approximately 10 minutes per
> aircraft) with the usual two petrol bowsers available: 1 to 1½ hours.
> Total time to rearm and bomb-up aircraft (approximately 15 minutes
> per aircraft) with two crews available working while the aircraft were
> also being refuelled: 1½ hours.
> Time for taxying out to the assembly point and take-off: 12 minutes.[25]

The only method whereby fighter-bombers could respond to
support requests in a space of time comparable to artillery was that of
flying continuous patrols over the battle area on CABRANK (see
Chapter 4 above). Some indication of the responsiveness possible with
CABRANK is shown by an incident during the Rhine crossing which
occurred on 26 March 1945. The 154th Infantry Brigade of 51st
(Highland) Division called up the FCP in their sector to report a
German strongpoint in some houses that was delaying their advance.
The Contact Car with the Brigade was authorised by the FCP to call
down a section of Typhoons from CABRANK and immediately
contacted and briefed the pilots. Within three minutes artillery
had marked the target with smoke, and within eight minutes of the
original request the Typhoons had successfully attacked.[26]

This, however, should be regarded as exceptional. An average
response time was more likely to have been similar to that recorded for
a request for air support made by the 9th Brigade of 3rd Canadian
Infantry Division during the same operation. The Canadians called up
the FCP controlling their sector giving a target of German tanks and
asking for the estimated arrival of aircraft over the target. Once the RAF
Squadron Leader at the FCP had checked aircraft availability and given
an estimated time of arrival the Canadians were asked when coloured
smoke could be fired to indicate the target. The Brigade replied that
they could 'smoke it this minute if you are ready', whereupon the decision was made to assign the mission to aircraft on CABRANK in the
battle area; briefing details and even an available air photograph of the
target area were passed to the controller who then briefed the pilots. In
an interesting link-up between the artillery and air support communications systems during the airstrike, contact was maintained between
the artillery and 9th Brigade by telephone and from 9th Brigade to the
FCP by radio-telephone, so that the fall of smoke could be immediately reported to the aircraft. Results of the airstrike were then passed to
9th Brigade, the entire operation taking 18 minutes from the original
request to reporting of results.[27]

CABRANK offered the immediate availability of fighter-bombers to engage targets, but for aircraft to achieve responsiveness on a par with artillery was hardly economic. Keeping aircraft continually over a given area of the battlefront was wasteful in both flying hours and petrol stocks, especially as fighter-bombers were frequently kept waiting in vain for targets and had to leave the CABRANK to attack an alternative target in the battle area for which the pilots had been briefed before take-off. Such alternative targets were no doubt important, but were obviously not of the highest priority and it is questionable whether attacking them in any way compensated for the absorption of air effort involved. An artillery weapon, when not required, involved no such wastage.

Moreover, the commitment of aircraft necessary to maintain a CABRANK inevitably resulted in a diminution of air effort at other sectors of the battlefront. For example, in Italy on 7 November 1944 the Desert Air Force flew no less than 309 sorties, most of them CABRANK, in support of the attack on Forli by the 4th and 46th British Infantry Divisions alone, while No.83 Group's effort in flying 233 sorties on CABRANK in support of Guards Armoured Division during the first day of Operation MARKET GARDEN in Holland on 17 September 1944 had required the commitment of ten squadrons.[28] Even in the CABRANK sector the weight of air attack against targets was often diminished, because in order to maintain continuous patrols fighter-bombers were seldom able to operate in more than sections of four aircraft.

BATTLEFIELD EFFECTIVENESS

Having established that, at a high cost in air resources, fighter-bombers could be as responsive as artillery to requests for support, an obvious question arises as to whether their attacks were as effective as artillery fire. There are two criteria of effectiveness: the destructive effect, referring to the level of destruction and casualties inflicted, and the morale effect.

Against such typical close support targets as gun positions, strongpoints, and field works, the effects of fighter-bomber attack and artillery were remarkably similar. Pinpoint targets, such as individual gun positions, were not easily destroyed. This was largely a question of accuracy, as neither artillery nor the air delivered bombs and rockets of 1944–45 were precision weapons, while such targets proved quite resilient to near misses. The following shows the limited amount of destruction achieved by Typhoons against German gun positions in North-West Europe, during operations WELLHIT, the assault on Boulogne in September 1944, and INFATUATE, the capture of Walcheren Island in November 1944: [29]

TABLE II

LIMITED EFFECTIVENESS OF ROCKET ATTACKS ON POINT TARGETS

TARGET	NUMBER OF ROCKETS FIRED	NUMBER OF STRIKES ON TARGET	% OF STRIKES
4 Heavy & 6 Medium Gun Emplacements }	216 (27 Typhoon loads)	2	0.9%
3 Heavy & 4 Medium Gun Emplacements }	104 (13 Typhoon loads)	9	8.6%
4 Medium Gun Emplacements	62 (8 Typhoons – 1 with 6 RPs)	2	3.2%
4 Heavy Gun Emplacements	47 (6 Typhoon loads)	1	2.1%

Similarly, during Operation UNDERGO, the assault on Calais in September 1944, it was subsequently discovered that no damage to weapons had been achieved in 12 separate Typhoon attacks on six gun positions, involving the expenditure of 375 rockets.[30] This level of destruction improved little as the campaign progressed. ORS 2nd TAF investigated a number of German gun positions attacked by Typhoons in response to requests from the forward British troops in Germany in April 1945; they found that only three guns had been damaged out of 64 attacked in 12 positions.[31]

Against similar targets artillery apparently had only slightly more destructive effect. This was discovered by No.2 ORS when they investigated the density of artillery fire and the damage caused by British and Canadian medium guns engaged in counter-battery fire against German 88 mm guns at Boulogne in September 1944.[32] In shelling a German 88 mm battery of five guns the artillery put down 3,600 rounds in a circular area 300 yards across, or one round per 20 square yards, but knocked out only one gun. During engagement of a six gun battery 5,700 rounds were fired into a similar area. In this case one round per 12 square yards eliminated only two guns. It was also found that even if a medium shell landed in a German gunpit, the chance of putting the gun out of action remained small.[32]

Much the same level of destruction was found in Italy when the British Army's No.1 ORS examined the effects of counter-battery fire on German field gun and 'nebelwerfer' multiple-barrel mortar positions. They found that of 44 guns and nebelwerfers in 22 positions only eight (18 per cent) were damaged.[33]

The lethality of artillery and air attack was also variable. Against fieldworks the effectiveness of rockets and bombs was questionable. In 1945, after analysing operational data from the fighting in Germany, ORS 2nd TAF discovered that

> open positions consisting of trenches and fox-holes suffered little or no damage from this type of attack.[34]

Bombs needed direct hits to destroy such positions, while the anti-personnel value of rockets was limited against troops in fieldworks. In 1945 the joint No.2 ORS/ORS 2nd TAF investigation of Typhoon effectiveness admitted that the 60 lb semi-armour-piercing (SAP) rocket, with which Typhoons were equipped, can

> only be seriously lethal if it happens to catch men inside a building which it penetrates; against troops in the open it penetrates too far into the ground to be dangerous.[35]

In the same report the ORS noted that they found only one instance of significant personnel casualties being inflicted by rockets. This occurred during the assault on Calais (Operation UNDERGO) where a Canadian Medical Officer reported that he had attended to 70 German casualties, 12 of whom (17 per cent) were thought to have been rocket victims.[36] In fact it was found that only strafing attacks had been successful in inflicting significant casualties upon troops in fieldworks, the higher degree of accuracy possible and the larger number of rounds fired offering an increased chance of rounds penetrating trenches and foxholes and finding a mark.[37]

The level of personnel casualties inflicted by artillery was also variable, but most evidence suggests that relatively few casualties would be caused by even heavy bombardment to troops occupying well-protected positions. This can be seen in an example of German artillery engaging Allied troops which was considered to be of sufficient interest for the US Army to record it. On the night of 2 October 1944 some 200 US troops occupying deep and well-protected foxhole positions were subject to a bombardment by German mortars and artillery in preparation for an attack by German assault engineers and infantry. Between two and three thousand high-explosive rounds were fired and covered the US positions in an area 1,500 by 1,000 yards, yet the US casualties caused by this and the subsequent fighting amounted to only eight men, or four per cent.[38]

But troops less well protected or in the open could expect heavy casualties from artillery. In early 1944 No.1 ORS of the British Army reckoned that if enemy troops occupied only slit trenches, and were subject to a rate of fire of one 25-pounder shell per 10,000 square yards per minute for a period of some 4 hours, then about 17 per cent casualties would result. If the more lethal airburst shells were employed, then 30 per cent casualties could be expected.[39] An example from the Italian campaign seems to confirm this. On 19 September 1944 a regiment of British 25-pounders fired 432 rounds in an hour on each of two German hill top positions in the GOTHIC LINE near Casaglia. The fire was observed from an OP and was seen to cover an area 300 by 300 yards. Later ground examination showed that one shell had burst every 6 yards. Early the following day British troops captured six prisoners from the position who stated that their company had sustained 23 casualties during the shelling and had afterwards withdrawn, taking their casualties with them. Most of the German troops had occupied slit trenches only one or two feet deep, while some had been in the open without any cover at all.[40]

Such artillery bombardments, of some duration, are not really comparable with fighter-bomber attack. Unlike fighter-bomber pilots, artillery gunners had the opportunity to correct aim and bring their targets under prolonged fire.[41] However, if a rapid concentration had to be put down quickly in response to a request for fire, pinpoint accuracy would not be possible. Similarly, when conducting counter-battery fire against enemy gun positions with the intention of silencing them, the object was to saturate the target with fire. In this respect, the effectiveness of both artillery and fighter-bomber attack depended not so much on the target being destroyed, but neutralised – in other words the effect on morale could be more important than the destructive effect.

Early in 1944 the British Army attempted to analyse the morale effect of artillery fire. The following quotation from a report by No.1 ORS suggests that opinion varied as to whether a sudden, short, but heavy bombardment would have a more pronounced effect than one of longer duration:

> Psychologists consider that if men are exposed to sufficient strain for a sufficient length of time they will be brought to a state of moral collapse such that for a considerable period they will be unable to fight

effectively... The essence of the kind of collapse intended is that it takes a considerable time to recover from it. Men may be petrified with fright by a short, intense bombardment and yet recover in a minute or two after the shelling ceases. But according to the psychologists...a much less frightening experience (though still above a certain minimum of strain), if continuous and prolonged, will ultimately produce a break-down from which recovery will be a matter of hours.[42]

Whether a morale effect was achieved at all depended upon a number of variables. One was the nature of the defences protecting the target troops; they had to feel vulnerable. A British Army report on artillery fire in 1944 noted that

It has been established...that if men are in such strong defences that casualties cannot be inflicted they are not likely to be demoralised by any bombardment, however long sustained, and such bombardments are a waste of ammunition.[43]

Another variable was the quality of the troops under bombardment. Troops of poor morale, especially of low grade formations, or who were inexperienced, might be more susceptible to demoralisation. In contrast, troops of high quality often proved remarkably resilient, obvious examples being the German paratroop defenders of Cassino and the SS troops containing the British and Canadian troops around Caen – both of whom offered determined resistance to Allied attacks even after saturation bombing by heavy bombers and the heaviest artillery bombardments.

Some weapons caused a greater level of demoralisation than others. By the end of 1944 Allied gunners were employing the radar proximity fuse (originally developed for anti-aircraft use) which had a greater lethality than conventional shells. This was first employed by US forces during the fighting in the Ardennes in December 1944 and proved very deadly, especially against troops caught in the open. When a German battalion attempting to cross the Sauer River was caught by a concentration of airburst shelling US troops subsequently counted 702 bodies, an incident which moved General Patton to write that the advent of the proximity fuse would compel armies to devise a new method of warfare.[44]

By the end of 1944 ground-based rocket systems for saturation fire were also being employed in North-West Europe. British 21st Army Group had submitted a requirement for a weapon capable of delivering a very large weight of shell in a short period of time, resulting in twelve 'Rocket Projectors, 3 inch, Mark I', enough to equip one battery of two troops each of six projectors, being sent to First

Canadian Army. Known as 'Land Mattress', they were a development of the Royal Navy's 'Sea Mattress' rocket system used to provide area concentrations in support of seaborne landings. Each wheel-mounted projector had 30 barrels arranged in five banks of six. Fired electrically by remote cable control, Land Mattress could fire either single rounds or a 'ripple' and had a maximum rate of fire of 30 rounds in 7¼ seconds, the time between salvoes being some ten minutes.

Land Mattress could quickly saturate an area with fire; it was calculated that one salvo from a regiment of 36 projectors in 7¼ seconds could neutralise an area of 350,000 square yards, whereas an equivalent salvo from medium artillery required sixty regiments of 5.5 inch guns. Moreover, the destructive effect of the rockets, each equivalent to a 100 lb shell, was great due to their large high-explosive content, while the noise of the rockets in flight and their detonation had a pronounced demoralising effect on the enemy. German prisoners stated that they considered Land Mattress far superior to their own Nebelwerfer rocket projector, and that it was greatly feared. The rockets also had a heartening effect on friendly infantry, particularly as experience during attacks proved that they were able to advance safely within 500 yards of their impact, thereby giving the enemy little time to recover. Land Mattress had two major drawbacks, however: a slow rate of fire compared to orthodox artillery and the long period of time needed to assemble ammunition. It took a detachment of nine men some 1½ hours to unload, unbox, assemble and replace 30 rounds carried in a three-ton lorry and this could not be reduced by dumping as the rockets were affected by moisture. First Canadian Army remained the sole user.[45]

One problem regarding the morale effect of such special ground-based weapons was that their particular properties could go unnoticed amidst the general unpleasantness of a bombardment when they were employed with conventional artillery, as was usually necessary. This was discovered after the heavy preliminary artillery concentrations at the outset of VERITABLE, the operation to clear between the rivers Maas and Rhine by First Canadian Army in February 1945, to which both radar proximity shells and Land Mattress had contributed. Subsequent interrogation of prisoners revealed that the Germans had been completely unaware of them – including a specialist artillery observer who had monitored the bombardment from an OP in the Reichswald.[46]

In contrast, fear engendered by air-to-ground weapons tended to be more pronounced. One would expect that fear of a weapon would be linked to its lethality, and a British prisoner of war interrogation report from Normandy confirmed that German troops feared strafing above all and that the terror effect of this form of attack varied in inverse proportion to the altitude from which it was delivered, strafing from low level being particularly feared.[47]

The Americans also discovered the demoralising effect of strafing. The US XIX Corps reported an occasion when its light armoured units were trying to take a wooded hill strongly defended by anti-tank guns and machine guns; supporting fighter-bombers bombed the position but German resistance remained such that the US tanks still could not advance:

> The squadron was asked to come down again and strafe the positions after which the position was taken. POWs said the bombing was not so bad, but when the 'Jabos' strafed them they lost all will to fight and tended to make the men scatter for protection regardless of orders. Many were found hiding below the ground and they didn't offer much resistance. Many were killed at their guns and in their foxholes by the strafing.[48]

Similarly, during the fighting in the Colmar Pocket in January 1945, the advance of the US 3rd Infantry Division was held at a canal by German troops firing across it from a wood. All available fighter-bombers of XII TAC were called up and strafed the wood for 30 minutes, after which 'what was left of the enemy came to the bank of the canal with hands up'.[49]

American fighter-bombers were also equipped with what was probably the most terrifying air-to-ground weapon of all: napalm. Apart from the fearsome nature of the weapon, its morale effect was enhanced by the fact that it could cause considerable damage and casualties, especially when employed in conjunction with more conventional bombs or even artillery fire. Napalm was used extensively by the US Ninth Air Force in North-West Europe, and in early 1945 its ORS described how napalm considerably reduced German defence effectiveness:

> heavy artillery and/or GP [general purpose] bombing destroys or damages buildings, communication facilities, prepared defences; consequently, the enemy must utilize masses of rubble and smashed houses as...defense positions. Napalm...upon the devastated area renders these temporary emplacements untenable, causes fires to take hold in the wreckage, and drives the enemy into the open... The enemy troops who

are not evacuated have, in a majority of cases, taken refuge in cellars, and are subject to assault without being able to offer effective resistance.[50]

When attacking German positions in woods, US commanders preferred supporting fighter-bombers to be equipped with napalm rather than with conventional fragmentation bombs. This was because on the arrival of the fighter-bombers German troops always took cover in their slit trenches which normally afforded them good protection, whereas napalm caused casualties and generated unbearable heat which forced the Germans out of these positions.

While targets such as dense wet woods, stone and concrete buildings, and concrete and steel pillboxes proved resistant to napalm's destructive effect, their occupants were not immune to fear of the weapon. After the assault on the Siegfried Line in October 1944 the US 117th Infantry Regiment reported that, although little damage was done to pillboxes by either general purpose or napalm bombs, the napalm

> had a tremendous psychological and physical effect upon the enemy troops occupying the defenses outside the pill-boxes. These outer defenses were given up because of the napalm attack forcing the enemy troops into the pill-boxes. This...enabled our attacking troops to get to the rear of these fortificatons, utilize pole charges and seize the pill-boxes... POWs stated that napalm did not bother them while they were in pill-boxes; however, the demoralizing effect was great and fear of further attack by 'fire bombs' persuaded them to stay in their pill-boxes.[51]

Yet a weapon did not need to have a high lethality in order to have a pronounced morale effect, as the German attitude to rocket fire proved. For their joint investigation of Typhoon effectiveness No.2 ORS and ORS 2nd TAF questioned about 100 German prisoners, and discovered that

> ... all who had been attacked by rockets expressed their dread of the weapon.

In view of the limited destructive effect of the rockets against defence positions the ORS were somewhat at a loss as to why this should be so, and concluded that it was

> quite definite that it is the nature of the attack that upsets the Germans and not the physical damage which it causes. None of the prisoners had seen any damage or casualties caused by the attacks which had so scared them.[52]

Three reasons were suggested to account for this fear of rockets. One was that exaggerated tales of the effects of rocket attack had spread among German troops; another was the noise generated by a diving Typhoon, and the third was the unnerving sight of the approaching rockets.[53]

With regard to close support of attacks by infantry and armour, it was vital to know what scale of effort was likely to be required to neutralize the target and for how long the German defenders were likely to be affected. In both North-West Europe and Italy experience showed that the morale effect of bombardment, either by air or artillery, was of short duration and that if it was to be exploited it was imperative to attack immediately or as soon as possible after the airstrike or artillery bombardment. But operational data from these campaigns also indicates that air attack was able to achieve such a morale effect quicker than artillery, and that it was likely to be of longer duration.

Much depended on the quality, motivation, and level of immunity from physical danger of the German troops on the receiving end of any bombardment, but, as one example, an Unteroffizier (Sergeant) of the German 578th Grenadier Regiment, taken prisoner at Il Casone in Italy on 30 September 1944, told his British captors that artillery concentrations were terrifying while they lasted but had no such effect within about three minutes after they had ceased. He also stated that German troops manned their defence positions and weapons as soon as the shelling was over as they knew the British infantry would be attacking.[54]

This can be contrasted with what could be achieved by fighter-bombers. The American experience with napalm related above suggests a morale effect of much longer duration, while the joint RAF/British Army ORS investigation of Typhoon effectiveness calculated, on the basis of combat experience, that,

> if three flights of 4 [Typhoons] attack a position at intervals of 15 minutes, there is probably a period of 10 to 20 minutes afterwards during which enemy are in no condition to offer stiff resistance to attack by ground forces.[55]

A typical example was cited which had occurred on 13 October 1944 during the heavy and prolonged fighting for Overloon in Holland. That morning a battalion of the 3rd British infantry Division attacked a German-held wood some 300 yards from their own woodland positions. This was unsuccessful and they were driven back across the

open ground with some casualties. Air support was then requested and
a Typhoon strike made on the German positions at 2 p.m. The battalion immediately advanced and took the position, this time without
opposition, its commanding officer reporting afterwards that not only
had the rockets

> successfully unnerved the enemy...they had also put new vigour into
> his own men who were somewhat disconsolate after the casualties of the
> morning.[56]

This is but one of a number of recorded examples which indicated
that, apart from having a morale effect of longer duration, air attack
could also cause a sudden change in the determination of German
troops to resist at all. For example, the US 90th Infantry Division
recorded of its attack on Lightenborn in Germany in 1945 that

> German troops surrendered after short skirmishes only after two air
> attacks on positions...while before they defended the objective for 24
> hours with bitter resistance.

The US 9th Infantry Division recorded simply that 'Every time we
have an air mission the rate of surrender goes up'.[57]

The most striking examples of this occurred when fighter-bombers
precipitated the surrender of German positions without the need to
attack. During the assault on the Crozon Peninsula in Brittany by the
US 8th Infantry Division a German strongpoint refused to surrender,
but on the approach of fighter-bombers white flags immediately went
up. Similarly, later in Germany, the US VII Corps reported how the
town of Nastatten capitulated after being only 'buzzed' by fighter-
bombers.[58] Similar experiences were recorded by British and Canadian
forces. On 1 November 1944 the 8th (Canadian) Reconnaissance
Regiment demanded the surrender of a German strongpoint on the
island of North Beveland, which was refused. Air support was
requested from 2nd TAF's No.84 Group which, while committed at
that time to the Walcheren operation, agreed to send a squadron of
Typhoons over the island as a show of strength. The Commander of
the 8th Recce Regiment warned the Germans that his supporting
aircraft would make one pass without firing, but that afterwards they
would attack. The 18 Typhoons appeared on schedule, flying low
across the island, and as soon as they had passed over the first
Germans came out to surrender, the 8th Recce Regiment taking 450
prisoners in all.[59]

Apart from the morale effect, there were also more practical reasons
why Allied troops came to prefer close air support to that of artillery.

One was that fighter-bombers could deliver in a relatively short space of time a very heavy weight of firepower, which in itself must have been a contributory factor to the enhanced morale effect, but it is also true that the fire of many artillery regiments could be concentrated on a particular target and in both campaigns TOT ('Time on Target') fire, the bringing to bear of all guns within range to fire on a single target simultaneously, became a frequent practice.[60]

However, this type of fire was less useful than fighter-bomber strikes because artillery bombardments did not permit the assault troops to approach as near to their objective, so as to take maximum advantage of the neutralisation or morale effect before those enemy troops not killed or wounded recovered from the shock of bombardment. The US study of air support compiled by Twelfth Army Group discussed the merits of artillery and fighter-bomber attacks in close support and observed that

> best results were obtained from fighter-bombers in their close support role when the...attack was concentrated on key points of resistance within very close range. Range dispersion of our heavy artillery capable of firing an equivalent weight of projectile, that is, the 240 mm howitzer or the 8 inch gun or howitzer, would not permit fire this close, even if this artillery or the ammunition therefor were always available. On the contrary, effective bombing with 500 lb GP or 260 lb fragmentation bombs was conducted by fighter-bombers against close-in enemy positions sometimes within 300 to 500 yards of our own forward elements. Moreover, it was felt by many commanders that the terrific destructive effect on personnel, matériel, and morale of a fighter-bomber attack concentrated on close-in enemy positions was worth more than any artillery preparation, if the air attack was followed immediately by a determined infantry attack.[61]

To what extent infantry became accustomed to exploiting fighter-bomber support was demonstrated to the RAF by Canadian troops in Northern France in 1944. Two pilots from No.84 Group were attached to a battalion in order to see close air support from the ground. They were taken to a viewpoint 150 yards from an isolated German pillbox which an infantry company was about to assault after a planned airstrike by Typhoons. Having seen the target, they asked the company commander when they were to move back to watch the strike go in, knowing that the danger zone extended far beyond their present position. They were surprised to be told that the strike was expected in five minutes and that there they would stay. The Typhoons arrived on schedule, their rockets hit the target area, and the infantry immediately attacked and took the position without loss. The incident did not conform to current theory either in the attack position of the infantry or the effectivess of the rockets, but the company commander had witnessed previous airstrikes and was more confident of the result than the RAF pilots, who had failed to appreciate that experienced infantry preferred the risk of casualties from their own aircraft to the greater danger of lengthening the time and distance of the assault.[62]

In much the same way attacking infantry were prepared to 'lean on' an artillery barrage, a belt of fire moving across enemy positions, by following very closely upon the bursting shells in order to arrive on the objective before the Germans had time to recover. A textbook example of British artillery successfully neutralising a German defence position occurred during Operation CLIPPER, the attack on the Geilenkirchen salient by 43rd (Wessex) Division in Germany. On 18 November 1944 the 5th Dorsets attacked the village of Bauchem, held by some 200 German troops positioned in open trenches around the village, and cleared it at the cost of only seven casualties, while taking 180 prisoners. A subsequent ORS report on the attack observed that the Germans

> offered not the slightest resistance, and (were) described by the attacking troops as looking 'absolutely yellow coloured'. P.W. interrogated later were clearly very shaken physically and said they had felt quite overwhelmed with a sense of helplessness in the face of immense superiority.[63]

Such effective neutralisation by artillery generally took much longer to achieve than that by fighter-bombers. The fire support for the Dorsets had consisted of ten minutes' artillery fire followed by fire from mortars, 20 mm and 40 mm guns, and tanks lasting for three hours and finally by a further bombardment of artillery lasting just over 30 minutes – or 185 tons of high explosive delivered over a period of hours. This had not inflicted heavy casualties, German losses amounting to between 10 and 15 per cent, while so closely had the Dorsets 'leaned on' the final barrage that four of their seven casualties had been caused by their own artillery.[64] That artillery was unlikely to achieve effective neutralisation without such prolonged and heavy fire was indicated by other attacks during the same operation. The objectives of the 7th Somerset Light Infantry, 1st Worcesters, and 5th Duke of Cornwall's Light Infantry were the villages of Neiderheide, Rischden, and Hochheid respectively. All three objectives were bombarded for only 20–40 minutes, and the artillery fire was not followed up quickly – the 7th Somerset Light Infantry being 30 minutes behind their concentrations. Although the objectives were taken, the difference in the level of fire support and the speed of the follow-up between these attacks and that at Bauchem is reflected in the casualties on both sides. This time German casualties were estimated to have been only five per cent, while those of the British were reported as having been several times greater in each battalion than had been sustained at Bauchem.[65]

To achieve effective neutralisation artillery bombardments required a lavish outlay of ammunition. As preparation for the opening of Operation VERITABLE on 8 February 1945, the area assaulted by twelve British and Canadian battalions with tank support had been bombarded by field, medium, and heavy artillery from 5.00 a.m. to 9.20 a.m., while at the same time the German forward defences were the target of a 'Pepperpot', harassing fire from every available tank gun, mortar, anti-tank gun, anti-aircraft gun and medium machine-gun. At 9.20 a.m. a barrage was started by field and medium artillery which lasted for six hours. In all 1,050 artillery pieces fired some 91,330 shells (1,596 tons) in the bombardment and 160,388 shells (2,793 tons) for the barrage. Yet, of the total of between 2,250 and 2,700 German troops of the 84th Infantry Division holding the front in extensive field defences, a subsequent British Army ORS investigation estimated that less than 60 had become casualties to shellfire. Even the neutralisation had been patchy, No.2 ORS adding that,

> when the fire support was followed up closely, the enemy surrendered at once, but the effect...was transitory. Three battalions got well behind the shelling for one reason or another and found the enemy recovering and beginning to resist.[66]

The price of failing to exploit the temporary neutralisation was high. While 1,115 Germans were taken prisoner and many of them reported themselves quite shaken by the bombardment, British and Canadian casualties amounted to 349 (459 if those caused by mines are added). Similar use of artillery on a lavish scale persisted throughout the course of VERITABLE, but some felt this to be counter-productive. The commanding officer of 1st Gordon Highlanders complained on 26 February that artillery fire was excessive, causing too much mud and destruction, and that it warned the enemy of impending attack; he called for shorter fireplans with the infantry closer behind.[67]

This was the crux of the problem of artillery in close support. Not only were barrages expensive in ammunition, they also demanded precise timing which could often be a matter of considerable difficulty. A post-war British study of wartime artillery tactics noted that experience proved the planned rate of advance rarely achieved in practice.[68] Mostly the problem was that the barrage advanced too fast, leaving the infantry behind. This is what occurred on one occasion at Cassino, when a barrage advancing at 100 yards in six minutes began to leave the infantry behind from the start. Similarly, during the attack on Caumont in Normandy, British tanks had to push on far ahead of the infantry they were supporting in order to even reach and cross the start line for the attack before the effects of the barrage had worn off. Occasionally the barrage could instead be too slow. After an attack during the fighting at Overloon in Holland British infantry complained that the barrage, fired by three divisional artilleries and moving at a rate of 100 yards in five minutes, had actually delayed their advance.[69]

One solution to this problem, which proved successful in both Italy and North-West Europe, was to extend the barrage by employing waves of fighter-bombers to provide what amounted to a moving belt of fire support in the path of an attack. With artillery indicating the target area, the fighter-bombers were able to give the closest possible support to infantry and armour, while retaining sufficient elasticity, lacking in pre-timed artillery barrages, to conform with the ground situation at any time during the progress of an attack.

The first such example occurred in Tunisia in March 1943. During the battle to break through the MARETH LINE, the New Zealand Corps of the British Eighth Army was confronted by a valley stretching northwards between two ranges of hills and leading to the village of El Hamma. The Italian infantry defending this 6,000 yards bottleneck had been reinforced by the German 164th and 21st Panzer Divisions with anti-tank guns and minefields, so that a formidable obstacle blocked the route to Gabes. On learning of the problem, Air Vice-Marshal Broadhurst, then commanding Western Desert Air Force, conceived the idea of exploiting the Allied air superiority by using all available air units in a concentrated attack upon this narrow front with the object of paralysing the defences for long enough to allow the New Zealand infantry, followed by armour, to break through. Broadhurst's plan was welcomed with enthusiasm by Eighth Army, but not so by Broadhurst's immediate superior, Air Marshal Sir Arthur Coningham, commanding Allied North-West African Tactical

Air Force, who had no wish to accustom soldiers to having such air resources subordinated to their operations and who was also concerned about losses likely to be incurred by aircraft attacking at the very low level suggested by Broadhurst. However, because such use of aircraft could be justified in view of the small threat by then posed by the depleted Axis air forces, the Desert Air Force plan went ahead.[70]

At 3.30 p.m. on 26 March three formations of light and medium bombers struck the Axis positions from low level, pattern-bombing with the aim of creating disorganisation and severing telephone communications. They were followed immediately by the first relay of fighter-bombers, bombing and strafing from low level, the target area being indicated by artillery firing red and blue smoke while the New Zealanders burned yellow smoke to indicate their own positions. A strength of two and a half squadrons of fighter-bombers was maintained in the battle area, fresh relays arriving every 15 minutes with the pilots bombing specific targets and then strafing gun positions. For the first time they were receiving radio instructions during their attacks from an RAF officer observing the battle from an OP with the forward troops. At 4 p.m. the infantry attacked under cover of a barrage moving at the rate of 100 feet a minute, the main object of which was to define a bomb-line for the fighter-bombers that were continually bombing and strafing in front of the line of bursting shells. This 'air blitz', as it was termed, lasted for 2½ hours and a total of 412 sorties were flown for the loss of 11 aircraft. The operation was successful, the infantry and armour having broken through and advanced 6,000 yards by dusk with only light losses.[71]

The next occasion when Desert Air Force fighter-bombers were similarly employed occurred in Northern Italy. By 11 November 1944 the British V Corps had cleared Forli and advanced to the line of the River Montone, but further progress was held up by German positions on the east bank occupied by troops of the 278th Infantry Division supported by tanks and self-propelled guns. The terrain in the area was well suited to defence, being low lying and too soft to allow armour to deploy off the roads, and dotted with numerous farms and houses which had been turned into strongpoints. The V Corps decided to clear these positions employing the 12th Brigade of 4th Infantry Division, but also requested close air support from Desert Air Force and, in particular, a solution to the problem of safe bombing over a fluid bombline. The RAF response was 'Timothy'.

On 12 November the 12th Brigade attacked in three phases of approximately 1,000 yards advance. First artillery laid a coloured-

smoke bombline as instructed by the ROVER control 300 yards ahead
of the forward troops. At 7.30 a.m., 8.30 a.m., and 9.30 a.m. fighter-
bombers, in flights of 12 aircraft arriving every ten minutes, bombed
and strafed everything in sight to a depth of 1,000 yards parallel to,
and 1,000 yards either side of, the brigade axis of advance. After a few
minutes the intensive 'blitz' was lifted and the infantry advanced. By
the end of the day the 12th Brigade had advanced over 2,000 yards and
taken 106 prisoners at the cost of 13 casualties.[72] On the following day,
after a further six 'Timothy' attacks by 12 squadrons, including
rocket-firing US P-47 Thunderbolts, German resistance collapsed,
the enthusiastic commander of 12th Brigade reporting that his
casualties were the lightest for such an operation in his experience.
Eighth Army was equally enthusiastic, describing 'Timothy'

> as the greatest step forward in air/ground cooperation since the innova-
> tion of the Rover controls.[73]

Meanwhile, similar attacks had been carried out in North-West
Europe, where they were referred to as 'Winkle'. On 1 October 1944
No.84 Group RAF noted of 'Winkle', only recently introduced, that

> This type of operation involves the employment of aircraft in a very
> close support role, where the forward line of our own troops is
> identified by a line of white smoke extending for 1,000 yards, 2,000
> yards, or 3,000 yards. This line of smoke clearly defines the area beyond
> which pilots are free to attack. Normally such an operation is laid on in
> connection with a ground offensive, with the object of destroying and
> disrupting the enemy's defences and reducing morale, in order to
> facilitate an immediate advance. On the one or two occasions when this
> method of support has been employed, success has been evident...In
> difficult country where it is not possible, or where it is very difficult, for
> ground OPs to locate exactly the position of mortars and defended
> posts, it is usually a somewhat haphazard procedure to attempt to
> indicate pinpoint targets by the use of red smoke. 'WINKLE' is
> considered to be the better method in these circumstances, even though
> it may entail a certain waste of effort.[74]

On 20 October 1944 Typhoons of No.84 Group carried out a particularly successful 'Winkle' on the immediate front of the Canadian
2nd Infantry and 4th Armoured Divisions. This was in support of
Operation SUITCASE, the attack towards Esschen as part of the
advance to clear South Beveland in Holland. Some 59 sorties were
flown by rocket-Typhoons and Typhoon bombers during the day, the
Operations Record Book of No.263 Squadron recording that

Bombing was good, nearly all falling on selected targets by the road side. A message was received later from Army H.Q. to say the attack was very successful as many enemy strongpoints had been wiped out, and they had been able to advance to within one mile of Esschen.[75]

Further approbation was received from 10th Canadian Infantry Brigade, whose troops reported finding the bodies of 42 German troops killed during the 'Winkle' on their front alone.[76]

By the end of the year a further variation had been introduced in Italy. On 14 December 1944 the 1st Canadian Division, advancing towards the River Senio, encountered stiff German opposition in the area of the Naviglio Canal. A request was made to Desert Air Force for a 'Timothy', but weather conditions precluded bombing. Rather than leave the Canadians unsupported, Desert Air Force suggested a 'Timothy' without bombs, a strafing attack by three squadrons. In the afternoon infantry of the Westminster Regiment supported by tanks of Lord Strathcona's Horse attacked northwards along the canal road. Just ahead of them Spitfires strafed the German positions on each side of the canal, this support being so close that spent cartridge cases from the Spitfires' guns fell among the Canadians. By evening the German positions had been cleared at the cost of four Canadians killed and 16 wounded, over 100 German prisoners being taken. Strafing 'Timothies' were afterwards referred to as 'Pigs'.[77]

The advantage of 'Timothies' and 'Winkles' was that the fighter-bombers could neutralise German positions to greater depth than the single belt of fire of an artillery barrage, and added the more pronounced morale effect of air attack. They also permitted greater flexibility in the advance. Even when, as a result of unexpected opposition, the advance did not conform to plan, the fighter-bomber pilots could still directly support the infantry. The air attacks on 12 November in Italy were timed to coincide with the infantry advance, but in subsequent operations fighter-bombers attacked with equal success at prearranged intervals, irrespective of the line reached by the forward troops, the smoke safety-line being put down to conform with the ground battle at any given time. The smoke line could also be put down diagonally to the axis of advance, and pilots were briefed for this eventuality. Moreover, particularly troublesome strongpoints could be singled out for attack in the usual way through the FCP.[78]

As with CABRANK, such operations could be expensive of air effort. At least 260 sorties were flown in close support of 12th Brigade in Italy on 12 and 13 November 1944, albeit with only one aircraft being lost. Moreover, mass air attacks on generally defined areas instead of specific targets necessarily involved a certain waste of effort, with much of the bombing and strafing being directed at areas unoccupied by German troops. As employment of 'Timothies' became extensive, their advantages became negated by misuse. In 1945 Eighth Army reported of 'Timothy' that it was intended as air support for offensive operations, but that

> it was...NOT always used as such, and there was a tendency for it to degenerate into a mere 'area blitz'.[79]

Partly as a result of excessive caution and partly because in some formations the mechanics of 'Timothy' were insufficiently under-stood, the artillery smoke line was often put down between 500 and 800 yards ahead of the leading British troops. This was too far, and meant that the fighter-bombers did not attack the forward German positions, but instead, as German prisoners affirmed, bombed and strafed targets some 400 yards to the rear of the German front line. After reviewing a number of cases, I Canadian Corps advocated that the smoke bombline be put down no further than 300 yards from the forward troops.[80]

Most close support strikes involved some form of artillery participa-tion. Usually this took the passive form of indicating targets or the bombline to the aircraft but, when possible, guns had the more active role of assisting the aircraft by suppressing known German flak positions, airburst shells being effective in inducing flak gunners to remain in cover. Attaching an artillery FOO to the staff of an FCP also proved profitable, for this officer was on hand to engage a target rejected as unsuitable for air attack and, for those targets accepted for airstrike, could arrange smoke indication more rapidly. This led to combining programmes of air attack and artillery bombardment, such as shelling a target area a few minutes after an airstrike with the intention of catching the German troops just as they were emerging from cover.[81]

As time went on, a method of more direct artillery/fighter-bomber co-operation evolved and, as with many air support innovations, it first appeared in Italy. At the height of the battle for Rimini in September 1944 it was found that the two FCPs working on the Eighth Army front (ROVER DAVID and ROVER PADDY) could not cope with the number of targets submitted by Divisions and Brigades. Moreover, as many of these targets were German gun and mortar positions, it became imperative to ensure as far as possible that those attacked by fighter-bombers were those actually engaging the British troops. In effect, an improved method of passing accurate counter-battery data to the fighter-bomber pilots was necessary, requiring specialised artillery involvment.

The solution was the creation of an FCP entirely concerned with air attack on enemy guns – ROVER FRANK – situated at an AGRA headquarters where artillery counter-battery officers worked together with an RAF air controller. The AGRA furnished the FCP with a regularly updated list of active German battery positions, and when aircraft were given a target of German guns they were to check in with ROVER FRANK, who confirmed that those particular guns were still active. If they were, then the airstrike went ahead, but if not ROVER FRANK directed the strike upon an active battery. ROVER FRANK went into operation on 18 September, directing a series of airstrikes at 15 minute intervals which succeeded in reducing considerably the volume of fire from 11 German batteries firing on Canadian troops from the Trebbio–Marecchia valley.[82]

Fighter-bomber attack on German batteries proved effective by suppressing German fire even if the guns themselves were not destroyed. Mediterranean Allied Air Forces ORS reported that

> During and after fighter-bomber attacks on enemy gun positions, the shelling activity of these guns is reduced; either because material damage has been caused, or firing has ceased during the attack, or because the battery attacked has moved to avoid further attack.[83]

Precisely how effective such attacks were was discovered by an intensive ORS analysis of fighter-bomber support for British V Corps operations in Italy between October and December 1944. From this data, having particular regard to the level of casualties inflicted by German shellfire and a comparison of the volume of this fire on days when fighter-bombers had attacked the German guns with days when air support was reduced or unavailable, it was found that ten fighter-bomber attacks, amounting to some 50 sorties, directed against German gun positions during a day approximately halved their activity. When 100 fighter-bomber attacks, equivalent to some 500 sorties, were carried out 60 to 90 fewer British troops were killed and some 200 to 300 fewer wounded by German shellfire. The cost to the RAF of these 500 sorties, calculated under the operational conditions of the time, would have amounted to 2.6 pilots killed or missing, 0.3 pilots injured, and 4.5 aircraft lost in a total of some 600 flying hours.[84]

The saving of nearly 400 army casualties seems a fair return for such losses, but the necessary commitment of air effort, amounting to over one sortie per army casualty saved, was high. As with all the close air support methods discussed above, such commitment of air resources was possible only as a result of the Allied air forces possessing complete air superiority and having available large numbers of tactical aircraft. This aside, the figures suggest that German batteries were seriously disrupted by air attack.

In fact, there is evidence to suggest that air attack was considerably more effective than artillery counter-battery (CB) fire. In a comparison analogous to that between airstrikes and artillery concentrations in close support of attacks, it can be seen that neutralisation achieved by artillery against German guns tended to be of shorter duration than that achieved by fighter-bombers. For example, after the capture of Boulogne in September 1944 an investigation by No.2 ORS observed of artillery CB that

> Discussion with Infantry and Artillery personnel served to confirm once more...that while an accurate concentration on a well-located battery invariably silenced it for the duration of the concentration, the effect seldom lasted for any length of time afterwards.[85]

That this was realised at the time and acted upon is reflected in the setting up of ROVER FRANK in Italy, which was itself a reflection of the number of close-support requests with German gun and mortar positions as their target. Indeed, one artillery specialist has recently observed of the campaigns in 1944–45 that aircraft came to assume the greater responsibility for counter-battery work, adopting the role carried out by heavy artillery in the First World War and leaving field artillery to concentrate on the close-in battle.[86]

There appears to be a paradox resulting from this analysis. The Allied armies were well equipped with artillery which was able to provide fire support rapidly in response to requests from forward troops. They were also supported by fighter-bombers of the tactical air forces which normally could not respond to support requests with anything like the same speed without a considerable commitment of air resources to the battle area, and whose attacks offered little significant advantage over artillery in terms of destruction. Yet fighter-bomber attack appears to have been significantly more effective than artillery in terms of neutralisation, and the above examples from both Italy and North-West Europe indicate that against close support targets neutralisation, albeit temporary, was just as important as destruction, indeed more so in view of the small likelihood of the latter being achieved.[87]

Fighter-bomber attack frequently proved to have a greater morale effect than that of artillery and, moreover, could cause this demoralization of the enemy more rapidly. This in turn was also likely to be of longer duration than that caused by artillery bombardment. The reason was partly the shock effect of the weight of firepower that fighter-bombers could deliver in a comparatively short space of time. In addition, the Allied ORS investigations suggest that, in general terms, being subjected to air attack was genuinely more frightening for troops than being subjected to artillery bombardment and induced a greater feeling of helplessness.

In this respect fighter-bomber close air support was invaluable for Allied troops about to attack German positions, but only if the assault troops were so placed as to take maximum advantage of the shock effect by attacking as soon after the airstrike as possible. While the shock effect of air attack may have been of longer duration than that caused by artillery, it was, as the ORS calculated, unlikely to last beyond 20 minutes. Depending upon such variables as the nature and weight of air attack and the quality of the German troops and their level of protection, it could be considerably less. Very often it was not possible for the assault troops to take immediate advantage of airstrikes, even had it been planned that they should do so. A study of the message logs of British Army formations reveals numerous occasions when there was a considerable lapse of time between a requested airstrike and an attack going in.

The reason was what the nineteenth-century military philosopher Carl von Clausewitz termed the 'friction' of war, the propensity of the unforseen to intervene to upset plans.[88] Battalions waiting to attack could be delayed by the fact that another battalion detailed to clear the area of their start line encountered unexpectedly heavy resistance. Armour in support could be delayed in moving up due to road congestion or the presence of mines. Orders and timings could be changed at short notice due to circumstances beyond the knowledge and control of units detailed to attack. All these could occur with too little notice to alter air support timings, or even after the airstrike had been made. Occasionally the airstrike could go in at a time other than that originally intended due to the threat of adverse weather closing in, while it proved impossible for the army to speed up its own preparations. Occasionally the fighter-bombers could inadvertently attack the wrong target. Often, particularly during major operations, there was no attempt to exploit the morale effect of many of the air attacks, fighter-bombers being directed to engage German positions in general 'softening-up' attacks not closely co-ordinated with specific ground assaults.

Under such conditions the greatest value of close air support, that of neutralisation, was wasted. The soldiers learnt how important it was to exploit airstrikes rapidly, yet they could hardly be expected to desist from requesting air support on occasions when it was known that such exploitation was neither possible nor intended. In 1943–45 Allied troops became accustomed to a lavish scale of air support, and the fact that it could be requested meant that it would be. During their joint investigation of Typhoons in 1945, ORS 2nd TAF and No.2 ORS observed that British and Canadian troops had become so dependent upon Typhoons that

> when, for reasons not always obvious to the front line troops, a request for close support Typhoons has to be turned down, a feeling of dissatisfaction is apt to arise.[89]

When close air support was not exploited on the battlefield the fighter-bombers might have been more profitably employed against targets beyond the battlefront. This is the subject of Chapter 8.

NOTES

1. Martin Blumenson, *Breakout and Pursuit* (Washington, DC: Dept. of the Army, 1961), p. 178.
2. Advanced Headquarters, RAF Desert Air Force, ORB Nov. 1944 – Jan. 1945, PRO AIR 24/443 and AIR 27/444.
3. Shelford Bidwell, *Gunners At War: A Tactical Study of the Royal Artillery in the Twentieth Century* (London: Arms & Armour, 1970), p. 139.
4. Bidwell, pp. 232–3; Ian V. Hogg, *The Guns*, in *Tanks & Weapons of World War II* (London: Phoebus, 1973); Ian V. Hogg, *British and American Artillery of World War 2* (London: Arms & Armour, 1978).
5. RAF Desert Air Force Report, *Fighter Bombing* (1944), in *Employment of Fighter-Bombers – Policy*, PRO AIR 23/1826.
6. Bill Colgan, *World War II Fighter Bomber Pilot* (Blue Ridge Summit, PA: Tab Books, 1985), p. 150.
7. General Omar N. Bradley and the US 12th Army Group Air Effects Committee, *Effect of Air Power on Military Operations, Western Europe* (15 July 1945), p. 42, PRO AIR 40/1131.
8. RAF Desert Air Force Report, *Fighter Bombing*.
9. Bradley and 12th Army Group Air Effects Committee, p. 43.
10. Royal Armoured Corps Pamphlet: *Armoured Operations in Italy, May 1944 – January 1945*, p. 77
11. Organisation tables, British and US divisions (1944), in 'The Allied Armada', by Major-General R.H. Barry, in *History of the Second World War* (London: Phoebus, 1973), pp.1742–3.
12. Bidwell, p. 138.

13. Ibid., p. 142.
14. Kenneth Brookes, *Battle Thunder: The Story of Britain's Artillery* (Osprey Publishing, 1973), p. 217.
15. A.L. Pemberton, *The Development of Artillery Tactics and Equipment* (London: The War Office, 1951), p. 215.
16. Bidwell, *Gunners at War*, p. 143; J.B.A. Bailey, *Field Artillery and Firepower* (Oxford: The Military Press, 1989), pp. 202–3.
17. Bailey, *Field Artillery and Firepower*, p.192.
18. Major-General J.A. Crane, 'Full Use of Field Artillery', in *Field Artillery Journal*, Volume 35, No.6 (June 1945), pp. 354–8.
19. Ken Wakefield, *The Flying Grasshoppers: US Liaison Aircraft Operations in Europe 1942–45*, (Leicester: Midland Counties, 1990), pp. 75–6. British development and use of Air OP squadrons is detailed in Major-General H.J. Parham and E.M.G. Belfield, *Unarmed Into Battle: The Story of the Air Observation Post* (Chippenham: Picton, 1986).
20. Desmond Scott, *Typhoon Pilot* (London: Arrow, 1988), p. 115.
21. Hilary St. G. Saunders, *Royal Air Force 1939–45*, Vol. III (London: HMSO, 1954), p. 117.
22. The AAF Evaluation Board in the ETO, *The Effectiveness of Third Phase Tactical Air Operations in the European Theater, 5 May 1944–8 May 1945* (Feb. 1946), p. 339, PRO AIR 40/1111.
23. Christopher Shores, *Ground Attack Aircraft of World War II* (London: Macdonald & Jane's, 1977), p. 132.
24. RAF Desert Air Force Report, *Fighter Bombing*.
25. Ibid.
26. British 21st Army Group Report (May 1945), *Air Support for Operations Plunder, Flashpoint, and Varsity*, Part III, *The Forward Control of Aircraft during Plunder/Varsity*, PRO AIR 40/313.
27. Ibid.
28. RAF Desert Air Force ORB, 7 Nov. 1944, PRO AIR 24/443; No.83 Group RAF, Intelligence Summary No.94 (0001 hours 17 Sept. to 0001 hours 18 Sept. 1944), PRO AIR 25/705.
29. No.2 ORS/ORS RAF 2nd TAF Joint Report No.3 (1945), *Rocket Firing Typhoons in Close Support of Military Operations*, in *Operational Research in North West Europe*, PRO WO 291/1331.
30. No.2 ORS Report No.16, *Air and Ground Support in the Assault on Boulogne* Appendix "E" discussing Operation UNDERGO (Calais) in *Operational Research in North-West Europe*.
31. ORS RAF 2nd TAF Report No.32 (December 1945), *Fighter-Bomber Attacks on Guns and Strong Points in the Closing Phase*, PRO AIR 37/61.
32. No.2 ORS Report No.16, *Air and Ground Support in the Assault on Boulogne*.
33. No.1 ORS (British Army, Italy), Report 1/28, quoted in Army Operational Research Group Report No.282 (1945), *A Study of Casualties and Damage to Personnel and Equipment Caused by Some Air and Artillery Bombardments in European Operations*, PRO WO 291/262.
34. ORS RAF 2nd TAF Report No.32, *Fighter-Bomber Attacks on Guns and Strong Points*.
35. No.2 ORS/ORS RAF 2nd TAF Joint Report No.3, *Rocket Firing Typhoons in Close Support*. In Normandy, a team of investigators from No. 83 Group examined the results of rocket-Typhoon attacks against German strongpoints in villages around Caen and at Carpiquet airfield. The village buildings were rugged rural dwellings with walls about 20 inches thick. The RAF team found that instantaneously fused rockets had blown holes up to nine feet in diameter in these walls, but in the light of comments from Canadian and British infantry officers they reported that even direct hits were insufficient to render them untenable. Typhoons had also fired some 56 rockets at a château strongpoint to the north-west of Caen, but the RAF team found evidence of only 12 effective hits, and no evidence that the defence had been impeded by the explosions or debris. At Carpiquet the Germans had fought tenaciously to hold the airfield. On 4 July during Operation WINDSOR, the attempt by 3rd Canadian Division to capture it, the Royal Winnipeg Rifles sustained 132 casualties in attacking German strongpoints which, later in the day, were rocketed by 44 Typhoons. Here the air attacks had been more effective; the airfield buildings had brick walls some two feet thick, but rocket hits had sprayed their interiors with lethal splinters of stone and steel. No.83 Group concluded that a much-increased scale of air attack was necessary to achieve adequate levels of destruction. The usual practice of attacking village strongpoints with totals of 60–100 rockets (8–12 Typhoons) was inadequate, and they suggested that the scale

of attack be such as to ensure that each house was hit by four rockets. Attacks against isolated strongpoint buildings, such as the château, required saturation by at least 120 rockets (15 Typhoons). Appendix C to No.83 Group Operations Record Book (1944), *Effect of RP Attack Against Villages (Strong Points)*, PRO AIR 25/704. Canadian losses from C.P. Stacey, *The Victory Campaign* (Ottawa: 1960).

Similar conclusions were reached by Allied ORS investigating close air support in the Far East. In 1945 a report compiled by the USAAF operating in support of British Fourteenth Army in Burma noted that

High percentages of casualties can be achieved only by higher concentration of bombs on the target than are obtainable with the normal strikes (of a squadron or fewer of fighter-bombers). When the enemy can be contained in the target area for a considerable period of time (that is, long enough for several such strikes on the same positions), the effects of such strikes are cumulative. Killing more than 5–10 per cent of the enemy in a position is, therefore, normally something that can be achieved by fighter bombers only in a static battle, or a very slowly moving one.

US Army Air Forces, India Burma Theater (2 June 1945), *The Effectiveness of Air Strikes as carried out by 221 Group in Co-Operation with Fourteenth Army*, PRO AIR 23/4359.

36. No.2 ORS/ORS RAF 2nd TAF Joint Report No.3, *Rocket Firing Typhoons in Close Support*.
37. Ibid.
38. US 12th Army Group Battle Experiences No.62 (9 Oct. 1944), quoted in British Army Operational Research Group Report No.282, *A Study of Casualties and Damage*.
39. No.1 ORS British Army, Report (February 1944), *Bombardment to break Morale*, PRO WO 291/1327.
40. No.1 ORS British Army Report No.1/24 (1944), *Effects of Artillery Fire – Italy*, PRO WO 291/1317.
41. See Chapter 3.
42. No.1 ORS British Army, *Bombardment To Break Morale*.
43. British Army Report (1944), *The Probability of Hitting Targets with Artillery Fire*, PRO WO 291/1330.
44. General Patton to General Campbell, quoted in Roby Vattisuom, *Present and Future Artillery Fuzes*, in *Defence Today*, No.87–8 (Aug. 1985), pp. 311–16.
45. British Army Battle Analysis Study (1945), *Role of Rockets as Artillery Weapons, 1944–45*, PRO WO 232/49.
46. No.2 ORS Report No.26 (1945), *Fire Support in Operation Veritable*, to be found in No.2 ORS *Operational Research in North-West Europe*.
47. Prisoner of War Interrogation Report, ADI (K) Report No. 382/1944 (24 July 1944), PRO AIR 37/760. With conditions and theatres of war this varied. Japanese troops in bunker positions had little to fear from strafing. A captured Japanese Intelligence Officer questioned on the effects of air attack stated that troops were nervous of bomb hits but that when strafing started, which usually followed bombing, it was time to relax and 'light up cigarettes'. No.10 ORS (Fourteenth Army) Report (March 1945), *Interrogation Of A Japanese Officer*, PRO AIR 23/2829.
48. US XIX Corps, quoted in The AAF Evaluation Board in the ETO, *The Effectiveness of Third Phase Tactical Air Operations*.
49. Ibid., p. 230.
50. ORS US 9th Air Force, (9th February 1945), *Use and Effectiveness of Napalm Fire Bomb*, PRO AIR 37/956.
51. Ibid.
52. No.2 ORS/ORS RAF 2nd TAF Joint Report No.3, *Rocket Firing Typhoons in Close Support*.
53. Ibid. German troops may have heard rumours of casualties and damage caused by Typhoon rocket attacks against troops and motor transport caught in the open, when casualties would have been greater.
54. No.1 ORS British Army Report No.1/24, *Effects of Artillery Fire – Italy*. It is also true that attacks by fighter-bombers tended to be less predictable than artillery. The cessation of an artillery bombardment was very likely to presage an attack by Allied troops, whereas the departure of fighter-bombers did not necessarily mean that all Allied aircraft had left the battle area.

55. No.2 ORS/ORS RAF 2nd TAF Joint Report No.3.
56. Ibid.
57. US 90th and 9th Infantry Divisions, quoted in The AAF Evaluation Board in the ETO, *The Effectiveness of Third Phase Tactical Air Operations*, p. 231.
58. Ibid., quoting US VIII Corps.
59. Jeffery Williams, *The Long Left Flank* (London: Leo Cooper, 1988), pp. 131–2.
60. Bailey, *Field Artillery and Firepower*, p. 205.
61. Bradley and 12th Army Group Air Effects Committee, *Effect of Air Power on Military Operations*. In a post-war USAAF analysis the US XVI Corps stated of close air support strikes against fortified villages and strongpoints within artillery range that 'The desired results in many cases can be obtained more quickly and effectively by air'. Quoted in The AAF Evaluation Board in the ETO, *The Effectiveness of Third Phase Tactical Air Operations*, PRO AIR 40/1111.
62. Incident related by Jeffery Williams (author of *The Long Left Flank*) in letter to I.R. Gooderson, 19 Feb. 1990.
63. No.2 ORS Report No.22, *The Effect of Artillery Fire on Enemy Forward Defensive Positions in the Attack on Geilenkirchen*, in *Operational Research in North-West Europe*.
64. Ibid.; War Diary, 5th Dorsetshire Regiment, Nov. 1944, PRO WO 171/1287
65. No.2 ORS Report No.22.
66. No.2 ORS Report No.26, *Fire Support in Operation Veritable* in *Operational Research in North-West Europe*.
67. Pemberton, *The Development of Artillery Tactics and Equipment*, p. 267. Over 3,000 guns were assembled for the crossing of the Rhine in March 1945. One regiment alone during this operation, the 13th Royal Horse Artillery, on 23 March fired without cease for ten hours, and by just over 15 hours had fired 16,800 rounds of high-explosive. Brookes, *Battle Thunder*, p. 221.

   Such colossal expenditure of ammunition resulted in periods of artillery famine either through shortage or because rounds were being conserved for a major assault. In Italy before the assault on the GUSTAV LINE in May 1944, for which 1,060 guns were assembled, the British 25-pounders were restricted to 15 rounds per gun per day and the medium guns only 10 rounds per day. Pemberton, pp. 212–13.

   John Ellis points out that Allied artillery expenditure in 1944–45 was on a par with the First World War. In North-West Europe alone US artillery fired some 48 million rounds, equivalent to 25.6 per cent of the 187 million rounds fired by the British Armies on the Western Front between September 1914 and November 1918. See *Brute Force: Allied Strategy and Tactics in the Second World War* (London: André Deutsch, 1990), p. 536.
68. Pemberton, p. 235.
69. Ibid. But experience showed that an increasing use of 'on call' targets instead of timed programmes brought occasions when the infantry found it difficult to decide when and where to call down fire support. When command was not centralised, there was the risk that one unit by calling for fire support might bring down fire on to another that had advanced further. In the event of communications failure, the absence of a timed programme could result in no artillery support at all.
70. I.S.O. Playfair and C.J.C Molony, *The Mediterranean and Middle East*, Volume IV (London: HMSO, 1966), pp. 344–50.
71. Ibid.; No.211 Group RAF Operations Record Book and Appendices, March 1943, PRO AIR 25/848 and PRO AIR 25/849; RAF Narrative, *The North African Campaign, November 1942–May 1943*, pp.175–9, PRO AIR 41/33.
72. War Office Narrative, *Italian Campaign*, Section 4, *Winter Oct. 1944 – March 1945*, p. 104, PRO CAB 44/147; Air Historical Branch Narrative, *The Italian Campaign 1943–45*, Vol. II, *Operations June 1944 – May 1945*, pp.217–18; RAF Desert Air Force ORB, Nov. 1944, PRO AIR 24/443.
73. Eighth Army G (Air) Narrative, Aug. 1944 – May 1945, PRO WO 204/8120.
74. No.84 Group RAF ORB, 1 Oct. 1944, PRO AIR 25/709.
75. No.263 Squadron ORB, Oct. 1944, PRO AIR 27/1548.
76. No.84 Group RAF ORB, 21 Oct. 1944.
77. Air Historical Branch Narrative, *The Italian Campaign*, Vol. II, p. 219; G.W.L. Nicholson, *The Canadians In Italy 1943–1945* (Ottawa: 1957), p. 631.
78. Air Historical Branch Narrative, *The Italian Campaign*, Vol. II, p. 219.
79. Eighth Army G (Air) Narrative.

80. Air Historical Branch Narrative, *The Italian Campaign*, Vol. II, p. 218.
81. Ibid.
82. Ibid.
83. Mediterranean Allied Air Forces ORS, Report No.36 (July 1945), *The Reduction of Enemy Artillery Activity, and the Resultant Saving of Army Casualties, by Fighter-Bomber Attacks on Hostile Batteries*, PRO AIR 23/7455.
84. Ibid.
85. No.2 ORS Report No.16, *Air and Ground Support in the Assault on Boulogne*.
86. Bailey, *Field Artillery and Firepower*, p.197.
87. By 1945 artillery tactics in North-West Europe emphasised neutralisation, with many favouring the development of longer range guns with a lighter (20-lb) shell. But gunners in the Far East were disdainful of neutralisation, having learnt that the only way to deal with formidable Japanese field defences was to destroy them and their occupants. See Bailey, *Field Artillery and Firepower*, p.230, and Pemberton, *The Development of Artillery Tactics and Equipment*, p. 320. An emphasis on destruction can also be discerned in the records of Allied tactical air forces in the Far East, and much work was done by RAF ORS Air Command South East Asia and by the RAF's Jungle Targets Research Unit in attempts to determine the most effective method of destroying Japanese bunker positions and fieldworks from the air. Their papers are in the PRO AIR 23 files.
88. Carl von Clausewitz, *On War* (Harmondsworth: Penguin, 1986), pp. 164–5.
89. No.2 ORS/ORS RAF 2nd TAF Joint Report No.3, *Effects of Artillery – Italy*.

The Cost Effectiveness of Close Air Support: A Comparison with Armed Reconnaissance

The single most important ground attack mission rivalling close air support in terms of the commitment of Allied fighter-bomber effort in 1943–45 was armed reconnaissance. There are two dimensions to the following discussion, cost and effectiveness, and the object of drawing a comparative analysis is to show which of the two mission types incurred the heaviest losses in aircraft and pilots, and to determine precisely what the Allied fighter-bombers achieved when directed against ground targets other than in the close air support role.

THE ALTERNATIVE MISSION: ARMED RECONNAISSANCE

In 1944 RAF Desert Air Force in Italy described armed reconnaissance (usually abbreviated to armed recce in contemporary documents) thus:

> Pilots are given a general area, usually well behind the enemy lines, in which to find and attack with bombs and machine-gun fire, any target of tactical value. They use their own discretion and initiative as to the targets they select for attack. These targets include...M.T. [motor transport], bridges, camps and barracks, trains, defence works, airfields, ships or barges and fuel dumps...[1]

This was an intensely offensive use of tactical air power, but that there was an element of reconnaissance involved was confirmed by RAF 2nd TAF which reported of armed reconnaissance in 1945 that

> fighter aircraft are sent out to look for ground targets and attack them. At the same time, pilots bring back any possible information about the enemy ground situation.[2]

While the impact of close air support was felt at the battlefront, that of armed reconnaissance was felt sometimes far behind it, as fighter-bombers brought the German rear areas and lines of communications under attack. This was in fact interdiction, even when not part of a deliberate interdiction campaign, and was in effect a continual air offensive demanding a consistently large commitment of sorties.

In North-West Europe, more sorties were flown on armed reconnaissance than on close support by the Allied tactical air forces. Shortly after the end of the war in 1945 ORS 2nd TAF produced a summary showing that during the eleven month campaign of 1944-45 the fighters and fighter-bombers of 2nd TAF had flown 80,957 sorties on fighter-escort missions and patrols, 52,975 sorties on close-support missions, and 73,406 sorties on armed-reconnaissance missions.[3]

A predominance of armed-reconnaissance sorties can also be seen in the operations of the US tactical air forces in this theatre. Between October 1943 and May 1945 fighters of the US Ninth Air Force flew 73,123 armed-reconnaissance sorties, while those committed to 'dive bombing' and 'rocket-projecting and bombing', which embraced close support, amounted to a combined total of 55,983 sorties – strikingly similar to the corresponding 2nd TAF totals.[4] Close support apparently took second place to armed reconnaissance in the operations of the 1st US (Provisional) TAF, supporting the US Sixth Army Group in the Alsace-Lorraine area and later in Germany between November 1944 and May 1945. In this period the P-47 Thunderbolt squadrons of 1st TAF flew 14,479 armed-reconnaissance sorties, as opposed to 5,563 sorties listed as 'ground support'.[5]

Armed reconnaissance also accounted for a high percentage of sorties during the campaigns in Sicily and Italy. However, with regard to the Mediterranean theatre it is difficult to determine precisely the balance between close air support and armed reconnaissance because Mediterranean Allied Air Force (MAAF) did not employ these terms. This problem has been pointed out by American historian Alan Wilt, who observes that during the campaign in Sicily tactical sorties by fighters were either listed as 'offensive sweeps' or 'ground attacks'. Thus between 9 July and 17 August 1943 some 4,000 Allied fighters flew 45,173 sorties of which 13,309 were listed in these categories. Professor Wilt observes that, as far as can be discerned from available sources, most of the sweeps and attacks reflected interdiction missions rather than close air support. During the period of the offensive on Rome (Operation DIADEM) from 12 May to 22 June 1944, MAAF categorised fighter tactical operations as either 'fighter-bomber' or 'strafing and sweep' missions. Of the 32,291 such sorties flown during this period, Professor Wilt estimates that about half were directed against interdiction targets, with the other half, or 24 per cent of the DIADEM total, being in close air support.[6]

COMPARATIVE LOSSES

The attrition rate of pilots and aircraft among fighter-bomber squadrons engaged in attacking ground targets during 1943–45 was high. Bill Colgan, a former P-47 Thunderbolt pilot who served with the US 79th Fighter Group in Italy, wrote of the period May to June 1944 that losses in the Group during May were such that, had they continued at the same rate over a period of months, the entire pilot strength of the squadrons would have had to be replaced every three to four months.[7] Similarly, Charles Demoulin, a Typhoon pilot who served with the RAF in North-West Europe, recalls of the autumn of 1944 that the average survival rate for a rocket-Typhoon pilot engaged on low-level ground-attack missions was about 17 missions, after which he was considered to be living on borrowed time. Veterans stood more chance of surviving than the younger inexperienced pilots, whose average number of missions before being shot down was no more than five.[8] In fact, the hazardous nature of low-level attack was acknowledged by the RAF in December 1944, when the tour of duty for such pilots was reduced from the normal fighter-pilot tour of 200 operational sorties to 80 – a reduction of no less than 60 per cent.[9]

The scourge of Allied fighter-bombers was flak. From the point of view of the Allied tactical air forces, the most unwelcome consequence of the German armies having to adapt to operating in the face of Allied air superiority was the great increase by 1943–44 in the amount of light automatic anti-aircraft firepower possessed by German formations. An infantry division was typically equipped with at least eighty-four 20 mm light anti-aircraft guns, while a panzer division of

the type encountered in Normandy was equipped at full strength with
up to 21 self-propelled, 55 towed, and 32 lorry or half-track mounted
anti-aircraft guns. Most were of 20 mm and 37 mm calibre with a high
rate of fire. In both cases this was in addition to hundreds of lighter
calibre machine guns and small-arms that could engage low flying aircraft.[10] Table I lists the principal German flak guns and their characteristics.

TABLE I

GERMAN LIGHT ANTI-AIRCRAFT ARTILLERY[11]

TYPE	MAXIMUM ELEVATION (Degrees)	RATE OF FIRE (rds/min)	MAXIMUM VERTICAL RANGE (Feet)
20 mm Flak 30	90	280	7,000
20 mm Flak 38	90	450	7,000
20 mm Flakvierling	100	1800 *	7,000
30 mm Flak 103	80	400	15,400
37 mm Flak 18	85	160	15,700
37 mm Flak 36	85	160	15,700
37 mm Flak 43	90	250	15,700
37 mm Flakzwilling	90	500 **	15,700

* four-barrelled   ** two-barrelled

Fighter-bomber pilots thus had to contend with a highly dangerous
low-attack environment. This is emphasised by the former Typhoon
pilot quoted above, who states with regard to Normandy that the
Germans had an undisputed flak supremacy, estimated at some 20,000
batteries of anti-aircraft guns of 105 mm, 88 mm, 40 mm, 37 mm and
20 mm calibre. He estimates that this gave the odds in favour of the
Germans at 4 to 1 against the number of Allied aircraft, but that when
concentrated to defend key points these odds reached 20 or 30 to 1 in
favour of the defenders, an explanation of the fact that up to 95 per
cent of air losses in attacks on ground targets were caused by flak
defences, while only five per cent of losses could be attributed to the
Luftwaffe.[12]

While aircraft such as the Typhoon and Thunderbolt were rugged,
they could not normally be expected to survive a direct hit from flak,
especially of the 37 mm variety. Indeed, Bill Colgan points out that
rounds from guns ranging from 20 mm to 40 mm calibre could be
expected to down a fighter-bomber with a good hit.[13] The likelihood
of receiving such a hit was high, particularly when flak was concentrated to defend a particular target, as gunners could lay a curtain of
fire through which the aircraft had to fly in order to press home their

attacks. A former Typhoon pilot recalled that German gunners could put up a dense curtain of 20 mm and 40 mm fire at between 3,000 and 4,000 feet through which pilots had to dive.[14] In fact the lethality of light flak was confirmed by ORS 2nd TAF during an investigation into squadron damage reports in July 1945, which concluded that

> practically all the damage sustained on operations due to enemy action was caused by light flak.[15]

Further proof came in another post-war investigation, which discovered that many of the fighters posted as missing on operations were likely to have been victims of light flak. On repatriation to the UK fighter pilots who had been prisoners of war were interviewed by ORS personnel as to the cause of their aircraft loss. This included pilots who had not been engaged in ground attack, and covered the entire 1940–45 period. From a total of 1,002 cases, of which 672 (67 per cent) occurred in the period 1943–45, a sample of 770 were selected for analysis. Of these, 369 (48 per cent) had been light-flak victims (most of which were in the 1943–45 period), 335 (43½ per cent) had been air-combat victims, while the remaining 66 (8½ per cent) losses were attributed to 'unknown flak'.[16]

There is conclusive evidence that armed reconnaissance was more dangerous than close air support. In 1945 ORS 2nd TAF compared the close-support and armed-reconnaissance operations of Nos. 83 and 84 Groups between January and April 1945. The latter were found to be approaching twice as hazardous.[17] (See Appendix.)

These figures represent a period in the campaign when, operating over German soil, pilots found flak highly concentrated. Squadrons flying armed reconnaissance, searching for targets, often paid a heavy price. Pierre Clostermann, a French pilot serving with the RAF led a Tempest wing of No.83 Group at this time which was employed mainly on armed reconnaissance. He later recalled that Germany was 'lousy with flak' and that, with German road convoys confined to routes whose lengths were covered by light-flak batteries, the extent to which Tempests should be risked in order to destroy lorries became questionable.[18]

German airfields were also armed-reconnaissance targets, but by this time the remaining German operational fighters were harrying Allied troops from heavily camouflaged secondary airstrips. These were protected by up to a battalion of light flak guns, often enabling the German aircraft to take off and land under a curtain of protective fire. Attempts to bomb and strafe these airfields could be extremely costly, and Clostermann records leading such an attack on the airfield at Schwerin in April 1945 which resulted in six of the eight attacking Tempests being shot down.[19] Not surprisingly, awareness of flak came to dominate the lives of pilots engaged on such missions, and Clostermann recalls that pilots returning from a mission were always sharply questioned as to the density of the flak and the location of gun positions by those who were about to set off. [20]

That it was armed reconnaissance, and attacks on specific targets beyond the battlefront, rather than close air support that exposed pilots to the fiercest flak concentrations is reflected in the losses. An indication of the level of casualties sustained on close support strikes during this same period is shown in Table II, which lists a number of operations by British and Canadian troops to capture defended towns or villages and the air support provided.[21]

TABLE II

CLOSE AIR SUPPORT OPERATIONS, APRIL 1945

DATE	OBJECTIVE	ARMY FORMATION	LEVEL OF AIR SUPPORT	AIR LOSSES
2/4/45	Nijmegen Island	49 (West Riding) Div.	31 Typhoon sorties	none
8/4/45	Voltlage	52 (Lowland) Div.	4 Typhoon sorties	none
10/4/45	Deventer	3 (Cdn) Inf. Div.	27 Typhoon sorties	none
11/4/45	Rethem	53 (Welsh) Div.	22 Typhoon sorties	none
12/4/45	Arnhem	49 (West Riding) Div.	131 Typhoon and Spit-bomber sorties	none
12/4/45	Friesoythe	4 (Cdn) Armd. Div.	32 Typhoon sorties	1 Typhoon lost – pilot baled out
13/4/45	Altenwahlingen	53 (Welsh) Div.	4 Typhoon sorties	none
14/4/45	Winsen	11 Armd. Div.	12 Typhoon sorties	none
17/4/45	Eitze	53 (Welsh) Div.	8 Typhoon sorties	none
24–25/4/45	Bremen	3 Inf. Div.	25 Typhoon sorties	none

The principal reason for the difference in casualties is that flak was concentrated to defend such typical armed reconnaissance targets as airfields, headquarters, supply dumps, and vital points in the communications network. In the front line, except in support of heavily defended key positions, flak was likely to be far less concentrated and flying against such close-support targets as small defended posts, pill-boxes, and gun positions which were often well dispersed, there was considerably less. Moreover, during close-support strikes friendly artillery was often on hand to suppress flak. Armed-reconnaissance pilots were denied this help, though strikes against heavily defended targets could be supported by additional aircraft – often rocket Typhoons – specifically tasked with flak suppression.

These anti-flak Typhoons usually operated in pairs, one pair drawing German fire while another pair spotted for gun flashes and dived to attack. Guns opening fire on the second pair were then rocketed by a third pair of Typhoons orbiting the area. This was in itself very hazardous, for while flak gunners were often shy of artillery fire they were rarely afraid of air attack. A former Typhoon pilot recalls of such attacks that the German gunners were very courageous, and would continue to fire throughout the dive and subsequent attack.[22] In fact the high quality of German flak gunners was acknowledged at the time by No.2 ORS, who observed after the capture of Calais (Operation UNDERGO) in September 1944 that the morale of the Luftwaffe flak gunners was the highest among the entire garrison.[23]

Apart from the anti-flak aircraft being themselves at risk, and their presence representing a greater demand on air resources, they were not always effective even when employed in large numbers. This was seen especially during the crossing of the Rhine in March 1945, when both Nos.83 and 84 Groups maintained strong anti-flak patrols by Typhoons equipped with rockets and anti-personnel cluster bombs in the area of the Allied airborne landing. Subsequent investigation by No.2 ORS discovered that not only had very few of the flak guns been destroyed, which was no surprise as by then the problem of accuracy was well known, but also that there had been no appreciable slackening of the flak fire during the airborne drop. This was considered to be because there were not enough Typhoons available to maintain the constant attacks deemed necessary to effect neutralisation, and the fact that they obviously could not operate during the drop itself.[24]

An important question to be asked with regard to the above data is whether the comparative close-air-support and armed-reconnaissance casualties from early 1945 are representative of the campaign in North-West Europe as a whole. While there is no comparable ORS data for earlier in the campaign, the available evidence does suggest that armed reconnaissance was consistently more costly. Table III is based on the Daily Intelligence Summaries produced by No.83 Group of 2nd TAF for the period August 1944 until February 1945 and which give details of each day's operations in terms of sorties per mission type and also of battle casualties. Although it is not specified on what type of operation each casualty was sustained, these statistics show that the number of aircraft casualties in a given number of sorties was greatest during those months when most sorties were flown on armed reconnaissance.[25]

TABLE III

No.83 GROUP (RAF 2nd TAF) ARMED RECCE AND CLOSE SUPPORT EFFORT, AUGUST 1944 – FEBRUARY 1945

IMMEDIATE AND PREARRANGED SUPPORT SORTIES		ARMED RECONNAISSANCE	AIRCRAFT CASUALTIES*	SORTIES PER CASUALTY
August 1944	4,538	8,516	103	126.7
September 1944	1,471	2,344	51	75.5
October 1944	3,026	1,861	34	143.7
November 1944	2,285	1,315	36	100.0
December 1944	967	2,298	66	49.4
January 1945	639	3,709	55	79.0
February 1945	2,231	4,126	70	90.8

* Computed on aircraft destroyed or damaged, not on pilots. Does not include casualties sustained in combat with enemy aircraft or those not due to enemy action. The majority of the above casualties were listed as caused by flak.

The same trend can be discerned in US tactical air operations during the campaign. Table IV shows the number of sorties by mission type each month between November 1944 and April 1945 for the P-47 squadrons of the US 1st (Provisional) TAF, while Table V gives their losses for each month. This shows that, during the two months when the most armed reconnaissance sorties were flown, March and April 1945, the number of aircraft lost to flak and to 'unknown causes' (presumably on deep armed-reconnaissance missions beyond the German front line) was considerably greater.[26]

A more detailed picture can be obtained by a study of losses at squadron level sustained throughout the campaign in North-West Europe by No.609 (West Riding) Squadron. This Typhoon fighter-bomber unit served throughout the campaign in No.84 Group of RAF 2nd TAF, being employed almost entirely in the ground-attack role.

TABLE IV

P-47 SORTIES, US 1st (PROVISIONAL) TAF, NOVEMBER 1944–APRIL 1945

	DIVE BOMBING	ARMED RECCE	GROUND SUPPORT	FIGHTER SWEEPS	ESCORT	MISC*
Nov. 44	1,905	250	415	20	520	15
Dec. 44	2,345	2,030	311	54	400	120
Jan. 45	2,211	673	1,291	153	222	29
Feb. 45	4,656	1,191	674	117	468	39
Mar. 45	5,185	4,436	1,586	516	653	496
Apr. 45	3,127	5,575	958	388	1,064	843

* Refers to leaflet dropping, weather reconnaissance, and patrols.

TABLE V

LOSSES OF P-47s OF US 1st (PROVISIONAL) TAF,
NOVEMBER 1944 – APRIL 1945

LOSSES DUE TO:	FLAK	FLAK & ENEMY AIRCRAFT	ENEMY AIRCRAFT	ACCIDENT	UNKNOWN	TOTALS
November 1944	6	1	6	0	7	20
December 1944	9	0	11	5	19	44
January 1945	8	0	12	1	8	29
February 1945	11	1	0	3	20	35
March 1945	33	0	1	10	25	69
April 1945	33	0	7	9	22	71

Only losses sustained as a result of enemy action have been considered, and all such losses, with one possible exception, were caused by flak. Aircraft that sustained flak damage but which were able to return to base have not been included. Armed reconnaissance and attacks beyond the battlefront against specific targets (such as headquarters, radar sites, and bridges) have been compared with close air support. The experience of 609 Squadron confirms that attacks beyond the battlefront were more dangerous, with seventeen of the 24 aircraft and pilots lost, or 70 per cent, being sustained on such operations. The ratio of sorties per battle casualty was 170.2 sorties per casualty for close support and 102.1 sorties per casualty for armed reconnaissance/deep penetration.

Of the total of 24 pilots lost, 13 (54 per cent) had carried out less than 20 operations by the time that they were shot down. Seven pilots (29 per cent) had carried out over 30 operations, and of these only three pilots (12 per cent) had carried out over 50 operations. This tends to confirm Charles Demoulin's assertion, quoted above, that the less-experienced pilots were most at risk.[27]

All the above evidence suggests that the further fighter-bombers operated beyond the battlefront, the higher their losses were likely to be. Confirmation of this was provided by ORS 2nd TAF in 1945 during an investigation into armed reconnaissance. While not directly relevant to a comparison with close air support, the results are worth noting because they proved that armed reconnaissance itself could be more dangerous depending on how deep behind the German lines the aircraft patrolled. In February 1945 No.83 Group's armed-reconnaissance effort was seen to be conveniently divided into two sections, deep and shallow penetration, the areas being separated by a line some 60 miles behind the German lines running through Hamm, Munster, Rheine, Almelo, and Zwolle. This provided an ideal opportunity for comparison, and the ORS findings are summarised in Table VI. While the table does not indicate a significant increase in the risk from flak to pilots flying deep-penetration missions, it is likely that the higher number of losses due to 'unknown cause' in this category reflects flak losses.

TABLE VI

No.83 GROUP ARMED RECONNAISSANCE EFFORT, FEBRUARY 1945

	TOTAL SORTIES		PER 100 SORTIES		PER AIRCRAFT LOST	
	Deep	Shallow	Deep	Shallow	Deep	Shallow
No. of Sorties	2,210	1,878	100.0	100.0	48	75.1
LOSSES						
Total	46	25	2.1	1.3	–	–
Due to enemy a/c	5	0	0.2	0	–	–
Due to flak	15	11	0.7	0.6	–	–
Not due to enemy action	11	9	0.5	0.5	–	–
Unknown cause	15	5	0.7	0.3	–	–

At the time the justification for such deep penetration missions was considered to be that pilots were presented with more targets and, judging by their claims, inflicted more damage. This is shown in Table VII. Nevertheless, the findings of this investigation resulted in 2nd TAF curtailing the number of deep-penetration missions, and increasing the number of aircraft when such missions were flown.[28]

TABLE VII

No.83 GROUP ARMED RECONNAISSANCE CLAIMS, FEBRUARY 1945

	TOTAL SORTIES		PER 100 SORTIES		PER AIRCRAFT LOST	
	Deep	Shallow	Deep	Shallow	Deep	Shallow
No. of Sorties	2,210	1,878	100	100	48	75.1
CLAIMS						
Aircraft *	32:3:33	17:0:8	1.4:0.1:1.5	0.9:0:0.4	0.7:0.1:0.7	0.7:0:0.3
Locomotives *f*	124:598	37:105	5.6:27.1	2.0:5.6	2.7:13.0	1.6:4.2
Heavy Trucks *f*	198:1140	215:534	9.0:51.6	11.5:28.4	4.1:24.6	8.6:21.5
Motor Transport *f*	135:505	120:321	6.1:22.9	6.4:17.1	2.9:10.9	4.8:12.8
Tugs and Barges *f*	15:120	14:41	0.7:5.4	0.8:2.2	0.3:2.6	0.6:1.6
Rail Track Cuts	12	19	0.5	1.0	0.3	0.8

* Figures indicate destroyed:probably destroyed:damaged
f Figures indicate destroyed:damaged

THE IMPACT OF ARMED RECONNAISSANCE

Having established that armed reconnaissance accounted for more sorties than close air support, and that it was the more dangerous ground-attack mission, an important question arises as to the extent to which it assisted the Allied armies. First, it will be helpful to draw a parallel with close air support. Close air support was firepower applied at the decisive time and place in order to enable friendly troops to achieve set objectives – to take a village, to clear a wood, or to repel a counter-attack. Like artillery, it was used as and when necessary to achieve short-term ends. As the previous chapters show, its success usually depended upon its effects being rapidly exploited on the ground. In contrast, armed reconnaissance was continuous, for only by the exertion of constant pressure could it bring results. Its objectives, and its effects, were usually of a longer term nature.

Armed reconnaissance by fighter-bombers was one aspect of air interdiction, as a post-war US study observed:

> All types of aircraft have played a part in interdiction: reconnaissance planes through surveillance and bomb-damage assessment; fighter-bombers on armed-reconnaissance patrols, mediums and heavies by obstruction of the arteries of movement and destruction of the things to be moved.[29]

When the object of armed reconnaissance was, as part of a concerted air offensive, completely to cut off the German front line forces from reinforcement and supply, it was unsuccessful. A good case study to illustrate this is Operation STRANGLE, a deliberate interdiction campaign waged over two months by the Allied tactical, strategic, and coastal air forces in an attempt to paralyse the supply and transportation system in northern and central Italy in the spring of 1944. STRANGLE was intended to compel the withdrawal of the German armies from central Italy in the period while the Allied armies were preparing a major offensive (DIADEM), and commenced on 15 March. Over 50,000 sorties were flown and 26,000 tons of bombs delivered.[30] Yet, despite the destruction and disruption of many Italian road, rail and port facilities, the German armies continued to receive sufficient supplies – in fact those of ammunition and fuel actually increased in the period.[31]

When it was realised that STRANGLE would not compel the Germans to withdraw before DIADEM was launched, it was decided to continue the air campaign during the offensive. Fighter-bombers had mainly been employed in attacking road transport, and for this new stage the interdiction belt was placed closer to the German front lines where, it was thought, they could engage such transport more effectively. The object remained supply-denial, with the intention of creating shortages among German front-line units while they were under pressure from Allied ground action. This too failed in its object, mainly because the previous STRANGLE effort had been conducted at a time when the German forces were not heavily engaged. They had therefore been able to accumulate sufficient stocks of ammunition and fuel in the forward area so that shortages never became critical.

STRANGLE proved the necessity of closely integrating any interdiction attempt with ground operations, but interdiction proved a very demanding goal to achieve. For STRANGLE Allied planners estimated that the level of supplies needed by the German armies in Italy amounted to no more than some seven per cent of the total normal capacity of the railway system. They thus set themselves the target of reducing this capacity by more than 93 per cent. In fact they had overestimated German supply requirements, and it has since been reckoned that for interdiction to have been successful the rail system would have had to be reduced to no more than one or two per cent of its peacetime capability.[32]

It is questionable whether the fighter-bombers of 1943–45 were capable of consistently destroying enough transport vehicles, railway locomotives and rolling stock, or of effecting enough road and rail cuts, to make the Germans feel the bite of interdiction in the tactical area.[33] The limitations of fighter-bomber weapons and their accuracy have been discussed in Chapter 3. With regard to attacks on road transport, the data from the ORS investigations in Normandy (discussed in Chapter 5) confirm that fighter-bomber weapons were lethal to softskin vehicles. However, maintaining a continual armed reconnaissance meant that there were long periods when targets were relatively few, when the battlefront was static, and with less frequent periods when targets were prolific. It is interesting to compare claims made by pilots flying armed reconnaissance during these varying periods. Taking a typical fortnight in the Normandy campaign – 30 June to 16 July – as an example we find that 83 Group of 2nd TAF flew some 1,614 close support sorties and 2,819 on armed reconnaissance. As a result of the latter there were claims of the destruction of 266 vehicles and the damage of 366. Only 632 hits on 2,819 sorties – one every four – appears an expensive use of air power. It might be added that on one day only in the same short period did close support missions exceed those of armed recce.[34]

Fighter-bomber pilots of 1943–45 ultimately depended upon the visual sighting of targets. There could be no guarantee of finding them and many armed-reconnaissance patrols in such a period would have seen little or no German movement at all. Only when the German army was on the move, either during an offensive (the mounting of which interdiction was intended to make impossible) or during a retreat, could the fighter-bomber pilots expect to find targets on a large scale. Indeed, a similar study of the sorties and subsequent claims made by the fighter-bombers of 2nd TAF flying armed reconnaissance missions during the German offensive through the Ardennes between 23 and 26 December 1944 show a ratio of only one sortie per vehicle damaged or destroyed.[35]

The experience of 609 Squadron illustrates the trend in more detail. In each of June and July 1944 with the battlefront relatively static the squadron flew rather more than 60 armed recce sorties with claims of 47 hits, but in August as the Germans fell back from Falaise the total exceeded 200 while claims jumped to 110 vehicles of all types. This trend continued during September as the Germans retreated further into northern France and Belgium.[36]

All the evidence indicates that, with regard to road movement, effective interdiction, if it demanded the prevention of all or very nearly all supplies reaching the battlefront, would have been very difficult to impose.

Given that interdiction efforts such as STRANGLE were not
sufficient in themselves to compel a German withdrawal, then the
value of a continual armed reconnaissance during periods when the
battlefront was relatively static, with no large-scale German
movement, becomes questionable. Indeed, the fact that in a single
fortnight during the Normandy campaign there was only one day on
which close air support sorties exceeded those of armed reconnaissance, begs the question as to the extent to which the constant
patrolling of the German rear areas offered an effective means of
assisting Allied troops.

The answer is that armed reconnaissance did not need to consistently destroy large numbers of German vehicles in the tactical area in
order to reduce the ability of the German armies to fight effectively.
As with close air support, neutralisation was often more important
than destruction. Armed reconnaissance rendered all German movement in and around the battle area potentially vulnerable to air attack.
In his 1972 study of STRANGLE, F.M. Sallagar suggested that while
the air offensive failed in its interdiction objectives, it nevertheless
reduced and occasionally paralysed German freedom of movement in
the combat area, with field commanders unable to move units to
strengthen threatened sectors or to seal off Allied breakthroughs without penalty.[37]

There is much evidence to support this view. Both in Italy and in
North-West Europe German movement in and beyond the tactical
area was severely disrupted by air attack or the threat of it. In May
1944 the headquarters of Field Marshal Kesselring, commanding
German forces in Italy, reported that in the face of Allied air
superiority it was impossible to make any computation of the time
factor in movements.[38] General von Vietinghoff, who succeeded
Kesselring in March 1945, later admitted that the presence of Allied
fighter-bombers paralysed all movement.[39]

German forces in North-West Europe experienced similar
difficulties, from the very outset of the fighting in Normandy. On
10 June 1944 Field Marshal Rommel, commanding Army Group
B, while driving towards the battlefront, had to jump out of his car
and dive for cover no less than 30 times.[40] It is not surprising that
on the same day he echoed those German commanders in Italy by
complaining that the Allies had total command of the air for up to
some 60 miles behind the battlefront, and that in daylight
practically all traffic on roads, tracks and in open country was
pinned down and movement paralysed.[41]

The extent to which the threat of air attack affected German freedom of movement is seen in a POW interrogation report that was being studied by 2nd TAF planners in May 1944 based on information from Poles and Alsatians captured while serving in German units. This revealed that, when air attack was likely, German motorised units moved only at night whenever possible, with movement taking place by companies at half-hour intervals and with distances between individual vehicles – sometimes as much as 50 metres – rigidly maintained. Units marching on foot in daylight posted air sentries to front and rear, and marched with an average distance of 500 metres between companies, and sometimes with a distance of 20 metres between each man. Halts, such as for meals, were made dispersed under cover whenever possible.[42]

Failure to observe these elaborate precautions invited disaster, but in the initial stages of the campaigns in Italy and North-West Europe German troops were unprepared for an enemy air force that would seek to attack them as they moved towards the battlefront. For example, the history of the 29th Panzer Grenadier Division records of its deployment against the Allied landings at Salerno in September 1943 that the air attacks to which the Division was subjected exceeded all previous experience, and that it was considered an achievement if a single vehicle was able to make a short journey unscathed.[43] In Normandy, a staff officer of 17th SS Panzer Grenadier Division described how his division learnt the same lesson soon after the Allied landings, when in an unexpected attack of 15 minutes duration fighter-bombers destroyed several of the Division's vehicles, completely disrupted its march column, and left the troops badly shaken.[44]

German formations soon learnt not to present such targets to the air, but inexperienced formations arriving in Normandy later in the campaign occasionally fell victim to such attacks. On 9 July 1944 a regiment of parachute-infantry was moving forward to reinforce Bayerlein's Panzer Lehr Division. Their march discipline was poor and, when near Les Champs de Losque, they were pounced upon by ten fighter-bombers which bombed and strafed them for five minutes – leaving over 200 killed and wounded out of 1,500 men. According to Bayerlein the survivors had been so shaken by this experience that he could never afterwards regard the unit as reliable.[45]

Only severe weather brought respite from air attack in daylight, and the Germans were compelled to move mainly at night. A post-war US study of air support in North-West Europe suggested that the ability to move unmolested at night largely redressed the balance:

There was one deficiency in tactical air action that was evident throughout the campaign in Europe. That was the dearth of night-fighter and
night-intruder operations. When weather permitted, the two night-
fighter squadrons turned in a good performance, but there was never
enough. From the early days in NORMANDY when reports from
POWs, French civilians and our patrols showed that the enemy formed
his columns at last light preparatory to moving throughout the night,
through the ARDENNES Counter Offensive phase, during the early
stages of the REMAGEN Bridgehead over the RHINE, and to the end,
it was apparent that a lack of night air activity allowed the enemy the
freedom of movement which he had lost by day and permitted him to
redispose and resupply his forces with little danger of interference.[46]

While it is true that the Allies had few night-fighter aircraft available
in North-West Europe, it is questionable whether an increase in their
numbers would have had any appreciable effect on German movement. Radar with the ability to detect road and rail movement did not
then exist, and attempts to operate by the light of flares dropped by
accompanying bomber aircraft had only limited success.[47] In terms of
interdiction, night movement ensured that at least a certain level of
supplies reached the battlefront.[48] Yet, in operational terms, night
movement was a very poor substitute for total mobility, particularly in
summer with few hours of darkness. For example, Bayerlein recalled
that in Normandy it took 36 hours to get his Panzer Lehr Division to
the battlefront, a journey which would have required no more than 12
hours had daylight movement been possible.[49]

Granted that armed-reconnaissance patrols severely disrupted
German tactical movement, one might still argue that this was not of
great importance if the German formations, albeit with difficulty and
perhaps losses, could still reach their destinations in time to achieve
their purpose, for example to reinforce a portion of the battlefront. It
is certainly true that there were occasions when the Germans had time
on their side, that formations arriving at their destinations after long
and difficult journeys nevertheless had time to reorganise without
being under great pressure from Allied ground action. But there were
also occasions when time was absolutely crucial to the Germans,
such as when an offensive was to be mounted or an Allied breakthrough sealed off, and when daylight movement had to be hazarded.
Then armed reconnaissance could not only take a fearful toll of the
German formations but also ensure that they arrived in no state to
fight effectively.

Such was the experience of the Hermann Goering Division in Italy, which was employed against the Anzio beachhead at the end of May 1944, but whose journey to the battlefront from the Leghorn area between 23 and 27 May was disrupted by air attack. Its commander, General von Greffenberg, reported that his division had been subject to unceasing low level attacks and had sustained considerable losses, eventually reaching its intended concentration area with only 11 tanks. More tanks arrived piecemeal, but of the division's original 60 only 18 reached the battlefront.[50] Given the limited accuracy of Allied air-to-ground weapons (see Chapter 5), it is likely that few of these tanks were lost as a result of direct rocket or bomb hits, but rather due to the wear and tear of making long detours on poor roads on their tracks, the difficulties of repairing damaged tanks on the march, and shortages of spare parts and fuel due to their supporting softskin vehicles being continually shot up from the air. This also explains the fact that, of the 18 tanks that did get to Anzio, only some eight or ten of them were fit for action at any one time and they had little effect on the outcome of the battle.[51]

Similarly, in Normandy, on the night of 1 August 1944, the 9th SS Panzer Division began to move across the River Orne from the Caen sector in order to counter the thrust of British VIII Corps towards Flers. Daylight movement was imperative, and on the afternoon of 2 August the main body of the division was found by 83 Group fighter-bombers along the roads between Thury-Harcourt and Condé-sur-Noireau. They flew 271 sorties in the area and claimed the destruction of 10 tanks and 50 MET and the damaging of 13 tanks and 76 MET.[52] Even allowing for overclaiming, the losses inflicted on 9th SS were considerable. Moreover, the division could not go into action as a cohesive body but only as a series of small battlegroups; and by 4 August it was fighting in a purely defensive manner.[53]

Also in early August, in preparation for the German counter attack at Mortain (see Chapter 5), the 1st SS Panzer Division began to move on 3 August from the Caen area to opposite the US forces near Avranches. This also demanded daylight movement and Allied fighter-bombers turned the march into a nightmare, harrying the division relentlessly to the extent that one source states that losses amounted to 30 per cent of strength.[54] Long delay was also caused, especially when a fighter-bomber, shot down by the Division's flak, crashed on to the lead tank as the column was moving along a narrow defile, blocking the road. It took several hours for the tanks to extricate themselves and find an alternative route, and only scattered elements arrived in time to start the offensive on 7 August. Armed reconnaissance was thus responsible for a significant reduction in the tank strength available for the offensive's initial thrust.[55]

Extensive armed-reconnaissance patrols throughout the course of the offensive also resulted in heavy losses among the transport vehicles feeding the tanks, and very little fuel reached the armoured spearheads. On 11 August an ULTRA intercept of a message from XLVII Panzer Corps headquarters, directing the operation, revealed that the Germans were critically short of fuel. On the following day a further intercepted message reported that 30 tanks of Panzer Lehr were immobilised for lack of it.[56] Similarly, during the Ardennes offensive, losses to motor transport as a result of fighter-bomber attack were decisive in denying both supply and mobility to the German armoured spearheads, which could draw upon only limited stocks of fuel as a result of the bombing of oil production facilities and communications by the Allied heavy bomber forces. One consequence of this was described by Bayerlein, who recalled that he had to abandon 53 tanks of his Panzer Lehr Division by the roadside during the withdrawal from the Ardennes salient in January 1945, mainly because of losses to the lorries bringing forward his fuel and spare parts.[57]

Such were the penalties of attempting to fight a mobile war in the face of an enemy's air superiority. The roads beyond the German forward positions were usually devoid of movement in daylight. This amounted to continual neutralisation. While armed-reconnaissance sorties did not always find targets, and could not entirely prevent German supply and reinforcement, they perpetuated the threat of air attack. There is no means of computing how much German movement did not take place, or how many operations were not attempted, as a result.

While the evidence confirms that ground attack was costly, it also shows quite conclusively that the heaviest aircraft and pilot losses were not sustained on close air support missions but on armed reconnaissance or as a result of attacks upon specific targets beyond the battlefront. This should not be surprising, for the targets vulnerable to armed reconnaissance, such as supply dumps, airfields, arteries of communication leading to and from the battlefront, and concentrations of troops and armour in reserve, were vital and could be expected to have priority in flak defences. In contrast, many close-support strikes were against relatively small front line targets. Even allowing for the massive German investment in automatic flak by 1943–45 it was still impossible for every pillbox, small gun position, or slit trench to be so protected. In effect, the most dangerous flak concentrations were not at the battlefront, but behind it.

This is not to suggest that German troops in the forward area were totally denuded of flak cover, but an important factor – perhaps not given sufficient attention in previous discussion of this subject – is that when aircraft were engaging targets at the line of contact friendly artillery could play a vital role in neutralizing any known flak positions that were in range. Allied gunners were adept in the art of counter-battery fire, and by 1943–45 could bring targets under fire very rapidly (see Chapter 7 above); those German flak positions that gave away their position by engaging aircraft could expect swift concentrations of airburst shelling.

The fact that Allied fighter-bombers flew considerably more armed-reconnaissance sorties than close air support missions begs the question as to how the relative priorities were accorded. There was no pronounced tension over allocations between the two mission types in either Italy or North-West Europe, mainly because the Allied tactical air forces in 1943–45 had at their disposal large numbers of fighter-bombers and pilots, and a steady flow of replacements for both. This enabled a sizeable allocation of air effort to both armed reconnaissance and close support at any one time. For example, on 11 June 1944 RAF Desert Air Force (DAF) in Italy reported that

> The policy for the employment of our fighters and fighter-bombers remains the same...that is, attacks on road movement, certain rail and road bridges, and having A/C available for close support.[58]

The extent of armed reconnaissance varied according to the situation at the battlefront but was greatest during those periods when there was relatively little intensive ground fighting. Operations such as STRANGLE were mounted while Allied troops were preparing for a major offensive, but whenever circumstances forced a lull in the ground battle armed reconnaissance was reasserted. One example occurred in Italy during January 1945, when Desert Air Force reported:

> The most noticeable feature of our activities has been the switching of the major part of our effort from the direct support of the Eighth Army in the battle area, to the interdiction of the enemy's communications...With the present stalemate on the battle front, brought about by atrocious ground conditions, it became obvious our forces could be better employed elsewhere.[59]

The level of armed reconnaissance also rose when, after an Allied ground offensive, a breakthrough had been achieved and German forces were compelled to withdraw, as in Normandy during August 1944. This enabled the fighter-bombers to take advantage of the increased number of targets, there being in any case by then a reduction in the number of close support requests.

This is not to suggest that when conducting armed reconnaissance the tactical air forces were waging a totally separate campaign, unrelated to the requirements of the Allied armies. In fact armed reconnaissance was acknowledged by the soldiers to be an extremely valuable form of air support, and many such missions were carried out at their request. For example, on 14 June 1944, during a period when the battlefront in Italy was static, the Advanced Headquarters of Desert Air Force noted that

> there is no change in the Army's requests for armed recces behind the battle area, there being very few calls for support by forward troops.[60]

Ground offensives saw a considerable rise in the number of close support sorties to meet army demands, a situation that often lasted for periods of several days. Yet, despite the amount of close support required on any given day, the armed-reconnaissance offensive, albeit on a reduced scale, was never compromised to the extent that the threat of air attack in the German rear areas came to be ignored. This was true of tactical air operations in both Italy and North-West Europe, but the daily Operations Record Book of RAF Desert Air Force in Italy provides some interesting examples from the period of the assault on the formidable German GOTHIC LINE during August and September 1944. On 26 August Desert Air Force reported:

> A maximum effort was put up today and a total of 664 sorties were flown in support of the Fifth and Eighth Armies. By far the largest effort was against targets in and around the GOTHIC defences...

but the DAF report also added that

> Continuous armed recces were flown throughout the day covering the enemy's lines of communication but little movement was observed.

Similarly, on 1 September 1944, Desert Air Force reported a further heavy commitment to close support:

> A maximum effort was achieved today, a total of 690 sorties being flown. By far the greater number were in close support of the 8th Army who were attacking and advancing through the GOTHIC Line defences in the Pesaro area.

Nevertheless, the daily report adds that,

> Apart from the close support work, armed recces of roads and rails behind the battle area were flown throughout the day to deny the enemy much-needed reinforcements.

The same situation prevailed on the following day, 2 September:

> Almost our entire effort was once again concentrated upon the enemy immediately in front of the 8th Army who are advancing through the GOTHIC Line. Fighter-bombers attacked gun positions, strong points, troop and tank concentrations, and flew constant armed recces over roads and rails in the enemy's rear.[61]

That a significant scale of armed reconnaissance could be conducted at a time when army demands for a heavy scale of close support were also being met was due primarily to the air resources at the disposal of the tactical air forces. There was also, to some extent, a merging of roles. Much of the close support for such offensive operations was provided on CABRANK, and aircraft detailed for this task, if no close-support target was given, often had armed reconnaissance of a specified area as a prearranged alternative mission. Moreover, VCPs or FCPs controlling the CABRANK aircraft, if there were no targets at the battlefront requiring immediate attention, would frequently request an armed-reconnaissance of the area immediately behind it. In this way many armed-reconnaissance missions were directed from the battlefront.

It would be incorrect to suggest that, whatever the situation at the battlefront, close-support requests were in general denied in order to maintain the armed-reconnaissance offensive, despite the overall higher number of sorties for the latter. Very often the opposite was true, as shown by the procedure in use by the Allies in 1944–45 of diverting aircraft proceeding on armed reconnaissance to respond to unforeseen requests for close support. The frequency of this procedure is confirmed by the fact that among many US army formations it became the preferred method of ensuring close support precisely when and where needed as opposed to relying on prearranged missions (see Chapter 2 above). Close air support and armed reconnaissance were in effect complementary aspects of the same highly flexible tactical air offensive. This was most evident during mobile operations, when RAF fighter-bombers on CABRANK, and their American counterparts flying Armored Column Cover, often provided a combination of close air support and armed reconnaissance by patrolling considerable distances ahead of the armoured spearheads when close-in targets were lacking.[62]

While the strength of the Allied tactical air forces averted a serious tension between the resources that could be allocated to close support and armed reconnaissance, the potential for such tension existed. There were occasions, albeit relatively few, in both campaigns when it was necessary for the tactical air forces to provide simultaneously a major close-support effort and also prevent large-scale German movement to the battle area. This was especially true when Allied troops were fighting on the defensive. Such was the case in Italy during the defence of the Salerno and Anzio beachheads against German counterattack in September 1943 and March 1944 respectively, and in North-West Europe during the German counterattack at Mortain and the Ardennes offensive. These operations demanded maximum efforts by the Allied tactical air forces which, despite their resources, were stretched in order to meet both demands.

Such emergencies were often of short duration, demanding only a few hours or a day of intensive effort which could be provided by working pilots and ground crews to the limit to achieve the necessary sorties. An example was the crisis on the first day of the Mortain counterattack, which was met by an afternoon of concentrated effort by No.83 Group of 2nd TAF and the US IX TAC. Such operations, necessitating a reduction of air effort in other sectors of the battlefront, could not be sustained for more than very limited periods, and the tactical air forces could not cope with crises of longer duration without reinforcement. For example, the extent of Allied tactical air operations, both at and beyond the battlefront, during the German Ardennes offensive was made possible only by the involvement of 2nd TAF, the reshuffling of US fighter-bomber units in order to reinforce those TACs supporting the US armies directly engaged, the intervention of the Allied heavy bomber forces against interdiction targets leading to the battlefront, and the temporary posting to the continent of two Groups of the Eighth Air Force's Mustang fighters to reinforce the IX and XXIX TACs of Ninth Air Force.[63]

The ability of the tactical air forces to draw upon resources of fighters normally employed in ensuring air-superiority was an important factor in maintaining fighter-bomber strength. This was shown in August 1944, when the Allied landings in Southern France (Operation DRAGOON) resulted in the armies in Italy losing the support of the US XII TAC, while RAF Desert Air Force became responsible for the whole of the Italian front shortly before the launching of a major offensive against the GOTHIC LINE. Desert Air Force was reinforced, but the almost total lack of German air opposition meant that the loss of XII TAC was also offset by several fighter squadrons being converted to fighter-bombing, among them four squadrons of Spitfires of No.244 Wing which had been gaining experience in the role since the end of June.[64]

The Allied tactical air forces were also able to concentrate fighter-bomber strength in sectors of the battlefront demanding intensive effort, by temporarily assigning units to the area from quieter sectors. For example, in early 1945 Desert Air Force was expecting demands for a heavy scale of close air support from Eighth Army, which was preparing to take the offensive. All fighter-bomber squadrons were expected to be fully occupied and, for Desert Air Force to maintain its operations, it was thought that reinforcement would be necessary. A Desert Air Force study noted that

> This can be provided by the temporary transfer of fighter-bomber air-craft from 22nd TAC, provided that 5th Army is not on the offensive at the same time.

It was even suggested that such a step might provide a surfeit of resources, for the same study added that,

> If it so happens that 5th Army do not undertake major offensives at the same time, then the total of DAF plus 22nd TAC is almost certainly too great.[65]

In 1943–45 the Allied armies enjoyed a lavish scale of air support both at and beyond the battlefront. An indication of how their operations would have been curtailed had they been denied the support of powerful tactical air forces is shown by an incident which occurred in Italy. In December 1943 four US fighter groups of North-West African Tactical Air Force (NATAF) were about to exchange their P-40s for P-47 Thunderbolts. Headquarters Mediterranean Allied Air Forces (MAAF) decided that, after conversion, they would be transferred to the Fifteenth (Strategic) Air Force for fighter-escort duty. Air Marshal Coningham, then commanding NATAF, warned of the consequences of such a step:

> Experience in the Mediterranean theatre has proved conclusively that the fighter-bomber, owing to its versatility, hitting power, and powers of self-defence, is the most important single factor which consistently contributes to success on land ... without fighter bombers it would be impossible to provide the necessary support for an advance... The fight-er bomber force in TAF has long experience and is highly specialised. The present standard is due to continuity and the inculcation of a fighter-bomber mentality born of more than two years offensive trial

and error with armies. It is a difficult task which has to 'grow' on a unit
... to take these units away from their specialised offensive role and con-
vert them into a defensive escort to long-range bombers is unthinkable.

Coningham also warned that the Allied armies would become more
vulnerable to a strong German counterattack directed upon either
Foggia or Naples. This was because

> The preventive factor is the air war on enemy supply and communica-
> tions, and the killing element in every enemy attack is the fighter
> bomber. This is especially the case in Italy where the weight of the
> attack depends upon roads.[66]

The strength of Coningham's argument was that, if MAAF held to its
decision, the result would have been to reduce the overall fighter
strength of NATAF by 60 per cent, thereby reducing the number of
fighter-bombers supporting Eighth and Fifth Armies by 66 per cent
and 50 per cent respectively. Largely due to Coningham's intervention, the decision was not implemented. Had it been, a serious tension
between the number of aircraft available for armed reconnaissance and
close air support would have been inevitable, with NATAF unable to
maintain sufficient armed-reconnaissance patrols to disrupt German
tactical mobility, while lacking the resources to provide more than a
limited close-support effort.

With regard to the effectiveness of the two mission types, it can be
seen that in each case the effects – neutralisation and delay – were
temporary. The inevitability of adverse flying weather on some days
and the inability to operate at night ensured that armed reconnaissance could never completely sever the German forward troops from
reinforcement and supply. Its effect on German tactical mobility,
however, was undeniably very great and sometimes decisive; it was
for this reason that in 1945 ORS 2nd TAF concluded that armed
reconnaissance was

> the most important of all tactical air force work, because of the restric-
> tions it imposes on enemy movement.[67]

Yet in order to have this effect armed reconnaissance had to be
continuous, not just to engage targets but to make credible the continual threat of air attack which paralysed the German army.

This was an advantage over close air support, for an armed-
reconnaissance mission contributed to this psychological effect even if
the pilots found no targets. It could thus be argued that such a mission
was not wasted, and that even for the aircraft to be seen over the

German rear areas had some effect. This was not true of close air support to the same extent. While the presence of Allied fighter-bombers over the battle area undoubtedly curtailed German fighting efficiency by preventing movement and inducing artillery and mortar crews to desist from firing, this was of limited assistance to Allied ground units about to attack German troops already occupying fighting positions. In this situation, as the previous chapters have shown, each close-support strike that failed to destroy or neutralise such positions, or which, having done so, was not exploited on the ground, was wasted.

NOTES

1. RAF Desert Air Force Report (1944), *Fighter-Bombing*, in *Employment of Fighter-Bombers – Policy*, PRO AIR 23/1826. The present concept of armed reconnaissance in the RAF is broadly the same. See Royal Air Force, *Air Power Doctrine* (AP 3000), 2nd Edition, 1993, p. 64.
2. ORS 2nd TAF Report No.30 (July 1945), *Armed Reconnaissance by Aircraft of 2nd TAF in the Western European Campaign*, PRO WO 291/1357.
3. Ibid.
4. USAAF 26th Statistical Control Unit Report (1945), *Statistical Summary of Ninth Air Force Operations, 16 Oct. 1943–8 May 1945*, PRO AIR 40/1096.
5. USAAF Statistical Control Unit Report (June 1945), *First Tactical Air Force Operations (Provisional): Summary of Operations 1 Nov. 1944 through 8 May 1945*, PRO AIR 40/1097.
6. Alan F. Wilt, *Allied Cooperation in Sicily and Italy 1943–45*, in Benjamin F. Cooling (Ed.), *Case Studies in the Development of Close Air Support*, Office of Air Force History (Washington, DC: 1990), pp. 223–5.
7. Bill Colgan, *World War II Fighter-Bomber Pilot* (Blue Ridge Summit, PA: Tab Books: 1985), p. 90.
8. Charles Demoulin, *Firebirds: Flying the Typhoon in Action* (Shrewsbury: Airlife Publishing, 1986), p. 155.
9. Desmond Scott, *Typhoon Pilot* (London: Arrow, 1988), p. 144.
10. Eric Lefèvre, *Panzers in Normandy Then and Now* (London: After The Battle, 1983), p. 17.
11. *The Illustrated Encyclopedia of 20th Century Weapons and Warfare*, Volume I (London: Purnell, 1977), pp. 107–18.
12. Demoulin, *Firebirds*, p. 219.
13. Colgan, *World War II Fighter-Bomber Pilot*, p. 103.
14. J.G. Simpson, quoted in Franks, *Typhoon Attack* (London: William Kimber, 1984), p. 204.
15. ORS 2nd TAF Report No.40 (July 1945), *Vulnerability of 2nd TAF Aircraft*, PRO AIR 37/61.
16. ORS Fighter Command Report No.679 (Sept. 1946), *Analysis of Reports on the Causes of Loss of Their Aircraft by Pilots Missing on Operational Flights*, PRO AIR 16/1047.
17. RAF 2nd TAF Reports (1945), Summaries and Comparisons of Effort and Casualties for Nos. 83 and 84 Groups, Jan.–April 1945, PRO AIR 37/869.
18. Pierre Clostermann, *The Big Show: Some Experiences of a French Fighter Pilot in the RAF* (London: Corgi, 1970), pp. 217–18.
19. Ibid., pp. 234–5.
20. Ibid., p. 240.
21. The sources for Table II are many: British and Canadian Divisional and other unit records for North-West Europe are in the PRO WO 171 and PRO WO 179 files respectively. Those for RAF squadrons are in the PRO AIR 27 files.
22. L.H. Lambert, quoted in Franks, *Typhoon Attack*, p. 205.
23. *Morale and Types of P.W. and The Effects of Supporting Arms at Calais (Operation Undergo)*, Appendix E to No.2 ORS Report No.16, *Air and Ground Support in the Assault*

on Boulogne, in *Operational Research in North-West Europe* (1945), PRO WO 291/1331. This observed that the flak gunners were the most youthful element in the German garrison of Calais.

24. No.2 ORS/ORS 2nd TAF Joint Report No.3, *Rocket Firing Typhoons in Close Support of Military Operations* (1945), in *Operational Research in North-West Europe*.

    Had these German guns (dual-purpose 88 mm) been engaging Allied troops and been manned by troops other than trained anti-aircraft gunners, then the Typhoon attacks may well have neutralised them. There is evidence to suggest that trained and experienced anti-aircraft gunners were immune to the fear of air attack engendered in other troops. In British experience this was seen regarding the anti-aircraft gunners of Malta and Tobruk earlier in the war. This phenomenon may have been linked not only to the discipline engendered by training and experience but also to the ability to hit back offsetting fear. In North Africa British troops were exhorted to fire back at attacking aircraft even with their small-arms, this being more for reasons of British morale than any serious hope that enemy aircraft would be hit. See *Direct Support of the Army in the Field: Miscellaneous Reports*, PRO AIR 37/760.

    General Messervy, commanding 4th Indian Division in North Africa at the time of Operation CRUSADER in Nov. 1941, insisted that his men should not dive for the nearest slit trench during dive-bombing raids but should stand their ground and engage the aircraft with their weapons. For an account of Messervy setting a personal example see Henry Maule, *Spearhead General* (London: Corgi, 1963), pp. 141–2.

25. Statistics taken from No.83 Group RAF (2nd TAF) Daily Intelligence Summaries, Aug. 1944 – Feb. 1945, Appendices to No.83 Group ORB, PRO AIR 25/704, AIR 25/705, AIR 25/706 and AIR 25/707.

26. USAAF Statistical Control Unit, *First Tactical Air Force Operations*.

27. No. 609 Squadron ORB, June 1944 – May 1945, PRO AIR 27/2103.

28. ORS 2nd TAF Report No.30, *Armed Reconnaissance by Aircraft of 2nd TAF*. Note that the total of armed reconnaissance sorties for February 1945 arrived at by ORS 2nd TAF, a total of 4,088, differs from that shown in Table III. Table III is based on the daily intelligence summaries of No.83 Group, which record a total of at least 4,126 armed reconnaissance sorties during February 1945.

29. General Bradley and the US 12th Army Group Air Effects Committee, *Effect of Air Power on Military Operations, Western Europe*, 15 July 1945, p. 58, PRO AIR 40/1131.

30. Wesley Frank Craven and James Lea Cate (Eds), *The Army Air Forces in World War II*, Volume III, *Europe: Argument to V-E Day* (Washington, 1984), pp. 373–84.

31. F.M. Sallagar, *Operation Strangle (Italy, Spring 1944): A Case Study of Tactical Air Interdiction*, RAND Report R-851-PR (Santa Monica: Rand, Feb. 1972), p. vi.

32. Ibid., pp. 24–32.

33. Accuracy was not the only limitation with regard to fighter-bomber attack upon railway targets; there was also the question of weapons-effectiveness. Trials held in the UK in 1944 discovered that even a direct hit on a section of track by a salvo of Typhoon rockets would only cause such damage as could be rapidly repaired within two hours. The trials concluded that, to keep a railway line out of operation, air attacks would have to be multiplied at various points along the line. Ministry of Home Security, Research and Experiments Department, *Comments on TAF trial at Shoeburyness, 21 Feb., 1944*, PRO AIR 37/805.

    Rockets and bombs, provided they hit the target, could be relied upon to destroy or damage carriages and freight trucks. This was apparently not true of locomotives, however. Between Feb. and April 1945 fighter-bomber pilots of 2nd TAF attacked some 500 locomotives with rockets, claiming 176 destroyed and 185 damaged. Subsequent investigation by ORS 2nd TAF found little evidence of locomotives damaged by rockets and, of the hundreds of locomotives found and examined, only four had possible rocket damage. The ORS were inclined to believe assurances by German engineers that even a direct rocket hit would not destroy a locomotive, though it was considered that rocket damage would take about a month to repair, or twice the amount of time needed to repair damage caused by strafing. ORS 2nd TAF concluded that the claims for locomotives destroyed were overstated, and that locomotives were in fact very difficult to destroy. ORS 2nd TAF Report No.31 (July 1945), *RP Attacks on Locomotives by Aircraft of 2nd T.A.F.*, PRO AIR 37/61.

34. Daily Intelligence Summaries, No.83 Group RAF (2nd TAF), June – July 1944, PRO AIR 25/698.

35. ORS 2nd TAF Report No.19 (April 1945), *The Contribution of The Air Forces to the Stemming of the Enemy Thrust in the Ardennes, 11–26 Dec. 1944*, PRO AIR 37/1208.

36. No. 609 Squadron Operations Record Book, PRO AIR 27/2103. This indicates the frequency with which road movement targets were seen by pilots. On many such missions when no road movement was seen the pilots attacked other opportunity targets (i.e. railway lines, stations and marshalling yards). In coastal areas, ships or barges were often attacked.
37. Sallagar, *Operation Strangle*, p. vi.
38. Quoted in John Ellis, *Cassino, The Hollow Victory: the Battle for Rome January–June 1944* (London: Andre Deutsch, 1984), p. 435.
39. Quoted in Hilary St. G. Saunders, *Royal Air Force 1939–45*, Volume III, *The Fight is Won* (London: HMSO, 1954), p. 232.
40. David Irving, *The Trail of The Fox: The Life of Field-Marshal Erwin Rommel* (London: Weidenfeld and Nicolson, 1977), p. 345. Rommel's career in Normandy was terminated by 2nd TAF on 17 July 1944 when Spitfires patrolling the roads near Vimoutiers strafed his staff car. Rommel suffered a fractured skull. Ibid., pp. 381–2.
41. B.H. Liddell Hart (Ed.), *The Rommel Papers* (London: Collins, 1953), pp. 476–7.
42. Interrogation Report (British Army), on 17 Polish Division and 2 Alsation Division, May 1944, PRO AIR 37/831.
43. Quoted in C.J.C. Molony, *The Mediterranean and Middle East*, Volume V (London: HMSO, 1973), p. 315.
44. Quoted in Warren Tute, John Costello and Terry Hughes, *D-Day* (London: Pan Books, 1975), p. 239.
45. Bayerlein Interrogation, in The USAAF Evaluation Board in The ETO, *The Effectiveness of Third Phase Tactical Air Operations in the European Theater, 5 May 1944 – 8 May 1945* (1946), p. 259, PRO AIR 40/1111.
46. Bradley and the US 12th Army Group Air Effects Committee, *Effect of Air Power on Military Operations*, p. 45.
47. Richard P. Hallion, *Strike From The Sky: The History of Battlefield Air Attack 1911 – 45*, (Shrewsbury: Airlife, 1989), p. 204.
    The night intruder operations by RAF Mosquito aircraft could never match the armed reconnaissance effort possible by day. There were never more than eight Mosquito squadrons in 2nd TAF (only six until early 1945) and they averaged only 170 sorties per month, 88 per cent of this effort being at night. ORS 2nd TAF Report No.37 (1945), *The Effort and Accuracy of Tactical Bombers in 2 Group Jan. 1944 – May 1945*, PRO WO 291/1362.
    Night-fighter operations, though few, could delay German formations moving by night. A German soldier of the 899 Reserve Regiment taken prisoner in Normandy told his captors of an occasion when his company was moving by bicycle at night. Two night-fighters flew over, dropping flares, and his company immediately dispersed into cover. Although the aircraft departed without attacking, and did not return, the company remained in cover for 20 minutes. Prisoner of War A.D.I. (K) Report No. 382/1944 (24 July 1944), PRO AIR 37/760.
48. During his post-war interrogation, Bayerlein told how German formations were resupplied at night, though the difficulties of night movement and the short summer nights made supply uncertain. In winter, due to the longer period of darkness, supply was better. Bayerlein Interrogation, p. 264.
49. Ibid, p. 262.
50. Quoted in John Ellis, *Cassino, The Hollow Victory*, p. 423.
51. Ibid.
52. No.83 Group RAF, Intelligence Summary No.50, 2 Aug. 1944, PRO AIR 25/704. Chester Wilmot in *The Struggle For Europe* (p. 441) mentions this incident and gives the figure for 83 Group sorties as 923, but this was the total of all 83 Group sorties during the day including close support, fighter patrols and conventional reconnaissance. He observes that the claims are 'broadly substantiated' by German sources.
53. Ibid.; also Lefèvre, *Panzers in Normandy*, p. 144.
54. James Lucas and James Barker, *The Killing Ground: The Battle of the Falaise Gap August 1944* (London: 1978), p. 76.
55. Ibid.; Ralf Tiemann and Rudolf Lehmann, *Die Leibstandarte*, Band IV/1 (Osnabrück: Munin Verlag, 1986), p. 206 (DOAC translation).
56. Ralph Bennett, *Ultra in The West: The Normandy Campaign of 1944–45* (London: Hutchinson, 1979), p. 120.
57. Bayerlein Interrogation, p. 261.
58. RAF Desert Air Force, ORB, June 1944, PRO AIR 24/443.

59. Ibid., Jan. 1945, PRO AIR 24/444.
60. Ibid., June 1944, PRO AIR 24/443.
61. Ibid., Aug.–Sept. 1944, PRO AIR 24/443.
62. See Chapter 4 above.
63. Craven and Cate, *The Army Air Forces in World War II*, p. 690.
64. RAF Desert Air Force, ORB, July – August 1944, PRO AIR 24/443; Christopher Shores, *Ground Attack Aircraft of World War II* (London: Macdonald and Jane's, 1977), p. 128.
65. Mediterranean Allied Air Forces ORS Report N.32 (1945), *Observations on the Strength and Balance of Desert Air Force*, PRO AIR 23/7513.
66. Air Marshal Coningham, to Headquarters Mediterranean Allied Air Forces, 29 Dec. 1943, *Memorandum on the Effect of Withdrawing Fighter-Bombers from Tactical Air Force*, PRO AIR 23/1529.
67. ORS 2nd TAF Report No.30, *Armed Reconnaissance by Aircraft of 2nd TAF.*

Conclusion

The RAF and the British Army, and later the US Army and the USAAF, entered the war completely unversed in close air support, and lacking worthwhile experience, equipment and doctrine. Yet by 1944 the British and Americans each had in operation joint army/air force machinery providing for the swift handling of air-support requests and the command and control of aircraft extending from airfield to battlefront. The Allied air-support systems were remarkable achievements, yet while the British and Americans each created a workable air-support machinery, neither attained the highest level of potential efficiency. For air support to work the armies and air forces had to be very closely co-ordinated, and to achieve this only at the operational level, and not always then, was not enough.

Opposition, or at least lack of commitment, to the principle of close air support on the part of the RAF and USAAF was a major contributory factor, but so too was an almost complete lack of understanding of the nature of air support on the part of the US and British Armies. While junior air and ground commanders learnt by experience, at staff level this situation prevailed until the end of the war. This meant that the extra effort necessary to make the system work to full efficiency was never forthcoming. It was unfortunate, too, that training in close support for the Allied troops and air forces preparing for OVERLORD was minimal, with very few joint exercises, largely due to the fact that the air forces were continually fighting to secure the air superiority necessary for the invasion to take place. The success of air support in North-West Europe ultimately depended upon the innovation and imagination of those air commanders at a lower level, such as Broadhurst of 83 Group and Quesada of IX TAC, who had learnt air support in the Mediterranean, and who were prepared to support the army despite censure from their superiors.

The test of battle inevitably exposed weaknesses in both the US and British systems, but many of the problems, particularly those that cost lives such as poor bombline discipline and air-ground recognition procedure, could have been minimised had adequate training been possible. It was only too obvious in Normandy, just as it had been in Sicily and early in Italy, that air and ground forces were unfamiliar with each other. In each case examining and finding solutions to the problems with close air support that were likely to be encountered had been accorded too little priority.

The air suppor' systems depended upon an extensive communications network and the rapid accumulation, processing, and dissemination of data and of instructions based upon it. Both the British and US systems had problems with this. At the time much of the fault was considered to be due to individuals – for example in the US system the army Ground Liaison Officers (GLOs) attached to air squadrons were criticised by some army formations for not keeping the air units sufficiently informed of the ground battle situation. Yet, while variations in individual performance could adversely affect efficiency at all levels, in 1943–45 the real problem lay in the breaks in the data flow, where a man at a desk, be he an air force or army officer at a joint control centre, an air force headquarters, or at a fighter-bomber airfield, had to sift through and act upon a continuing mass of data from the battlefront. Delays here were inevitable, as was the fact that by the time ALOs or GLOs at the airfields briefed the fighter-bomber pilots their information was to some extent out of date. It must be remembered, too, that the communications systems of the time were unreliable and cumbersome, and prone to breakdown.

The fighter-bomber squadrons were the cutting edge of the Allied tactical air forces, but despite the immense effort and manpower both within the air-support systems and the air forces needed to maintain these squadrons, to direct them to the battlefront, and to control them once there, they were in fact blunt instruments.

The fighter-bomber of 1943–45 was certainly flexible and versatile, able to be directed against a wide range of targets, but what it actually achieved when it reached them was a different matter altogether. This was due to the limitations of the air-to-ground weapons with which it was equipped, principally their inaccuracy. Rockets and free-fall bombs, even when delivered by experienced pilots, could not be depended upon to hit their target, be it a gun position, a tank, a building, or even a bridge. With regard to close air support, when many of the targets could be expected to be small and camouflaged, this was a significant drawback. Precision attacks, if not completely beyond the capabilities of fighter-bombers of the time, were at best very difficult to achieve, and the main value of the fighter-bomber was its ability to bring to the battlefront a considerable weight of firepower with which to saturate a target area.

This ability was particularly important when fighter-bombers had to act as a substitute for artillery by flying close air support for armoured thrusts and airborne operations, this being the only means of providing fire support in such operations.

With regard to the former, close air support offered two important advantages over conventional artillery support. One was that the fighter-bombers could keep pace with the advance, and the other was that they could engage targets that were very close to the advancing tanks. Yet it is apparent that it was the morale effect of air attack, rather than the destruction caused or number of casualties inflicted, that was decisive in overcoming German resistance.

Although the Typhoon attacks in support of GARDEN undoubtedly caused some casualties among the German troops, the war diary of the Irish Guards clearly describes how it was the resulting shock and demoralisation that caused the German defence to collapse. This was confirmed by the fact that the Typhoons proved equally effective in inducing German troops to surrender by making dummy attacks, after their rockets and cannon ammunition had been expended. Similarly, after CYGNET, the subsequent Royal Armoured Corps report noted how the fighter-bomber attacks on German defended buildings caused a 'temporary disorganisation' which enabled the British tanks and infantry to close in and clear them with few casualties.

The problem with such neutralisation, as opposed to outright destruction of the enemy, was that it only lasted while aircraft were overhead. Once they had departed, the effect soon wore off. Both on the first day of GARDEN and throughout CYGNET the air support was continuous, but the lack of progress made on subsequent days during GARDEN when the Typhoons were unavailable revealed to what extent the Germans were prepared to fight stubbornly. With Armored Column Cover there were occasions when, after fighter-bombers had neutralised German positions to enable the US armour to bypass them, the occupants of these positions had subsequently recovered to offer resistance to the following US infantry.

All this suggests that, particularly when armour was advancing in terrain favouring defence, or was confined to roads, success depended upon the provision of close air support, but to maintain a CABRANK or Armored Column Cover demanded the commitment of considerable air effort. The Allies were fortunate in having air superiority and large numbers of fighter-bombers available, but even so such commitment could not be sustained for more than limited periods.

Turning to airborne operations, there were obviously problems with regard to providing close support to troops operating beyond the established front line, particularly that of pilots correctly identifying friend from foe on the ground and the paramount need to maintain communications. Given that close air support was the only means of augmenting the firepower of lightly armed airborne troops when beyond the protection of friendly artillery, it is remarkable that the Allied airborne forces were so poorly served until nearly the end of the war.

Both the US and British airborne troops in Normandy were denied much potential air support, not because the aircraft were unavailable but because the means of contacting them was lacking. Even as late as September 1944, the British 1st Airborne Division went to Arnhem unversed in the close air-support procedure that had been in use with British troops on the Continent since D-Day, and lacking adequate means to contact tactical aircraft. The subject had been given very little thought and accorded no priority, a situation that was not corrected until early 1945.

However, while it was inexcusable that little consideration had been given to close air support of the Allied airborne forces, the case can be overstated. It would have been inappropriate for airborne troops to be utterly dependent upon such support. Had 1st Airborne Division gone to Arnhem superbly equipped and trained for the utilisation of close air support, this would have been of little use had adverse weather kept the fighter-bombers grounded. Moreover, it is hard to see how the Typhoons could have intervened in the confused fighting at Arnhem without great risk to friendly troops. When they did appear, towards the end of the battle, their attacks proved to be of limited practical use and certainly not of a decisive battle-winning nature. Once again it was a case of fighter-bombers causing neutralisation instead of destruction. The presence of the Typhoons kept the German troops in cover, but little advantage could be taken of this under the prevailing circumstances and ultimately the Typhoons provided the airborne troops with only a temporary respite from German fire.

Conclusion 231

In fighter-bomber attacks against armour, the underlying theme remains the morale effect of air attack. The ORS ground surveys at la Baleine, Mortain, the Falaise Pocket, and in the Ardennes prove that fighter-bombers, despite the claims of their pilots, did not destroy many German tanks. This was not because their weapons lacked destructive capability, but because they could not be relied upon to hit the target. What is also apparent, however, particularly with regard to la Baleine and Mortain, is that air attack could disrupt concentrations of armour and cause widespread panic and demoralisation among tank crews.

At Mortain both American and German accounts of the battle acknowledge that the intervention of the fighter-bombers, particularly the rocket-Typhoons, was decisive. Given the evidence from the ORS ground surveys of the battle area, which seems conclusive, this could only have been as a result of the air attacks disrupting the enemy attack and causing panic – hence the number of German tanks subsequently found abandoned. Thus the reputation of the Typhoon as an effective 'tank killer' was really based upon the quite terrifying effect of salvoes of the 3-inch rocket and the fact that, despite its lack of pinpoint accuracy, the weapon could nevertheless be placed with more accuracy than free-fall bombs, thereby enabling the Typhoons to engage German armour which was very close to the positions of Allied troops.

Turning aside from tanks specifically, there is more reason to believe that fighter-bombers wrought great destruction among German soft-skin transport. This was mainly by strafing, for cannon and machine gun fire was far more accurate than bombing or rocket fire, and had a high lethality against soft-skin and even lightly armoured vehicles. Moreover, bombs or rockets did not need to actually strike such vehicles to destroy or seriously damage them, for they were vulnerable, as tanks were not, to the blast and shrapnel caused by a near-miss. It was by attacking such targets that fighter-bombers were really most effective against armour concentrations, for if the fighter-bombers could not easily destroy the tanks they could certainly reduce the softskin vehicles keeping them supplied with fuel and ammunition.

In short, with regard to close air support, the effectiveness of fighter-bomber attack against armour on the battlefield ultimately depended upon the disruption and morale effect. In armed reconnaissance attack on armour that was not closely engaged with Allied troops, their effectiveness depended upon disruption and the destruction of those vehicles keeping the tanks supplied.

The success of heavy and medium bombers in the close support role also depended upon the disruption and demoralisation caused by bombing, and the extent to which this could be exploited, rather than the amount of destruction or casualties inflicted. Against pinpoint targets, such as individual gun and battery positions, heavy and medium bombing was too inaccurate to be relied upon to score the requisite number of direct hits, while defended positions constructed of concrete and steel often proved impervious to the heaviest calibre bombs. Bombing in support of offensive operations in open country usually found the German defenders too well dispersed for the number of casualties and losses in equipment inflicted upon them to be decisive, while bombing of urban areas proved almost wholly counter-productive and a positive hindrance to the troops it was intended to assist.

What, then, could such bombing achieve? The answer can only be that bombing amounted to the saturation of German defence positions with a tremendous weight of fire that, while it did not necessarily cause great destruction or massive casualties, did cause widespread disruption, shock and demoralisation and left the machinery of defence vulnerable and temporarily unable to function. If this could be exploited at once by Allied troops, then significant gains could be made at less cost.

However, this was not always sufficient to secure success. GOOD-WOOD, for example, failed not only because sufficient German forces survived in the bombed areas to offer resistance which slowed the British advance, but also because the German defence zone was of such depth that the initial heavy bomber strike was insufficient to blast a way through it. The entire operation was mounted on the basis of faulty intelligence and it is questionable whether a breakthrough could ever have been achieved. In contrast the bombing that initiated COBRA, while it did not completely eliminate German resistance or obviate hard fighting by the US troops, did make a breakthrough possible because the German defence that had been initially disrupted lacked depth and could not be restored.

The decision to bomb urban areas in the path of Allied troops, especially after the experience of Cassino, is difficult to comprehend. The resulting obstruction prevented the assault troops from taking advantage of the disruption of the defence, while the German troops were presented with a series of new and well concealed positions. Some of the operations in open terrain also reveal a lack of awareness on the part of the soldiers of what bombing could be expected to achieve.

The reason was that the soldiers were anxious to make progress while saving casualties, but did not understand sufficiently the implications of heavy bombing in varying terrain. They were unwilling to heed the warnings of the senior airmen, and therefore exposed themselves, when operations failed, to the not unjustified charge that the strategic bomber forces were being used not to secure decisive result but simply to save army casualties. With hindsight the saving of soldiers' lives does not seem so reprehensible a justification, but in fact the senior airmen had some cause to oppose any diversion of the strategic bomber offensive against Germany. In 1944–45 this offensive, for which the Allied heavy bomber forces had been created, was at long last beginning to show positive results – most notably in the targeting of Germany's synthetic oil plants and the attrition of the Luftwaffe.

It is ironic that this should have occurred only after the Allied armies had landed in France, an event which both Harris and Spaatz had intended to make unnecessary through bombing. Demands from the soldiers for heavy bomber close support thus began to occur at the worst possible time for the airmen – when their strategic offensive, which had already been disrupted by the bombing programme leading up to D-Day in support of OVERLORD, was beginning to show results, and when they had to meet yet another, even more urgent, demand for the bombing of German flying-bomb sites.

This, coupled with the fact that the strategic airmen were doctrinally opposed to close air support, meant that such support was provided reluctantly. Hence the bitter recrimination, such as after CHARNWOOD and especially GOODWOOD, when it appeared to the airmen to have been wasted. Their determination that the strategic air forces should not be at the disposal of the army, and the fact that their forces were continually engaged, ensured that little was done until late in both the Italian and North-West European campaigns to educate the soldiers as to the nature of heavy bombing, or to solve the likely command and control problems which cost so many lives in the short-bombings.

Yet, while a more positive attitude towards close air support on the part of the senior airmen might have seen some of the command and control difficulties avoided, thereby preventing some of the short bombing tragedies, they were fundamentally right in their contention that the heavy bombers were unsuited to the role. It is hard to see, given the nature of bombing and the ways in which it could be effective, how any of the heavy bomber operations could have been more successful than they were, or how any further such employment could have been justified.

The COBRA bombing was vindicated by the success of the operation, while the GOODWOOD bombing was condemned by the operation's failure. Yet the bombing for GOODWOOD was no less effective in what it actually achieved than that for COBRA, while the latter operation could hardly have succeeded had the US forces been confronted with a German defence as formidable as that which had defeated GOODWOOD. Even operation QUEEN, for which the US Army and Eighth Air Force working together eliminated the risk of short-bombing, ultimately failed due to the depth of the German defence. The employment of heavy and medium bombers in close support proved to be of value only in the initial stages of set piece attacks, and for the gaining of limited objectives. If rapidly exploited, such bombing could enable Allied troops to break into German defence localities at reduced cost, but it could not ensure a break-through any more than could the massive artillery bombardments of the First World War to which it was analogous. In short, the answer to defence in depth could only have been more, and yet more, bombs.

When comparing the effectiveness of fighter-bombers and artillery in close support, it would seem that close air support could only be justified on the grounds of the pronounced morale effect of air attack.

Artillery was on hand to provide support day and night, in all weathers. Fighter-bombers could only be called upon during daylight, and then were at the mercy of the weather, making the provision of close air support highly questionable. Moreover, the Allied artilleries by 1943–45 were adept at providing fire support very rapidly, and had attained a responsiveness that could be matched by aircraft only by the expensive provision of standing patrols in the battle area. With regard to destructive effect and lethality, air weapons were little more effec-tive, if at all, than artillery fire against troops with a reasonable level of protection. Against troops unfortunate enough to be caught in the open, both air attack and artillery fire could be very lethal. But in the battle area German troops were rarely caught at such a disadvantage in daylight and, being on hand and well within range, it was usually artillery that was best placed to take advantage of such occurrences.

Yet, fighter-bombers offered several advantages over artillery. One was that their attacks enabled Allied troops to approach closer to the objective than could normally be possible during an artillery bombardment. Another was that air attack could achieve the neutrali-sation of an enemy position more quickly, with effects of longer duration, than could be achieved by artillery. Both these considerations were vital, for experience in European operations proved that it was not how many Germans a supporting bombardment killed or wounded that was critical, but how quickly they could be rendered incapable of fighting, through shock or panic, and how long this state was likely to last. In attacks by Allied troops upon German positions it was time that cost lives, the time, a matter of a few vital minutes, during which the German defenders could recover from the effects of bombardment and emerge from cover to man their positions. Fighter-bombers saved time.

The TIMOTHY and WINKLE methods of co-ordinating airstrikes to support the various stages of an advance exploited these advantages on a wider scale. They provided deeper and more flexible fire support throughout the course of an attack than an artillery barrage alone, as not just the German forward defence localities to be assaulted but also those positions and gun areas immediately beyond were subject to air attack and the consequent disruption. Neutralisation was therefore more extensive, and was renewed at intervals.

Were these advantages enough to justify the commitment of aircraft to the ground battle area to support armies generally well equipped with artillery? Many of the airstrikes carried out in close support against German positions negated the advantages of fighter-bomber attack because they were not co-ordinated with attacks by Allied troops. Except in situations where artillery was lacking or its ammunition was in short supply, the air support offered no appreciable advantage and was wasted. Yet, because close air support, when rapidly exploited, could enable German positions to be overcome rapidly with fewer casualties there were occasions when such support was not only justified but vital.

Whether this contribution could be made without compromising the effectiveness of those air operations conducted beyond the battle-front leads to the wider question of cost effectiveness, and inevitably to a comparison with the role rivalling close air support in terms of commitment of air effort: that of armed reconnaissance.

North-West Europe and Italy in 1944/45, and particularly the former, constituted the most flak-intensive environment confronting Allied fighter-bomber pilots during the war. Losses in aircraft and pilots among squadrons engaged in ground attack were high. Yet, despite the preconceived tenet held by both the RAF and USAAF that close air support was the most costly of tactical operations (see

Chapter 2 above), statistical evidence from North-West Europe proves that close air support was significantly less dangerous than armed reconnaissance. In effect, the data suggests that the further beyond the battlefront that fighter-bombers operated, the higher their losses. Armed reconnaissance itself varied in the losses sustained, deep penetration missions proving more costly than those conducted closer to the battlefront.

Not only was armed reconnaissance more expensive than close support in terms of losses, it was also more expensive in terms of air effort, with significantly more fighter-bomber sorties being committed to this mission type. The question remains whether the cost of armed reconnaissance in both respects was justified by the results achieved.

With regard to both close air support and armed reconnaissance these results were temporary in nature in that it was neutralisation rather than destruction that was ultimately more important. Armed reconnaissance was a continual daylight air offensive over the German rear areas but, as interdiction operations such as STRANGLE proved, it was unrealistic to expect fighter-bombers to prevent all German road, rail and river movement and to cut off the German forward troops from all reinforcement and supply. However, their disruptive effect on German movement, due to the ever-present threat as much as the actual attack, was great. This was continual neutralisation, and the air effort involved was commensurate with what was achieved. So too were the losses. Supply traffic, ammunition and fuel dumps, airfields, troop concentration areas, and those units compelled to move by daylight were of vital importance and heavily defended by flak – it was unthinkable that they should not be brought under attack, but they could not be attacked without penalty.

Close air support losses were also commensurate with the nature of the targets. Nothing was more important than the next enemy pillbox, trench, or defended house to those Allied troops whose task it was to assault it. They were similarly important to the German troops defending them, but their priority for anti-aircraft protection was low and the vast majority of such targets were undefended by flak. Moreover, flak positions in the battle area could be suppressed by Allied artillery.

In the wider perspective armed-reconnaissance targets appear undeniably more important than those of close support. Yet in the 1943–45 period there is little evidence of serious tension in determining the allocation of air units to either role, though certain trends are apparent. When the battlefront was static and the Allied armies not engaged in large-scale offensive operations the amount of close air support requests was relatively small, allowing a considerable commitment to armed reconnaissance. Once offensive operations were under way, particularly in the initial stages, the amount of close support increased, but never to such an extent as to make armed reconnaissance impossible and thereby to lessen the threat of air attack in the German rear areas. Once a breakthrough had been achieved, or the battlefront had stabilised, the priority of armed reconnaissance was reasserted.

In fact close support and armed reconnaissance were complementary aspects of the same tactical air offensive, which remained highly flexible. The air-support systems allowed for the diversion of aircraft from armed-reconnaissance missions to answer unforeseen requests for close support, and in the US system this became the favoured method of responding to such demands. Similarly, during large-scale close support operations involving CABRANK or Armored Column Cover, aircraft were frequently directed to armed reconnaissance when close-in targets were lacking. In fact, even during set-piece offensive operations as opposed to rapid armoured advances, the FCP and VCP controllers with the forward troops were responsible for directing a high proportion of the armed-reconnaissance missions carried out in the areas immediately behind the German front line positions.

In effect, it was quite normal for fighter-bomber pilots assigned to close air support to find themselves flying armed reconnaissance, and for pilots setting out on an armed-reconnaissance mission to be diverted to close air support. It would be a mistake to consider that the fighter-bomber squadrons assigned to either mission type were somehow waging separate campaigns, for they were not. A study of the major ground offensive operations reveals that, in addition to the squadrons assigned to close support, those assigned to armed reconnaissance were also indirectly supporting the operation, as well as maintaining the attack upon the German rear areas, by flying armed reconnaissance over the roads leading to the battle area.

In Italy and North-West Europe during 1943–45 which of these roles was the most vital was found to depend, in practice, not upon preconceived dogma but upon the prevailing circumstances in the battle area. It is true that the disruption of German tactical mobility and of supply and communications could only be achieved by air attack whereas, in theory at least, the soldiers should have been able to achieve their objectives without close air support. Experience proved otherwise: there was an unforeseen requirement for close air support not only in emergency situations, such as at Mortain, but also to exploit the particular advantages that supporting aircraft could bring.

THE EFFECTIVENESS OF CLOSE AIR SUPPORT

The effectiveness of close air support depended upon its responsiveness and its ability to destroy or neutralise targets. Aircraft could not normally respond rapidly to requests for close air support. With close support by heavy and medium bombers, the question of responsiveness does not arise as they could only be employed according to a rigid timetable, for example at the outset of a major attack. With fighter-bombers, at the very least time had to be allowed for the request to be passed from the forward troops through the air-support control system to the airfield, where further time was needed for a rapid briefing of pilots. Still more time was taken by the aircraft in taking-off, forming-up when airborne, and proceeding to the battlefront.

Under these conditions, even with a squadron whose aircraft and pilots were at readiness, the forward troops would have been extremely fortunate to see their supporting aircraft arrive within an hour of the original request. This was clearly unsatisfactory, as far as the troops were concerned, for dealing with German strongpoints and pockets of resistance that were encountered during the course of an advance. In order to save time and casualties such positions had to be dealt with rapidly, and in most circumstances artillery, providing it was available, was the more effective solution. In 1943–45 the British and US artilleries possessed fire control systems whose responsiveness could not normally be equalled by aircraft.

There were two methods whereby the Allied air-support systems could respond faster than by relying upon squadrons at airfield readiness. One was to contact aircraft that were already airborne in or near the battle area, divert them from their mission and direct them to respond to the request. Normally such aircraft, providing they happened to be available, were proceeding on armed-reconnaissance patrols. However, time would be needed for them to change course and proceed to the particular sector of the battlefront, where on arrival they would report to the ground controller at the FCP or contact car. The pilots would then have to be briefed before they could attack the target. There were two drawbacks to this method. One was the obvious disruption to air force planning, in that in order to respond to the close-support request the assigned mission had to be dropped. The other relates to the quality of the resulting air support. Pilots diverted in this way were unlikely to be as familiar with the sector of the battlefront, the ground situation, and the relative positions of enemy and friendly troops as those of squadrons originally assigned to close-support tasks and who had been given a more detailed briefing.

The second, and most important, method of responding rapidly to close-support requests was to maintain standing patrols of aircraft in the battle area. Examples of this are CABRANK and, for mobile operations, Armored Column Cover. In this case the pilots would have been well briefed for operating in the battle area and made familiar with the ground situation and the positions of enemy and friendly troops. They could also respond on a par with artillery, as they could be directed on to targets as they arose. For fighter-bombers to achieve this level of responsiveness, however, demanded such a commitment of air resources that the Allied tactical air forces in 1943–45, despite their possession of large numbers of aircraft and pilots, could not sustain such efforts for more than limited periods.

Moreover, such operations were inefficient, and involved a certain amount of waste. Maintaining constant patrols in a single area meant that many of them were not required for close-support targets. In effect, supply exceeded demand and pilots were frequently directed to attack pre-briefed alternative targets or to carry out armed-reconnaissance patrols in the area immediately behind the German positions. Such patrols may have reduced German defence effectiveness by discouraging movement and inducing gun positions to remain inactive. But equally very few worthwhile targets were to be found immediately behind the German positions during a battle, particularly at a time when German troops knew the sky to be full of Allied aircraft, and that the aircraft could have been more profitably employed, in either the close-support or armed-reconnaissance role, in other sectors which had been denuded of both types of air effort.

Yet there was no realistic alternative. Viable close air support demanded a rapid response to support requests, and this could only be achieved if the pilots were kept overhead waiting for targets. In 1943–45 the Allied tactical air forces were able to attain a high degree of responsiveness in close air support only as a result of the considerable air resources at their disposal, and at the ultimate expense of cost effectiveness.

A problem with regard to close air support never solved in the period 1943–45 was that of destructive capability. It was extremely difficult for Allied aircraft to destroy the targets that they were called upon to engage at the battlefront.

The bomb patterns of heavy and medium bombers were intended to saturate wide target areas. Yet it was consistently found that such bombing was uneven, with some areas overhit and others relatively untouched. This simply meant that when bombing German defence localities and gun areas in the field, some positions would be destroyed and others not. In fact the number of men and amount of equipment that could survive saturation bombing appear to have been a constant surprise to both Germans and Allies alike. This was not a question of accuracy alone. Dispersion did much to negate the effectiveness of the bomb patterns, but it was also found that troops well dug-in had little to fear from near misses. The destructive effect of a high-explosive bomb extended little beyond its crater, while fragmentation bombing, lethal to unprotected troops, was considerably less effective against those that were. Heavily fortified positions of concrete and steel, such as encountered during the operations to clear the Channel ports, were impervious to even the heaviest calibre bombs. Bombing urban areas caused much devastation, but here too sufficient German troops could be expected to survive to mount a formidable defence.

Fighter-bomber effectiveness was compromised by the fact that the bombs and rockets of 1943–45 were so inaccurate that, when directed against precision targets, they were almost certain to miss them. Yet most close-support targets in the battle area were precision targets because they were small. They were also usually well camouflaged, in order to hide them from the air and from observation by Allied troops. Such targets included dug-in tanks, gun and mortar positions, strong-points and machine-gun nests. The heavy and medium bomber crews never expected to see such targets; they were intended to saturate the areas known to contain them and usually bombed from too high an altitude to distinguish anything but the most prominent landmarks. In contrast, the fighter-bomber pilot was expected to tackle such targets individually, yet he too rarely saw them. More often than not, diving at speed with only a few seconds to aim and release his bombs or rockets, and confronted with a battle area obscured by smoke, the pilot saw only the coloured smoke fired by friendly artillery that was intended to indicate his target. This, taken in conjunction with the inaccuracy of air-to-ground weapons, meant that very few such targets were actually hit.

But if they were not hit they would not be destroyed, as near-misses by bombs and rockets against dug-in troops and equipment, or tanks, were of little value. Only strafing appears to have had the potential to inflict significant casualties, providing a large number of fighter-bombers were strafing an area containing a high concentration of troops lacking overhead protection. In effect, close air support could never be relied upon to achieve the outright destruction of targets, and attempts to ensure even a reasonable chance of such destruction demanded an inordinate scale of air attack by all aircraft types.

The battlefield effectiveness of close air support depended not upon its destructiveness, but upon the fact that air attack had the potential to neutralise targets more effectively than Allied ground weapons. This really amounts to saying that air attack was more terrifying, and that the German troops subjected to it were likely to remain in a state of shock, and incapable of fighting effectively, for longer than those subjected to ground-based fire support. The evidence is persuasive.

With regard to fighter-bomber attacks, accounts from British and US troops and ORS investigations all affirm that it was this temporary morale effect of air attack, rather than any destruction and casualties caused, that was decisive. There was also the very important practical consideration that fighter-bomber strikes could permit assault troops to approach closer to their objective than possible with supporting artillery fire, enabling them to take maximum advantage of the morale effect. For mobile and airborne operations close air support was the only means of supplementing the limited firepower of Allied units, and its success was crucial. But here too air support proved highly effective in the temporary neutralisation of targets, rather than in their destruction.

The situation was slightly different regarding heavy and medium bomber operations, in that more destruction and casualties were likely to be caused than by fighter-bomber strikes due to the weight and scale of attack involved. Nevertheless, this was never in itself decisive, and the progress made by Allied troops at the outset of such operations was due primarily to the morale effect of bombing. Many German troops subjected to carpet bombing survived, but they were often found to be suffering from vibratory shock, deafness and complete disorientation. Equipment may not have been destroyed, but in the period immediately following a bomber strike many of the tanks and guns were rendered temporarily unworkable by being toppled into craters or buried under dirt and debris. The problem was that the nature of such bombing often prevented Allied troops from exploiting this effect. Crater bombs ploughed up German defence localities in the field, but they also slowed the progress of Allied troops, particularly armour. Bombing defended urban areas completely disrupted the German defences, but caused such obstruction that Allied troops could not reach their objectives. In both cases, by the time the Allied troops had negotiated the obstruction caused by bombing, those Germans that had not become casualties or prisoners had recovered.

The justification for using fighter-bombers in close air support despite their lack of destructiveness was their success in enabling Allied troops to secure their objectives more rapidly and with fewer casualties than would have been possible with ground-based fire support. Attacks upon German gun and battery positions which, though they destroyed few guns, significantly reduced German fire on the Allied assault troops were thus equally justifiable.

Yet the success of close air support for Allied attacks depended upon the air support being rapidly exploited on the ground, and in very many instances this was not done. When such exploitation was attempted but not achieved for reasons beyond the control of Allied troops, one may say that the air support was wasted but that its employment was nevertheless justified. However, a very large proportion of close air-support strikes were directed at German front line targets, within range of friendly artillery, but were not closely integrated with ground operations. Such attacks amounted to an unjustified waste of effort.

Turning to heavy and medium bomber operations, few can be justified by success. The bombing of heavily protected gun batteries, such as at Walcheren, or concrete and steel fortifications, such as at Le Havre and Boulogne, when such raids were not integrated with an assault, proved to be a waste of bombs. Similarly, the bombing of urban areas, even immediately prior to an assault, proved counterproductive. After the experience of Cassino in March 1944 further such employment of the heavy and medium bomber forces seems inexcusable.

In field operations, heavy and medium bombing enabled Allied troops to overcome German defence localities in the initial stages of a major attack, but, when Allied troops were confronted with a German defence in depth, such bombing could not be decisive by ensuring a breakthrough. It was therefore not justified by results, though as this could not be foreseen at the time one might argue that the attempts were reasonable. Each of the joint heavy and medium close-support bombing operations was intended to be decisive, and the bombing that initiated Operation COBRA finally was because it made possible the breakout from Normandy. Yet, in terms of what the bombing actually achieved it had not been markedly more successful than that for GOODWOOD a week previously. It is therefore simplistic to condemn the employment of the bomber forces for the latter operation simply because it ultimately failed, while at the same time acknowledging the contribution of the former to Allied success.

AN UNWARRANTED DIVERSION OF EFFORT?

To the question as to whether air support proved to be of more value when directed against targets beyond the battlefront, the answer must be that, in general, it did.

This is most relevant to fighter-bombers, which were certainly more likely to be able to destroy the targets found beyond the battlefront than those in the immediate battle area. German motor transport was extremely vulnerable to fighter-bomber weapons, as were fuel and ammunition dumps. Concentrated attacks upon buildings used as headquarters were likely to achieve sufficient hits to make them untenable. That such targets could be destroyed by fighter-bombers is not in itself a justification for stating that attacks on them were of more value than close support. However, such targets were of vital importance to the Germans, and this is reflected in the losses in aircraft and pilots sustained by the Allied tactical air forces in attacking them. Moreover, armed reconnaissance and attacks upon specific targets beyond the front line maintained a continual threat of air attack that reduced German fighting ability, with tactical mobility and supply being impossible in daylight without severe penalty.

Attaining this dominance over the German rear areas was undoubtedly vital, but it must be observed that there were occasions when close air support was necessary – for example in an emergency situation such as Mortain. In 1943–45 the Allies were fortunate in that, having achieved air superiority, they possessed sufficient aircraft and pilots to provide both a high level of close air support and also maintain a continuous armed-reconnaissance offensive. While priorities varied according to circumstances in the battle area, the Allied armies were never denied the support of one mission type at the total expense of the other. The German armies in Italy and North-West Europe were under the continual threat of air attack both at and beyond the battlefront. Had circumstances been different, however, with fewer

Allied air resources and a formidable Luftwaffe to be countered, then despite the advantages that it could bring to the battlefield, close air support on the scale enjoyed by the Allied armies in 1943–45 would have been impossible – and rightly so.

Turning to heavy and medium bombers, the latter must be considered as tactical, rather than strategic, weapons. Mediums were rarely employed in close support except in conjunction with the heavy bombers. They were mainly employed to bring under attack such German communications and supply targets that were beyond fighter-bomber range, and thus represented the deep-strike capability of the tactical air forces. They were also employed, with some effect, to disrupt German troop concentrations and gun areas beyond the battlefront which demanded a heavier scale of bombing than was possible with fighter-bombers. Extensive use of the medium bomber squadrons in the close air-support role, when large numbers of fighter-bombers were available, would have resulted in many vital targets beyond the battlefront being neglected. Moreover, lacking the flexibility and responsiveness of fighter-bombers, and their ability to attack targets in very close proximity to friendly troops, the mediums could have brought little advantage to the close-support role, for which they were unsuited.

With regard to the heavy bomber forces, there can be little doubt that the strategic role for which they were created, that of disrupting Germany's economic and industrial base, was of more vital importance than close air support. Ultimately heavy bombers proved of limited effectiveness on the battlefield. Whereas their use was justified on a very few occasions in assisting Allied troops at the outset of a major offensive, the problem was that, particularly in Normandy, employment of the heavy bombers escalated as such operations failed in their objectives. This placed the senior airmen in a dilemma. They were prepared to sanction a limited diversion of the strategic forces to support the army if the result was to be decisive – such as to achieve the breakout from Normandy. Yet when such operations failed they were obliged to sanction further diversion.

Given that the extent of close air support by the heavy bomber forces in 1944–45 was small, it might be argued that this limited effort did not in any way compromise the effectiveness of the strategic offensive. Yet the same bomber effort accorded to operations such as GOODWOOD and COBRA might have been used to render an oil plant inoperable for several weeks, or to render a railway marshalling yard unusable for days with consequent disruption to the German transportation network. The opportunity to attack strategic targets depended upon suitable weather, and the effectiveness of the offensive depended upon regular repeat attacks. Seen in this light the effort devoted to close air support seems far less inconsequential, and harder to justify.

Another argument might be that the strategic offensive was compromised by the Allied air forces failing to determine targeting priorities, for example whether to direct the offensive against the German oil industry or transportation targets, and that its overall effectiveness was therefore questionable. It is beyond the scope of this book to determine which strategic target was the most appropriate for the heavy bombers, but suffice to say that such an argument is not a sufficient ground, given their battlefield effectiveness, for stating that further close support would have been desirable or justified.

To sum up, the strategic bomber offensive against Germany's war effort and the armed-reconnaissance tactical air offensive against German movement and supply behind the battlefront were both vital roles for Allied air power in 1943–45. Close air support was not, though it did undoubtedly provide certain advantages that could be exploited by Allied troops. However they were highly variable, and were to a great extent incidental and made apparent only as a result of the Allied air forces possessing large numbers of aircraft for employment in the close-support role.

Appendices

EXAMPLE OF DIVE BOMBING ATTACK AS CARRIED OUT
BY BONFIRES AND BOMPHOONS OVER AN AREA
WHERE FLAK IS LIGHT.
12,000 - 7,000 feet or below.

1st PHASE ~

TARGET

APPROACH

2
1
3
4

2ND PHASE ~

TARGET

1
3
4
2

ECHELON STBD

3RD PHASE ~

2

4

3

1

Not to scale.

LINE ASTERN

Explanatory Notes:

When in vicinity of target, section changes to echelon starboard. The
leader when over the target allows it to pass under the leading edge of his port
wing as in second phase in diagram. When the target reappears at the trailing
edge, the leader executes a semi-stalled turn to port, followed by the other
aircraft of his section. The result of this manoeuvre is a line astern attack at a
steep angle on the reciprocal of the original course as shown in the third phase of
diagram. After releasing bombs, all aircraft make a violent evasive turn in a pre-
arranged direction and reform in a section line abreast.

NOTE: In the above attack a half-roll can be executed as an alternative to the
semi-stalled turn.

APPENDIX TO CHAPTER 3 (DIAGRAM IV)

Example of Dive Bombing Attack as carried out by Banshoons 12,000 – 7,000 ft. over target where intense flak is anticipated.

1st Phase ~

2nd Phase ~

3rd Phase ~

Not to scale.

APPENDIX TO CHAPTER 5

ALLIED FIGHTER-BOMBERS VERSUS GERMAN ARMOURED FORCES

Sorties and Claims by Allied Tactical Air Forces: Falaise 'Pocket', August 1944

	RAF 2nd TAF	US Ninth AF	Total
Sorties	9,896	2,891	12,787
Claims for MT destroyed	3,340	2,520	5,860
Claims for armour destroyed	257	134	391
Total Claims	3,597	2,654	6,251
Claims per sortie	0.36	0.91	0.49

German Armoured and MT Vehicle Losses in the Falaise 'Pocket', August 1944

Type	Rockets	Bombs	Cannon/MG	Abandoned/ destroyed by crew	Total
Tanks, SP Guns, AFVs	11	4	18	100	133
Lorries, cars and motor cycles	4	43	278	376	701
Guns	–	–	1	50	51
Totals	15	47	297	526	885
Percentages	1.7	5.3	33.5	59.5	

German Armour Losses in the 'Shambles' Area, August 1944

Type	Armour-Piercing Shot (Allied ground fire)	Rocket	Crew	Abandoned	Unknown Cause	Total
Pzkw VI (Tiger)	–	–	9	3	–	12
Pzkw V (Panther)	3	0	8	11	–	22
Pzkw IV	2	2	12	6	–	22
Pzkw III	2	–	1	1	1	5
SP Guns	1	–	8	12	–	21
Totals	8	2	38	33	1	82
Percentages	9.7	2.2	46.3	40.2	1.2	

German Armour Losses in the 'Chase' Area, August 1944

Type	Armour-Piercing Shot (Allied ground fire)	Crew	Abandoned	Unknown Cause	Total
Pzkw VI (Tiger)	–	7	4	–	11
Pzkw V (Panther)	2	23	1	2	28
Pzkw IV	3	16	7	2	28
Other tanks	–	–	2	1	3
SP Guns	3	9	12	4	28
Totals	8	55	26	9	98
Percentages	8.1	56.1	26.5	9.1	

Source: No.2 ORS Report No.15, 'Enemy Casualties in Vehicles and Equipment during the Retreat from Normandy to the Seine in Operational Research in North-West Europe', PRO WO 291/1331.

APPENDIX TO CHAPTER 6

HEAVY AND MEDIUM BOMBERS IN THE CLOSE SUPPORT ROLE

Number of Heavy Bombers and Bombs Needed to Cause Obstruction of a 100-Yard Circle
(from No.2 ORS Report No.14 'Heavy Bombing in Support of the Army'
in PRO WO 291/1331)

	Bombs per acre	Number of Bombers (RAF)
Heavily built-up areas	5	50
Lightly built-up areas (villages)	10	100
Open suburban and level open country areas	40	400
Close country (woods, hedgerows)	10–15	100–150

Short Bombings: Allied Casualties in Major Incidents

Operation/Date	Air Forces	Allied Troops	
		Killed	Wounded
Cassino 15.3.43	Mediterranean Allied Strategic AF	96	200
COBRA 24/25.7.44	US Eighth AF and 9th Bomb Division	101	463
TOTALISE 8.8.44	US Eighth AF	86	286
TRACTABLE 14.8.44	RAF Bomber Command	112	376
BUCKLAND 9.4.45	US Fifteenth AF	40	120

Source: See Note 92, page 163, above.

APPENDIX TO CHAPTER 8

THE COST EFFECTIVENESS OF CLOSE AIR SUPPORT:
A COMPARISON WITH ARMED RECONNAISSANCE

Armed Reconnaissance and Close Air Support Missions of RAF 2nd TAF,
January–March 1945

		No.83 Group	No.84 Group	Totals
Sorties in period		9,825	9,221	19,046
Casualties		110	52	162
Sorties per battle casualty		89.3	177.3	117.6
Sorties per battle casualty by role:				
Typhoons:	Armed Reconnaissance	76.8	126.2	
	Close Air Support	143.2	248.3	
Spitfires:	Armed Reconnaissance	94.2	135	
	Close Air Support	181.4	193.1	
Tempests	Armed Reconnaissance	57.1	36	
	Close Air Support	2.7		

Armed Reconnaissance, Close Air Support and
Fighter Patrol Missions of RAF 2nd TAF, April 1945

	No.83 Group				No.84 Group			
	Spitfire	Typhoon	Tempest	Total	Spitfire	Typhoon	Tempest	Total
Armed Reconnaissance sorties	3,153	1,350	940	5,443	3,461	976	865	5,302
Close Air Support and Fighter Patrol sorties	4,560	2,304	529	7,393	1,847	1,505	135	3,487
Aircraft destroyed/Pilots lost:								
On Armed Reconnaissance	35/24	27/26	21/19	83/69	34/29	22/20	12/11	68/60
On Close Air Support and Fighter Patrols	14/10	12/11	7/6	33/27	9/6	11/10	2/2	22/18

Source: RAF 2nd Tactical Air Force (1945), 'Summaries and Comparisons of Effort and Casualties for Nos. 83 and 84 Groups, January–April 1945', in PRO AIR 37/869.

Note on Source Material

OPERATIONAL RESEARCH

Contemporary operational research (OR) material is the single most important data source consulted. In fact, had no attempt been made at the time to determine the effectiveness of weapons and what particular operations had achieved, it is hard to see how any worthwhile historical analysis of close air support could be possible.

Contemporary army records vary considerably in the extent to which the value of air support was acknowledged. Some battalion and regimental war diaries, such as that of the Irish Guards during operation GARDEN, are quite effusive. Others, such as those of the battalions which took part in the first TIMOTHY operation in Italy, actually make little mention of the air support. The reason for this is that compilers of war diaries varied in a number of ways; in temperament, in what they considered important to record of their battalion's activities, and also in the amount of writing time available to them. Moreover, in some operations the air support may not have been so obvious to the troops being supported as in others.

Turning to the air force records, what is the historian to judge of the effectiveness of an airstrike on reading the bald statement that all bombs or rockets fell in the target area, or that the target was well covered with strikes? What inference is to be drawn from the fact that in one afternoon in Normandy, during the German armoured counter-attack at Mortain, Allied fighter-bombers claimed the destruction and damage of more German tanks than the latter actually possessed for the attack?

These questions would be impossible to answer satisfactorily were it not for operational research material. With regard to the destructive effect of weapons, their accuracy, and the identification of their effect on morale the ORS investigations are beyond price. Yet OR material has its limitations. As the experience of No.2 ORS and ORS 2nd TAF shows, there were too few ORS members and too little time was available for a fully comprehensive and quantitative study of close air support to be made. Battlefield examinations, sometimes instigated without clear directives from higher authority, were more a process of trial and error than systematic study – not least because the staff of the ORS did not know what evidence to look for until they found it. Rather these investigations, and the more general reports, offer a series of qualitative examples by which other such operations may be measured. They provide an idea as to how air attacks could be effective.

But, given the lack of time and resources for quantitative study, are the OR data contained in a collection of qualitative examples reliable? The answer to this question is, broadly, yes. The attribution of damage and destruction to air weapons as a result of battlefield examinations can be regarded as accurate – for example the evidence indicating whether a tank had been knocked out by an air or a ground weapon was usually conclusive. From such evidence of weapons effectiveness, added to what was known of weapons accuracy, a fair idea could be deduced of what these weapons were likely to achieve in terms of destruction.

Beyond this point caution has to be exercised. It would be a rash historian or analyst who suggested that, because air-to-ground weapons were found to have had a certain destructive effect on one or even a few occasions, they would have the same effect on all such similar occasions. The morale effect of weapons was even more variable. There was simply not enough OR work done on air support to enable the OR scientist then, or the historian now, to state more than that under a given set of circumstances certain weapons and methods of attack had the potential to achieve a certain result.

The risk of unreliability lies not so much in the OR material itself, but in the conclusions that the unwary may draw from it. For example, because they found few German dead during their investigations of heavy bombing operations, No.2 ORS concluded that such bombing did not cause many casualties to German troops in defensive positions. Evidence from German sources (such as from GOOD-WOOD and Cassino) certainly confirms that heavy bombing did not cause such casualties as to completely obliterate a defence, but it also confirms that more were killed than were subsequently found by the ORS. Moreover, the ORS discounted the fact that when possible the Germans removed their dead to prevent their discovery by Allied troops.

The impact of OR at the time was slight, and in retrospect this is not surprising. To begin with, there was little worthwhile experience of utilising ORS, and little idea of what they should be asked to do. This was found by No.2 ORS soon after arriving in Normandy, and the section began much of its work, including that on heavy bombing, on its own initiative. The fact that they were given such a free hand suggests that they were tolerated, perhaps even indulged – until they produced an unpalatable report, such as No.14 questioning the effectiveness of heavy bombing, for which they were censured, or when their reports caused embarrassing inter-service conflict, such as over fighter-bomber claims.

It is questionable whether there was much likelihood of the discoveries made by the ORS with regard to air support resulting in a change of operational methods. First, as the history of No.2 ORS observes, there was no mechanism for ensuring that OR data was read or acted upon. Second, it is by no means certain that this would have been appropriate. For example, the ORS convincingly pointed out that heavy and medium bombing of gun batteries and German 'Fortress' positions destroyed few, if any, guns and did little damage to fortifications, and that such bombing was really only of use immediately before an assault when its morale effect could be exploited. But what was the alternative when, as at Boulogne, artillery resources were limited? It was unthinkable to leave such formidable German positions unmolested in the period while an assault was prepared, and the soldiers could never be convinced of the futility of bombing, as the enduring resentment at what they perceived to be the lack of bomber support in some operations, such as Walcheren, shows.

This gap between theory and practice was the greatest obstacle to OR data being of practical use at the time. Experienced British and Canadian battalion commanders, their company officers and men, did not need an ORS scientist to tell them that the sooner they advanced after a Typhoon attack the more shaken and demoralised would they find the enemy – in fact it was only by talking with such men that the ORS formulated their ideas. It was another matter, however, for ORS reports pointing out the limitations of air-ground weapons, outlining their morale effects and the wastefulness of airstrikes uncoordinated with ground action, and advocating a rapid follow-up of airstrikes, to have much impact at Corps and Division level. Even if such reports reached that level and were read, it was simply not possible in all cases to ensure that airstrikes were immediately exploited. Battles are not conducive to such stage-management or to rigid timetables, and much that was unforeseen could occur to prevent an attack going in exactly on schedule. Moreover, as the ORS admitted, the effect on morale of air attack lasted a matter of a very few minutes at most.

When circumstances allowed, airstrikes were rapidly exploited, but operational planning could not be predicated solely on the likely morale effect of weapons, and there was much Army and RAF opposition to suggestions that weapons be developed with a pronounced morale effect at the expense of destructive capability. Nor could there be any question of the army ceasing to demand air attacks on known enemy positions when air support was available simply on the grounds that they were not yet ready to attack them. In short, tried and trusted methods were unlikely to be forsaken by fighting formations on the basis of OR reports, even had they been aware of them, and much of the OR data from 1944–45 is of more practical use to the historian now than it was to the soldiers and airmen then.

ARCHIVAL SOURCES

Although OR forms the bedrock of the material used, extensive reference has also been made to the operational records of the British Army and Royal Air Force, and the considerable amount of USAAF material available to researchers at the Public Record Office at Kew.[1]

The War Diaries of British Army Divisions, Brigades, Infantry Battalions, Artillery and Armoured Regiments are to be found in the WO 171 files for North-West Europe and WO 170 for Italy. They contain a daily narrative of operations, though the amount of detail provided can vary considerably. However, these sources confront the researcher with a major stumbling-block in that, with relatively few exceptions, War Diaries at Battalion and Regimental level generally make little or no reference to how useful air support had been during particular operations. In fact War Diaries at this level often make little or no reference to air support at all. This can be frustrating, particularly when it is known that close air support was an important feature of the operation being researched.

War Diaries at Brigade and Divisional level are more useful. Daily Intelligence Summaries detailing each day's operations, usually compiled at Divisional level but occasionally also at Brigade level, invariably mention air support, and may give some indication of how useful it had been. Message Logs, usually contained in the War Diaries at Corps and Divisional level, can include messages from battalions reporting airstrikes on their front, sometimes indicating any noticeable effects but more often simply reporting that the bombs or rockets had been seen to fall in the target area. They can also be useful for giving an indication of timings, with the message requesting air support and that reporting the airstrike usually being recorded.

Useful sources of data to supplement material contained in War Diaries are published regimental histories. These also vary in the amount of detail provided, but the best of them are extremely detailed, describing events affecting the unit almost day by day. They have obviously used the War Diary as their principal source, but they often contain additional details and can be valuable for references to air support, and general comments as to how useful it had been, that may be lacking in a War Diary.

The operational records of the RAF are contained in the Operations Record Books (ORBs) maintained by RAF formations at the following levels: Commands (AIR 23 & 24 files); Groups (AIR 25 files); Wings (AIR 26 files); and Squadrons (AIR 27 files). All contain a daily narrative of operations, an example being that compiled by RAF Desert Air Force in Italy, which provides detailed summaries of each day's activities and which is an essential source for a study of its operations (this is to be found in AIR 24). The ORBs of RAF Groups, and in particular the daily Intelligence Summaries to be found in the appendices to Group ORBs, can be quite detailed with regard to air-support operations and usually record the number of sorties and aircraft losses.

The most detailed air accounts of particular close support operations are to be found in the ORBs of the squadrons concerned. These not only list the number of aircraft involved and any losses incurred but also contain the observations of the pilots who carried out the attacks and their assessment of damage and casualties inflicted upon the enemy, though often they were able to report only that their bombs or rockets had fallen in the target area. The amount of detail in squadron ORBs varies. In general those of squadrons which served in Italy are far more detailed than those of squadrons which served in North-West Europe. In addition, both Group and Squadron ORBs may include messages from Army formations expressing gratitude for particularly successful air support missions, and these sometimes give an indication of the effect of the air attacks by recording the number of enemy dead and amount of destroyed or damaged equipment subsequently found by the troops.

Major operations, and some of lesser scale but which were particularly successful, were often the subject of separate Army and/or RAF reports. Most of such operations involved close air support, and the reports are now to be found among the Headquarters papers of the Army and Air Force concerned. The reports are either straightforward narratives, or analyses. The latter are more useful, as some attempt was made to evaluate the effectiveness of the air support, and these were often carried out by Operational Research Sections. One example from North-West Europe of an operation given extensive coverage is Operation VERITABLE, which was the subject of separate reports by British 21st Army Group, the ORS of RAF 2nd Tactical Air Force, and No.84 Group RAF.

Contemporary RAF and British Army tactical memoranda and reports are an important source for how close air-support operations were conducted. Numerous reports on the tactics employed by aircraft when attacking ground targets were compiled by the RAF in Italy and North-West Europe, and those compiled by the USAAF that are available at the Public Record Office have also been consulted. In addition, there are studies by both the RAF and British Army detailing the organisation and method of operation of the systems for providing and controlling close air support employed in both theatres. In this regard, a most important source is British Air Ministry *Air Support, Air Publication 3235 (The Second World War 1939–1945: Royal Air Force)*, 1955, a copy of which is held at the Air Historical Branch.

Comments on the campaigns and the air operations involved are contained in the despatches of senior commanders, most notably the Notes for General Eisenhower's Despatch and the Despatch on air operations in North-West Europe by Air Chief Marshal Leigh-Mallory, both to be found in PRO CAB 106/980, and Air Marshal Coningham's Report on 2nd Tactical Air Force Operations from D-Day to VE Day to be found in PRO AIR 37/876. Also referred to was Field Marshal Alexander's Despatch on the Italian Campaign, a copy of which is to be found in PRO AIR 8/1790.

Important input has also been found in data from the German side. The Imperial War Museum holds copies, some in translation, of the War Diaries and message logs of some of the principal German formations that fought in North-West Europe. Many of these are incomplete, but they yield useful information. In the post-war years the Air Historical Branch also compiled translations of contemporary German documents, some of the most useful being the weekly situation reports issued by German Army Headquarters (such as the Seventh Army in Normandy). In addition, Prisoner of War interrogation reports, many of them intrinsic to Allied ORS studies, were consulted. Recent years have seen the publication of a number of detailed German unit histories, which provide an interesting, and often revealing, alternative perspective on many actions. All these sources have been helpful in providing an indication both of what it was like to be on the receiving end of Allied air attack and what such attack achieved, and they have been referenced throughout.

PUBLISHED PRIMARY SOURCE MATERIAL

Data can also be extracted from the published memoirs of former fighter-bomber pilots. These provide useful descriptions of tactics employed on close support missions, which are often a revealing contrast to the contemporary official RAF tactical studies mentioned above, and for their first-hand accounts of the hazards inherent in the low-level attack role. Those particularly useful regarding RAF operations in North-West Europe were *Firebirds: Flying the Typhoon in Action* by Charles Demoulin,[2] *Typhoon Pilot* by Desmond Scott,[3] and John Golley's *The Day of The Typhoon*.[4] A valuable compilation of Typhoon pilot memoirs is provided in *Typhoon Attack* by Norman Franks,[5] while Christopher Shores in his book *Ground Attack Aircraft of World War II* includes an interesting synopsis of Typhoon tactics by the distinguished Belgian Typhoon pilot Colonel R.A. Lallement.[6] Not surprisingly, these can give a somewhat biased view of the amount of destruction inflicted by Typhoon attacks. Bill Colgan's *World War II Fighter-Bomber Pilot* provides an American perspective and is somewhat more balanced. It is especially valuable in being concerned with the Italian campaign, and Colgan includes a useful chapter relating his experience as a Forward Air Controller in Italy.[7]

For the chapter on the use of heavy bombers in the close support role an important source was the memoirs of the British Army's Liaison Officer at RAF Bomber Command Headquarters – *Soldier at Bomber Command* by Charles Carrington.[8] This in turn indicated a number of contemporary reports on the subject compiled by Lieutenant-Colonel Carrington when serving in this capacity and which are now accessible at the Public Record Office. The autobiography of the Commander-in-Chief of RAF Bomber Command, *Bomber Offensive* by Air Chief Marshal Sir Arthur Harris, was also consulted, as was that of Lord Zuckerman.[9] An important source detailing British Air Observation Post (AOP) operations, referred to in the chapter comparing fighter-bombers and artillery, was *Unarmed into Battle*, the history of the AOP by Major-General H.J. Parham and E.M.G. Belfield, originally published in 1956 but reissued in 1986.[10]

References to the employment of air support in North-West Europe are also to be found in the memoirs of senior commanders, examples being Eisenhower's *Crusade in Europe,* Montgomery's *Normandy to the Baltic,* and De Guingand's *Operation Victory.*[11]

SECONDARY SOURCE MATERIAL

Literature specifically on the subject of close air support in North-West Europe and Italy is scant, and the most useful overviews are those by Richard Hallion, who discusses support by heavy, medium and fighter-bombers in both campaigns in the relevant chapters of *Strike from the Sky,* and the work edited by Cooling, both referred to in the Introduction to this book. Two other extensive studies are invaluable sources for American air support operations in North-West Europe, and fortunately copies of both are available in the UK. One covers the *Effect of Air Power on Military Operations, Western Europe* and was compiled by General Omar Bradley's Air Effects Committee of the US Twelfth Army Group in 1945. The other is *The Effectiveness of Third Phase Tactical Air Operations in the European Theater, 5 May 1944 – 8 May 1945* compiled by the US Army Air Force's Evaluation Board in 1946.

This Board was one of five such separate groups of officers assigned to the major theatres by the US War Department during the summer of 1944, with the task of preparing reports enabling assessments to be made of the effectiveness of USAAF training, doctrine, and organisation. After the creation of the Strategic Bombing Survey later that year, these boards concentrated upon tactical air operations. The board assigned to the European Theatre of Operations (ETO) was requested, in February 1945, by the USAAF Headquarters in Europe, to carry out an analysis of close air support or 'Third Phase' operations as this was styled. The result was the above report, completed in the summer of 1945, which drew upon data provided by US air and ground forces but which mainly reflected the experience of the US Ninth Air Force.

Both the above reports outline the air-support system employed to support the US armies. They give detailed summaries of operations along with comments from US Army formations and also from German prisoners. These are contemporary historical documents and could be described as primary source material. However I have listed them as secondary sources because, as their titles suggest, they were attempts to analyse the effectiveness of air support. Copies of both are held at the Public Record Office.[12]

Detailed narratives of both campaigns were compiled in Britain after the war by the Cabinet Historical Section and the Air Historical Branch of the Air Ministry.[13] The former are mainly narratives of ground operations and the latter of air operations, though both give details of air support. Recourse was also had to the British, Canadian and American Official Histories of both campaigns.[14] In addition, a number of relevant campaign histories were consulted. A major source for operations in North-West Europe is Chester Wilmot's *The Struggle for Europe*, while another is Milton Shulman's *Defeat in the West*.[15]

Sources used for Normandy included *Overlord* by Max Hastings, *Six Armies in Normandy* by John Keegan, and *Decision in Normandy* by Carlo D'Este.[16] Max Hastings' *Das Reich* and Ralph Bennett's *Ultra in the West* give useful indications of the effect of air attack on German movement, the former detailing the experience of the 2nd SS Panzer Division during its move to the Normandy battlefront and the latter relating intercepted German signals traffic.[17] Sources used for the latter part of the campaign in North-West Europe included *The Long Left Flank* by Jeffery Williams, which is a very useful history of the operations of First Canadian Army, and Major-General Essame's *The Battle for Germany*.[18] Both are written from the point of view of the soldier, and refer with acerbity to occasions when, in Army opinion, the Air Forces declined to provide a sufficient scale of air support.

The role of the Air Forces involved in both campaigns is well described in John Terraine's *The Right of the Line*, Roderic Owen's *The Desert Air Force*, and Christopher Shores' *Second Tactical Air Force*.[19] A greater level of analysis is provided in an immediate post-war study of the US Ninth Air Force in North-West Europe – *Condensed Analysis of the Ninth Air Force in the European Theater of Operations* compiled by the Office of the Assistant Chief of the Air Staff in Washington in 1946. A copy is held at the Public Record Office.[20] For the chapter examining heavy bomber operations two

sources giving statistical data on a daily basis for RAF Bomber
Command and the US Eighth Air Force were *The Bomber Command
War Diaries* by Martin Middlebrook and Chris Everitt, and *The
Mighty Eighth War Diary* by Roger Freeman, Vic Maslen and Alan
Crouchman.[21]

An important overview of the air war as a whole is Professor
Overy's *The Air War 1939–1945*, while a recently published (1990)
general study of air bombardment in the Second World War is
Bombing 1939–45 by Karl Hecks.[22] The latter covers tactical as well as
strategic air operations, and summarises the developments in close-
support weapons and tactics by all the belligerents. Among the sources
referred to for the chapter on fighter-bombers and artillery two were
particularly useful – *Gunners At War* by Shelford Bidwell, for its
detailing of the evolution and employment of the method of fire control employed by British artillery in 1943–45, and *Fire-Power* by
Shelford Bidwell and Dominick Graham for its discussion of the
British air support system.[23]

NOTES

1. The Public Record Office holds USAAF tactical studies and memoranda from the campaigns in Italy, North-West Europe and Burma. These are usually found among the RAF
papers relating to these campaigns. There are also some ORS reports from North-West
Europe (Ninth Air Force) among the RAF 2nd TAF files (AIR 37). These have been
consulted and referenced accordingly. UK researchers should be aware of the extensive
collection of 8th USAAF papers, particularly detailed mission reports, held at the PRO in
the AIR 40 (Directorate of Intelligence) files.
2. Charles Demoulin, *Firebirds: Flying the Typhoon in Action* (Shrewsbury: Airlife Publishing
1986/87).
3. Desmond Scott, *Typhoon Pilot* (London: Arrow Edition, 1988)
4. John Golley, *The Day of the Typhoon* (Patrick Stephens, 1986)
5. Norman Franks, *Typhoon Attack* (London: William Kimber 1984)
6. Christopher Shores, *Ground Attack Aircraft of World War II* (London: Macdonald and
Jane's, 1977).
7. Bill Colgan, *World War II Fighter-Bomber Pilot* (Blue Ridge Summit, PA: TAB Books,
1985).
8. Charles Carrington, *Soldier at Bomber Command* (London: Leo Cooper, 1987).
9. Sir Arthur Harris, *Bomber Offensive* (London: Collins, 1947); Sir Solly Zuckerman, *From
Apes to Warlords* (London: Collins, 1988).
10. Major-General H.J. Parham and E.M.G. Belfield, *Unarmed into Battle: The Story of the Air
Observation Post* (Chippenham: Picton Publishing, 1986).
11. Dwight D. Eisenhower, *Crusade In Europe* (London: William Heinemann, 1948); Field-
Marshal The Viscount Montgomery, *Normandy to the Baltic* (London: Hutchinson, 1958);
Major-General Sir Francis De Guingand, *Operation Victory* (London: Hodder and
Stoughton, 1947).
12. The Army Air Forces Evaluation Board in the European Theater of Operations, *The
Effectiveness of Third Phase Tactical Air Operations in the European Theater, 5 May 1944 –
8 May 1945* (Feb.1946), PRO AIR 40/1111; US 12th Army Group Air Branches of G-3 and
G-2, Weisbaden, Germany, July 1945, *Effect of Air Power on Military Operations, Western
Europe*, PRO AIR 40/1131.

13. Air Historical Branch Narratives are held at the Public Record Office, AIR 41 files; Cabinet Office Narratives in the CAB 44 files.
14. Official Histories consulted were: Brigadier C.J.C. Molony, *The Mediterranean and Middle East*, Vol. V (London: HMSO, 1973); General Sir William Jackson, *The Mediterranean and Middle East*, Vol. VI (London: HMSO, 1988); Hilary St. G. Saunders, *Royal Air Force 1939–1945*, Vol. III (London: HMSO, 1954); Major L.F. Ellis, *Victory in the West* Volumes I and II (London: HMSO, 1962); Colonel C.P. Stacey, *The Victory Campaign* (Ottawa: 1960); Martin Blumenson, *Breakout and Pursuit* (Washington, DC: Department of the Army, 1961); Wesley F. Craven and James L. Cate (Eds), *The Army Air Forces in World War II*, Vol. III, *Argument to VE Day* (Chicago: 1951).
15. Chester Wilmot, *The Struggle For Europe* (London: The Reprint Society, 1954); Milton Shulman, *Defeat in the West* (London: Secker & Warburg, 1947).
16. Max Hastings, *Overlord: D-Day and the Battle for Normandy 1944* (London: Michael Joseph, 1984); John Keegan, *Six Armies in Normandy* (London: Jonathan Cape, 1982); Carlo D'Este, *Decision in Normandy* (London: Pan, 1984).
17. Max Hastings, *Das Reich* (London: Papermac, 1993); Ralph Bennett, *Ultra in the West* (London: Hutchinson, 1979).
18. Jeffery Williams, *The Long Left Flank* (London: Leo Cooper, 1988); H. Essame, *The Battle For Germany* (London: Batsford 1970).
19. John Terraine, *The Right of the Line* (London: Sceptre, 1988); Roderic Owen, *The Desert Air Force* (London: Hutchinson, 1948); Christopher Shores, *Second Tactical Air Force* (Osprey, 1970).
20. Headquarters Army Air Forces, Office of the Assistant Chief of the Air Staff-3, Washington, March 1946, *Condensed Analysis of the Ninth Air Force in the European Theater of Operations*, PRO AIR 40/1095.
21. Martin Middlebrook and Chris Everitt, *The Bomber Command War Diaries* (London: Penguin edition, 1990); Roger Freeman with Vic Maslen and Alan Crouchman, *The Mighty Eighth War Diary* (London: Arms & Armour, 1990).
22. R.J. Overy, *The Air War 1939–45* (London: Papermac, 1987); Karl Hecks, *Bombing 1939–45* (London: Robert Hale, 1990).
23. Shelford Bidwell, *Gunners At War* (London: Arms & Armour, 1970); Shelford Bidwell and Dominick Graham, *Fire-Power* (London: Allen & Unwin, 1985).

Bibliography

I. SECONDARY PUBLISHED SOURCES

Specific Close Air Support Titles

Cooling, Benjamin Franklin (Ed.), *Case Studies in the Development of Close Air Support* (Washington, D.C.: Office of Air Force History, 1990).

Hallion, Richard P., *Strike from the Sky: The History of Battlefield Air Attack 1911–1945* (Shrewsbury: Airlife Publishing, 1989).

Smith, Peter C., *Close Air Support: An Illustrated History, 1914 to the Present* (New York: Orion Books, 1990).

Air Operations

Bekker, Caius, *The Luftwaffe War Diaries* (London: Macdonald, 1967).

Bingham, Victor, *Blitzed! The Battle of France May–June 1940* (New Malden: Air Research, 1990).

Craven, W. F. and Cate, J. L., *The Army Air Forces in World War II*, Volume III, *Argument to VE Day* (Chicago: 1951).

Drew, E. and Kozaczka, F., *Air Interdiction: Lessons from Past Campaigns* (Santa Monica: Rand, September 1981).

Freeman, R. with Crouchman, A. and Maslen, V. (Eds), *The Mighty Eighth War Diary* (London: Arms and Armour, 1990).

Gerbig, Werner, *Six Months To Oblivion: The Eclipse of the Luftwaffe Fighter Force* (London: Ian Allan, 1975. Originally published in Germany by Motorbuch Verlag, Stuttgart, 1973).

Guedalla, Philip, *Middle East 1940–1942: A Study in Air Power* (London: Hodder and Stoughton, 1944).

Hastings, Max, *Bomber Command* (London: Pan, 1981).

Hecks, Karl, *Bombing 1939–45: The Air Offensive against Land Targets in World War II* (London: Robert Hale, 1990).

Infield, Glenn, *Big Week!* (London: New English Library, 1976).

Kohn, R.H. and Harahan, J.P. (Eds), *Air Superiority in World War II and Korea* (Washington, DC: Office of Air Force History, 1983).

—— *Air Interdiction in World War II, Korea, and Vietnam*, USAF Warrior Studies (Washington, DC: Office of Air Force History, 1986).

McFarland, S. L. and Newton, W.P., *To Command The Sky: The Battle for Air Superiority over Germany, 1942–1944* (Washington and London: Smithsonian Institute Press, 1991).

Mason, Air Vice-Marshal R.A., CBE, MA, RAF, *Air Power: An Overview of Roles* (London: Brassey's, 1987).

Mead, Peter, *The Eye in the Air: History of Air Observation and Reconnaissance for the Army 1785–1945* (London: HMSO, 1983).

Middlebrook, M. and Everitt, C., *The Bomber Command War Diaries: An Operational Reference Book 1939–1945* (London: Penguin, 1985).

Mierzejewski, Alfred C., *The Collapse of the German War Economy 1944–1945: Allied Air Power and the German National Railway* (University of North Carolina Press, 1988).

Overy, R.J., *The Air War 1939–1945* (London: Papermac, 1987).

Parham, Major-General H.J. and Belfield, E.M.G., *Unarmed into Battle: The Story of the Air Observation Post* (Chippenham: Picton Publishing, 1986).

Price, Alfred, *Battle over the Reich* (Shepperton: Ian Allan, 1973).

Sallagar, F.M., *Operation STRANGLE (Italy, Spring 1944): A Case Study of Tactical Air Interdiction* (Santa Monica: United States Air Force Project Rand, February 1972).

Saunders, H. St.G., *Per Ardua: The Rise of British Air Power 1911–1939* (Oxford: 1944).

Saunders, H. St.G., and Richards, Denis, *Royal Air Force 1939–1945*, three volumes, *The Fight is Won* (London: HMSO, 1953 and 1954).

Smith, Peter C., *Dive Bomber: An Illustrated History* (Ashbourne: Moorland Publishing, 1982).

—— *Into The Assault: Famous Dive Bomber Aces of the Second World War* (London: John Murray, 1985).

—*Jungle Dive Bombers at War* (London: John Murray, 1987).

Wakefield, Ken, *The Flying Grasshoppers: U.S. Liaison Aircraft Operations in Europe 1942–1945* (Leicester: Midland Counties Publishing, 1990).

Walker, Air Vice-Marshal John R. (Ed.), *The Future of Air Power*, RUSI Military Power Series (Shepperton: Ian Allan, 1986).

Webster, C. and Frankland, N., *The Strategic Air Offensive against Germany*, Volume III, *Victory* (London: HMSO, 1961).

Air Forces and Units

Caldwell, Donald L., *JG 26: Top Guns of the Luftwaffe* (New York: Orion Books, 1991).

Cooper, Matthew, *The German Air Force 1933–1945* (London: Jane's, 1980).

Johnson, C.R., *The History of The Hell Hawks* (US 365th Fighter Group which served in North-West Europe), Southcoast Typesetting, 1975.

Killen, John, *The Luftwaffe* (London: Sphere, 1970).

Kohn, R.H. and Harahan, J.P. (Eds), *Condensed Analysis of the Ninth Air Force in the European Theater of Operations*, USAF Warrior Studies (Washington, DC: Office of Air Force History, 1984).

Owen, Roderic, *The Desert Air Force* (London: Hutchinson, 1948).

Shores, Christopher, *Second Tactical Air Force* (London: Osprey, 1970).

Smith, Peter C., *Stuka Squadron: Stukagruppe 77 – The Luftwaffe's 'Fire Brigade'* (Wellingborough: Patrick Stephens, 1990).

Terraine, John, *The Right of the Line: The Royal Air Force in the European War 1939–1945* (London: Sceptre, 1988).

Aircraft

Angelucci, E. with Bowers, P.M., *The American Fighter: The Definitive Guide to American Fighter Aircraft from 1917 to the Present* (Sparkford, Somerset: Haynes Publishing, 1987).

Green, William, *Famous Fighters of the Second World War* (London: Macdonald, 1960).

Gunston, Bill, *The Illustrated Encyclopedia of Combat Aircraft of World War II* (London: Tiger Books, 1990).

Shores, Christopher, *Ground Attack Aircraft of World War II*

(London: Macdonald and Jane's, 1977).

Smith, Peter C., *Vengeance – The Vultee Vengeance Dive Bomber* (Shrewsbury: Airlife, 1986).

Wagner, Ray (Ed.), *American Combat Planes* (New York: Doubleday, 1968).

General Titles

Air Ministry Publication 3368, *The Origins and Development of Operational Research in the Royal Air Force* (London: HMSO, 1963).

Ambrose, Stephen E., *The Supreme Commander* (London: Cassell, 1970).

Bailey, J.B.A., *Field Artillery and Firepower* (Oxford: The Military Press, 1989).

Bidwell, S., *Gunners at War: A Tactical Study of the Royal Artillery in the Twentieth Century* (London: Arms & Armour, 1970).

Bidwell, S. and Graham, D., *Fire-Power: British Army Weapons and Theories of War 1904–1945* (London: Allen & Unwin, 1985).

Brookes, Kenneth, *Battle Thunder: The Story of Britain's Artillery* (London: Osprey, 1973).

Bryant, Sir Arthur, *The Turn of The Tide 1939–1943: A Study Based on the Diaries and Autobiographical Notes of Field Marshal The Viscount Alanbrooke, K.G., O.M.* (London: The Reprint Society, 1958).

Fergusson, Bernard, *The Watery Maze: The Story of Combined Operations* (London: Collins, 1961).

Fitzsimons, Bernard (Ed.), *The Illustrated Encyclopedia of 20th Century Weapons and Warfare*, Volume I (London: Purnell, 1977).

Fraser, David, *And We Shall Shock Them: The British Army in the Second World War* (London: Sceptre, 1988).

Hogg, Ian V., *British and American Artillery of World War 2* (London: Arms & Armour, 1978).

Irving, David, *The Trail of The Fox: The Life of Field Marshal Erwin Rommel* (London: Weidenfeld & Nicolson, 1977).

Jones, R.V., *Most Secret War* (London: Hamish Hamilton, 1978).

Liddell Hart, B.H. (Ed.), *The Rommel Papers* (London: Collins, 1953).

Pemberton, A.L., *The Development of Artillery Tactics and Equipment* (London: The War Office, 1951).

Postan, M.M., Hay, D., and Scott, J.D., *Design and Development of Weapons* (London: HMSO, 1964).

Saunders, H. St.G., *The Red Beret* (London: New English Library, 1975).

Waddington, C.H., *OR in World War 2: Operational Research Against the U-Boat* (London: Elek, 1973).

White, B.T., *Tanks and Other Armoured Fighting Vehicles 1942–45* (Poole: The Blandford Press, 1975).

Campaign Studies - General

Ellis, John, *Brute Force: Allied Strategy and Tactics in the Second World War* (London: Andre Deutsch, 1990).

Ellis, Major L.F., *The War in France and Flanders 1939–1940* (London: HMSO, 1953).

Shulman, Milton, *Defeat in The West* (London: Secker & Warburg, 1947).

Wilmot, C., *The Struggle for Europe* (London: The Reprint Society, 1954).

Campaign and Battle Studies – Mediterranean Theatre

Blumenson, M., *Anzio: The Gamble That Failed* (London: Weidenfeld and Nicolson, 1963).

Böhmler, R., *Monte Cassino* (London: Cassel, 1964).

Ellis, J., *Cassino – The Hollow Victory: The Battle for Rome January–June 1944* (London: Andre Deutsch, 1984).

Jackson, General Sir William, *The Mediterranean and Middle East*, Volume VI, Part III (London: HMSO, 1988).

Majdalany, F., *Cassino: Portrait of a Battle* (London: Longmans, Green, 1957).

Maule, Henry, *Spearhead General: The Epic Story of General Sir Frank Messervy and His Men in Eritrea, North Africa and Burma* (London: Corgi, 1963).

Molony, Brigadier C.J.C., *The Mediterranean and Middle East*, Volume V, *The Campaign in Sicily 1943 and The Campaign in Italy 3 Sept. 1943 to 31 March 1944* (London: HMSO, 1973).

Nicholson, Lieutenant-Colonel G.W.L., *The Canadians in Italy* (Ottawa: 1956).

Playfair, Major-General I.S.O., *The Mediterranean and Middle East* Volumes III and IV (London: HMSO, 1960 and 1966).

Stewart, I. McD. G., *The Struggle for Crete 20 May – 1 June 1941: A Story of Lost Opportunity* (Oxford: 1966).

Tute, Warren, *The North African War* (London: Sidgwick & Jackson, 1976).

Vaughan-Thomas, Wynford, *Anzio* (London: Pan, 1963).

Campaign Studies and Battle Studies – North-West Europe

Bennett, Ralph, *Ultra in the West: The Normandy Campaign of 1944–45* (London: Hutchinson, 1979).

Blumenson, Martin, *Breakout and Pursuit* (Washington, DC: Department of the Army, 1961).

D'Este, Carlo, *Decision in Normandy* (London: Pan, 1984).

Ellis, Major L.F., *Victory in the West*, Volumes I and II (London: HMSO, 1962 and 1968).

English, John A., *The Canadian Army and the Normandy Campaign: A Study of Failure in High Command* (New York: Praeger, 1991).

Essame, H., *The Battle for Germany* (London: Batsford, 1969).

Hastings, Max, *Overlord: D-Day and the Battle for Normandy 1944* (London: Michael Joseph, 1984).

—— *Das Reich: The March of the 2nd SS Panzer Division through France, June 1944* (London: Papermac, 1993).

Keegan, John, *Six Armies in Normandy* (London: Jonathan Cape, 1982).

Kershaw, Robert J., *It Never Snows in September: The German View of MARKET-GARDEN and The Battle of Arnhem, September 1944* (Marlborough, Wilts.: The Crowood Press, 1990).

Lefèvre, Eric, *Panzers in Normandy Then and Now* (London: After The Battle, 1983).

Lucas, James and Barker, James, *The Killing Ground: The Battle of The Falaise Gap August 1944* (London: Batsford, 1978).

Powell, Geoffrey, *The Devil's Birthday: The Bridges to Arnhem, 1944* (London: Papermac, 1985).

Rawling, Gerald, *Cinderella Operation: The Battle for Walcheren 1944* (London: Cassell, 1980).

Roskill, Captain S.W., *The War at Sea 1939–1945*, Volume III, *The Offensive*, Part II, 1 June 1944 – 14 August 1945 (London: HMSO, 1961).

Ryan, Cornelius, *A Bridge Too Far* (London: Hamish Hamilton, 1974).

Stacey, C.P., *The Victory Campaign* (Ottawa: 1960).

Tute, Warren, Costello, John, and Hughes, Terry, *D-Day* (London: Pan, 1975).

Whiting, Charles, *A Bridge at Arnhem* (London: Futura, 1977).

Williams, Jeffery, *The Long left Flank: The Hard Fought Way to the Reich 1944–1945* (London: Leo Cooper, 1988).

II. PUBLISHED PRIMARY SOURCES

Memoirs

Bradley, Omar N., *A Soldier's Story* (London: Eyre & Spottiswoode, 1952).

Carrington, Charles, *Soldier at Bomber Command* (London: Leo Cooper, 1987).

Clostermann, Pierre, *The Big Show: Some Experiences of A French Fighter Pilot in the R.A.F.* (London: Corgi Books, 1970).

Colgan, Bill, *World War II Fighter Bomber Pilot* (Blue Ridge Summit, PA: TAB Books, 1985).

De Guingand, Major-General Sir Francis, *Operation Victory* (London: Hodder and Stoughton, 1947).

Demoulin, Charles, *Firebirds: Flying the Typhoon in Action* (Shrewsbury: Airlife Publishing, 1986/87).

Eisenhower, Dwight D., *Crusade in Europe* (London: William Heinemann, 1948).

Foley, John, *Mailed Fist* (London: Granada 1982).

Franks, Norman (Ed.), *Typhoon Attack* (London: William Kimber, 1984).

Golley, John, *The Day of the Typhoon* (Patrick Stephens, 1986).

Hagen, Louis, *Arnhem Lift* (London: Severn House, 1977)

Harris, Sir Arthur, *Bomber Offensive* (London: Collins, 1947).

Horrocks, Sir Brian, with Belfield, E. and Essame, H., *Corps Commander* (London: Sidgwick & Jackson, 1977).

Luck, Hans von, *Panzer Commander: The Memoirs of Colonel Hans von Luck* (New York: Praeger, 1989).

Montgomery, Field Marshal the Viscount, *El Alamein to the River Sangro* (London: Hutchinson, 1948).

—— *Normandy to the Baltic* (London: Hutchinson, 1947).

Scott, Desmond, *Typhoon Pilot* (London: Arrow Books, 1988).

Urquhart, Major-General R.E., *Arnhem* (London: Pan Books, 1960).

Zuckerman, Solly, *From Apes to Warlords* (London: Collins, 1988).

Army Unit Histories – British

Chadwick, Sergeant, *Seconds Out: A History of the 2nd Royal Tank Regiment* (The Regiment: undated, but likely 1945). Copy held at the Imperial War Museum, London.

Foster, Major R.C.G., *History of The Queen's Royal Regiment,* Volume VIII, 1924–1948 (Aldershot: Gale & Polden, 1953).

Liddell Hart, B.H., *The Tanks,* Volume II, 1939–1945 (London: Cassell, 1959).

Nicolson, N. and Forbes, P., *The Grenadier Guards in the War of 1939–45,* Volume I (Aldershot: Gale & Polden, 1949).

Regimental Committee, *The 10th Royal Hussars in The Second World War 1939–1945* (Aldershot: Gale & Polden, 1948).

Rosse, The Earl of, and Hill, Colonel E.R., *The Story of The Guards Armoured Division* (London: 1956).

Army Unit Histories – American

Hewitt, Robert L., *Work Horse of The Western Front: The Story of The 30th Infantry Division* (Washington: Infantry Journal Press, 1946).

Mittelman, Captain J.B., *Eight Stars To Victory: A History of The Veteran Ninth U.S. Infantry Division* (Ninth Infantry Division Association, 1948). Copy held at the Imperial War Museum, London.

Army Unit Histories – German

Lehmann, Rudolf, and Tiemann, Ralf, *Die Leibstandarte,* Band IV/1 (Osnabrück: Munin Verlag, 1986).

Strauss, Franz Joseph, *Geschichte Der 2 (Weiner) Panzer Division* (Neckargmünd: Kurt Vowinckel Verlag, 1977).

III. ARTICLES

Copp, Terry, 'Scientists and The Art of War: Operational Research in 21 Army Group', *RUSI Journal,* Winter 1991.

Corum, James S., 'The Luftwaffe's Army Support Doctrine, 1918–1941', *The Journal of Military History,* January 1995.

Greenhous, Brereton, 'Aircraft versus Armor: Cambrai To Yom Kippur', in Travers, Tim, and Archer, Christan (Eds), *Men at War* (Chicago: Precedent, 1982).

Hallion, Richard P., 'Battlefield Air Support A Retrospective Assessment', *Airpower Journal*, Spring 1990.

Jacobs, William A., 'Tactical Air Doctrine and AAF Close Air Support in the European Theater, 1944–1945', *Aerospace Historian*, Spring, March 1980.

Price, Alfred, 'The 3 inch Rocket: How Successful was it against the German Tanks in Normandy?', *RAF Quarterly*, Summer 1975.

Staff Group 4B, CGSOC Class of 1986–87, 'Operation Cobra and the Mortain Counterattack', *Military Review*, July 1988.

IV. PRINCIPAL OPERATIONAL RESEARCH REPORTS

The following Operational Research reports are held at the Public Record Office, Kew.

The work compiled by No.2 ORS, British 21st Army Group, in North-West Europe during 1944–45 is contained in a single volume entitled *Operational Research in North West Europe*, PRO WO 291/1331. Reports pertaining to close air support are:

No.3 *Investigation of an Attack on a German Column near La Baleine.*
No.5 *Bombing of Caen, 7 July 1944.*
No.6 *Bombing in Operation GOODWOOD.*
No.7 *Bombing in Operation BLUECOAT.*
No.8 *Bombing in Operation TOTALISE.*
No.9 *Effect of 90 lb Fragmentation Bombs.*
No.14 *Heavy Bombing in Support of the Army.*
No.15 *Enemy Casualties in Vehicles and Equipment in the Retreat from Normandy to the Seine.*
No.16 *Air and Ground Support in the Assault on Boulogne.*
Joint Report No.1 (with ORS 2nd TAF), *Air Attack on Enemy Armour in the Ardennes.*
Joint Report No.3 (with ORS 2nd TAF), *Rocket-firing Typhoons in Close Support of Military Operations.*
Joint Report No.4 (with ORS 2nd TAF), *German Flak and Allied Counter-flak Measures in Operation VARSITY.*

The following reports, compiled by ORS 2nd TAF in 1944–45, are to be found among the collected ORS 2nd TAF papers in PRO AIR 37/61:

Report No.1, '*Investigations of the Operation of TAF Aircraft in the Mortain Area – 7th August 1944.*

Report No.9, *Air Attack on Gun Positions.*

Report No.30, *Armed Reconnaissance by Aircraft of 2nd TAF in the Western European Campaign.*

Report No.32, *Fighter Bomber Attacks on Guns and Strong Points in the Closing Phase.*

Report No.36, *The Operational Accuracy of 2nd TAF Fighter/Bomber and RP Aircraft, October 1944–April 1945.*

Report No.37, *The Effort and Accuracy of Tactical Bombers in 2 Group, January 1944–May 1945.*

Index

CPSIA information can be obtained at www.ICGtesting.com
Printed in the USA
LVOW10s1248050614

388739LV00002B/15/A

9 780714 642116